DISCARD

VAS YOU EVER IN ZINZINNATI?

VAS
YOU EVER
IN ZINZINNATI?

BY DICK PERRY

DOUBLEDAY & COMPANY, INC., GARDEN CITY, NEW YORK

1966

F
499
.C5
P38

Dedicated to GEORGIA GLYNN, *who
said one afternoon, "Why don't
you write a book about Cincinnati?"*

CONTENTS

To those of you now studying history, we have one word of consolation. Think how much toil and trouble and killings and misery went into making it. There are times when we feel like inaugurating a National Let's Do Nothing Week. If it works, maybe we can make it a month, and if THAT works . . .

OLLIE JAMES
Cincinnati *Enquirer*

VAS YOU EVER IN ZINZINNATI?

1

Fortune magazine said Cincinnati "is the best run big city in the United States." *Life* said, "Cincinnati has one of the best police forces in the country." *Time,* on the other hand, once called Cincinnati "dowdy." To Indians, Cincinnati was a calamity; to slaves, a promised land; and to children on skates, a hilly impossibility. To the Reds, its a place to play ball; to Procter & Gamble, a place to make soap; to the Ohio River, a place to flood; and to starlings, a place to drop in. Which Cincinnati you know depends upon your point of view. There are as many viewpoints as there are people, and I can only write of this city from mine. I happen to be fond of Cincinnati.

Is this any way for a person to feel about a *city?* Yes. To me, Cincinnati is more than a dot on an atlas or an accumulation of people. My heart and my sinuses are attuned to this grab bag of hills, valleys, smelly creeks, factory districts, and gentle parks. To me, Cincinnati is a living thing. Sometimes it charms me. Sometimes it bores me. Sometimes I love Cincinnati. Sometimes I hate it. Now and then I leave it, swearing never to return, but I always come back. This is the way love affairs are.

But the love story I'm writing will not be complicated. This book is divided into two distinct parts. The first part tells about Cincinnati's yesterdays. The second part tells about Cincinnati today. Because I am not a historian, I must ask your indulgence. I am a novelist; love stories are my meat. But history—unlike fiction—cannot be rearranged by an author or his editor to make the ending happy or the tale more exciting. We must take Cincinnati as it was and as it is.

Cincinnati is unlike any other city. It hasn't the hurry of New York, the anger of Chicago, or the buttoned-down sophistication that San Francisco affects. I suggest that what Cincinnati has is innocence. It

1

is the innocence of Fountain Square. It is the innocence of old ladies lugging shopping bags. It is the innocence of typists preening themselves in store-window reflections. It's an innocence expressed by nuns hurrying along Fifth Street and by hordes of teenage girls in Catholic-school uniforms. Cincinnati's innocence has a voice. Its voice is Kentucky drawls, Hoosier twangs, here and there a German guttural, Negro laughter, and the newsboy's garbled cry.

Not *all* Cincinnati has retained this innocence. Beyond the downtown area and the near-in communities of Cumminsville, Riverside, Linwood, Brighton, and the rest, Cincinnati's innocence has been bulldozed away and ticky-tacky houses have taken root. In such lookalike subdivisions on this city's periphery, Cincinnati has traded in its innocence as down payment on a power mower. By the time our great-great-grandchildren are middle-aged, Cincinnati—and all cities—will have ceased to exist as separate and distinct personalities. There will be no way to tell one from the other. American cities, as television programs do now, will look alike. Even now in Cincinnati this is happening. When gathering material for this book, I drove through many neighborhoods, old and new. In some neighborhoods I had the uneasy feeling of being in New York, St. Louis, Kansas City—or anywhere. The houses were the same. The streets were the same. The KEEP OFF THE GRASS signs were the same. The exception, which later developers will rectify, is elevation: some neighborhoods are hilly and some are not. A bulldozer can solve this nonsense. Then all communities—everywhere—*will* look alike.

If some outlying communities have no innocence or personality, areas closer in that possess these charms are losing them. Great houses the size of castles are being sliced into apartments. Do you doubt me? Check the brow of Price Hill. Check Clifton. Witness the twilight of mansions. The ones that remain are the last of their tribe. When they go—and they will—there won't be any more. Each year more one-family dwellings are rendered into apartments, eventually to decay and to be torn down. Meanwhile on the outskirts of this city, the ticky-tacky houses multiply like rabbits.

Forgive me. Being in love with this city, I sometimes quarrel with its intentions. But when I quarrel with Cincinnati—its innocence, its silliness, and its wisdom—recognize my quarrel for what it is: a lover's quarrel and nothing more. But who am I, you ask, to quarrel this way with Cincinnati or to presume to write its love story? If I may qualify myself via antiquity, let me say that our family Bible—*circa* 1864, with pages musty, brown, and crackly—shows that my father's family has been in Cincinnati since 1815. They might have been here longer, but that's as far back as the notations go. Two great-uncles of mine died of cholera when they were babies here: one died in 1849, when he was eleven months old; the other

2

died in 1851, when he was sixteen months old. Their graves must be in the area somewhere. I don't know exactly where. Graveyards have a way of giving way to roads that must be widened. Except for a flyer at silver mining in Colorado, my father's family has been in the Greater Cincinnati area for 150 years. My mother's family came from Aurora, Indiana, where her father drove a team of horses that pulled a Standard Oil tank wagon. Also, my mother's side of the family was part Indian. I don't know which tribe, but my mother insisted that being part Indian was better than coming over on the *Mayflower*.

"Our ancestors," she liked to say, "were here to *meet* the boat!"

I was born in Cincinnati. I smoked my first cigar here. I got my first traffic ticket here. My sister was born here. I met my wife here, and my three children were born here. I met my wife in an apartment she shared with two other charmers. The apartment was the Grey Manor, 188 East McMillan Street. But that ramshackle valentine of a building has since been bulldozed into oblivion. Where on long-ago summer nights young couples used to sit in backyard shadows, drink beer, and talk love, now the Ohio Life Insurance Company has its building. Also, I stood one stormy night on the Ida Street Bridge in Mount Adams and asked the girl to marry me. Lightning crackled, thunder boomed, she said yes, and we got drenched. I list these items not to make this book into a soap opera. These items are my credentials. If you're not sentimentally inclined, I'll add that the Ida Street Bridge was built in 1931, cost $100,000, is 440 feet long, and was the first bridge in Cincinnati to be equipped with indirect lighting: thirty-three 200-watt lights recessed in the concrete railing.

Come with me now to the observation deck atop the Carew Tower and let's give this Cincinnati of ours a quick once-over. First, picture a football stadium that's completely round. Put yourself in the last row—way up there. The players look like ants. The stand directly opposite you is two and a half miles away. It is, you must admit, a whopper of a stadium. Get the picture? Now, do this. Change the stadium into hills and let the playing field be the valley. Add a river. Let it flow from goal to goal, east to west, via broken-field running, and we'll call it the Ohio. North of the river—in that half circle of hills—is Cincinnati. The playing field is the basin district which is downtown Cincinnati. South of the river is Kentucky and more hills. And *that*, oversimplified, is Greater Cincinnati's topography.

Time and civilization have made hash of our amphitheater's natural lines. A thousand spring rains have whittled gulleys and passes in the hills. And people, past and present, flattened this part, smoothed off that part, chewed away at this hill, dumped dirt into that valley, the better to build their city. But no matter. From the top of the Carew Tower, which we'll place in the center of the field, smack on the 50-yard line, and north of the river, we can stare in all directions. For the technical at heart, we note that Cincinnati is 540 feet above sea level, extends a zigzaggy 25 miles along the northern bank of the zigzaggy river, sometimes as far as 15 miles inland, has 71.9 square miles within its corporation limits, an average summer temperature of 75 degrees, and winter temperatures that average between 30 and 40 degrees.

The 48-story Carew Tower, built in 1930, is Cincinnati's tallest building. It rises 574 feet above the intersection of Fifth and Vine Streets and can be seen from every direction. From the observation deck the area seems to spread out before you like a smoky map. The trip to the top is fast. Automatic elevators *whooosh*—and there you are. The tower once had pretty girls to run the cages. Some were sex kittens, some were not, but when you caught the right car, the *whooosh* was satisfying. By New York standards our Carew Tower is penny-ante stuff. Its first six floors are gray limestone. The rest of the structure is yellow brick.

Madame Tournaire's Circus used to be where the Carew Tower stands. That was before the Civil War. Delegates to the 1856 Democratic Convention here were hard-pressed to keep their minds on the convention; they were more fascinated by "Professor" Pulley's balloon ascensions. But they did stop long enough to nominate James Buchanan. Then they gaped at the professor some more. After the Civil War the Palace Varieties took up where the circus left off. The Varieties was a noisy and beery collection of acrobats, gambling, cigar smoke, and a mishmosh of everything that would attract a crowd. Now the wildest sight you can see on the corner of Fifth and Vine Streets is a Pogue window dresser twist the arm from a naked dummy, or—when the wind is brisk—a secretary's skirt flap like a pennant.

Face south. From the observation deck you can see the Ohio River and the Kentucky dormitory communities of Covington, Newport, Dayton, and the rest. Some are sad little waterfront towns filled with old houses, the smell of mildew, and memories: grandeur that went to seed. Others are trim little neighborhoods that cling to hillsides or slumber in valleys behind the hills you see. Each Kentucky town is a separate entity. Each possesses its own police chief, its own mayor, its own mood, and its own preoccupation with whether to be naughty or nice. Although some Cincinnatians label these places "bedroom towns" for those who cross the river each day to work in Cincinnati, some of these communities are self-contained and have industries of their own. At one time, not too long ago, some of these industries had to go underground each time the grand jury was in session. Also, not too long ago, little green streetcars used to groan through the Kentucky valleys and climb up the Kentucky hills. They were shy and vague little trolleys that would forsake the street the moment your back was turned, hum an electric hum, and clatter off somewhere through a stand of trees. They didn't care for streets too much.

Now, observe the Ohio side of the river. As far as you can see is Cincinnati. It occupies a lot of Hamilton County. It's also the county seat. Each year more than 2000 babies are born here, more than 5000 couples get married, nearly 1000 die, and more than $23,000,000 is spent on booze. Once our city was nothing more than a gathering of log cabins at the river's edge, where the Public Landing is now. The flatland that stretches out from the river to meet the hills was forest, not a parking meter anywhere. No houses grew on the sides of the close and distant hills. But that didn't last long. Trees were chopped down. Soon the valley was crisscrossed with streets, there flowed the canal from Lake Erie, and frame houses, as well as factories belching smoke, were everything. The only Indians left stood in front of cigar stores.

I take that back. Even today there are Indians in Cincinnati. Si Cornell's "Town Talking" column in the *Post & Times-Star* notes that Indian Pete, seventy-three, has operated as a medicine man in Cincinnati for thirty-seven years. His teepee is a storefront on Central Avenue, his full name is Peter William Whitson, and—surrounded by buffalo heads and muzzle-loading rifles—this full-blooded Cherokee peddles Indian Pete's Tonic @ $1.50 an eight-ounce bottle. According to Mr. Cornell, most of Indian Pete's customers buy roots, leaves, and herbs which the Indian learned about from his grandfather in the Great Smoky Mountains.

Another, but less communicative, Indian operates from his base on Thornton Circle in Fernbank, which is Cincinnati's most western river community. But this Indian is not real. He is cast iron, holds a bow longer than any Indian ever used, and spends his days staring into space with a worried expression. He had reason to worry. In 1940 an automobile clobbered him and he was sold for junk, but Fernbank citizens were so fond of him, he was rescued and put back together again.

See the hill to the east, the one with the high-rise on it? That's Mount Adams. It's festered with tenements. An incline railroad used to hoist streetcars up its slope, but the streetcars no longer run, and the incline has been torn down. Mount Adams is going through a trying period. As I write this, Mount Adams doesn't know what it's going to become: the slum area it was, a beatnik monstrosity, or—cross your fingers—another Nob Hill. Now it's an accumulation of frame houses, a high-rise apartment that seems out of place, a bookstore that features a bar and jazz combo, and roller-coaster streets that take your breath away. As you look north and west from

5

Mount Adams, the hills are more distant and more gentle. To the far west the valley ends at State Street with a thud—and Price Hill takes over. The seven hills? Which are they? Some say they are Mount Adams, Walnut Hills, Mount Auburn, Fairmount, College Hill, Fairview Heights, and Vine Street Hill. Some say Cincinnati has not seven, but seventy hills. Don't ask. Each time you do, you'll get a different answer.

Instead, look straight down in front of you: the sprawling "downtown" district, now rebuilding, with its department stores, dime stores, chili parlors, theaters, and parking lots. To the north from downtown is Central Parkway, which, before they drained it in 1920, was a canal that separated downtown from the Mohawk, that slum area between the Parkway and the bottom of the hills. Long ago the Mohawk was a compact community of cozy red-brick houses flush with the sidewalk. This was where the Germans used to gather when the Parkway was the Miami-Erie Canal and the air each morning was sweet with the scent of empty beer kegs. Now the district is filled with jukebox noise and a secondhand melancholy that neighborhoods acquire when purpose and dignity are gone.

Had you wandered through the Mohawk in 1843, however, you would have seen the community in its prime. Also, you would have seen hordes of men, women, and children—all wearing frightened looks and white muslin—heading for Brighton Hill, that hazy blob beyond the tenement chimney pots. These people were the Millerites, their destination a hastily constructed wooden platform on the hillside, and—at sunset—eternity. It was Doomsday, the Second Coming predicted by William Miller of Pittsfield, Massachusetts. The idea captured the imagination of many Cincinnatians. But as they stood on the crowded platform, watching the sun go down, and seeing that things were still going on, they began to feel foolish. When church bells in the Mohawk rang out their tinny supper calls, the people climbed off the platform and went home. Miller said he had miscalculated. It would be the year 1844, he said. So in October 1844 most everybody went back to the platform and waited some more. But Doomsday laid an egg. A lot of stuff like that has happened here. Cincinnati, you'll discover, can be silly as well as sad. It can also be mixed up.

For one thing, if as you stare down on the city the multiplicity of architectural styles confuses you, say so. Everyone else does. Paul Landfair, architect and assistant professor of architecture at Miami University in Oxford, Ohio, says that to him "Cincinnati is a town of little red-brick houses." He's thinking of the Mohawk and the rest, not the antiseptic suburbs, and certainly not downtown. Downtown Cincinnati might be considered a designer's hodgepodge. Cincinnati,

6

like Pittsburgh, is suffering right now a renaissance called Core Redevelopment. Herbert Kubly, in *At Large*, wrote that "Pittsburghers like to compare their renaissance with that of Florence centuries ago . . . but Pittsburgh is a Florence without Lorenzo." Cincinnati lacks a Lorenzo, too. For instance, is the Kroger high-rise at Vine and Central Parkway a structure that expresses Cincinnati best? If so, no quarrel. That blue and many-windowed thing Kroger put up has charm. But if the Kroger building expresses Cincinnati best, does the funny-colored City Hall with its turrets belong? Others don't get too enthusiastic about Procter & Gamble's office building. They say it is dull and lacks imagination. Still others maintain that the Procter & Gamble building makes architectural sense because its designers had the imagination to capture the essence of what Cincinnati is. Look at Fourth and Vine Streets. The Sinton Hotel—ornate, old-fashioned, and folksy—has been demolished to make way for a modern high-rise. Yet, across the street stands the Central Trust Tower. Will the two be compatible? If a modern high-rise is logical, the antique tower is not. Or, could it be the other way around? Each of us has his own idea of what our city should be.

Some of us poke fun at buildings. Some of us poke fun at vacant lots. Grownup nonsense is nothing new to Cincinnatians. Consider the intersection at Oak Street and Reading Road. At the turn of the century, on one corner was a residence named *Jewel*. On another stood another residence named *Hopewell*. That's where Ursuline Academy is now. But let's keep going. Where Bethesda Hospital stands on the third corner of that intersection there used to be a private hospital operated by T. A. Reamy. When he called his hospital *Getwell*, the neighborhood wags couldn't leave well enough alone. They called the vacant lot on the fourth corner *Staywell*.

More nonsense? Consider the Mack Sennett donnybrook in 1851. Ten fire companies responded to a lumberyard blaze, got into a fistfight over which company should douse the fire, and by the time they resolved the issue, there was no issue to resolve.

So much for nonsense. To the west, between the new expressway, which is also Intrastate 75, and Mill Creek in the distance, is a low-lying commercial area crisscrossed with new streets. This area used to be the West End, the Negro ghetto. As a child I used to walk through this section with my parents because the Negro section contained the cheapest groceries. We were on relief and had to make every penny count.

Now the West End is gone. Demolished. The Negroes have moved away. The West End was not a beautiful place in its last days; better the bulldozer came. But where did the Negroes go? And in what bar do some sit now? And in what ghetto are the Negro

7

children trapped? These items are part of my Cincinnati love story, too. All is not lollipops in my hometown. Big cities have big aches.

Cincinnati is big in lots of ways: in size, in ideas, in happiness, and in hurts.

How big is Cincinnati in numbers? Actually, there are *two* Cincinnatis. First is incorporated Cincinnati, defined by city limits and the surveyor's sidewalk markings, a legal area beyond which the Cincinnati police dogs aren't supposed to growl at you. Second is Greater Cincinnati, which includes incorporated Cincinnati plus certain Kentucky counties, one in Indiana, and as many in Ohio as might seem reasonable to you at the time. Many of these "outside" communities have a fierce pride. "We are *not* Cincinnatians," one will say; "*we* live in Cheviot." Or: "*We* live in Norwood . . . or Ludlow . . . or Rabbithash." Yes, there is a Rabbithash. It's in Kentucky, close by. Other people on the periphery of incorporated Cincinnati couldn't care less; they think of themselves as Cincinnatians. If there's a quarrel, it's an amiable one. Sometimes Cincinnatians tease Norwood because Norwood is a three-square-mile city entirely surrounded by Cincinnati. Norwood has no hotels, no hospitals, and no cemeteries. It depends on Greater Cincinnati for these things. On the other hand, Norwood residents tease Cincinnatians right back. During the 1937 flood it was Norwood's well—and waterworks—that helped quench Cincinnati's thirst. Cincinnati's waterworks had been flooded.

While corporate Cincinnati struggles to maintain a population of a half-million people—we count each family carefully because, if 100 people move to the suburbs, we can't claim that—Greater Cincinnati has a million and a half people. In others words, there are twice as many Cincinnatians who don't live here as do. But we must be fair. To tell how large a city is in such loose terms is the same as if New York City included Newark, New Jersey, in its population; and Chicago included Gary, Indiana.

No matter. We're all Cincinnatians—and I'm not alone in these sentiments. General Electric, for example, located for the most part in Evendale, Ohio, a separate corporate area, because the facilities GE needed were available there. Yet, GE doesn't sell its transplanted executives on Evendale's beauty. Evendale, unless you look carefully, is nothing but a Greater Cincinnati industrial complex out in the valley—a traffic jam waiting to happen. When shifts change, Evendale doesn't smell of roses. It smells of car exhaust. That's why GE wooes its labor force into this area by singing the charms of Cincinnati. The opening statement of its booklet *Hello! and Welcome to Cincinnati* says:

> We have been here a few years now and we're happy to
> make Cincinnati our home . . .

Hardly a word about Evendale as a place to raise children. Kind words throughout, though, for Cincinnati and its neighboring Norwoods, Terrace Parks, and Ludlows.

Bypass-highways and smoothly regulated traffic link these communities with GE-Evendale.

Procter & Gamble feels the same. In its *Your Introduction to Cincinnati* the soap company says, "There's never a lack of something to do in Cincinnati" and proceeds to list Cincinnati's 1476-acre Mount Airy Forest, Cincinnati's Zoo, Cincinnati's theaters, Cincinnati's 3700-seat Music Hall, the Cincinnati Reds, the Cincinnati Royals, and the Cincinnati May Festival. While P&G's general offices are in downtown Cincinnati, purists point out, its manufacturing facilities, for the most part, are not even in the city. Ivorydale—that sprawling last-century industrial heap that's as modern inside as it is ancient outside—is in St. Bernard, a corporate entity. Its Miami Valley Laboratories are near Ross, Ohio. And so on. But let the purists get technical if they choose. Tell anyone that P&G is not a Cincinnati company, and he'll chase you with a net. So much for bickering.

Instead, look again from the top of the Carew Tower. That blob that looks like a dirty tennis ball cut in half? Well, that's our Cincinnati Union Terminal, now in the Queensgate area. At one time Cincinnati had a bunch of railroad stations. In 1933, at a cost of $41,000,-000, the Terminal was built and combined them all. When it was going full-blast, the Terminal had activity in every one of its 24 buildings. Its nearly 300 acres of track were in constant use. The station had a capacity of 216 passenger trains each day, but that was back then. As far as passenger-train service goes, the railroad's golden age is over. At least here in Cincinnati. Mostly the great Terminal broods in silence now. Its breathtaking dome—180 feet in diameter and 160 feet straight up—no longer hatches passengers by the train-load. When the Terminal's public-address system speaks, it speaks to an almost empty concourse, a great room 80 feet wide and 450 feet long that used to throng with thousands.

Now, look straight down! Fifth and Vine Streets. To me, this intersection is the true *center* of Cincinnati—*my* Cincinnati. Sedamsville streetcars used to inch through rush-hour traffic and stop at Fifth and Vine, where I climbed on board. I must have waited for a thousand Sedamsville streetcars on that corner. Then the orange trolley would lumber through the West End (which isn't there anymore), roll west through the narrow river valley to Sedamsville (which isn't there anymore), and finally reach the end of the line at Anderson Ferry, where connections could be made for Aurora, Lawrenceburg, and Harrison at the interurban depot (which isn't there anymore). Yes, forty-eight floors straight down is the intersection I knew as a

9

child and as a man. Before that, it was the intersection where balloon ascensions were made and where, one evening, crowds gathered to hear Abraham Lincoln speak, and before that, where Charles Dickens, strolling along, got caught in a temperance parade.

But how did it all begin?

I'm glad you asked that question. To begin with, the Ohio River is only forty or fifty thousand years old. When it was young . . .

2

The Ohio River is only forty or fifty thousand years old. When it
was young, it was a crazy, mixed-up little stream that flowed in
every direction, including the wrong one. Its mother was the Teays
River, and its father was the Paleozoic era. By the end of that
era—230 million years before television—much of our present Ohio
Valley emerged from the bottom of the sea. Marshes and puddles
were everywhere. The earth, drying out, adjusted itself the way a
woman squirms into her girdle. There were earth tremors, sighs,
upheavals, shudderings, howling winds, the scent of salt, and before
the first dinosaur could rummage around Fountain Square, there was
one whopper of a movement—and the Appalachian Mountain chain
was born. Cincinnati at that time was not the best place to raise
children.

You would have noticed that the Ohio River—then, the Teays—
was not behaving as it should. It didn't follow the course the Ohio
River does now. It flowed west from Pittsburgh all right, but at
Lunken Airport it got kittenish and turned north, sloshed through
Madisonville, Mariemont, and Oakley until it reached Norwood. But
that's not all. The Licking River had a mind of its own, too. Instead
of meandering through Kentucky and dumping its waters into the
Ohio River, it shot out of Kentucky with such force that it ran up
Mill Creek, following Intrastate 75 generally, to join the Ohio River
near Norwood. In other words, Mill Creek ran backwards. The Ohio
River, reinforced by the Licking River, pushed north from Norwood
to Hamilton, and then turned west to the Great Miami River Valley.
There the waters flowed south through the Great Miami Valley to
Cleves, turned west, and followed the course they do today. Add
to the confusion by calling Mill Creek the Ancient Manchester River;

11

the Great Miami, the Ancient Cincinnati River. And then wait for the glaciers to come and clean up the confusion.

A few hundred thousand years ago, the winters in Cincinnati got longer, the temperatures dropped lower, and before you could turn up the thermostat, ice caps from the north were inching noisily across Ohio and Indiana, aimed straight at the Carew Tower. Some say the glaciers reached Cincinnati. Some say the glaciers stopped north of Cincinnati. Whichever happened, Cincinnati wasn't threatened with one glacier but a bunch of them. The ice would retreat, regroup, and try again. Each time it came, the glacier pushed rock and soil ahead of it. This debris filled in river valleys, opened gaps where no gaps had been, reshuffled the landscape, and flattened the terrain in places, the way bulldozers do now.

The glaciers, though, made sense out of the Ohio River. After the last glacier, the Teays River, the Ancient Manchester River, and the Ancient Cincinnati River were no more. What remained was the Ohio River, Mill Creek, a gurgling Licking River, plus the Great and Little Miami Rivers. So if you've memorized those earlier names, forget them. The older names will not help you with navigation. They will only help you win bar bets.

How did Cincinnati *look* back then? First, scrape away civilization: houses, farms, intrastates, and Izzy Kadetz. Look out your window and pretend you see nothing but fog—because for hundreds of years after the glaciers left, that is all you would see. Cincinnati was warming slowly, but the air was still nippy. Every time you went outside you would have slipped on ice. You can't defrost a refrigerator fast. Don't expect Cincinnati to work miracles, either. In fact, had you lived in those days you would have stayed inside by the fire and watched television, and you wouldn't have gone out until you had seen the last of the arctic elephants. Those elephants —hairy beasts with the intelligence of prehistoric sleepwalkers—were as plentiful for a while as mice. Your calendar would have indicated that you were in the Mississippian Period of the Paleozoic era. And if you like pets, you would have found some weird ones to feed and water. The Pennsylvanian Period, which followed the Mississippian Period, was another grabber. You would have got your kicks each time a 40-ton dinosaur rooted up your pea patch. Some dinosaurs were 90 feet long, walked on birdlike hind feet, and laid eggs. Some were toothless, but this didn't make them harmless. They could have gummed you to death.

Now and then, when shooing a dinosaur out of your garden, you might have stumbled over a pleiosaurus—and would have run for your life. This reptile grew up to 25 feet long in this area, 42 feet long in Kansas. He had teeth for gnashing and tearing, and it is said swallowed stones to aid his digestion. Be glad you weren't in

Colorado. That's where the diplodocus used to hang out. He had a 3-inch brain to power a 52-foot-long body that weighed 20 tons. He looked like death warmed over. Each day, to keep in trim, he munched a half ton of vegetables.

Also potting around in the primeval ooze of early Cincinnati was that confused reptile with a fishlike body: the ichthyosaurus, sometimes called the fish-lizard. This rascal grew to be 30 feet long. The closest thing to a parakeet, the pterodactyl, would have been another bad dream. Its wing span was 22 feet, it hung by its feet like a bat, had scales instead of feathers, and swallowed its food whole.

Why did these creatures come to Cincinnati? Well, after the sea went down and the glaciers went away, Cincinnati—and most everywhere else, for that matter—was ideal for such critters. There were marshes and ponds everywhere. The underground springs contained salt from the ancient seas. If a cow likes salt, why shouldn't a dinosaur?

Other livestock which grazed during this period were the giant elks, tapirs, and sloths.

Eventually, you would have had people for neighbors, but you wouldn't have alerted the Welcome Wagon. It is said that the first humans to arrive at Fifth and Vine Streets came here from Asia, via the northern tip of America. Some, of course, came to Cincinnati. When they got here, they huddled, without too many clothes, under the rocks the Paleozoic era had left them. They had terrible eating habits. They were fond of shellfish, which were plentiful—and when the shellfish were scarce, they were inclined to eat one another. The men were short (five feet, four inches) and the women were shorter (five feet, one-half inch). These were Cincinnati's first families —a grubby sort—gaping at the sun and eating shellfish. They didn't have tools and they didn't invent any. Life for them was chilly and dangerous, and when grandmother was invited to dinner, sometimes she was the main course.

A thousand years ago, when the Moslems were conquering Spain and everyone was taking potshots at the Byzantine Empire, the Mound Builders came to Cincinnati and built houses that looked like upside-down wicker baskets. These suburbanites grew corn and flattened their heads as the Aztecs did. The Hopewell Culture, which followed them here, went them one better. They built houses inside of stockades, hunted, fished, and farmed—but they still flattened their heads. Actually, their mothers flattened their heads for them when they were babies—as in old China the feet of women were bound in infancy. The Mound Builders were the last of Cincinnati's earlier settlers. After them, the Indians came, then Uncle Al, and here we are.

In passing, though, let's note that the members of the Hopewell tribe dressed better than the Indians who followed them. When the

Hopewell men dressed up, they looked like members of Amos n' Andy's Mystic Knights of the Sea. R. E. Banta says that the men wore wooden skullcaps; their ears were pierced and yo-yo earrings hung from them; they wore a choker decorated with fresh-water pearls around their necks; a copper breastplate was the main garment and covered a poncho-style covering made of linen-like cloth; and over this Halloween costume they wore a cloak made from sewed-together feathered skins, the feathers still there and tickling.

The Hopewell ladies dressed even gaudier.

The Mound Builders hung around until 1700. Then their civilization got swallowed up by the Cherokees and Shawnees, their tailor got discouraged, and that was that.

We're getting closer to the present. Cincinnati, so far, has endured the wet at the bottom of the sea, shivered through the glaciers, had dinosaurs for pets, said hello to the first humans, seen the Mound Builders come and go—and at this point is waiting for the first white man to paddle down the Ohio River. The Iroquois, chased from New York State, were in upper Ohio. Now and then a hunting party of theirs would have padded across your front lawn, but mostly there was only the silence of the forests. Trees were everywhere. No field had been cleared. At night, from your front porch, you would have seen the shadowy shapes of buffalo and bear heading for a water hole. Deer flitted in and out among the trees. Turkey and grouse ran wild. Food was for the taking: quail, pigeon, squirrel, rabbit, and fish. The woods swarmed with bees. You might have heard the cry of a cougar or the howl of a wolf. You would have seen birds you don't see loose anymore: green and gold parakeets, flying free. And sometimes the sky would have been dark with passenger pigeons—flocks a hundred miles in length—flying somewhere dark and mysterious.

Mostly, the air was still. A silence filled the land. Cincinnati was waiting, holding its breath, for a Frenchman to paddle his canoe down the Ohio River from the East. Some say his name was René Robert Cavelier. He was destined to be terribly disappointed. He thought he could paddle west—straight to the Pacific Ocean.

Some know-it-all Indian had told him he could.

Before the United States was the United States, England and France bickered over which of them owned the Northwest Territory, part of which was Ohio. First the French, aided by that Frenchman paddling west on the Ohio River, claimed the Territory. Next, the British, peeping over the Allegheny Mountains at the biggest fur factory they'd ever seen, claimed it. One thing led to another, trappers from both countries invaded the Territory, and thus, by the eighteenth century, the Ohio River Valley became well known. There were contretemps with Indians who also claimed the Territory. The French tried to make friends with the Indians so the Indians would shoot arrows at the British trappers; and the British tried to make friends with them so the Indians would shoot arrows at the French trappers. All of this confused the Indians, the French, and the British.

In 1774, delegates from the British colonies of New York, Pennsylvania, Maryland, and Virginia met in Lancaster, Pennsylvania, with an Iroquois chief, everyone got sauced, and the Indians sold to the British the red man's rights to the northern bank of the Ohio River—which includes Cincinnati. As lawyers might say, this was somewhat after the fact. It seems that two years before the Lancaster meeting, the Ohio Company of Virginia had been formed, the King had approved its charter, and the charter granted the company a half-million acres on both sides of the river.

Meanwhile, the French didn't sit idly by and allow the Midwest to get away from them. They organized what R. E. Banta called "a Gilbert and Sullivan" force to travel through the Territory, making speeches, waving banners, and whooping things up for France. Joseph Céloron de Bienville headed this comic-opera army down the Ohio River. Now and then the army would pull ashore and bury lead plates noting that the valley belonged to the French. These plates, in part, said:

> [We] have buried this plate . . . as a token of renewal of possession . . . of the aforesaid Ohio River, of all the streams that fall into it, and all lands on both sides of the source of . . . said streams.

The French party traveled along the Ohio River, passed Cincinnati, which wasn't there, and when they reached the mouth of the Great Miami River below Cleves, Ohio, they turned north, heading up that stream until they ran out of water. After that, they walked overland to Fort Wayne, Indiana, which wasn't there, either. However, as they moved through the Great Miami Valley, they ran into a chief of the Miamis. The chief's name was *La Demoiselle,* which means "young lady." Whether the French commented on what are said to be the feminine tendencies of the chief, and whether the chief commented on the crazy attire of the French, are not recorded. Some say, in an attempt to keep grownup history at child's level, the French didn't translate the chief's name correctly. They say the chief's real name, properly translated, was "Dragonfly." But have you ever seen a dragonfly flit around? Well, there you are again.

While the French were having problems with dragonflies, the Governor of Virginia, Robert Dinwiddie, sent George Washington into the Ohio Valley to look around. George Washington was then twenty-one years old, a planter, a surveyor, and a major in the Virginia militia. He climbed over the Allegheny Mountains, walked around a lot, noted the influence of the French, and climbed back over the mountains to report this to the Governor. The Governor called for volunteers to chase the French out of the Territory. Why didn't he call the militia? Well, the Virginia militia had a strong union. It refused to fight, march, or do anything five miles beyond the Virginia boundary. The Governor realized that when the militia reached the five-mile limit, it would stop, the men would stand around, grumble, and that no amount of urging would get them to move in any direction but back to Virginia. Hence, the call for volunteers.

The real end to the French influence here came with the 1763 Treaty of Paris. This treaty ended the Seven Years' War between England and France. The splitting up of the western territory, frankly, was no more than an afterthought in the treaty; Europe was more concerned with Europe than with the New World.

Then there was the Revolutionary War, Bunker Hill, Valley Forge, Paul Revere, and all that; our side won, and here we are in Cincinnati, in the good old U.S.A.

If you had been up late one night back then you might have seen—or, at least, *heard*—Ben Stites gallop through your backyard. And, if you had been on the patio at the time, he might have asked if you had seen a bunch of Indians with a bunch of stolen horses. Then, off he'd have gone, galloping through the forest in search of his prey.

Ben Stites wasn't a U.S. marshal. He was one of the first peddlers to drift west on the Ohio River. In 1786 he left Brownsville, Pennsylvania, with a boatload of odds and ends to sell the settlers. He wasn't worried about the lack of customers. The Revolution was over, but our country wasn't well heeled; its only cash crop was land, which it passed out as pay to its veterans. By the time Stites was drifting west, more than 100,000 settlers had drifted west ahead of him. He floated past where Wheeling, Charleston, and the Frederick Hotel in Huntington, West Virginia, now are. The Kentucky side of the river was more populated than the Ohio side because Ohio was still considered Indian country.

The voyage for Stites was lonely. Traveling four miles an hour with the current, he was surrounded by silence. Now and then he could see smoke rise from a cabin hidden by the thick forests, but that was all. Eventually he left the river and took a wagon trail headed to Lexington, Kentucky, where (rumor had it) the action was. He didn't reach Lexington. Along the trail he met men unhappy because Indians had stolen their horses. He was leading the posse to find the Indians when you saw him in your Cincinnati backyard. He went up the Little Miami River 60 miles, swung west to the Great Miami River, and turned south back to the Ohio River. He saw neither the Indians with the stolen horses nor that chief of the Miamis,

16

which, considering what they say about the chief, was just as well. Instead, he saw the wonder of the virgin land through which he passed. That ended forever his chance to become the West's first Fuller Brush Man.

Instead, he hustled back east and got John Cleves Symmes steamed up about the real estate possibilities around here. Symmes went right to work.

Symmes put out his Trenton Prospectus and ran newspaper ads touting the glories of Ohio. He offered, with each parcel of real estate purchased, additional free lots in the city he planned to build, plus free logs to build a cabin *and* a half-year's supply of Indian grain. But there was one fly in the ointment: The land wasn't his to sell. Still, he was not alone in such schemes. Others were doing the same. However, to keep the record straight, before Symmes got into hot water, the Treasury Department okayed his two-million-acre claim —which he immediately went out and purchased. For the record, also, note that Symmes was a New Jersey congressman.

Down the Ohio River everybody came! Ben Stites, rewarded with ten thousand acres, pulled ashore at Lunken Airport. With him were twenty-six men, women, and children. They waded to land on November 18, 1788. The men knocked apart the rafts, erected quick shelters, and named their community Columbia. The women cooked. Three days after Christmas, Israel Ludlow, who was Symmes' surveyor, landed at the foot of Sycamore Street with twenty-three men, and started Losantiville, the original Cincinnati. Why Losantiville? Well, *L* for Licking River that the community was across from; *os*, meaning *mouth* in Latin; and *anti*, which means *opposite*. Put them all together, tack on a *ville*, which means what you think it means, and there you are. A month later, Symmes himself drifted by Columbia, found it flooded, drifted by Losantiville, found it wasn't, and drifted on with his family and a handful of soldiers to North Bend, Ohio. It seemed to Symmes that North Bend was the perfect place to build a city.

Poor Symmes! According to legend, Fort Washington, the military post that was the making of Cincinnati (then Losantiville), should have been built at North Bend. It is said that Ensign Luce, an army engineer, came to the valley to pick the fort's site and ran into Symmes. Symmes rolled out the red carpet, convinced Luce that North Bend was best for the fort, and the deal was practically locked up. Unfortunately, Luce began to feel natural urges for the wife of a North Bend settler, which, understandably, irritated the lady's husband so much that he moved to Losantiville and took his wife with him. But the soldier followed. While in Losantiville, the officer laid out the fort, his one accomplishment, and Symmes sat drumming his

17

fingers in North Bend, feeling terribly put out. As you can see, the history of Cincinnati has love stories, too.

The first years for the three villages weren't good. Some foods were scarce. Settlers had to develop a taste for flour made from bear-grass root. Fishing was good, though, and if your aim was steady, you could eat all the turkey you wanted. But salt and whiskey were hard to come by. As towns go, Columbia, up by Lunken Airport, grew faster than Losantiville, at the foot of Broadway. Poor Symmes, becalmed in North Bend, watched both places grow bigger than his town. But Columbia was spread out over the river flatlands. Its growth wasn't visible to the eye. Losantiville, on the other hand, was crowded together at the foot of Broadway, its back against the hills. To those passing west on the river, Losantiville, with its cabins bunched together, seemed a bigger community than Columbia. The upriver community was considered the area's grainery—thanks to the flatland of Turkey Bottom, now approximately Lunken Airport. Wilmer Avenue, which runs by the Airport today, was Turkey Bottom Road. All Losantiville had at the river's edge were pawpaw thickets. All Symmes had was the uneasy knowledge that he had goofed.

The three towns began to settle down. Two taverns opened. A ferry service operated to Kentucky. The first recorded crime was stealing cucumbers. The convicted thief got twenty lashes. When General Josiah Harmer arrived with 300 soldiers for Fort Washington, the entire population of Losantiville turned out to greet him: eleven families and twenty-four single men. When the governor of the territory stepped off a flatboat to dedicate the fort, he took a dim view of the town's name. The Governor—Arthur St. Clair, an officer in the Revolution—is supposed to have said:

"Losantiville! What an awful name! God damn it, call it Cincinnati!"

This was in honor of that organization of Revolutionary War officers called the Society of the Cincinnati.

St. Clair later proved no better at Indian fighting than he was with tact.

Life in those hairy days was not all peashell beer and bear-grass biscuits. Indians resented the intrusion. Now and then an Indian would sneak up and cause trouble. St. Clair would have none of that. He sent east for troops so he could put down the Indians once and for all. More than a thousand soldiers poured into Cincinnati, business boomed, and soon the soldiers marched north to tell the redskins off. The troops traveled through most of Ohio, but the first time they encountered Indians, the soldiers lost sixty men. General Harmer sent 400 soldiers back to surprise the enemy—and lost 183 more. So things didn't look too bright for the three settlements of Columbia, Cincinnati, and North Bend. Gloom was everywhere. The dinky villages became armed camps, and feelings between the military and the settlers ran high. It was not the time to start a USO—or anything else, for that matter. So Governor St. Clair did. He personally took charge of the Indian fighting. He should have stood in bed.

The Governor led an army of 1400 soldiers north through the woods. His army looked for Indians to fight, and each morning he held assembly and parades. Unfortunately for the Governor, the army ran into a mess of Indians in Mercer County who didn't wait for the morning ceremonies to conclude. Two thousand Indians—whooping and hollering—charged from the woods and attacked. The Indians captured the Governor's artillery; and the militiamen, huddled together, were shot down like ducks in a shooting gallery. The battle was noisy, messy, and tragic. Six hundred and thirty soldiers died in that fiasco, and 300 of those who escaped were wounded.

If the settlers had been simply gloomy before, now they were filled with despair. Forty Cincinnati families gave up and moved across the river to Kentucky's safety. Ringing the three villages were collections of farmers in "outpost" stations: self-contained stockades that housed families and, at times, a soldier or two. One station was near Terrace Park, another in Cumminsville, and one a lonely affair a dozen miles up the Great Miami River. In January 1791, a station called Dunlap's was attacked by Indians, and if one man hadn't sneaked away for help, the station would have been destroyed.

But we're nearing the end of the eighteenth century in Cincinnati, so let's give it a happy ending. There was need for happiness then. Smallpox had broken out. Cincinnati was plagued with squirrels and caterpillars. At the swampy water's edge, millions of mosquitoes hummed their malarial hum. When you slept at night—if you could— you would have been awakened by the glumping of a thousand frogs. So if ever a city needed a happy ending, that city was Cincinnati.

The happy ending came in the person of General Anthony Wayne, a no-nonsense soldier and Indian fighter who knew his trade. In 1794, he marched his troops north, laying waste to fields of Indian corn as he went. By August he was near the mouth of the Maumee River at Fallen Timbers. There waiting for him were 1300 Indians. But the General played it cool. He didn't rush into battle. He dallied, killed time, and pretty soon the Indians got hungry. When 500 redskins got bored with the waiting and wandered off to look for a square meal, Wayne attacked the Indians who remained. The Indians hid behind trees and crouched behind logs—and were ready. But the sight of soldiers advancing with fixed bayonets unsettled them. Two hours after the battle began, it ended with the Indians routed.

The following summer, 1795, the defeated Indians met General Wayne in Greenville, Ohio, to work out a treaty. Talk went on for weeks. The treaty: The Indians had to get out of all but the northwest tip of Ohio. Twenty years of Indian fighting was over.

Greenville, Ohio, is noted for another thing besides being the site of the treaty signing. It has a duck pond.

19

3

In 1805, fifty keelboats were on the Ohio River—and the first steamboat that came along, in 1811, didn't scare them off. Instead, by 1815, there were 150 keelboats being pushed between Cincinnati and Pittsburgh. Keelboats were tiny cargo craft no bigger than today's outboard pleasure boats. They floated downstream with the current, but going the other way they were "poled" along by keelboat huskies. A round trip took two months. A keelboat could make three round trips during the navigation season. Keelboat men were tough, noisy, and nasty gentlemen who had terrible thirsts. When these bruisers stormed ashore, they played rough games. Sometimes they got involved with "ladies of the pave." When keelboat men fought, they gouged out eyes, bit off ears, and ripped open mouths. If they became irritated with a tavern they would, upon occasion, push the tavern into the river, or if the tavern was too far from the water's edge, they would dismantle it and start a bonfire. In later years, when steamboats replaced them, some keelboat men came ashore and, with effort, turned respectable. Most, however, ended up decayed river relics who lived in Bucktown with women they had neglected to marry. Simply put, they were hardly the sort one made "family" movies about, but they reckoned without Walt Disney, who turned Mike Fink into Mr. Clean. The real point is, when on December 31, 1799, Cincinnati rang out the old century and rang in the new, it was to be, for a while, not exactly the Cincinnati we see today. It was a rough-hewn community, a frontier town, a brawling river point. The Cincinnati of today was a long time coming.

How was life at the turn of that century? Charles Cist wondered, too; and he was less than fifty years from it. He published a book, *Cincinnati 1841*, in which he wrote:

20

I propose to furnish an extended narrative of the incidents of the early settlement . . .

But "extended narrative" proved to be a bit much. Sorry he had mentioned the matter, he added:

. . . I shall substitute [what I call] the *Early Annals of Cincinnati* compiled from the . . . newspaper press then . . .

This meant he was going to copy advertisements, news items, and notices from Joseph Carpenter's *Western Spy and Hamilton Gazette*, which began publishing May 28, 1799. Let's do the same.

From Griffith Yeatman, then a person but better known now as a bar in the Sheraton-Gibson Hotel, came this notice:

Observe this notice. I have experienced the many expenses attending my pump, and any family wishing to receive the benefits thereof for the future may get the same by sending me 25¢ each Monday morning.

Help was hard to get:

There is a vacancy at present in the *Spy* office for an apprentice to learn the printing business, which has been most beneficial to mankind since its discovery. [You] would do well to embrace the present opportunity. A lad from 14 to 15 would meet generous terms. One from the country would be preferred.

And help was even harder to keep: Robert McGinnis advertised that his apprentice, Philip Drum, had run away. Mr. McGinnis offered a reward of a sixpence worth of cucumbers for the boy's return.

Just as the *Enquirer* and *Post & Times-Star* do now, the *Spy* offered recipes. With liquor at a premium, the paper printed one for peashell beer:

Pour six gallons of water in a bushel of peashells and boil . . . until the shells are insipid to the taste. Pour off the water, which will be very sweet, into a clean tub or keg, and add a pint [of] yeast and two ounces of ginger. Fermentation will soon take place and the beer be fit for use. Beer obtained in this manner is very clear, has a fine amber color, is pungent to the taste, and bears a fine head when poured into a tumbler. Is superior to molasses beer.

Does someone owe you money? In 1799, Cincinnatians advertised the fact in the *Spy*. Consider the plight of Mr. C. Avery:

OBSERVE. The undersigned, having a particular call to go to the Atlantic States, requests his customers pay off. In so doing they will not only be considered honest men but particular friends of their very humble servant . . .

A month later, Mr. Avery appeared again:

> My generous friends, it may seem like an absurdity to give you another call to assist me to perform my journy to the Atlantic States . . . Gentlemen, you are to say whether or not I shall go . . .

But Mr. Avery wasn't alone. Consider Dr. Homes:

> Those indebted to Dr. Homes are desired to remit him the sums due. He being confined in jail deprives him of the pleasure of calling personally on his friends. They will therefore particularly oblige their unfortunate friend by complying with this request without loss of time . . .

A flash from Dayton, Ohio:

> *Notice to Smiths.* A blacksmith is very much wanted at Dayton, there being none within 20 miles of the place, which subjects its inhabitants to great inconvenience. A smith might settle himself to good advantage there . . .

And a place to wet your whistle:

> Francis Menessier begs leave to inform the public that he has opened a coffee-house at Cincinnati, at the foot of the hill on Main Street, where he proposes to retail different kinds of liquors and all kinds of pastries. He will punctually attend the coffee-house, which will be open from 2 o'clock to 9 P.M. His sign is *Pegasus*, the bad poet, fallen to the ground. Also teaches the French language. School to begin on Monday at his home, teaching every evening, Saturdays and Sundays excepted . . .

Aaron Cherry's notice said:

> Whereas a certain woman who calls herself Mary, and has for a long time passed as my wife, but who is not, as we were never lawfully married, has eloped from my bed and taken with her my property . . . I hereby forwarn all persons not to trust her to my account as I will pay no debts of her contracting.

Other wives—well, whatever they were—tended to wander. John Bentley, a sergeant in the First Regiment, advertised that his wife, whose first name was Mary, too, had not only left his bed without just cause but had taken up with a fellow named Sylvannus Reynolds.
Another ad:

> A good schoolmaster wanted on the Great Miami. One with a family preferred . . .

An academy in Newport advertised that, besides the ordinary branches of education, it would teach the dead languages, geometry, plain surveying, navigation, astronomy, mensuration, logic, rhetoric, bookkeeping, and—perhaps?—television repair. The elementary course was $8 a year. The higher branches were peddled at one pound ($2.67) each quarter.

A fashion note from the 1800s:

It has been ascertained that within the last year throughout the United States, from the present fashion of muslin undresses, as many as 18 ladies have caught fire, and 18,000 have caught cold; both classes of accidents terminating in death . . .

A military ad:

Heads up, SOLDIERS. Those gentlemen who wish to join a volunteer light infantry company are requested to meet at Mr. Yeatman's tavern . . .

This was the first military company organized in Cincinnati. How well organized is shown by the following ad:

In consequence of the rain, the muster of the Cincinnati light infantry is postponed . . .

The hungry editors ran ads of their own:

To country subscribers: the printers want some turnips and potatoes for which a reasonable price will be allowed.

One correspondent complains:

Nothing is more disagreeable, either to the speaker or to the hearer, than the bawling of children [in church]. It would be well, also, if persons were to leave off hammering on frying-pans during the divine services . . .

And, finally:

Uncommon. There is in the garden of Colonel John Armstrong of Columbia a peach tree . . . There is fruit nearly as big as a half bushel and would weigh, it is supposed, from 20 to 25 pounds . . .

So how was life at the turn of that century? It was, at times, peachy.

People had begun to arrive to start the city rolling. For example, when he was only fifteen, Dr. Daniel Drake came to Cincinnati to study medicine under Dr. Goforth. Drake turned out to be a one-man chamber of commerce, attracting settlers and industry to his adopted hometown. He also helped build hospitals. His influence is still strong upon the area. Look at the University of Cincinnati. He helped start it.

Then Nicholas Longworth, twenty-one, arrived, stayed at David Wade's Boarding House on Front Street for $2 a week, read law under Jacob Burnet, dabbled in real estate, and by the time he was forty-six, gave up law to concentrate on his investments in land and in grape growing. Been to Eden Park lately? That's where his vineyards used to be.

In 1811, as we noted, the first steamboat came by Cincinnati. Built in Pittsburgh, it was a Tinker-Toy sidewheeler named the *Orleans.* Its speed: eight miles an hour. During its trip downstream, it encountered an earth tremor below Cincinnati. The river got wild, hills wobbled, but the boat chugged on because it seemed silly to tie up to a tree that was, itself, dancing the Charleston. While that was happening, Cincinnati was gaping at the sky: Halley's comet!

After 1800, James Kemper built that log cabin which is now at the Zoo.

In 1815, when Daniel Drake published his 250-page book *Picture of Cincinnati,* the city had 6000 residents. They lived in 1100 houses, most of which were unpainted. That was also the year Cumminsville, where there was horse racing, acquired the nickname "Helltown."

Interested in birds? John James Audubon was here in 1820 as taxidermist at the Western Museum. On his free afternoons, he wandered along the river bank and sketched wildlife. In October he took off for New Orleans and never came back. Cincinnati was suffering through a depression when he left: banks were failing and flour cost $3 a barrel. It was the same year Dr. Drake opened Cincinnati's first medical school: a faculty of four and a handful of students. Three years later, in 1823, Dr. Drake opened the Cincinnati Hospital and Lunatic Asylum.

LaFayette was rowed across the river in 1825 from Kentucky so he could say hello to Cincinnati. The city rolled out a red carpet for him—literally!—but when he came ashore he refused to step on it. He is reported to have said:

"The soil of America is good enough for me."

The same year he said that, a brewery began making suds in Fairmount's Little Italy, but then it wasn't Little Italy. The neighborhood tucked away in the western hills was German, with a scattering of French. Dotty Mack would have to wait more than a century to live there, but she wouldn't have liked it then. No pizza parlors.

Cops were around. They weren't called cops, though. After a fire in 1803, the city established a "night watch." Volunteers roamed the streets after dark. Their purpose: to sound an alarm should Cincinnati catch fire again. All male citizens over twenty-one were required to serve. Each carried a lantern and a rattle. In 1811, a paid marshal was appointed and empowered to make arrests. When that happened, the night watch turned in its rattles and went home.

Our Cincinnati love story is beginning to flesh out now. Many people have come along to add their part. In 1825, Thomas Lawson, a Main Street tin and coppersmith, decided to manufacture gas for lighting. He rigged an ornate elephant's head in front of his shop. The flame came out of the elephant's trunk! Later Mr. Lawson installed gaslights in the William Tell Tavern on Elm Street east of Main Street, but his attempt to be a public utility came to a screeching halt in 1831. The City Council ordered him to douse the flames. They considered his utility a fire hazard. Cincinnati would be without gas street lighting for a while. The Cincinnati Gas & Electric Company was thinking about being born, but years were to pass first.

Don't feel too badly about Mr. Lawson. He made out. Born in Yorkshire, England, he came to Cincinnati and worked hard; the result is the F. H. Lawson Company, which now manufactures different colors, styles, and sizes of everything from bathroom cabinets to equipment for gasoline stations. Seven hundred men and women are employed there.

Cincinnati was coming of age medically. The first Caesarean section operation performed in the United States is said to have been done on a wild and stormy night in Newton, April 22, 1827. According to Daniel Drake, the doctor who performed it was John Lambert Richmond, a lad who had been a janitor at Drake's medical school until his interest caught the eye of Drake himself. Richmond—later to start medical schools of his own—got the word the patient needed his attention at the same time the Little Miami River was flooding. The doctor had to row through the swift waters to the house and there, with only pocket instruments, performed the operation. But the operation was a success. In less than a month, the woman was back at work.

The year the doctor made medical history, 1827, was the year the Miami and Erie Canal reached as far as Middletown, Ohio. The canal went through Cumminsville, the one nicknamed Helltown. Cumminsville was then a rambunctious community—noisy and shrill—filled with honky-tonks, fights, and mayhem. Later, Cumminsville would evolve into an orderly neighborhood of tightly packed red-brick houses, but not yet. Anyway, Cumminsville had every right to a hairy fling. Its beginning was tough: as an outpost station that protected Cincinnati from the Indians. Knowlton's Corner was named for Ephraim Knowlton, who not only established a store on that corner but also supervised the building of the canal through the community. He was co-owner of Cumminsville's first canal boat: *Hannibal of Carthage*. Cumminsville, even with the canal on tap, remained relatively isolated from Cincinnati until 1851, when the first Cincinnati, Hamilton, and Dayton Railroad train tooted through—but we're getting ahead of our history.

By 1828, Cincinnati had 20,000 citizens, a stagecoach service to Cleveland, fifty-four foundries, four steam-engine factories, a powder mill, two paper mills, a sugar refinery, nine printing plants, and a steamboat docking with a passenger on board named Mrs. Thomas Anthony (Frances) Trollope. She had come up the river on the *Criterion* with some of her children. Her husband and the rest of her children, including author Anthony Trollope, remained in England, where the Trollope tribe had come upon troubled times. They had purchased an English farm with the money they hoped an uncle would leave them when he died. Unfortunately, the uncle remarried instead of dying, and there they were. Mrs. Trollope had come to Cincinnati to make her fortune. She had heard glittering reports of Cincinnati's beauty, but as she stood at the railing looking at the city, she had only one comment:

"An uninteresting mass of buildings!"

But don't frown at her. She changed Cincinnati's skyline.

On the other hand, frown if you like. Those who didn't like Mrs. Trollope had good reason: She wasn't the most pleasant female to visit Cincinnati. And after she left, she wrote things about this city that rankled. She considered Cincinnati ugly—and Cincinnatians, loyal lovers all, hated her guts. But Mark Twain is supposed to have said:

> Nearly all the tourists were honest and fair . . . felt a sincere kindness for us . . . [and] glossed us over a little too anxiously. . . . Mrs. Trollope dealt a strictly "square game." She did not gild us; and neither did she whitewash us.

She was a sarcastic woman with a shrill voice. She was fat, dumpy, and masculine. Being from England, where the world was older, more organized, and neater, Mrs. Trollope was no more prepared for Cincinnati than you would be for a weekend on Chicago's Skid Row. But she hadn't come to Cincinnati to be a tourist. She had come to make a buck.

Why Cincinnati? Actually, it could as easily have been Louisville, St. Louis, or anywhere. According to her, the tasteless midwestern natives were ripe for plucking. She was going to peddle culture. She was going to get our minds off the dollar and, at the same time, get the dollars from us.

"Every bee in its hive," she wrote, "is actively employed in search of that honey of Hybla, vulgarly called money. Neither art, science, learning, nor pleasure can seduce [Cincinnati] from its pursuit!"

Her plan: to build a bazaar that would wow the city. In it she would sell items her husband sent her from England. The *Cincinnati Guide* said that she thought Cincinnati wanted "domes, towers, and steeples," so that's how she constructed her odd-looking building on Third Street. The *Cincinnati Guide* also said that Mrs. Trollope "went about Cincinnati like a child at the zoo for the first time." She thought the people rough and uncouth, and given to strange practices.

"I seldom during my stay," she recalled later, "heard a sentence elegantly turned and correctly pronounced from the lips of an American."

The "eternal" handshake irritated her, as did the approach of men reeking of whiskey and tobacco. Also, the way we shopped shocked her:

> There are no butchers, fishmongers, or indeed any shops for edibles except "bakeries" as they are called. Everything must be purchased at the market. And to accomplish this, the busy housewife must go there early or she will find her hopes for breakfast, dinner, and supper for the day defeated, the market being well over by eight o'clock!

Just walking down the street rattled her thoroughly:

> I am sure I would have liked Cincinnati much better had the people not dealt largely in hogs. The annoyance came nearer this: if I determined upon a walk up Main Street the chances are 500 to one my reaching the shady side without brushing by a snout fresh dripping from the kennel. . . . Our feet literally got entangled with pigs' tails and jawbones.

Eventually she built her queer building at 411 East Third Street. If riverboats had souls, the building would have scared the wits out of them and caused their boilers to blow. It dominated the skyline. It had a cupola on top—Arabic, Oriental, take your choice!—and inside an exhibition gallery, a ballroom, and two salons.

Why did she build such a monstrosity and start such a business? Because she thought she could get away with it. And Cincinnati encouraged her in her beliefs. While getting the "feel" of our town, she had lent a hand to the Western Museum, which had been started a few years before her arrival by Daniel Drake and Martin Baum. By the time she got off the steamboat *Criterion*, the Western Museum, in the Cincinnati College building on the northwest corner of Fourth and Walnut Streets, was teetering on its last legs and going under fast. Joseph Dorfeuille, a New Orleans naturalist, was its curator, riding herd over a raffish assortment of fossils, mineral specimens, and Indian artifacts nobody wanted to see. To attract business, he added two-headed pigs and eight-footed lambs. Even this didn't work. Somehow he and Mrs. Trollope got together. First, she jazzed up the museum attractions with the "Invisible Girl," who would answer *almost* any question. One mustn't forget that Mrs. Trollope was a lady.

The *Advertiser* reported:

> In the centre [of the room] enveloped in clouds is suspended the trumpet by which the Invisible Girl, the oracle of the

cave, delivers her responses. . . . She promptly answers any question propounded to her, if it be not an improper or immodest one. To all such a peculiar sound proceeds from the oracle, indicative of her displeasure and refusal to answer.

Following the success of the "Invisible Girl," Mrs. Trollope helped create the Western Museum's *Infernal Regions:* transparencies in the background, and in the foreground statues which, if touched, gave out shocks. This wowed Cincinnati, too. Any wonder she thought Cincinnatians were ready to be taken?

So the bazaar was built. But when advised to study what the other Cincinnati stores were selling, she didn't. She would have found, by simply visiting them, that our stores were offering a greater variety of posh than she had shipped over from England—and at lower prices, too. Result: She went bankrupt the day she opened, the law was on hand to seize her stock for unpaid construction bills, and that was the end of Mrs. Trollope in Cincinnati. Shaken, she hustled back to England, where she wrote *The Domestic Manners of the Americans,* which, happily, made enough money to bail her family out of debt.

Her strange building on Third Street became, by default, a series of sad things: a hotel, a dancing school, a military hospital, and a house of prostitution. It was, also, at one time, a Presbyterian church.

4

Had Lieutenant Arthur Mehring, the helicopter traffic cop who hovers over Cincinnati each rush hour and broadcasts about the tangles he sees, his ulcer diet, and whatever else strikes his fancy over WLW, been up there in 1850, he would have concentrated on the Public Landing. In 1850, the Public Landing was as organized as a Chinese fire drill. Five thousand steamboats put in each year. Day and night, the Landing was at full cry. Negro roustabouts wrestled bales and barrels between ship and shore. Amid the confusion on the cobblestone landing, horse-drawn carriages and drays clattered. The cheerful lieutenant might have reported:

> You better use caution rolling those barrels around because there's a pig loose, running every way. I see the farmer chasing him. Listen, you farmers bringing pigs from Kentucky, watch this sort of thing. Keep an eye on your pigs. Once they run off, they're hard to find, and there go your profits. Besides, we have enough pigs running loose on Cincinnati streets now. Make sure your porkers don't join them.
>
> Well, the traffic on the river is as I suspected at this hour. It's building up to a Signal 24. There's one packet—I think she's from Louisville—looking for a place to land. If you're listening, fellow, the Landing is full up. There are thirty-two boats there now, but I think a couple of them are stragglers. They're either finished loading or unloading. No activity around them. Listen, boats, when you finish your business, move out of the way and make room for the other guy, will you? But you boats waiting out in midstream, there's no use blowing whistles. That's not going to make the traffic move faster.
>
> Well, the farmer caught his runaway pig, so we can scratch

that problem. I can see the farmer now, herding his pigs up Vine Street to the slaughterhouse. You men running drays, be on the lookout for him. Let's not scatter those pigs again. The poor guy has had enough trouble. Who knows? One of his porkers might be shipped as far as England. They say the English people sure smack their lips over Cincinnati hams.

Well, here come two more sidewheelers. It's rush hour now, but take it easy, fellows. Play it cool, and everything will work out fine and dandy. Now, back to WLW . . .

The announcer back at Ninth and Elm Streets, then, might have launched into a commercial about the *Magnetic Doctress Miss Tennessee Claflin*, who was, at that moment of the nineteenth century, selling her services in Cincinnati. She claimed to see into the past and to know everything there was to know about the present; if the price was right, she would also peer into the future. On the side, when not looking around, she moonlighted as a medical doctor. One of her claims was a cure for cancer. The sports announcer at WLW might have followed this commercial with updated news about baseball's grandpappy: townball. He would have touched upon other sporting events: the race tracks, the dog pits, and—if the spirit moved him—the shooting galleries, which in 1850 Cincinnati had lots of. The newscast that followed him would have told about a new landmark in Cincinnati education: German was being taught in schools for the first time. Germans, then, made up 20 percent of the population. In one court trial, for example, the entire hearing was conducted in German!

But there was no radio back in 1850. Radio in Cincinnati was more than seventy years away. There were magazines, though. Ladies would not have read *Secrets* or *Personal Romances*. Confessions were also to come later. Ladies would have read *Godey's Lady's Book* or the *Ladies Repository*. Hugh Hefner had not made the scene, either. Men, instead of looking at pictures of girls with staples in their stomachs, read *Harper's* and *The Atlantic Monthly*, not a bunny in the lot. James Book Store, which had opened in 1831, was *the* headquarters for reading matter. Still, had there *been* radio in 1850, WNOP's Leo Underhill might have been muttering things about Cincinnati's first bathtub, built for the Florentine Hotel on Vine Street between Sixth and Seventh Streets across from the Cincinnati *Enquirer*—which wasn't there at the time. The tub was immense and ornate. It was so immense that a derrick was needed to hoist it into place.

Had you been a visitor to Cincinnati in 1850, you would have arrived in time to stay at the brand-new Burnet House at Third and Vine Streets, now the Central Trust garage. It was a heady and big-domed structure with 340 rooms. The *Illustrated London News* called it the "finest hotel in the world."

But if you had been a visitor to Cincinnati then, a word of caution: Watch your step. Certain parts of our city were not considered nice. We'll explore them later. Right now, though, let's walk along Fourth Street of 1850. Ignore the Irish streetworkers. They are inclined to shout nasty things about your ancestors. At the moment, they're none too happy—and with good reason. Everywhere you look you see signs posted:

NO IRISH WANTED

The Irish came here by the ton in 1840, when a potato famine back home made life a sticky wicket. Now everywhere you look: Irishmen! But don't shout back at them if they shout at you. They are 13,000 strong, a touchy group, and we don't want a donnybrook. Keep your Pat-and-Mike jokes to yourself.

The Irish made up 12 percent of our population, the Germans 28 percent, the English a scant 4 percent, and Negroes a mere 2 percent. Cincinnati was too close to the South for the Negroes to feel at ease. More than half of the Cincinnati residents of 1850 considered themselves red-white-and-blue Americans. They came mostly from Virginia, New York, New Jersey, and Maryland. Cincinnati, in 1850, was a melting pot.

As you walk along Fourth Street, listen to the conversations of the businessmen we pass.

> . . . When a man invests in a slave, he doesn't want to lose his money to a mob of addle-brained abolitionists, or to a bunch of wild-hairs from Lane Seminary. Property is property!

Can you see why Cincinnati, then, was only 2 percent Negro?

> The stink from the packing houses! Somebody ought to *do* something about it!

Ignore that gentleman. Unlike Mrs. Trollope, no true Cincinnatian would have complained about the packing houses. Pigs meant dollars. Cincinnati was slaughtering more pigs than any other two cities in the world. Anyway, all the stench hadn't originated at the packing houses. You would have noticed that the gutters along the streets were no more than open sewers: distasteful rivulets of free-flowing human waste and garbage seeking the sea. When the gutters got clogged and when the noonday sun burned hot, the smell was worse. That's why you would have taken your stroll on Fourth Street in the evening. Now and then, surprise: a whiff of fresh air! But you wouldn't have strolled too far after dark. Only a few Cincinnati streets in 1850 had gaslights. Over on Sixth Street, that serene residential row of brick and stone townhouses side by side, the residents were supposed to set out oil lamps in front of every seventh house, but sometimes they forgot.

That clutch of businessmen on the corner, yammering at one another? Their immediate problem would have been the nonsense of building a bridge across the Ohio River. "We need high stacks on boats," one said. "Without high stacks, boats would have no power. And how can a high-stacked boat pass under a *swinging* bridge? That confounded structure will be more than a channel obstruction; it will stop *all* river traffic." The other men would have nodded agreement. To them, a bridge was an evil item that must not be built. They would have been talking about the suspension bridge to Covington—and, of course, the bridge *was* built. But not without a fuss. John A. Roebling, who built the Brooklyn Bridge (the twin sister of our own bridge) as well as the one across Niagara Falls, constructed it. His first plan called for eight or nine piers, with a drawbridge in midstream to let the steamboats go by. As you can see, his plans were revised. But back then, river captains and their fellow businessmen didn't like the project one bit. Captains favored high chimneys on their boats. The higher the chimney, the greater the draft for the boat's furnace; and the greater the draft, the faster the fuel burned; and, presto! the greater the speed—and speed was what they wanted.

Charles Dickens, who had visited Cincinnati, hadn't looked upon steamboats with the love of a steamboat captain. He thought they were always going to blow up—and some did. He wrote:

> To see the great body of fire exposed, raging and roaring beneath that frail frame of painted wood, the wonder is that *any* journey can be safely made . . . These western vessels are foreign to all the ideas we are accustomed to entertain about boats. They have no mast, cordage, rigging, or other such boat-like gear; nor have they anything in their shape calculated to remind one of a boat's head, sides, or keel. Except that they are in the water and display a couple of paddle wheels, they might have been intended to perform some unknown service, high and dry upon a mountain top . . .

Mr. Dickens, also, took a dim view of the dining arrangements aboard the riverboat:

> At each meal there were a great many small dishes with very little on them. So that although there is every appearance of a mighty spread, there is seldom more than a joint; except for those who fancy slices of beet-root, shreds of dried beef, complicated entanglements of yellow pickle, maize, apple

32

sauce, and pumpkin. Some people fancy these little dainties. They are generally dyspeptic ladies and gentlemen who eat unheard of quantities of hot corn bread, almost as good for the digestion as a kneaded pin-cushion.

But back to bridge building, which in Cincinnati had become something out of a Laurel and Hardy movie. Cincinnati's first bridge was a rickety footwalk across Deer Creek, built in 1800. But consider the adventures of bridging Mill Creek. In 1806, the first bridge was constructed of yellow pine that grew at the creek's mouth. It was a fine bridge and everyone was pleased with it, but along came high water. A boat tied under the bridge raised when the creek did, lifted the bridge from its moorings, and, when last seen, the $700 bridge was floating down the Ohio River. Five years later, another bridge was thrown across Mill Creek. High water got that one, too. Another, however, lasted ten years until the Great Flood of 1832. After the river crested at 64.2 feet in February, Cincinnati discovered that its third Mill Creek bridge was resting on an island a few miles upstream from Louisville. Fed up with the nonsense, the bridge builders had the bridge towed back to Cincinnati and reinstalled where it belonged. So don't feel too harsh toward river captains for cursing bridges. It was bad enough not to get under a bridge because of the steamboat's high chimneys, but it was a bit much to face the hazard of a bridge floating downstream and crashing into them. Imagine explaining *that* to the steamboat owners.

Look around at the city's industrial leaders *circa* 1850. These were the men who owned the foundries, packing houses, furniture factories, and clothing mills. Some were brewers and some were distillers. Here were men who started Cincinnati's readymade clothing industry, which hired 950 regular workers plus 9000 women who did piecework in their homes. That man over there? He manufactured stoves and transported them everywhere, as far as the river, canal, or railroad could reach.

There stood E. B. Hinman. His place of business was at 2 Market Street. He trafficked in oils, dyestuffs, window glass, drugs, medicines, paints, and David Landreth garden seeds—practically a shopping center unto himself. There went George W. Coffin, of the George W. Coffin Company at 194 Second Street. Bells were his business. His company was the first to handle brass castings of any weight up to 3000 pounds. One-day service, yet! Want a brass bell for your tavern or steamboat. See Mr. Coffin. Had you looked carefully, you might have seen the Procter & Gamble boys peddling their candles. They had already made enough tallow candles to light all of Cincinnati. And that man over there? Nathan Sampson, Cincinnati's leading importer, or so his advertising said. From his shop at 227 Main Street, Cincinnatians bought earthen china and glass-

33

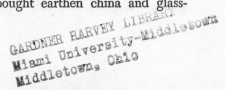

ware, as well as lamps, coasters, tea trays, knives, and the rest. Fourth Street, in 1850, was where such businessmen gathered. There was Mr. Jackson, who made carpets and mattresses. There was Mr. Dodsworth, who ran the coalyard on Front Street: Youghiogany, Brownsville, and Wheeling coal—for home or steamboat. There was the first Hertz-Rent-A-Car: Steavens and Cole, who had stables on Columbia Street between Sycamore and Broadway Streets. Rented horses, carriages, buggies, and barouches. Every horse well broken to the harness, of course. In 1850, Fourth Street was the center of commercial Cincinnati.

". . . That fool Roebling claims his bridge will be suspended by wire rope. Tell me, who ever heard of wire rope?"

"The bridge isn't the problem. It's the abolitionists!"

But except when they were irritated by the rantings of the more vocal abolitionists, the majority of thoughtful Cincinnatians pretended the slave issue didn't exist. True, some of the students from Beecher's Lane Seminary had made the issue difficult to ignore. The more agitated seminary students had formed societies and preached *instant* abolition. Some had gone so far as to walk through the streets with Negroes. One had actually spent the night with a Negro family. So enthused and so intense had his students become that poor Beecher himself was aghast. But his efforts to calm them had done little good.

Also, there would be—in 1850—talk of cholera, but you wouldn't have got *too* excited. You would have got excited, instead, about the California gold rush or, perhaps, the price of pigs. Besides, twilight was approaching. You would have felt the heat go away and you would have relaxed.

By twilight the basement saloons along Fourth Street were either half-empty or shuttered for the night. The real action was elsewhere. Several carriages moved over the cobblestones. And from the levee you would have heard the hoot of the nightboat pulling free of the landing for its nightly run to Aurora, Indiana. So there was really nothing to worry about. The man-on-the-street wasn't fretting about slavery. No one, he reasoned, would *do* anything about it anyway. The Irish were loud and capable, but they lacked organization. The Germans? They liked nothing better than to get organized, but they had not taken any action against slavery before, had they? The hare-brained nativists in the Know-Nothing party? Slavery wasn't their cup of tea. They were too busy damning the Irish and the Germans. No, the man-on-the-street wasn't worried about slavery. He had figured every angle.

So you would have kept a wary eye out for the pigs and enjoyed the twilight stroll; not the fat and slothful pigs headed for the slaughterhouse, but lean and hungry porkers that roamed the streets as free and sassy agents. They rooted in the gutters for sustenance. They were the city's garbage collectors, collecting the refuse that housewives had hurled out their front and back doors. Unlike today's garbage men, those of 1850 had been known to attack dogs and children.

Perhaps you would have paused in your stroll to step into a saloon and sample some of Cincinnati's best: wine from Longworth's Catawba grape. The grapes were grown in the vineyards in the dips and hollows of the Mount Adams ravines. The grapes were tended by Germans who had come from the Rhine Province—the *old* Rhineland—hill country not unlike Cincinnati. Entire families, chattering in German, used to swarm through the Mount Adams vineyards in advance of the first frost. They picked grapes with such care that hardly a grape was bruised. But the danger of mildew had always been present. Sometimes called "rot," sometimes called "black rot," it could have destroyed a season's crop. Already, in 1850, the grape industry in Cincinnati was entering its twilight, but the demand for wine from the Catawba had not lessened. The wine was so dry and such a delicate white that it rivaled the costly champagnes of Europe. But there had been rumors brought by canal-boat men that in the northern Ohio lake country the soil was richer and the climate less dangerous for grape growing than in Cincinnati. Just right for the Catawba, the rumors said, mentioning Sandusky and the tiny offshore islands in Lake Erie. So the grape industry, due to dry rot and rumor, eventually died, but not in 1850. It was still there then. You would have sipped the Catawba's light muscatine flavor and known that your wine had come from a cave deep in Mount Adams's crags. You would have been sampling the wine that Longfellow once praised in verse. In 1850, Cincinnati was more than a pig loose and talk of slavery; Cincinnati was the wine it made.

Had you been East, you would have heard New Yorkers refer to this wine as "better than the Rhenish or even the French sparkling wines." All this bouquet had come from an innocent grape found growing wild along the banks of the Catawba River in the Carolinas. But you would have drunk knowing that, although this wine was a luxury elsewhere, in Cincinnati it was not. Peddlers with wagons sold this wine in Cincinnati from door to door. The poor as well as the rich could slosh it down the hatch. The southern planters who crowded the Cincinnati hotels, wallowing in the grape, thought the world of it. Cincinnatians, on the other hand, could take it or leave it, which was more than most of them could do with beer and whiskey. No matter. You would have sipped another glass and listened to the conversation in the saloon:

"Take this cholera we had last year, for instance. Some say it's Asiatic cholera. Some say it's Lexington cholera. But nobody knows,

35

not even old Doc Drake. All any of us knows is, every time the weather turns warm, people dies of it . . ."

"Remember when the *Moselle* blowed up? Worst thing in river history. All her boilers went at once, killing 150 passengers . . ."

"I tell you Stephen Foster has written a new one. It's called *Summer Longings*. Prettiest tune I ever heard."

"Well, *I* long for summer to be over . . ."

And well you might, sir, and so do we. For cholera always came with summer. The year before, in 1849, the balmy weather was welcome, but death was not. Death had come anyway to begin its slow accumulation. Church bells had rung through the night heat. Each horse-drawn hearse warned Cincinnatians that cholera was again loose in the city. Each housewife was aware of it as she shopped in the teaming, rowdy Pearl Street Growers' Market. The Pearl Street Growers' Market was a mile-long open stall where milady could find everything she needed to feed her family—if, that is, she arrived early in the morning before the choice foods had been purchased; and if, that is, she discarded notions of fancy eastern fare.

But Cincinnatians had to eat. Housewives joined in the frantic race to be at the market first. Most of the ladies—mistresses and kitchen help alike—got there at dawn. Some came on foot. Some came in carriages. They shoved, elbowed, and bickered in the frenzied rush from farm wagon to farm wagon. The wagons themselves had arrived the night before loaded with country foods. Milady, also, might shop at the wagons heaped with fresh-caught river fish. Then, hurry, hurry, hurry! There's the wagon with the sausages that were so tasty! There's one with bacon! Finally, they hurried to the wagons where chickens cackled useless bellyaches. But always traveling with milady from wagon to wagon was the specter of cholera. Charles Dickens, who had strolled through the Pearl Street Market, was amazed at the multiplicity of wagons and the variety of foodstuffs. He had called the market a "horn of plenty." But Death was there, too.

By the time the sun came up, the choicer items had been purchased. It was impossible to say how many times the remaining vegetables and meats had been thumped and prodded by how many dirty hands. So, instead of rushing from wagon to wagon as the early shoppers did, the late shoppers moved with caution through the heat and they shopped warily. They hesitated, deliberated more, and closely analyzed each purchase, doubting its worth. Why had no one else bought it? As the day grew brighter, the light became better. But the daylight did not help them see what they wanted—and didn't want—to see: cholera. Would they, perhaps, then, bring death home in a market basket?

No one was sure what caused cholera. Was it a fish left too long in the sun? Was it that ear of corn which might have been touched by a hand that had—the night before—touched a body that was a body, and not a person, because of cholera? Milady didn't know where cholera came from; she only knew it came. Even then, above the cries of the vendors and the snorting of the horses and the rattling of wagon chains, milady could hear the faint tolling of church bells—and the bells reminded her to shop with care. And, in 1849, history proved her right. What had been anticipated as a normal "summer" sickness had turned into a full-scale plague.

Many claimed the cholera epidemic of '49 began with the arrival of a steamboat from New Orleans, Christmas Day, 1848. Aboard was one sick passenger. While most of the Queen City celebrated Christ's birth, the diseased intruder was taken to Commercial Hospital. His death there was hardly noticed. But the rattle of the doctors' carriages had been heard along the streets as early as January 1849. Still, the city didn't fret. The "sickness" seemed restricted to the waterfront.

By April 1849, the number of cholera cases had increased; the sickness was trespassing beyond the waterfront confines. The first case had been that of a seven-year-old girl.

"They say this doctor examined her (about the first of April). The very next day, her little brother was dying from the same thing. Within twelve hours, both were dead. Two days after that, another child in the same family was taken . . ."

Self-appointed nurses violated quarantines to go from one sickbed to another, comforting those who were conscious only of ceaseless vomiting and ceaseless seizures of cramps. In some homes these nurses found the floorboards so loose that pollution seeped up and in through the cracks. Many of these brave and nameless women themselves contracted the illness from those they could only comfort.

The Public Landing? Busy as ever. Barrels, bales, and bundles were heaped everywhere. The roustabouts sang. The pigs squealed. The boats hooted. It was business as usual. But from the city came the church bells' ringing. And the songs the Negroes sang were songs of voodoo. Makes sense. In 1849, voodoo was as good an answer as any other. It satisfied the frightened souls of Bucktown, Sausage Row, and Rat's Row. Negroes began to practice almost-forgotten African rites in the semisecrecy of their hovels. But later, as summer wore on, the rites were hardly secret: the noise was too loud. Lacking drums, the Negroes beat sticks upon sticks and chanted. At times the Public Landing resembled the African Coast, crowded with Negroes who chanted and swayed and prayed to ten thousand gods.

The Cincinnati City Council appropriated $3000 for fuel to be burned on all streets corners "to dry up or consume the noxious exhalations that brood about the city." Into these fires citizens dumped sulphur in hopes of destroying the cholera, which some actually be-

37

lieved was an evil spirit transmitted through the air. These fires themselves made the hot night air more sickening.

Where the canal turned east after its trip from the north (now Central Parkway and Plum Street), the Commercial Hospital stood. Every window gave out a yellow glow as doctors, nurses, and volunteers fought through the night against death. Wagons approached the hospital, deposited the sick, and hurried away for more. Workers carrying torches moved about among the new arrivals, carrying them into crowded rooms, crowded halls, and crowded offices. When the hospital opened in 1823, it was a three-story brick wonder of the medical world. But by 1849 it was no longer a place of glamor and wonder. Deterioration had set in—and it served too many functions. By day it was the central clearinghouse for those needing charity. It doled out food to the poor and, when available, money. It was, also, the almshouse for the city. It was the orphan's home. It was, in addition, the medical college and the insane asylum.

The smell that came from the brick structure hung like an ugly cloud over a three-block area and blotted out even the odors of roving pigs, the slaughterhouses, and the night street fires of sulphur. Screams rang out from the prison-like wards where, night and day, the insane were shackled to the floor, to be shackled there until God came. So many patients died in the Commercial Hospital that its superintendent acquired the nickname "Absalom Death."

But let us not quarrel with that hospital of Cincinnati's antiquity. In the summer of '49 it was the place where hundreds were crowded into its already crowded quarters. Epileptics convulsed unattended. Some patients, fired with cholera's anger, wandered listlessly from ward to ward. Others lay stiff and cold: exquisite almost-corpses with mouths frozen open, still breathing, hating to breathe, pleading in silence for death. Among these, the doctors, nurses, and helpers moved. They didn't know what to do, but they were brave people. They tried to stop the dying or, failing in that, tried to make the dying easier. Sometimes they, themselves, died. The only treatment they knew was bloodletting and leeching. The only drugs used were calomel and camphor. But the only answer they could depend on was death or—perhaps—the coming of autumn.

Certain records suggest that cholera had come to the continent many years before. They suggest that a handful of emigrants brought it. They suggest it traveled down the St. Lawrence River and then into the Great Lakes region. They suggest it inched through the Mississippi River Valley and came, finally, riding up the Ohio River in a proud, high-chimneyed steamboat. But others say no. They say it was picked up from the buffalo by Scott's troops en route to the Black Hawk War. It traveled, they say, by the fastest means available: riverboats, canal boats, overland stages, and finally in a railroad day coach. But it also struck down isolated areas not serviced by any of these. In reality, in 1849, there was no explanation at all. The theories about cholera were as many and as diverse as the poor souls who spread them. Some insisted it was caused by mineral poisoning. Others maintained cholera was an offshoot of malaria. One group said insects caused it. Another said mice. But these theories were not proved; and cholera continued to kill.

It was impossible to keep an account of deaths in the summer of 1849. Some doctors guessed that in July alone, 103 people died every day. But there was no official tally.

It was a torrid and feverish summer that year of '49. Now and then a thunderstorm would bring relief, but even then the violence of the lightning bursts seemed to enflame the cholera more. On most days the dry air suffocated. When the sun got hot at noon, the rivulets where the garbage flowed seemed to turn to steam.

Let's forget the summer of '49. May I get you another wine? Or shall we stroll some more along Fourth Street? Forget that summer is coming again . . .

5

Primed for a mid-nineteenth-century evening on the town? Where? "Over the Rhine?" The Public Landing? Sausage Row? Bucktown? Where? Cincinnati had many "kinds" of communities prior to the Civil War: some posh, some dinky, some delightful, and several that were downright depressing. Example: Bucktown.

Lafcadio Hearn came to Cincinnati in 1871, but he researched the pre-Civil War Bucktown section well. He arrived here from Ireland—shy, blind in one eye, but a friendly and chimerical soul—when he was twenty-one years old. He spent one day only as a messenger boy, quitting because the local rowdies twitted him about his birdlike stature. He slept in sheds, boxes, boilers, and once in a haymow. He spent his time reading and woolgathering. One day he met Henry Watkins, a printer who became his friend. The printer suggested that the Robert Clarke Company hire Hearn as a proofreader. To pay for his lodgings, Hearn worked as a waiter in a boarding house at 215 Plum Street. The stories about Hearn himself vary. Some say he married a mulatto girl named Althea Foley. Others say he didn't. No matter. He began to write articles for the local weeklies; they printed them, but paid him nothing. A shy critter, one day he approached *Enquirer* editor John Cockerill and handed the editor a manuscript. The editor liked it—and Hearn. Soon Lafcadio was a full-time staff writer. Six years after he came to Cincinnati, he boarded a train for New Orleans and never came back.

But let's rummage through his writings and reconstruct Bucktown.

The levee—Front Street between Broadway and Main Streets, where the Public Landing is—was a rowdy and obscene Valhalla. Blacksmiths and chandlers answered the needs of the steamboats. Saloons, restaurants, and hotels answered the needs of the travelers.

Sleezy rooming houses and even sleezier saloons answered the needs of the levee workers. But the section, once the heart of Cincinnati, had dwindled into a ramshackle world. Sudden rises in the Ohio River had driven the more genteel businesses to the high ground of Third and Fourth Streets. What remained was human debris: thieves, prostitutes, and other less fortunates—of every color. Sometimes "proper" Cincinnatians went slumming along the Public Landing to see the wickedness and to hear the noise, but invariably they hurried back uptown fast—counting their blessings and their jewelry as they went. According to one report, two policemen made 256 arrests in two years, about one every day or so, which shows how easy it was to look the other way. The waterfront was the Devil's Disneyland.

There was too much levee "life" for the levee itself to contain it. Some of it seeped west on Front Street to Main Street to a calamity of a neighborhood called Rat's Row. Some of it seeped east on Front Street to another calamity of a neighborhood called Sausage Row. These two "rows" contained a heady collection of businesses: saloons, boarding houses, barber shops, shooting galleries, and a few establishments that housed "ladies of the pave." History says that most of the bawdy houses were—within the framework of comparison—well behaved. Names like Charley Redman, Chris Meyer, and Maggie Sperlock were passwords to the amusements offered. Rat's Row was less exciting than Sausage Row, but when you consider Bucktown, the first two "rows" were as quiet as the library on Sunday afternoon.

Bucktown was a horny settlement filled with civilization's dropouts. It occupied a hollow bounded by Broadway, Sixth, Culvert, and Seventh Streets. So many murders were committed on the corner of Sixth and Broadway that the intersection was called "Dead Man's Corner." Bucktown bubbled to full flavor before—and for a little while after—the Civil War. Today, factories stand where Bucktown used to be, Sixth and Broadway is tamer, but now and then some of the old charm returns when men stroll by dressed as women.

Lafcadio Hearn himself wrote of Bucktown, calling it a noisy hollow,

> . . . a congregation of dingy and dilapidated frame houses and hideous huts. Shapeless dwellings often rotten with the moisture of a thousand petty inundations. Inhabited by the poorest poor and the vilest of the vicious. A little Gomorrah!
>
> In a certain low brothel there masked by a bar, a Negro levee hand blew a brother roustabout's brains all over the bar; and the waiter girl wiped the blood and white brains off the counter with a cloth—like so much spilt beer. . . .
>
> [The Bucktown residents] are Pariahs, Sudras, outcasts—often outlawed even from common criminal society. The mixture of race ceases to exist in the confines of Bucktown. White

and black are forced into . . . criminal fraternization. All are Ishmaels bound together by fate, by habit, by instinct, and by the iron law and the never-cooling hate of an outraged society. [They are] the harlot's bully, the pimp, the prostitute, the thief, the procuress, the highway robber—white, tawny, brown, and black. . . . [There are] those who have lost caste by miscegenation . . . and levee hands who live in a state of concubinage with mistresses who remain faithful to them. Of the former . . . it is scarcely necessary to say that white women wholly compose it—women who have conceived strange attachments for black laborers and live with them as mistresses. Also, women who boast black pimps for their masters and support them by prostitution. . . .

Gigantic Negresses stronger than men, neatly-built mulatto girls, slender octoroons . . . will be found among the crowd. The majority of the darker colored women are muscular and would have sold at high prices in a southern slave market. The lighter tinted are, in some instances, remarkably well favored. And among the white girls one occasionally meets with an attractive face bearing traces of what must have been uncommon beauty.

Bucktown by day is a little more than a collection of shaky and soot-begrimed frames, blackened old brick dwellings, windowless and tenantless wooden cottages, all gathered about the great mouse-colored building where the congregation of Allen Temple once worshipped, but which has long since been unused, as its . . . shattered windows attest. But by night this odd district has its picturesque points. A mass of many-angled shadows in the background relieved . . . by long gleams of light on some . . . porch or wooden stairway. Its doorways yawn in blackness, like entrances to some interminable labyrinth. The jagged outline of its dwellings . . . seem part of some mighty wreck. Its tortuous ways are filled with . . . shadows of . . . goblin form. The silent . . . nailed-up entrances and roofs jagged with ruin seem . . . specters. The gurgling gutter water seems blacker than ink with the filth it vainly [attempts] to carry away. The air is foul with the breath of nameless alleys . . .

The Sirens of Bucktown . . . walk abroad at all hours of the tepid summer night, disappearing from view by day into their dens. Dens, indeed, is the only term which can . . . be applied to many of their dwellings, whereof the roofs are level with the street and the lower floors are 30 feet underground like some . . . hideous haunts described in the Mysteries of Paris. . . .

Ten, 12, or even 20 inhabitants in one two-story underground den is common enough. At night even the roofs are occupied by sleepers, the balconies are crowded, and the dumps are . . . scenes of debauchery the most degrading.

The black hollows are foul, noisome, miasmatic! [They are] full of damp corruption and often under water—or, better expressed, liquid filth. . . . The alley which runs by old Allen Church on Fifth and Culvert some 20 feet below the fill is a long, stagnant pool of execrable stench . . . which never dries up. Insect life—the foulest and most monstrous—lurks in the dark underground shanties nearby. And ugly things—the most horrible—abound in the mud without. At the corner of Culvert and Sixth is a hole running into the sewer, a hole as deep as a well and as wide as a church door. . . . A splendid place to dispose a body in . . .

But perhaps the theater is more your style; the Losantiville Theater, of course.

When that elegant house opened its doors in the 1820s, it was hailed by Cincinnatians as the finest brick palace west—or east—of the Alleghenies. The sight of the theater's portico gave Cincinnati goose pimples, and its glittering chandelier, they say, defied description. A few clergymen and a few of their followers rejected the emporium as sinful. Their rejection was ignored. Before long, many of the objectors relented enough to be counted among those who occupied the theater's 800 seats. They, too, became enthralled with the chandelier, speaking of it as "the purest crystal, like an April shower of glittering glass drops." They were equally awed by the oil-fed footlights and the blue curtain which had woven into it a one-liner from Shakespeare. Each night the noisy and the noble of Cincinnati filled the theater's pits, boxes, and galleries.

Following the program the theater patrons—the washed and the unwashed—continued their evenings elsewhere. Rowdies hustled back to the riverfront to participate in the "fun and games" offered by Sausage and Rat's Rows. The Germans moved back across the canal to outer Vine Street and into their own "Rhineland." There, while singing waiters and orchestras bombarded them with popular melodies from *das Vaterland*, they would gather in beer gardens and reminisce. The more elite patrons of the theater usually gathered briefly in the theater's Punch Room, then singly into carriages and tallyhos, to return to the Sixth and Seventh Street townhouses. All the while, of course, Bucktown was going full-blast.

But consider the Punch Room a moment. There Cincinnati's emerging social set elbowed its way to the crowded bar to wet its whistle. The Punch Room was usually hip-deep with people who talked about London styles, the latest books, and the National Lottery. These were the rough-and-ready innocents of a hundred years ago who used imagination, fast footwork, and plain sweat to create the web of Cincinnati's growing industries.

Sooner or later, someone would have mentioned Levi Coffin. He was the Quaker from Richmond, Indiana, who had come to Cincinnati to operate a store on the northwest corner of Sixth and Elm Streets. They say tunnels connected his store with the waterfront. They say the tunnels were part of the Underground Railroad. They say that Levi Coffin, himself, was that railroad's president; and that before the end of the Civil War he had—directly and indirectly—rescued 3000 slaves from the South. In the Punch Room his name would have been mentioned at times with irritation and at times with compassion. Cincinnati, in the middle of the nineteenth century, was painfully aware of the slave issue that festered south of the river. But Cincinnati *faced* the South, did most of its business with the South, and thus practically owed its existence to the South. The businessmen who had gathered in the Punch Room had to concern themselves with southern opinion—if this city was to survive.

And always, murmured, there was talk of Levi Coffin and *that* railroad. . . .

Here they came, following the North Star. They were rough-hewn and haggard field hands, ignorant of most things, but they knew how to locate the North Star. They were soft-handed house servants, exhausted by flab, proud they knew where the North Star was. It was the star that beckoned them north. It beckoned fat women with babies sucking at their fat breasts. It beckoned high yellows with bewitching bodies. It beckoned some with skin so white they looked more like masters than slaves. By day this wandering horde hid in haylofts and in ditches. By night they crept north in scattered, shadowy groups. On moonless nights when the North Star refused to beckon, they prayed—and groped north aimlessly. They were always hungry. They were always tired. They were always frightened. To be captured meant to be turned back, to be whipped or branded or both, to be sold and separated from mother, father, husband, wife, children.

It is said that most of the slave chasers were disorganized hoodlums with nothing better to do. But some were honorable men maintaining a way of life. Some traveled in bands into the North on the trail of a particular runaway. Others were ruffians with southern accents, red-necked oafs whose palms itched for any reward dollar posted for any fugitive that they might capture. A few slave chasers were sheriffs, but not many. Several were no better than deputized tramps.

Cincinnatians at times hid the runaways in attics for months until it was safe to send them on to Canada. Other times it was essential to hurry the fugitive from the city the night he arrived. Though basically in tune with the South, Cincinnati was such that some of the runaways settled here and stayed. Often—too often—they would be discovered and secreted aboard a steamboat back to their masters.

In one manner or another, nearly every Negro completed his trip to freedom because of Levi Coffin's efforts. No one in the city could actually connect the little Quaker with the slaves, but it was common knowledge that he ran the "railroad." Rarely did any of the slaves themselves see him. He was too busy arranging their hiding places, arranging for wagons to get them to the next "transfer point," and too busy going from businessman to businessman, selling "stock" in the fictitious railroad so the railroad would have money to hire wagons. Other Quakers here were equally dedicated to the plight of the slaves. These early Cincinnati Quakers were pious souls—some merchants who had achieved wealth, and some who were poor. But they all pitched in.

While they murmured in the Punch Room, talking of this and that, a funeral procession moved without notice through the dark Cincinnati streets. It bumped on cobblestones as it passed through the Mohawk. In the Mohawk, no one noticed. The houses there were few and scattered. The hearse rattled north over the rutted stagecoach road to Hamilton. The procession moved into open country. Rural folk, talking at their gates, bowed their heads in respect as the hearse passed. But inside the hearse, instead of a coffin, three Negroes huddled in fear. Levi Coffin—was it Mr. Coffin?—had reasoned that no one would search a hearse. Such an act would have dishonored the dead.

Under normal conditions the Hamilton Road wasn't ideal. But spring rains had made it rougher. Travelers seldom used the road. Only farm wagons and the few remaining stagecoaches went along that washboard road in 1850. Stagecoaches were vanishing into history. The railroad and the canal represented the best passage to the North. Passengers seeking comfort and freighters with heavy loads traveled by rail or upon the water. A few of the roadhouses on that unused route continued to maintain rooms for infrequent overnight transients. But most of the roadhouses had closed or had become small stores that serviced the needs of the rural people around them.

The hearse stopped, the driver climbed down, went around to the back, and opened the doors. But for the next thirty minutes no one spoke. Then an owl hooted. It was the same as any one of a hundred owls in that lonely valley. Yet, it wasn't.

The driver smiled. The "railroad" had made another midnight connection.

As the Negroes headed northward from Cincinnati, perhaps you would have been riding your carriage to the "Rhineland" to sample more of Cincinnati's night life. But you would have had the feeling, as many Cincinnatians did, that time was running out on gaiety. And you would have hoped to keep the party going, aided by the Rhineland cheer. Well, it would have been worth a try. The Rhineland was that tight little community of Germans out Vine Street beyond the canal.

"Over the Rhine" had beer gardens, German restaurants, German theaters, German gambling haunts, and German singing halls. German was spoken there more often than English. In the daylight you would have seen neat red-brick houses lining the side streets. It was a ritual to scrub the stone steps each morning. Sidewalks were swept daily, too. You would have liked this Old World community where Bach chorales rang out from church towers and unpronounceable German names identified each store: *Bäckerei* for bakery, *Spezereihandlung* for grocery, and *Apotheke* for drugstore. And at the Armory Hall in 1850, the first *säengerfest!*

As your carriage crossed the canal, you would have ignored the unhappy language of the unhappy canalman. He was trying to convince his mules to pull his barge of Lake Erie ice to the icehouse. Enoch Scott ran the Northern Ice House on Twelfth Street. But the mules seemed more concerned with the texture of the grass that grew along the towpath.

Then the canal would have been behind you—and there you were: "Over the Rhine!" You would have tried the happy beer garden that seemed crowded with families. You wouldn't have criticized the bellowing. That was *Teutonic* singing. And you wouldn't have worried about the waiter with that trayful of beer steins. He never spilled a drop. Sometimes, above the din, you would have heard the string orchestra. But you would have hurried through the saloon to the grove outside where a table waited and a breeze blew. Entire German families would have been enjoying the cool of the garden. The young ladies were safe. At the first sign of rowdiness the bartender, tapping another barrel of beer, would have hurled himself over the bar with the grace of a ballet dancer, moved quickly through the room, and silenced the hubbub with a stare. Every bartender was a bouncer, too.

Night life in mid-nineteenth-century Cincinnati? That was the way it was, from Bucktown to the Losantiville Theater to Rhineland. Cincinnati, then, was trying to enjoy it while it lasted. Over Cincinnati, looking down, was the North Star. Though Harian Deihl shot off nightly fireworks displays from his fireworks factory on Mount Adams, none of his displays had the power of the North Star. Thus ended that long-ago night. The Losantiville Theater was silent and empty. A lone Negro had swept the Punch Room clean. The nation's hog butcher—long before Chicago won and lost the title—and the nation's largest producer of liquor was relaxing, drinking, and having fun. In Bucktown, in Rhineland, everywhere there were drunkenness and laughter. The saloons, beer gardens, dance halls, and restaurants brimmed with people. The din from the shooting galleries was constant. Guests in the new Burnet House strolled through its ornate lobby and out onto the street to seek the pleasures of the night. Somewhere a steamboat whistled for a landing. Somewhere Stephen Foster toyed with a new song. Somewhere in a German kitchen, a sleepy father slurped his kidney soup. But this was the twilight of Cincinnati's childhood—and the years flickered by so fast: 1850 . . . 1855 . . . 1860 . . . the twilight deepened. And then: the Civil War.

Cincinnati's wild, sweet childhood was over.

A month after Lincoln was sworn in as President of our side and two months after Davis was elected President of the other, General Beauregard began lobbing shells at Fort Sumter. As for Cincinnati's attitude, some say it was southern. Others say it was northern. General Sherman wrote that Cincinnati "furnishes more contraband goods than Charleston and has done more to prolong the war than the State of South Carolina." Charles R. Wilson, in *Cincinnati's Reputation During the Civil War*, wrote that "Cincinnati was really neither pro-Southern nor pro-Northern. Whatever sectionalism she revealed was Western, but as a matter of fact, she tended to discount even this in the interest of the Union. She was Unionist to the core." Dr. Louis Leonard Tucker, director of the Cincinnati History Society, looked into the matter and concluded that when the word of Fort Sumter reached Cincinnati, "if there had been doubt about Cincinnati's loyalty to the North, it was quickly dispelled . . . One persistent cry rang through the streets: Union, Union, Union!" He added that "one Southern sympathizer from Covington made defensive statements . . . and after being smashed in the face with an egg, found it expedient to leave the scene on the run." Dr. Tucker's book *Cincinnati During the Civil War* is crammed with such details, is well written, and sells for only $.75. Drop by the Cincinnati Historical Society in Eden Park and buy a copy. This is the same Eden Park through which streetcars used to run and where, on warm summer evenings, lovers walked and sometimes kissed.

Dr. Tucker noted that Cincinnati, at the start of the Civil War, was among the top five manufacturing areas of the nation. This made the city a prize to whichever side its loyalties favored. "A wide variety of products was manufactured from implements to willow wares," Dr. Tucker wrote:

> . . . Cincinnati could supply every human want including counterfeit money (and some did engage in this type of production). The city could boast 8 tent and awning establishments, 10 brass foundries, 10 boiler yards, 2 bolt factories, 474 boot and shoe makers, 25 candle factories, 32 carriage plants, 48 wholesale warehouses, 6 gunsmiths, 10 rolling mills, 56 saddlery shops, and 3 boatworks. The presence of 36 breweries and 33 major packing houses attests to the value of the spirits and foodstuffs among the manufactured commodities . . .

47

Before we get Cincinnati too involved in the Civil War, however, let's catch up on a few odds and ends to bring the city up to its war effort. Eight years before Fort Sumter got shot at, Cincinnati acquired its first steam-powered pumper for the fire department. The pumper was the handiwork of Alexander Latta, a Chillicothe-area native. On the New Year's Day when it was tested against a hand-pumper on Broadway Street hill between Fourth and Second Streets, crowds gathered. They wanted to see if the 12-ton steam-pumper could stop as it rolled down Broadway to the river—or end up in the drink. Happily, it managed to stop. Latta also designed and built a locomotive for the Little Miami Railroad. The same year he tested his steam-pumper, the first full-fledged insane asylum was established on the northest corner of Queen City and Harrison Avenues; there is no connection between the two events, however.

Seven years before the Civil War, the *Enquirer* began publishing its Sunday edition. Six years before the Civil War, the Know-Nothing party chased a German band from a Mary Street flat building, then invaded the "Over the Rhine" section itself, but were stopped by angry Germans shooting at them from second-floor windows. Five years before the Civil War, John C. Bruckmann started the Bruckmann Brewing Company at the southwest corner of Ludlow Avenue and the canal. Four years before the Civil War, the Ohio and Mississippi Railroad made connections both ways: from St. Louis to Chesapeake Bay; also, the first horsecars rattled sedately through the streets; and the Marietta and Cincinnati Railroad, less sedately, chugged through Oakley. But Oakley wasn't called Oakley then. It was called Schusterville, for Paul Schuster, who had purchased thirty-four acres there in 1853. *He* called it Oakley because of the neighborhood's oak trees.

We're getting closer now to the conflict. Three years before Fort Sumter, Charles McMicken, who had got rich as a merchant and a dabbler in real estate, died, leaving most of his money to the city so it could start a college that would major in "all the high branches of knowledge except denominational theology." But it wasn't until 1869 in rented quarters on Main Street that McMicken University began. Now McMicken is a building on the University of Cincinnati campus —and those stone lions out in front of McMicken Hall are whatever color the adventuring students can get away with.

Two years before the war, Pike's Opera House opened its thirteen doors. Samuel Pike, a distiller, had built the palace for Jenny Lind to sing in. Just one year before the war, the Germans could boast of twenty-one different singing societies; B. H. Kroger, who founded the Kroger grocery chain, was born; and the migration had begun from the crowded basin of the city to sparsely populated Walnut Hills, Clifton, Avondale, Mount Auburn, Price Hill, Westwood, College

Hill, and Glendale. On the other hand, in 1860, Silverton, where Aron Mathieu lives, was no more than a toll gate, an inn called the Eight Mile House, and a blacksmith facility. Cheviot, which had been laid out in 1800 as Cheviot Hills by Scotsman John Craig but had not been settled until 1818, held its very first Harvest Home Festival in 1860. The location: its seven-and-a-half-acre park, once the farm of Enoch Carson.

The year Fort Sumter was fired upon, Joshua Bates laid tracks for a horsecar line to carry passengers from Frenchman's Corner—Harrison and Queen City Avenues, where the insane asylum was—to Cumminsville. And these tracks became the first victims of the war—unintentional victims, that is. When General Henry Heth moved up through Kentucky to tear Cincinnati apart, Major General Lew Wallace was appointed to defend the city. One thing he did was suspend all business—all, that is, but the horsecar line and the horsecar drivers. This irritated the saloonkeepers, who had been forced to close. They became so irritated, they ripped up the horsecar tracks, reasoning: no tracks, no horsecars. Thus, the horsecar drivers would have to defend the city, too. *That* gives you an idea of the Civil War in Cincinnati. If the South didn't get you, the saloonkeepers did.

However long ago it was and however childish and antique some of the incidents appear in perspective, there was nothing childish about the havoc the war caused in nearly every home in the area. Men left Cincinnati to fight for the South—and for the North. Truly, here it was, at times, brother against brother. But let us look at the war as it touched upon the city itself.

As soon as word came about Fort Sumter, company after company was formed in Cincinnati to fight for the Union. Some, though, were more comic-opera than military companies. One such company, under the command of Judge Bellamy Storer, was called Storer's Rifles, but how much fighting his company did is questionable. Dr. Tucker writes that this company "had two distinctive qualities; they were splendidly dressed and equipped"—being mostly older and wealthy businessmen—"and they were conspicuously spherical in contour." Henry Howe, in *Historical Collections of Ohio*, told of a stuttering tailor named Platt Evans who had wisely refused to lead another company. The tailor said, "If-if I was m-m-marching you down B-B-Broad-B-B-Broadway you would all be in the r-r-river b-b-before I could ca-call ha-ha-halt!" The Cincinnati *Gazette* told of a 75-year-old man who volunteered not only himself but—without their knowledge —his sons, grandsons, and sons-in-law. Charles T. Grove wrote in the *Centennial History of Cincinnati and Representative Citizens* of the Montgomery Guards and the Sarsfield Guards. Each group was made up of men from the other. General Joshua Bates said, ". . . When [they] paraded at different times [they] were beautiful to behold, one

49

clad in Hibernian green and the other in our National blue; but when [they] paraded together, one of them was not there."

Dr. Tucker added that "the immigrant groups were particularly responsive to Lincoln's call for troops. The Irish community provided an entire regiment which became the 10th Volunteer Infantry . . . The much smaller French colony assembled at Gruhler's Garden and organized a 64-man 'Garde Nationale' . . . The Germans of Cincinnati were most enthusiastic . . . A mass meeting at Turner Hall . . . led to the formation of an all-German infantry regiment. To fill out the regiment, 1014 recruits were needed; over 1500 signed the muster roll. This unit later became the . . . 9th Ohio Voluntary Infantry—or *Die Neuner.*"

It was, at moments, a lighthearted war around Cincinnati. Canteens were constantly checked to see that the men had filled them with water and not the taste of bubbly. When the cavalry first got horses, men would get up on one side and immediately fall off the other. When the infantry was first issued rifles, so many rifles went off accidentally, the camps weren't safe. Although the Germans maintained a beery training area at Camp Harrison, the other camps around the city—Camps Clay, John McLean, Corwine, Colerain, and Dennison—were not exactly temperance gatherings. But no one worried. All felt the war would be over fast. But that wasn't in the cards.

And there *were* cards. You couldn't quite call it a defense industry, but near Foster's Crossing five brothers manufactured Cincinnati's first playing cards. They were the Longley brothers: Seretus, Septimus, Sirenius, Alcander, and Elias. Started in 1862, their playing-card business lasted a dozen years, then collapsed. Also started in 1862 was the Lunkenheimer Valve Company, by Fred L. Lunkenheimer. His business is still with us, trafficking in bronze, iron, and steel gadgetry, including valves and engine appliances. By 1862, while the soldiers were wetting their whistles at camp, the forerunner of the Cincinnati Gas & Electric Company was lighting Cincinnati streets with gaslights: 2450 street and park lamps that were turned on every evening and off every morning by a staff of 247 workers, lugging ladders. The company, in addition, had 8200 customers for its gas.

But 1862 was the year that scared Cincinnati out of its wits. In August, Confederate General E. Kirby came charging out of the South, aimed straight at the Queen City. All that stood between General Henry Heth's 10,000 rebels was a brace of Union regiments and the Ohio River. As noted, Major General Lew Wallace was assigned by the North to defend the Greater Cincinnati area. But when he arrived here in September to do it, he discovered the citizens too panicked to think about defending anything. Instead, they were packing clothes, burying silver, storing furniture, going to church more than usual, and drawing money from the banks. Stay and defend Cincinnati? No, thanks! They wanted out. Wallace didn't tolerate such nonsense. He proclaimed martial law and gave men only two choices: Show up with a gun to defend the city, or show up with a shovel to build the city's defensework. Somehow Wallace had electrified Cincinnatians with the idea that their city *could* be defended. Well, he didn't exactly electrify everyone. It is said that one man, caring neither for a shovel nor a gun, went around dressed as a woman to avoid conscription. But he forgot one thing. He forgot to shave off his mustache.

The defense of Cincinnati was not complicated. Cannon were placed on hills like Mount Adams and Price Hill, their snouts pointing south. A pontoon bridge was built across the river and men crossed it, lugging guns or shovels or both, to set up the first line of defense in the near Kentucky hills. Perhaps the hairiest group to defend Cincinnati was the Squirrel Hunters, who arrived the second day in September. They wore a mishmosh of uniforms: some tailored, some homespun, and some a raffish combination of the two. Carrying squirrel rifles, these men came from Ohio and Indiana, their arrival producing a whopper of a problem: how to feed them? where to bed them? When these tawny bruisers finally crossed the pontoon bridge into Kentucky, Cincinnati ladies lined the streets, waved handkerchiefs, and shouted,

"God bless you, boys!"

But the Squirrel Hunters, according to Dr. Tucker, received a chillier reception in Covington and Newport. There they were jeered and cursed.

In less than two weeks, though, the Squirrel Hunters—and everybody else—marched back across the pontoon bridge to Cincinnati. The invasion had proved a clinker. Cincinnati was relieved and so was the home guard. Other than a few skirmishes between guards, there had been no battle. The rebels had gone back into the South—and that was that.

The only real trouble Cincinnati faced was getting the Squirrel Hunters to go back to their homes. For a few days these lads were feted. Then they were mustered out of the service and given train fare home, but by then the lads had become too fond of Cincinnati. Hadn't the ladies waved pretty hankies at them? Anyway, they had come to fight, so they fought one another, fought saloonkeepers, and fought whoever else was handy. The ladies, though, no longer waved hankies and shouted, "God bless you, boys!"

Cincinnati's next scare came the next year, 1863. It was the same year that steamboats were converted into gunboats, and the year Avondale, named by Cincinnati and Chicago Railroad surveyor H. C. Freeman, was incorporated to protect the community from roving livestock. The scare, of course, was Morgan and his Raiders, who actually did less damage to the area than the livestock had done in Avondale. The Governor of Ohio declared martial law again as Morgan approached. He called the militia to active duty again. And on July 12, in Cincinnati, General Ambrose Burnside also declared martial law. But Cincinnati had grown blasé. Didn't Burnside have enough soldiers on tap to settle Morgan's hash? Wasn't Camp Dennison crawling with recruits itching to clobber the rebels? What was the fuss about?

The fuss was really nothing, unless you happened to live in Glendale, where, on July 14, Morgan and his Raiders galloped through. The Glendale residents hid behind locked doors and breathed a sigh of relief when Morgan's men kept right on going. By dawn his raiding party was near Camp Dennison. The invaders put a log on the tracks of the Little Miami Railroad, derailing a train and capturing 150 militia en route to the camp. Morgan let the militia go, figuring they would only slow him down. Other militia from Camp Dennison chased Morgan's party as far as Batavia, where the militia, said Dr. Tucker, "placed a tree across a road to check a possible retreat(!) by the Confederates . . ." So much for the war, *per se*, coming to Cincinnati. It never showed up.

But in 1864 the war elsewhere was going strong. In Cincinnati the price of a substitute soldier had risen to a new high: $500. James Hollenshade was manufacturing army wagons and pontoon bridges in what was the forerunner of the first assembly line. He made 80 boats and 160 wagons in less than a dozen days. Miles Greenwood's Eagle Iron Works had employed 400 to 700 men, changing 60,000 flintlock rifles to percussion caps at the rate of 800 rifles a day. This was 600 more a day than the National Armory at Springfield could do. Several times Greenwood's factory caught fire. Some said it was the work of southern sympathizers, but the fires actually caused little damage.

Although the surrender of Lee created cheering and wild celebration the day Cincinnati first got wind of the event (April 10), it was decided that Good Friday, April 15, would be the official day to celebrate, which gave some of the celebrants a few days to sober up and have another go at the bubbly. Celebrating was the key. Good Friday found Cincinnati doing little else. Factories had been closed. Schools had been closed. From the country, people poured into the city by every means of transportation available. Bonfires were set everywhere and church bells were poised to ring on cue—all church bells, that is, but the one in the steeple of the College Hill Presbyterian Church (then: the First Presbyterian Church); it had rung so long and so loud on April 10 that it had cracked.

Thomas Edison, who was seventeen at the time, was staying at the Bevis House, a hotel operated by Martin Bevis and W. H. Ridenour on the southeast corner of Court and Walnut Streets. He was the night telegraph operator who, at three in the morning, received word of Abraham Lincoln's assassination. And with the coming of that terrible word, Cincinnati's celebration ground to a halt and a silence. Junius Brutus Booth, Jr., had been playing a two-week engagement at Pike's when he was told, the next day at rehearsal, that his brother had killed the President. He fainted.

On April 17, Mayor Harris held formal memorial services in the same Pike's Opera House where the assassin's brother had been. There were eulogies by Bellamy Storer, Aaron Perry, Colonel C. F. Noyes, the Reverend J. F. Chalfant, and Samuel Cary.

6

Now that you have got through the Civil War, see if you survive the next thirty-five years to celebrate the arrival of the twentieth century. You would have survived—if, that is, you didn't get clobbered by a runaway horse, shot in the courthouse riot, burned to death in the Public Landing fire, nailed by a narrow-gauge railroad train, or drowned in the flood of '84. Also, it would have helped if you had avoided that nasty pack of hoods, the Deer Creek gang, and if you had stayed away from the Main Street incline on October 15, 1889, because the incline clutch didn't hold and—*crunch!* What did Cincinnatians do to survive those thirty-five years? They held their hats, they didn't stand up, they stayed out of Bucktown, and when crossing streets they looked both ways for runaway horses.

Example: In 1886, policeman Frank Morgan stopped a runaway team at Fourth and Race Streets; policeman Henry Eckerstaff stopped a runaway horse at Fifth and Walnut Streets; and at Gilbert Avenue near Grant, policeman Thomas McDonough stopped a runaway coal wagon. The following year wasn't any better. The music of a parade maddened a streetcar horse at 611 Main Street. Policeman John Donnelly stopped that one. Officer Patrick White stopped another horse, which had also maddened when it turned music critic. We have reports that year of a runaway team on Freeman Avenue; a runaway buggy horse (horse and buggy, that is) on Sycamore Avenue; a runaway ice-wagon horse on Plum Street; on John Street a runaway horse pulling a wagon that contained a very distressed lady; on Eastern Avenue a runaway horse pulling a wagon that contained not only a very distressed lady but two equally distressed children; a runaway express wagon horse on Main Street; and, to break the monotony, on

54

July 15, 1887, a pair of runaway mules. So much for the sport of kings. In those thirty-five years the city was growing fast.

In 1866, Major Peter Zinn platted the residential downriver community of Delhi to be, he said, "strictly residential." Then, across the river, Brooklyn and Jamestown merged to become Dayton, Kentucky. 1868 saw Westwood—which had been called Challengeville after early settler Reverend James Challenge—finally incorporated. Two years later, 1870, Cincinnati annexed a handful of communities: Price Hill, Pendleton, Sedamsville, Fairmount, Corryville, and Mount Lookout. In 1873, Cincinnati annexed another handful: Woodburn and Cumminsville—and knowing what we know about Cumminsville, then, you can see why it alone was a handful. In 1879, Home City, the next-door neighbor to Delhi, was incorporated. In 1885, the town that wasn't there—Industry—was annexed by Delhi. Originally platted to attract industry before the Civil War—1847, to be exact—the town of Industry attracted grief instead: a flood washed away its flour mill, its match factory went up in smoke, its cotton mill went bankrupt, and its foundry closed after the owner got free and easy with the petty cash. The town of Industry was located on River Road between Trautman and Delhi.

Norwood officially came into existence on May 10, 1888, but actually it began much earlier, 1809. It was, at first, a saloon operated by Samuel Bowman at Main and Smith Streets. John Sharp lived across the street from the saloon. Sharp was a retired Indian fighter, and in his honor and until the 1870s, the crossroads had been called Sharpsville. The same year Norwood began, so did Fernbank. Matthew Addy started the town west of Fernbank, calling it Addyston, platting it in 1889, incorporating it in 1891. His intention: to make Addyston a second Pittsburgh. The Addyston Pipe and Steel Company there was the first to use southern ore—and thus was partly responsible for the fact that Birmingham, Alabama, exists today. Terrace Park, where Don Leshner lives, was incorporated in 1893. In 1896, Cincinnati grabbed another handful of communities: Westwood, Avondale, Clifton, Riverside, and Linwood. Two years before the close of the nineteenth century, Cincinnati annexed Bloody Run—and there you are, at 1900!

Other things happened, though, between 1865 and the turn of the century. During this period Cincinnati invented Ivory Soap. Cincinnati watched workmen put the finishing touches on the Mount Adams incline, Music Hall, and the Hebrew Union College. So let's not rush. Let's sit in the shade of Philip Metz's winery tucked in the hills along Queen City Avenue, sample the bubbly, chat with Dotty Mack's ancestors, and watch thirty-five mellow summers drift by . . .

Some maintain that, after the Civil War, Cincinnati went into an eclipse. They point out, for example, murky politics. They mention

George B. Cox. When each city grew its own, Cox was Cincinnati's political "boss." The man cast such a long shadow over the Cincinnati political scene that it is not easy to convince some Cincinnatians—especially those who are Democrats and Charterites—that Cox is dead and no longer operative. Not too long ago one political figure suggested a political campaign based on the slogan: *Don't let them get away with it!* His cohorts knew—and understood! The charming part is, they agreed and were inclined to go along, doing battle with the long-ago Mr. Cox and his long-ago machine that is, in essence, nothing but murmurings from history. Cincinnati, some say, should update its political enemies. But this is no political thesis.

After the Civil War, Cincinnati completed the suspension bridge, opening it to traffic in 1867. But there was more than one way to cross the Ohio River. For fourteen days in February 1893, the river was frozen solid; people could walk over. The same thing happened in 1895. And consider 1877: From December 15, 1876, to January 14, 1877, the river was gorged solid for thirty-one days! And when the water was flowing, there the ferries were operating. Let's examine the history of one.

Since 1817, at Anderson Ferry on River Road, some sort of boat has always sloshed back and forth between Cincinnati and Constance, Kentucky—even though neither town was there at the ferry's start. Before 1817, it was an Indian crossing. John Wilson used to run a horse ferry at that point, but two years after, Charles Kottmeyer bought the ferry and built the steam-operated *Boone*. Even now there's a *Boone* chugging across the river at Anderson Ferry, an excellent shortcut from the western communities to the Greater Cincinnati Airport in Boone County, Kentucky.

The same year the *Boone* converted to steam, 1867, the Union Central Life Insurance Company began. It was founded by the Methodist Church, and employed preachers as agents. Before it changed its name, the Central Trust Tower used to be the Union Central Tower. Until 1930, that tower was, at thirty-eight stories, Cincinnati's tallest building. Then the Carew Tower came along.

The Cincinnati Work House, that antique city prison that looks, as you drive in on Intrastate 75, like a castle gone to seed, began in 1866 but wasn't open for customers until 1869. It's at 3208 Colerain Avenue, still going strong with a daily population of 400. Although there is no connection between the two, the year the Work House opened was also the year the Sisters of Charity began the College of Mount St. Joseph-on-the-Ohio. Among the College's newer structures is one of the most modern theater facilities this area has ever seen, but the real charm of the school is its serenity, its accumulation of some of the area's nicest nuns, and its collection of the prettiest girls you'd ever want to see. The school is perched on top of a hill that looks down on River Road in the western part of Cincinnati, its view of the river and the far Kentucky hills is spectacular, and its campus has enough trees to drive a woodpecker mad.

Thirsty? In 1870, George Wiedemann started a brewery in Newport that produced fifteen barrels of beer each day; later he bought the Constans Brewery on Monmouth Street; so drink up.

The Crane and Breed Casket Company, now at 1231 West Eighth Street and one of the last *old* buildings in the *new* Queensgate development, hit its stride after the Civil War. Its success actually came during the war itself, producing watertight and seepage-tight caskets. According to Dave Clark, casket authority, "massive shipments of caskets to the South during the Civil War for transferral of the dead to their northern homes were made possible by Crane and Breed." Mr. Clark points out that Abraham Lincoln was buried in a Cincinnati-made Crane and Breed casket and, also, that the local company was one of the first to tinker with a motorized hearse when horseless carriages came along.

Meanwhile, at Fountain Square in 1871, Governor Rutherford B. Hayes was speaking at the unveiling of the Fountain Square statue—the one that gets you wet on windy days. Now green with age, the statue was given to Cincinnati by Henry Probasco as a memorial to his brother-in-law. At the end of the First World War, a coffin that contained an effigy of the Kaiser was burned there. During the Second World War, Fountain Square became a "demolition depot." Tanks, jeeps, bombs, guns, and other military hardware were sold in exchange for War Bonds, but you couldn't take your purchase home. You had to let our side use it to win the war. When people gather for momentous events—the end of wars, the winning of league pennants—it is to Fountain Square they head. Where the Square is, a butcher's market used to be: rows of rickety stalls. The butchers didn't want to move out for the fountain to be built. One night city workers came along, ripped apart the butcher stalls, and ended the argument for keeps. But legally the Square is *supposed* to be a market, and to make certain that condition is fulfilled, once a year the mayor buys a flower there from one of the civic groups.

The Fountain Square statue itself is 43 feet high and was made in Munich. That 9-foot-tall gal on top holding her hands out is shapely all right, but some say that from certain angles she looks pregnant. Her title is "Genius of Water." Water dribbles from her hands, except on windy days, when the water is turned off. There are a bunch of lesser statues around the monument's base, each of them dribbling water, too. Now and then a country idiot will come along and pour detergent into the fountain's pool, saturating the city with bubbles enough to make downtown look like a Lawrence Welk rally, but in reality the effect is more irritating than uproarious. The *Cincinnati*

Guide sums up the scene best: "Fountain Square is the heart of Cincinnati—and its sentimental nosegay."

In 1872, the Norfolk and Western Railroad tooted through Hyde Park for the first time. In that year, the Main Street incline began to hoist passengers up Main Street hill—after the customers had ridden horsecars out Main Street from town. Also making noise that year was *Joe Bell,* the narrow-gauge puffer-belly that connected Mount Lookout Square with the outside world. It was a steam-powered dummy car that chugged one mile along the bank of Crawfish Creek (now Delta Avenue). The noisy and daring little railroad operated twenty-five years. Finally it went the way of most odd-gauged steam lines, but not before it had given the horses a good run for their money.

Horsecar lines—each a separate company—were expanding over the face of Cincinnati to connect the basin area with more isolated communities. Anyone could start a horsecar line. All he needed was $150 for a horse, a horsecar that would hold twenty passengers, and a franchise. To get the franchise, he had only to suggest a route the city engineer favored, agree not to charge too much, and build his track the proper gauge: five feet, two inches. It was a case of horsecar line eat horsecar line, however. In July 1873, most of the lines operating in the Queen City joined together. They called their collection of hay-burners the Cincinnati Consolidated Street Railroad Company.

Then, there was the Mount Adams incline—or, to give it its proper name: The Mount Adams & Eden Park Inclined Railway. One commentator, upon hearing that name for the first time, said:

"The builders proposed to build an incline hardly longer than its pretentious title."

The Mount Adams & Eden Park Inclined Railway was incorporated by E. M. Shield and others on June 26, 1873—and a few months later, *pow!* a major depression hit the land. Cincinnati was hit hard. The Queen City was no longer *the* Porkopolis; Chicago was. Cincinnati packed only 600,000 hogs; Chicago packed twice that number. But the incline builders crossed their fingers and looked to the future. Three years before, they reasoned, Eden Park had opened, and wasn't it destined to become popular? Eden Park, which formerly had been Longworth's vineyards, still lacked trees and shrubs to complete its charm, but the park was there. The trouble was, unless a Cincinnatian possessed a carriage, he had no easy way to reach it. And if he was a workingman who worked fourteen hours a day, as most did, he had little inclination after work to walk up a steep hill. So, they reasoned, an incline up the side of Mount Adams made sense. It would make the park available to all.

Hadn't the Main Street incline been a success? And what of the one in Pittsburgh? And consider the Price Hill incline then under construction. It would be a beauty. Cincinnatians could ride a horsecar out Eighth Street from town, then ride the incline up Price's Hill, as it was then called. The Price Hill incline was 800 feet long and climbed 350 feet up the steep slope. William Price had built his incline so well that the original steam engines he installed in 1874 kept going until electric motors replaced them in 1928. The hill was called Buttermilk Hill, because William Price didn't approve of drinking. Saloons at Eighth and State Streets at the base of his incline were marked with warning signs that announced:

LAST CHANCE!

In some Cincinnati saloons, women would sometimes come in and pray against demon rum. If the women had got their way, every hill in Cincinnati would have been a Buttermilk Hill, separated by Buttermilk valleys. However, some tipplers gave up the sauce without a whimper. In the basement of Robinson's Opera House, on the northeast corner of Ninth and Plum Streets, "Uncle Jon" Robinson wintered his circus animals. Tipplers who staggered by were never certain if the elephants they heard were real or imaginary. The Opera House, by the way, in the 1930s became a stumblebum hotel, and in 1936 was torn down.

The task of completing the Mount Adams incline fell to one of its first investors: a wealthy tanner named James E. Moody. He appointed Pennsylvanian George B. Kerper to the presidency of the hillside railroad, and from then on—*gangbusters!* Kerper has been described as a peppery but adaptable gentleman with a walrus mustache. He captured the imagination of Cincinnati as much as the incline itself had. When he took over, not much of the incline had been built. By the spring of 1874, only the smokestack and the depot at the top of the hill were there, one boiler had been installed, and two cars finished, but that was all. No tracks, no station at the bottom, nothing. Worse, there was no way to connect the inclined plane with existing horsecar routes. The railroad started at the top, where little was, and ended at the bottom, where nothing was. Kerper went ahead in spite of these problems. Soon the incline was making test runs.

While Kerper was testing his gadget, Cincinnati was involved in other matters. In the summer of 1875 the second May Festival was held. Reuben Springer offered to put up $125,000 to build an auditorium to house it, provided the public would put up an equal amount. Cincinnati school children scraped together pennies and nickels and did just that. The result: Music Hall. In another part of the city, meanwhile, Dr. Isaac Mayer Wise started the Hebrew Union College and would remain its president for a quarter of a century. The combined horsecar lines opened the Cincinnati Zoo, and out on Spring

Grove Avenue George N. Stone opened Chester Park, named after one of his race horses: *Lady Chester*. While all this was going on, there were forty-two gas ranges in Cincinnati. In ten years, there would be 3500.

In March 1876, Kerper started operating the Mount Adams incline. Passengers rode up and down on its two counterbalanced cars named *Nicholas Longworth* and *Martin Baum*. Kerper had also solved the problem of being out of touch with the world at the bottom of the hill. Against the grumbling of the Cincinnati Consolidated Street Railroad Company, he built his own horsecar line from the incline's base to Fountain Square. It was called Route 15.

As a next-door neighbor to the incline depot at the top of the hill, George W. Rapp designed Highland House, a two-story frame building that sported two towers. An ornate saloon, it at once added to Mount Adams' hodgepodge. The first floor was a 48×135-foot ballroom equipped with a brace of bronze fountains 7 feet tall and 10½ feet around! Upstairs were a smaller ballroom and a dining hall. Also included were a bowling alley, billiard room, bandstand, wine cellar, beer vault, and laundry. If Cincinnatians were daring, they could ride an elevator 80 feet up in one of the towers, rent binoculars, and stare at the city below. Though charming in its day, Highland House might seem like a Charles Addams nightmare now.

Two years after the incline began running, Kerper received permission to build a horsecar route from the top of the incline into Eden Park itself. That was in 1878. Much had happened in the interim. A freight incline had been added as a twin to the Price Hill passenger incline. The Physio-Eclectic Medical College had begun—only to flounder three years later. Also begun was the American Eclectic College, which lasted a bit longer as a medical school: exactly thirty years, at which point the state medical board shut it down as "not in good standing." By this time the Cincinnati & Westwood Railroad was tooting merrily along its narrow-gauge tracks to Cheviot, stopping long enough at Metz's Wine Cellars to unload tipplers; the Southern Railroad had tracks as far as Somerset, Kentucky; and Cox, irked by the way Democratic cops kept giving his saloon a hard time, ran for councilman, and, at twenty-four, was elected. This was the only time the "boss" ever held an elected office, but he ended up running the city anyway. While Cox was taking umbrage with the boys in blue, the newly formed Women's Art Museum Association, having exhibited in rented rooms, was trying to talk patrons into donating art or hard cash to start a permanent collection somewhere. That "somewhere" turned out to be Eden Park, where, in 1877, Kerper was chopping down trees so that his horsecars could get by.

How do you build a horsecar railroad through a public park? Well, you do as Kerper did. First, chop down the trees that stand in your way, level a roadbed, and put down iron plate for the road. Don't use T-rails; use wood strips covered with iron for your tracks. After all, horsecars don't travel fast—no more than six miles an hour—and they won't break the less expensive wood track. They don't weigh much either: never over two tons. And there's your horsecar railroad through the park!

The Eden Park line opened on April 18, 1878. It was a winner from the start. Writing later in the Cincinnati *Gazette* of a horsecar line through a public park, one New York visitor was surprised the line existed at all. "Of course," he wrote, "older and eastern cities would never allow a horse railroad through their parks. It would be a sacrilege."

But Kerper's problems hadn't ended. The horsecar line ran from the incline depot through the park—and that was it. His route to Peebles Corner in Walnut Hills had not been approved. But a year later he received the okay to extend the line, and when the permission came, he decided to overhaul his entire system. Why change cars? he reasoned. Why not ride *one* horsecar from Fountain Square, let the incline lift the horsecar up the hill, and away you would go, through Eden Park to Peebles Corner on the same horsecar you started out on downtown! This meant junking the incline's original passenger cars and installing platforms the horsecars could ride on. Hadn't the freight incline at Eighth and State Streets proved a success? It not only carried horsecars, but—when no horsecars needed lifting up the hill—drays as well. Thus, extra revenue. In November 1879, Kerper shut the incline down so he could rebuild it. It wasn't until the next spring that he was back in business again, but that was all right. Who wanted to visit Eden Park when the icy winds howled? Kissing wasn't best then.

While he tinkered with his incline, Procter & Gamble—making 200,000 cakes of soap a day—introduced Ivory Soap. Ivory Soap had been born of an accident, really. The workman who ran the blending machine had gone to lunch and forgotten to shut the machine off. The mixture blended itself silly. The result: a hard soap that could float! Customers who got the soap liked the way it floated and demanded more. To Harley Procter, though, the product was a cut above P&G's White Soap; it was a new world in soap and he wanted a new name for it. One morning in church he read in Psalm 45:8:

All thy garments smell of myrrh, and aloes, and cassia,
out of the ivory palaces, whereby they have made thee glad.

Ivory Soap had its name!

And while Mr. Kerper was rebuilding his incline and Mr. Procter was naming soap, the St. Frances De Sales Church was dedicated. But even in Cincinnati you couldn't win them all. When the 17½-ton bell, nicknamed "Joseph," was first rung in its 230-foot tower, the vibrations broke windows in the neighborhood. Since then, the bell has been rung by being clappered on its *outside* surface. It was Cincinnati's first sonic boom.

In 1880, the *Spirit of the Times* merged with the *Star* to become the *Times-Star*. The *Penny Paper* began publishing that year and eventually evolved to the *Post*, which merged with the *Times-Star* to become the present *Post & Times-Star*. The motto of the Scripps-Howard evening paper is "Let there be light," and the year the *Penny Paper* began, the light was supplied by the Maxim Electric Company of New York. The company demonstrated electric light for the first time in Cincinnati. An 8000-candlepower arc light was set up at Fourth and Elm Streets; its beam on that snowy night lit objects as far away as Fifth Street!

Had the light been aimed at Mount Adams, it might have shown Mr. Kerper sawing and hammering on his incline structure. But the rival Cincinnati Consolidated Street Railroad wasn't idle. It merged with an assortment of other horsecar lines: the Storrs and Sedamsville Railway, the Cincinnati and Spring Grove line, the Cincinnati and Clifton Incline Plane Company, and the Walnut Hills and Cincinnati Railroad. Its new name was the Cincinnati Street Railway Company, now the Cincinnati Transit Company. Kerper saw his company being surrounded by this new combination, but he refused to be eliminated by them. The only eliminating done that year was at the Atlantic Gardens on Vine Street. John L. Sullivan knocked out "Professor" Mike Donaldson in five rounds and earned $50 for doing it. The fight wasn't a crowd-pleaser. The Cincinnati police had insisted that the boxers wear gloves.

With 3300 manufacturing plants in Cincinnati in 1880, the horsecar lines were busy shuttling workers back and forth, and—when faced with hills—up and down. Commuting was a slow-motion adventure. The trip up Gilbert Avenue by horsecar took thirty minutes. Irked by the "bigness" of the Cincinnati Street Railway, Kerper decided to go for broke. Cable cars were faster than horsecars, he reasoned, so why not build a cable-car line? His proposed route was along McMillan, down Vine Street hill to Third Street, where the new railroad terminal was to be built, and then over to connect with the incline depot at the bottom of Mount Adams. He announced his plans in September 1881. Well, simply put, there was some behind-the-scenes dickering, some now-you-see-it-now-you-don't stock transfers, and the upshot was that Kerper's incline railroad and the Cincinnati Street Railway were the best of friends—partners, actually—working hand in hand, and that was that.

But you can't blame either company too much. To build a cable-car line would have taken more bucks than either, individually, could raise. For example, the Gilbert Avenue cable-car line had cost $100,-

ooo a mile; the cable alone, $1400 a mile. Regardless of the "merger," a lot of horses were to come and go before the first cable car, other than an experimental line, appeared. And a lot of other things happened in Cincinnati while Kerper and the Cincinnati Street Railway Company were working out details.

For one thing, electric lights were installed in commercial establishments. In February 1881, the Brush Electric Company rigged electric lights in Strobridge Lithographing Company's entire building. For the first time the company could operate at night. Electric lights were placed outdoors in front of the *Commercial* and the Grand Opera House. Elsewhere, nonelectrically speaking, B. H. Kroger started as a delivery boy for the Imperial Tea Company, at the age of twenty-one, and moved up quickly to become store manager at $12 a week, plus a percentage of the profits. When the company refused to make him a partner, he did the only honorable thing: He quit and started his own grocery.

Before the first cable car moved, another year passed, and Cincinnati was in 1882. The Andrew Jergens Company, 2535 Spring Grove Avenue, opened for business; and in Norwood, so did the Globe Wernicke Company. The Palace Hotel, on the northwest corner of Sixth and Vine Streets, took in its first customer. Ivory Soap was first advertised as "99 44/100ths% pure–it floats." Elias Kahn opened a butcher shop on Central Avenue, now the E. Kahn's Sons Company, 3241 Colerain Avenue. And for political watchdogs, note that Cox organized the votes in his ward, and *that*, some say, was the start of his political "machine"–which, they add, didn't turn out as pure as Ivory Soap.

The next year, 1883, B. H. Kroger opened his second store. His motto: "Do what your competitor neglects to do." He put price tags on merchandise, gave premiums for coffee and tea, and shocked shoppers by arranging his wares neatly.

That wasn't the only shock Cincinnati had that year. William Berner and Joseph Palmer hammered a horse trader to death for his gambling poke. On the night before Christmas they wrapped his battered body in burlap and dumped it into Mill Creek in Cumminsville. But what really upset Cincinnati more was when, the following year, Allen Ingalls and Ben Johnson murdered the Taylor family of Avondale–mother, father, and daughter–and peddled their remains to the Medical College of Ohio for $15 each. The doctor who bought the cadavers cut them into five parts each, and sold each part for $5, making a neat profit. The *Enquirer* headlined the grisly event:

COLLEGE OF MURDER

Ingalls and Johnson were locked in the county jail, which already contained our friends who had done in the horse trader. The jail

63

also contained two other murderers. One had killed his wife with a butcher knife, and the other had killed his with an ax. With that many murderers behind bars at one time, Cincinnati might have breathed easier, but when Berner, who helped kill the horse trader, got off with a light sentence, Cincinnati didn't have time to do a slow burn. It got angry fast. Thus: the Courthouse Riots of 1884, which took the United States Army to stop.

A mob of 10,000 assembled at the courthouse. They carried sticks and stones; a few carried guns. When they gathered, Hamilton County Sheriff Mort Hawkins acted. He secretly took Berner, focal point of the mob's anger, to the state prison at Columbus. But the mob seethed. Bricks were tossed, the jail door was battered with a beam, and before the first day was over, the frame building inside the courtyard had been burned, five men were dead, and nearly fifty were wounded. The next day federal troops arrived to face the mob which had established itself behind a barricade of mattresses, tables, and anything not nailed down. The mob charged the troops several times. Finally a flag of truce was raised, the wounded were carted off, and, the amenities having been observed, the battle resumed. By twilight the mob had piled furniture against the building and soaked the accumulation with kerosene. When night came, the fire was lighted. The mob noisily prevented firemen from putting the fire out. At dawn the Hamilton County Courthouse was a smoldering ruin. There was one final attack the third day, but in reality, the back of the mob had been broken. Three hundred men and boys had been wounded. An estimated fifty were dead.

The riot wasn't the only terrible event to plague the serene Cincinnatians in 1884. The Ohio River flooded, reached 71.1 feet—9 feet less than the flood of 1937, but still the second worst to clobber this town—and four thousand homes were under water. The Suspension Bridge was closed (it wasn't closed in 1937; it was our only link). Lights went out. Gas was shut off. Leaks from the gas mains presented a constant fire hazard. Every fire engine the city possessed was mounted on flatboats. For the first time, the Red Cross was active here. Clara Barton herself was on the scene.

But let's put the riots and the flood of '84 behind us and get on with the business of cable cars. After all, we *are* approaching the Gay Nineties, there hasn't been much to laugh about, and it wouldn't do to sit through the Gay Nineties as gloomy gusses, would it? What you would have needed was the adventure of a cable-car ride—and four days after the Fourth of July speeches in 1885, that's just what you would have taken: Cincinnati's first cable-car ride!

You would have ridden up Gilbert Avenue at a steady eight miles an hour. The 22-ton cable installed on July Fourth was working just fine. Of course, when you boarded the car downtown, it wouldn't have been a cable car but a horsecar. In reality, it was a cable car *pulled* by horses. At Court Street the horses were detached, the gripman pulled the gadget that hooked the charming little car to the continuously running cable in the slot, and, *zap!*, the car went scorching up Gilbert Avenue—eight miles an hour, naturally—leaving in its wake buggies and drays, and outdistancing all but street urchins, who ran alongside and made fun. At Nassau Street at the top of the hill, horses were attached again, and the car proceeded with clippety-clops to Peebles Corner.

You wouldn't have stared too hard as you passed the Deer Creek gang. You would have ignored them all: Flanagan, Walker, Skelly, Doherty, Kennedy, and the rest. They weren't nice. Allowing for an occasional absence caused by a prison term, the Deer Creek gang varied in membership from ten to forty. They sent their girls into Eden Park to make eyes at unwary males and lure the victims back into the Deer Creek area. Once there, if the victim lost only his wallet, he considered himself fortunate. Rumor had it that Dan Nuttle of that rat pack died a violent death, but no one kept score, so there was no way to make sure. Anyway, the gang was reaching its twilight. By 1886 they wouldn't be bothering Cincinnatians at all.

As you rode the cable car you might have listened to the conversations of the other passengers . . .

"I hear they're going to close the Physio Medical Institute—and after twenty-six years!"

"We've too many ward heelers in town now. I wish they'd start that Committee of One Hundred they're talking about."

"Pish! Cox will never let them do anything!"

"They say the Koehler Brewery has been sold. A man named Louis Hudepohl bought it."

"That's right. And they're going to call it the Buckeye Brewery."

"It's better than calling it Hudepohl! Who'd buy a beer with that name?"

Which shows, even then, not everyone was absolutely correct.

"We ought to get rid of the canal. It's getting to be an eyesore, and it stinks."

"Going to Chester Park next month? John L. Sullivan is fighting Dan McCaffrey."

"That'll be no fight. They're going to use the Marquis of Queensberry rules!"

"Here's Nassau Street. Say, look at the horses. I'm sure glad to see them. I don't trust cable cars. I mean, suppose the string broke?"

"But we got up the hill faster, didn't we?"

"If man was meant to travel eight miles an hour, God would have . . ."

And the cable, slapping in its slot, would have pulled you at a gentle eight miles an hour out of 1885 and into 1886. The Art Museum had opened in Eden Park. Charles West had put up $150,000 on the condition that the public match it. Cincinnati did, and the result was more customers on the Mount Adams incline. The cable-car line had been extended to Woodburn—no more changing to horses at Nassau Street. It extended, on the other end, into downtown. No more changing horses at that end, either. Drifting along at eight miles an hour, the cars moved silently along Sixth Street to Walnut, visited Fifth Street, then moved primly back to Gilbert Avenue to climb the hill once more.

As you passed them, you might have observed the stately policemen on the corners, proud and erect, swinging their billies. They were not the muttonhead flatfeet of earlier times. To become a minion of the law they had to attend school four days—four hours a day—before being loosed upon the public. Each carried a rosewood baton that had a red cord and tassel. Don't tangle with them. They're still the bust-em-up kind of cops. They keep in shape at the police gym at the Hammond Street Station between Third and Fourth Streets. And don't try to outrun them. Their speed has been tested on the gymnasium track. On the other hand, you might try slipping one a greenback. There are some things gymnasiums can't test.

Cox was entrenched in politics by then. He controlled 2000 patronage jobs. The word was "boss." The Committee of One Hundred? Well, the man on the cable car last year was right. The Committee fizzled out.

The Cincinnati & Westwood Railroad—that happy, little narrow-gauge that took Cincinnatians to Metz's winery—fizzled out, too.

Where could Cincinnatians go? Lots of places. There was always Ohio Grove. They advertised it as the "Coney Island of the West." James Parker, who owned the Grove and wrote the advertising copy, didn't know what he was starting, though. It's no longer the Coney Island of the West. It's simply Coney Island. Is there one in the East? Never heard of it!

Silently the cable car would have moved you into 1887, the year the Cincinnati Gas, Light & Coke Company made merging noises at the Cincinnati Electric Light Company. From the state legislature in Columbus came word that Negroes were to be admitted to public schools. If a telephone campaign had been organized in those days to fight for—or against—that legislation, the campaign would have fizzled. In 1887, the first telephone exchange had opened—with eighteen customers! This was also the year Procter & Gamble began experimenting. It gave a chemist a corner in its Ivorydale machine shop to conduct research. It experimented with employee relations, too. In 1887, William Cooper Procter started the P&G profit-sharing plan.

1887 was also the year of two calamities, one right after the other. The first was at Robinson's Opera House. Some nut shouted "Fire!" and the result was pandemonium. The second happened the very next day. On an Indian summer Sunday evening, thousands rode the cable cars down Gilbert Avenue, heading home after family outings. One car tried to disengage the cable at Court Street so it could stop, found the cable wouldn't release. The car's mechanical "grip" had caught in a kink in the cable—and the car kept right on going. It tooled around corners it should have coasted around. Passengers panicked. Some jumped, and the rest held on for dear life. The car, which had been moving at a steady pace, caught up with the cable car ahead, which had been starting, stopping, and slowing down, and off they both went, eight miles an hour, sweeping around curves, bucketing along straight stretches, until there were three cars racing in tandem. To make a long story short, there was a hairy pile-up at Fifth and Sycamore Streets: cable cars, horsecars, people, horses, and bewildered gripmen. More than 10,000 gathered to see the cars, horses, and people untangle. Happily, no one was killed. Still, October 1887 wasn't the best month that year.

The next year, 1888, saw the first *electric* streetcar. It operated on the Main Street line and left its competition in its wake. The last Gilbert Avenue cable car ran in February 1889. The line through Eden Park was electrified in 1890. The age of the hay-burners, except for one that clopped through the streets of Price Hill, was ended.

The age of the incline in Cincinnati almost ended, too. On October 15, 1889, the clutch at the top of the Main Street incline failed, and down the car came, crashing at the bottom and killing all but one passenger. People lost faith in the Main Street incline after that. Though remodeled, it never won back the business, and in 1898 stopped running.

But no strain. You could have gone back to Metz's winery in the hills along Queen City Avenue. James N. Gamble had purchased the defunct Cincinnati & Westwood Railroad, changed it to regular gauge, and ran a puffer-belly from the Westwood depot on Glenmore Avenue to the Sixth and Baymiller station in Cincinnati, stopping en route at the winery, of course. So there in the winery we would have sat, perhaps discussing the topics of the day.

"They're actually building a crematory on Dyxmyth Avenue . . ."
Or:
"Can you imagine it! P&G has 900 employees!"
Or:
"No matter *where* you look, another tennis club! There's one in Eden Park, Avondale, Price Hill, Covington, everywhere! They've even organized a thing called the Racquet Club!"

But as we entered 1890—the Gay Nineties—only 400 steamboats

still operated from the Public Landing, only 5000 arrivals and departures, a thousand *less* than ten years before. We were no longer Porkopolis—or even close: only 271,000 hogs were packed here. In twenty years our furniture industry had deteriorated 50 percent; the financial district had moved from Third to Fourth Street to get away from the river; and the West End was beginning to be a slum. Over the river, horsecars had been replaced by little green electric trolleys. So we welcomed the Gay Nineties with mixed feelings.

In this period—between 1890 and 1900—Cincinnati built 150,000 carriages and wagons each year, half the nation's needs. The Hotel Alms opened. Rookwood Pottery moved to Mount Adams. Proctor & Gamble began an employee stock-purchase plan. The Wheel Club, an assortment of bicycle nuts riding 54-inch front-wheel rattlers, held rallies. The Cincinnati Gym Boat Club became the Ohio River Launch Club. The Greenes bought a second riverboat, the *Argand,* and Mary Greene became a licensed river pilot. City Hall was built. The Old Carthage Distillery opened. *Billboard Advertising* began publishing. So did the Norwood *Enterprise.* In Ludlow, Lagoon Park opened. Harrison's statue was erected in Piatt Park.

But Highland House was torn down. Harriet Beecher Stowe died. The narrow-gauge railroad on Delta Avenue stopped running. And slowly, slowly the nineteenth century drew to a close, leaving the cable cars, the riots, and the narrow-gauge puffer-belly to old men sitting on park benches, muttering memories to themselves.

7

The first twenty-five years or so of the twentieth century were not the best years Cincinnati ever pasted into a scrapbook. One of the reasons was George B. Cox. But we must be fair: Cincinnati let him happen to it. Cox was the sort of political "boss" that Hollywood hatches in smoke-filled backrooms and nurtures with stuffed ballot boxes, patronage, and possible greed. When Joseph De Maistre wrote in 1811 that "every country has the government it deserves" he didn't realize that it would apply to city governments as well. Of that turn-of-the-century period of municipal government, Lincoln Steffens said, "You can't put all the known corruption of an American city into one book."

Cox, first teenage saloonkeeper and then keeper of the city, constructed a political machine so effective that it wasn't broken up until years after his death; and even today older members of the opposition dig up his bones to run against.

Because his father died when Cox was eight years old, Cox was forced to become the family breadwinner, working at odd jobs like selling newspapers, being a bootblack, driving a wagon, and finally being a bartender. By the time he was eighteen, he was a Republican challenger at the polls and soon was running his own saloon at Central and Longworth Avenues. He became a Republican because his father had been. Had his father been a Democrat, Cox would have been a Democrat, too. Chance played a great part in his career.

For instance, chance dealt him a bartender named Frank Kelly, described as a "sleek, dapper little man with a soul as cool and hard and shiny as a billiard ball." This gentleman regaled saloon customers with the glories of machine-run politics in Philadelphia —and Cox listened, too. That is, young Cox listened if the cops in the

69

ward—Democratic to the soles of their flat feet—were not raiding his saloon, an exercise they frequently performed because, as Cox fans say, Cox was a Republican and they were not. The fact that Cox ran a gambling session on the second floor might have had something to do with the police visits.

Chance also taught young Cox the political trade. While still "coming of age" he had only to look around and learn from his elders. Cincinnati elections back then were mostly farce and sometimes heavy-handed. Dr. Leonard Tucker, of the Cincinnati Historical Society, tells of an election in the early 1880s in which young gentlemen, Democratic by persuasion, voted often—and every chance they got. When confronted at one polling place by the official Republican challenger, they challenged him back, dragged him outside, worked him over, and in fifteen minutes were back inside, stuffing 125 votes into the ballot box. This shocked even the Democratic challenger's sense of proportion. He cried, "Hold up awhile! That's enough just now."

Gradually Cox moved into politics, beginning in the Eighteenth Ward, which each year put up a slate of thirty highly disorganized Republican candidates who promptly nullified one another in the city convention. This bothered Cox. The entire Republican organization of the city bothered him. It was little more than a ramshackle political sport so diluted it had little effect. The first thing he did was organize the candidates in his ward. From there, the rest was child's play. After organizing his ward, he organized the city convention. As chairman of the Hamilton County Republican Committee, he surprised the state machine by getting two Republican congressmen elected at a time when Hamilton County was considered a Republican wasteland.

Chance again entered his life via Dr. Thomas V. Graydon, an Iowa native who had come east to peddle a tuberculosis cure. Although one of the doctor's favorite pitches was to show photographs of patients he had cured, some skeptics say the patients were the doctor himself in various disguises. When not peddling remedies, the doctor won a seat in the Ohio legislature, got the ear of Governor Joseph B. Foraker, and came up with another cure-all: Get Cox entrenched in Hamilton County and, *presto!*, the county would be a gold mine of Republican votes. The Governor did just that. He abolished the *elected* Cincinnati Board of Public Affairs and made it into the *appointed* Board of Public Affairs, which immediately opened up nearly 2000 patronage jobs. Cox was appointed to distribute these jobs, and from then on, Cox was in the driver's seat. Said he:

"I had no ambition to become a boss when I entered politics . . . But because of my peculiar fitness, I became boss."

Businessmen—in love with bandwagons or frightened by Cox's building inspectors—made the machine run faster. They oiled it with dollar bills. Murmurs of protests were more squeaks than shouts. The real shouting was to come later. Cox did have some opposition, though. There was the Committee of One Hundred, which proved ineffective. Also, in 1911 the Democrats managed to break his stranglehold on the mayor's seat, booting the Cox mayor out and installing Henry T. Hunt, but Cox still held the majority of votes in council. Another protest came from an anti-Cox publication called *Side-Lights*, which ran this tongue-in-cheek ad in 1903:

WANTED! Candidates for the Republican nomination to the General Assembly. Seven of the men must be conscientious but incompetent, and the other seven must be competent but not conscientious. Inquire George B. Cox . . .

By Cox's fiftieth birthday he had reached a kind of zenith; such nitpicking didn't bother him. Lincoln Steffens had called his machine ". . . about the most perfect organization of the sort that I have seen or heard of." Cox himself had visited Tammany in New York to pick up a few pointers and had returned to Cincinnati with the heady knowledge that he was better organized than they were. So at his fiftieth birthday party, in 1903, he could relax, puff his stogie, and receive the gift of a $1600 gold chandelier from his friends, each of whom had been nicked $40, and to hear them sing that popular song of the day: "He's Been Mighty Good to Me." Of his opposition, Cox said:

"Their failings were born in them and they should not be blamed too much."

George B. Cox ran a malty machine. He knew each working part and what made it tick. At convention time, he personally selected the Republican candidates. His city and county workers paid the machine from 2 to 5 percent of their salaries. At election time he plastered city hall and the courthouse with Republican literature. Democratic literature, on the other hand, always seemed to vanish. It is said that on election day he opened the city Work House, freeing the prisoners. The prisoner who voted right got an instant pardon. Kentucky and Indian drifters, recruited from the Public Landing, were turned into citizens-for-the-day and given a vote. Two wards whose population had been decimated when a railroad right-of-way was built, actually showed a population increase on election day. In 1903, of the thirty-four voters registered at the National House on West Fifth Street, only five were listed in the city directory, many were not known at all, and one poor soul (may he vote in peace) had died six months before he cast his ballot. The *Cincinnati Guide* noted that:

. . . if an election promised to be close, it became the workers' unpleasant duty to register floaters . . . The practice, usually safe in the downtown wards, had to be avoided in the hills, where election officials were generally unimpeachable.

In 1905, when Cox machine faithfuls were praising the Cincinnati Water Works that the machine had built, they neglected to add that it wasn't as efficient as the one Cleveland had built, although it had cost three times as much to construct. In another matter, if a referendum hadn't stopped them cold, the machine workers would have peddled the city-owned Southern Railroad at a "sacrifice price."

Cox had two lieutenants: August Herrmann and Rudolph Hynicka. Of the three, Herrmann came out with the smallest bank account, but still he didn't end in a poorhouse. Anyway, Herrmann was the jolliest. He "radiated *Gemütlichkeit* at picnics, wedding parties, lodge suppers, and other social functions dear to the jolly Germans." He was forever sending people Cincinnati sausages. His letters usually began with the turn-of-the-century argot for "enclosed find sausage. . . ." Less cheerful was the machine's comptroller—comptroller of people as well as petty cash—Mr. Hynicka. It is said he kept a card file of Cincinnati voters, and made notes of whatever scraps of information ward workers could dredge up. Hynicka later made a mint with a string of burlesque houses—in the long-ago days when burlesque was cleaner than most city governments.

What kind of man was Cox personally? Well, Alfred Segal described him as a tall and fat man ("very fat around the belly") who answered questions in a gruff voice. "Most unfriendly," commented Mr. Segal. But George B. Cox had reason not to be a sea of gurgling glee when Mr. Segal appeared. Mr. Segal was then the amiable reporter for the Cincinnati *Post*, which was trying to take Cincinnati out of Cox's hip pocket. The Cincinnati *Commercial Tribune*, on the other hand, made Cox as palatable as Walt Disney's conception of Mike Fink. According to the *Commercial Tribune*, Mr. Cox favored marriage. One tale had him convincing an underling to cut out hanky-panky. Another tale, almost Lincolnesque, found a common laborer and a U. S. Senator waiting in Cox's outer office; when Cox entered he visited with the laborer first while the senator cooled his heels. Still another story had Cox giving away wads of money—anonymously. And another had him standing in the noonday sun in front of the Mecca Saloon, 431 Walnut Street, saying hoarse hellos to passers-by.

The Mecca Saloon was Cox's morning "home away from home." It was a place filled with man smells, tobacco smoke, beer, whiskey, and talcum powder. Lesser politicians dropped by each morning to wet their whistles and steal glances at whoever was going upstairs to have audience with Cox. In the afternoons, Cox went to Wieilert's Garden, 1408–10 Vine Street, and he usually spent his evenings there, too. The *Cincinnati Guide* says that Wieilert's "ranked with the best of the 'Over the Rhine' beer gardens in entertainment." But to Cox, when the party conventions were in progress, the real entertainment was at Turner Hall or Music Hall. He did not attend these events. Rather, runners hustled to Wieilert's to keep him posted. Why go? He knew the outcome. Hadn't he written the scenario himself?

In 1905, twenty-three of his twenty-four ward captains were on either the city or the county payroll. The one who wasn't enjoyed "gambling privileges." To show the nature of Cox's city council, this story has made the rounds: Someone once shouted into the council chamber, "Your saloon is on fire!" All the councilmen jumped up and ran out.

But the stories about George B. Cox are legion. If all of them had been established as truth in a court of law, he might have spent the rest of his life in the pokey. He didn't. Still, as more and more critics began to take potshots at him, he grew tired of being boss. He gradually backed away from the political arena and let his underlings have a go at the controls. They say he aspired to take Mark Hanna's place in politics. They say he aspired to control the state of Ohio as he controlled the city and the county, but these things never happened. A big fish in a small pond, he tried hard but could never control the state.

He retired from active politics in 1915, but his shadow was still seen everywhere, clouding the city government. Instead of spending his twilight years in jail or obscurity (grand juries found him clean), he spent them in his Clifton home at Wentworth and Brookline Avenues. There he toyed with theater projects as he had once toyed with government. Somehow or other the saloonkeeper had accumulated a bundle and had got interested in theater. The *Commercial Tribune* said he invested first $300,000, then $600,000 in the Shubert theater chain to become a major factor in its operation. The year after he retired from politics he suffered a stroke, lingered four months, then passed away. Poetically his political career might be summed up with the title of a feature picture he was supposed to have paid $30,-000 to control. The film was called *Traffic in Souls*.

The Cox machine refused to die. After World War I it still fiddled with the city and county. But some of the returned warriors were fed up with its political nonsense. One such veteran was Captain Victor Heintz, who had served both in Congress and overseas. He organized the Cincinnatus Association, made up of young business and professional men. Murray Seasongood made speeches to any group that would hear him. *Post* reporter Alfred Segal followed

73

Seasongood to every nook and cranny of the city, then came back to the city room to write stories that the voters suddenly wanted to read. Time for change was in the air. There was little joy in the city.

There was little joy in the Cox-built machine, either. It had come upon sad days. It had practically put the city into bankruptcy. And there was the Cincinnatus group, yapping at its heels. The yaps were effective. The Cincinnatus group pointed out how the per capita expenditure in Cincinnati was the fourth largest among the nation's leading cities. Cincinnatians, hearing this, got fed up. By 1923 the citizens had stopped doing a slow burn and started blowing their tops. When the machine tried to float a bond to cover the city's whopping deficit, the voters gave a resounding no. Piqued, the machine scrambled to cut expenses. Street repairs dwindled. No cash was the excuse. Street lights were turned out early. No cash. The machine wanted to shut down the Branch Hospital for tubercular patients. No cash.

Alfred Segal recalled that one Cincinnatian asked point-blank: "When will City Hall smell okay again?"

The machine had almost clanked to a halt, stopping the city with it. The next year, 1924, the machine uttered its last gasp. The machine which had been so well tended by Mr. Cox was helpless without him. But it didn't die a natural death. Irate voters of both political parties threw aside political differences and stomped the life out of it. The November election saw the last of a cumbersome city council. A new city charter called for a streamlined council of nine members instead of the dozens it had before. It called also for a city manager—then a radical idea of government—to run the city on "business principles." The mayor elected by the nine councilmen would be little more than an amiable figurehead when not functioning as a member of council. He could cut ribbons at openings, pass out keys to the city, make proclamations (Fishwife Day, Baseball Day, God-Mother-and-Home Day), but that was all. The salary for councilmen was raised from $1150 to $5000 a year—then good money—in the hope that councilmen would work fulltime and keep their fingers out of the till. The first mayor to be elected was Murray Seasongood, who had helped slay the dragon. It was Cincinnati's way of thanking him for a job well done.

The county, however, remained untouched, and the remnants of the giddier days of the county machine took a long time to erase. But now that generations have come and gone, the political picture in both city and county are much like the state and federal level: almost clean as a whistle. Utopia is difficult to legislate. Have things changed much here? Well, dead men have not voted for a long time. There are approximately 370,000 registered voters in Hamilton

74

County, and out of that total only once in recent years has a voter forged someone else's name.

The Charter party, that watchful combination of both parties that cleaned up the city, calls itself the Charter Committee, but functions as a party. It has, in essence, replaced the Democrats in the city government. The Republican party, licking its wounds after the machine debacle, regrouped and stayed around. However, for a long time its influence as a political machine was deader than a mackerel. Thus, even today in the city and county political establishments, there are bewildering contradictions. Because the Charter Committee is not active in the county scheme of things, the two active parties in county elections are the Republicans and the Democrats. But only recently in the city itself have the Democrats elected to run under their own banner instead of under the Charter banner, their co-workers under the Charter banner being disgruntled city Republicans. Come to think of it, the situation is still bewildering. However, with the city Democrats seeking identity of their own, Cincinnati may well end up with three political forces: Republican, Democratic, and Charter (Republican *and* Democratic politicians!). Or, some suggest, that the Charter group will eventually retire from the field. But that's wishful thinking. The charm and strength of the Charter Committee, party, or whatever you choose to call it, is this: it's made up of men of *both* parties, and these men, along with independents, believe that at the city level the important thing is not a party label but good government.

Other items occupied Cincinnatians in the first of the twentieth century. Once the largest city in Ohio, Cincinnati could no longer claim that distinction when the century began. That upstart Cleveland had taken the title away. Although Cincinnati still led the nation in the manufacture of whiskey and carriages, its carriage business in 1900 had dwindled to 75 percent of what it had been ten years before. Here and there were flashes of success. B. H. Kroger built his home on an acre tract at 3863 Reading Road. The arts were bubbling: Schuster-Martin School of Drama, originally the School of Expression, began. Years later, Tyrone Power would be graduated from it, to end in Hollywood and become a roaring success. Metropolitan Opera artists Melba, Schumann-Heink, Jean de Reszke, and Campanari were wowing Music Hall audiences. In 1902, trolleys began running to Cheviot; the Kemper Thomas Company in Norwood began manufacturing calendars; the Heekin Can Company got started; the Cincinnati Gas, Light & Coke Company changed its name to the Cincinnati Gas & Electric Company; and on a quick trip out saloon-ridden Vine Street, Carrie Nation was so stunned she refused to lug her ax along. "I would have dropped from exhaustion," she said, "before I had gone a block." In 1903, Alice Lee Roosevelt

75

married Nicholas Longworth II; the Cincinnati Country Club was incorporated; and the Mount Adams Cable Railways, which began running in the last chapter, stopped running.

Our first concrete skyscraper, the Ingall's Building, was built on the northeast corner of Fourth and Vine Streets in 1903. On Price Hill that year the last horsecar ran; Hyde Park became part of Cincinnati; and so did Evanston, Bond Hill, and Winton Place. In 1904, South Cumminsville was annexed; and Mary Greene gave birth to Tom Greene aboard the *Greenland*, rested a month, then piloted the riverboat 1200 miles from Pittsburgh to St. Louis. Procter & Gamble opened its first out-of-town plant, in Kansas City. Silverton—named in honor of Seth Haines, who helped the community get started and whose wife's maiden name was Elizabeth Silver—was annexed to Cincinnati. In 1905, Roselawn was annexed; Theodore Thomas, who had been with the May Festival since it began, passed away; and the Ursuline nuns bought the building at Reading Road and Oak Street for their academy. The Sunday *Enquirer* Editor George Randolph Chester's short story *The Strikebreaker* was acclaimed best of the year; he would later achieve even greater acclaim writing his J. Rufus ("Get Rich Quick") Wallingford yarns based on anecdotes told him by *Enquirer* Sports Editor Joseph Nolan. Also, in 1905, the city council passed Cincinnati's first speed laws. Downtown speed limit for autos was seven miles an hour; in the suburbs, fifteen miles an hour.

In 1907 the sternwheeler *Sprague* excited rivermen with its feat: it pushed a record tow of sixty coal barges loaded with 70,000 tons of coal from Louisville to New Orleans. *Billboard* magazine, a Cincinnati publication, added a movie section. There was no symphony for the 1906–07 season, due to trouble with the musicians' union. In 1908, William Howard Taft, fifty-one, stood on the front porch of his half-brother's house, 316 Pike Street, now the Taft Museum, and accepted the Republican nomination for the Presidency. He had previously lambasted George B. Cox, saying he wanted no part of the Cox machine. Meanwhile, in England, Sir Robert Baden-Powell had started the Boy Scouts of England, basing his organization on the outfit Dan Beard, of Covington, Kentucky, had originated and called the Sons of Daniel Boone. Beard, who lived at 322 East Third Street in Covington, merged his outfit with Baden-Powell's in 1910 and, as any self-respecting Eagle Scout can tell you, that was the start of scouting in America.

Much happened in 1909. Leopold Stokowski conducted the Cincinnati Symphony Orchestra. Taft, having defeated William Jennings Bryan, moved into the White House. Taft, they said, was the biggest man ever to occupy the place, but they always add, "in size and bulk." Recently his $1500 bathtub from the Taft mansion was discovered sitting "in battered splendor in a weed-tangled Boone County cow pasture," where it had served as a watering trough. On the commercial scene in 1909, the Cincinnati Milling Machine Company built its plant in Oakley, and the American Laundry Machine Company started in Norwood. The Yononte Inn of Kennedy Heights, one of Greater Cincinnati's more fashionable spots, was gutted by fire. Cincinnati capitalists George and James Bullock had built it for the (then) jet set of the world, including titled foreigners who jetted to Kennedy Heights in tallyhos.

The real excitement in 1909 was a gasser. On the first of July, the Cincinnati Gas & Electric Company stopped manufacturing artificial gas and opened a valve that introduced natural gas to its customers. CG&E gave the event a Hollywood touch. A man holding a 20-inch Roman candle shot colorful fireballs up into the air, his target the top of a pipe that jutted high in the sky. He finally made connection and, *poof!*, natural gas through a 183-mile pipeline from West Virginia was a fact in Cincinnati. The crowd along the Cincinnati waterfront who watched the demonstration was most impressed.

The following year was a mixed bag. The downriver community of Delhi was annexed to Cincinnati, and so was West Cumminsville and Langdon Farm Corridor. The present Hughes High School was completed. Ben Pitman died. Who was he? Well, Ben introduced his brother Isaac's shorthand method to the United States. Ben Pitman lived at 1852 Columbia Avenue, taught woodcarving at the Art Academy, and got so involved with woodcarving that his home, which already sported a front door with silver hinges, soon sported some wild touches Mr. Pitman had whittled into it. That year also saw a whopper of a fire that started in the shoe-factory district of Ninth and Sycamore Streets, quickly gutting the tinderbox buildings, and leaping alleys and streets to destroy a leather factory two blocks away. When the smoke cleared, the scene was sheer havoc, damage was estimated at $2,000,000, four people had been killed, and a dozen injured.

Had you been sitting in an "Over the Rhine" beer garden, you could have capsuled 1911 by the beery conversations you overheard.

"Jake Schmidlapp! Know what he's done now? He's starting a thing called low-cost housing out there on the corner of Park Avenue and Chapel. A day's wage for a week's rent, he says. And that's not all. He stands around looking at the building and says, 'This is my church. Here I worship God.'"

"I see they finally annexed College Hill to Cincinnati so Cox could have some more tax money to play with."

"And they annexed Sayler Park, too."

"And Carthage."

"And Madisonville."

77

Or, if you weren't there, you might have been out at the Maketewah Country Club, which opened in 1911, too—all 150 acres of it.

The Cincinnati Reds in 1912 built the grandstands they're using today, but the stands have been prettied up since then. Billy Sunday came to Cincinnati and took the city by storm with his sermons against demon rum. He was partially effective, too. Shortly after, a law was passed that limited the number of saloons to one for each 500 persons—and 700 saloons were forced to close. Thus the shadow of Prohibition was creeping across the sunny land, and that other faint noise in the distance was the noise of war drums in Europe. Gilbert Avenue viaduct opened. The last Green Line trolley ran around Fountain Square. That Indian statue was erected in Fernbank. Fernbank as well as Hartwell and Pleasant Ridge were annexed to Cincinnati. William Howard Taft was defeated by Woodrow Wilson —and 1912 dwindled to a halt. But there was talk of building that whopper of a structure called the Union Central Building at Fourth and Vine Streets. And, now and then, the mutterings of the trolley motormen and conductors were heard, talking strike. All of this brings us to 1913, when there were a flood and a streetcar strike.

Cincinnati in those days was a streetcar city. Though horses were still about and horseless carriages were not rare, the commonest form of transportation was the trolley car. But on Friday, May 9, 1913, Cincinnatians gaped in consternation at *Times-Star* headline:

TROLLEY STRIKE CALLED FOR 9 P.M. FRIDAY NIGHT
Traction Officials Will Try To Keep Cars Running

Another story failed to divert the readers. The same day the trolley strike was announced, a druggist, once president of the school board, had been arrested for "selling opium." Shades of Dr. Fu Manchu! But Cincinnatians felt they could survive without opium. Without streetcars was a horse of a different color. Thus, with their serenity coming unglued, Cincinnatians buttoned down for the weekend. Before the trolley strike was over, Cincinnati would lose its serenity completely. May 1913 proved to be a melancholy month both for streetcar lovers and Cincinnati's dignity.

The strike was caused by money. The motormen and conductors wanted a raise. The Cincinnati Traction Company didn't want to pay it. The crews went on strike. So far, no strain.

But the Cincinnati Traction Company imported strikebreakers from other cities to man the trolleys. This irritated the strikers. The strike began Friday at 9 P.M. on schedule. Mayor Hunt called it "an outrage for the city to be tied up." The police hastily deputized seventy-five men. The trolley company said that 90 percent of its motormen and conductors were loyal, but nonetheless the strikers were effective. As crews brought their trolleys into the barns on

Friday night, the strikers shouted mean things at them and convinced them to join the strike, too. They did.

Saturday morning found thirteen trolleys running on the Avondale line instead of the usual sixteen. Not running at all were the Sedams-ville, Vine-Norwood, Gilbert Avenue, Warsaw, Elberon, and those other Norwood cars: Norwood, North Norwood, and South Norwood. Fortunately for the traction company, the powerhouse men—firemen and engineers—did not strike, so there was always electricity on tap. The strikebreakers, though, had a hard time from the start. For one thing, Cincinnati streetcars possessed not one but two trolley poles. This rattled the men used to running cars that had only one. Cincinnati powered its traction cars by double trolley wires because, when the first electric car appeared, the city was afraid that using the rail as a "ground return" to complete the circuit would contaminate its underground sewer and water pipes.

The strike itself couldn't have come at a worse time as far as Pogue's was concerned. It was in the middle of its 50th Anniversary Sale!

On the other hand, some turned the unhappy event into quick profit. One newspaper ad told of two carloads of horses—"draft and general-purpose"—that were arriving at the Union Stock Yard, Spring Grove and Hopple Avenues, for auction.

Sunday was quiet. Those who had expected to ride trolleys to Chester Park for "Flood Relief Day" rode the Cincinnati, Hamilton & Dayton train, or the Baltimore & Ohio train.

On Monday the city came apart at the seams. Everything happened. First, the interurbans declined to run inside the city. These majestic country trolleys hesitated at the city's edge and then nervously retreated. The only trolley that ran unhampered throughout the entire strike was a boxy little car with no windows. Marked on its side was the sign: U. S. MAIL. They say its motorman got a kick out of clanging his bell and seeing the startled looks on the faces of the people. The activity centered at the Avondale car barn, where strikebreakers had arrived to pilot the cars. At 9 A.M. the strikebreakers maneuvered a pair of genteel and prim little summer cars out onto the street where a crowd of strikers stood. All didn't go well. Unused to the double-trolley system, the motormen raced the cars outside, the trolley poles flipped off the overhead wires, and the cars were stalled. "Scabs!" shouted the strikers. Finally the motormen managed to get the trolleys working, and down the street went the cars—followed by a crowd of 200 angry strikers and a police auto filled with four policemen. The passengers were three: two frightened men and one frightened woman. The two streetcars didn't get far.

Track obstructions were everywhere: two-by-fours, barrels, planking, rocks, bricks, and even trucks that presumed to have engine

79

trouble on the right-of-way. Since the cars couldn't swerve around, they were forced to wait. And while they waited, other reports began to filter in:

At Sixth and Sycamore Streets two more streetcars had been stopped by a mob and set afire.

The same thing happened to a car that emerged from the Brighton barn. A brewery wagon blocked its path, and seething onlookers set that trolley afire, too.

At another intersection, a horse-drawn wagon veered against a moving trolley, the wagon's driver sprayed gasoline on the car's front platform, someone lit a match, and *poof!*

Two John Street trolleys were stoned at Twelfth and Central Avenues and forced to turn back.

Another car, deserted by its strikebreaking crew, had every window and its headlight smashed. A fourteen-year-old boy threw its controller into a sewer.

Thus ended Monday. No trolleys moved after dark.

The quiet that prevailed most of the week was a fooler. Though the streetcars ran, their only passengers were policemen. The company had thoughtfully raised the wages of its powerhouse, barn, and substation crews to keep them on the job. The first streetcar to explore downtown Cincinnati that Tuesday moved timidly along as people on the sidewalk and from the windows stared at it in stony silence. If the newspapers were troubled by the events of the days before, their editorial pages for the most part failed to reflect their fretting. The *Times-Star*, for instance, ran one editorial that said how pleasant the coming of spring was along the Little Miami River Valley. Its lead editorial, captioned "Stop It," was headier fare. Smoke from the Burnet House smokestack, 100 feet away from the spanking new Union Central Building under construction, was getting the new structure smudged. The editorial asked that something be done about it. Thus, the week was a fooler all right. Even the Avondale trolleys operated by strikebreakers were moving right along on a schedule that was practically normal.

Friday was quiet—until noon. Twelve o'clock found an amiable trolley poking along around Fountain Square. Then someone—it was never established whether the "someone" was man, woman, or child—shoved a city refuse can in front of the streetcar, the can tangled with the car's high fender, got mashed underneath the front trucks, and the car was stalled. Instantly the noonday crowd's mood changed. They tried to pull the motorman from the front platform and down into the street the better to work him over, but he wanted no part of the celebration. Dodging their outstretched hands, he dived inside the streetcar, locked the doors, pulled the shades, and—together with the policemen passengers and other strikebreakers—huddled until help came. His retreat wasn't exactly a crowd-pleaser.

Some estimate that by then the crowd numbered 10,000. Their anger was apparent. They threw everything they could find at the beleaguered trolley: mostly wadded-up pieces of paper and sticks. Two policemen outside the car tried to disperse the crowd but were shunted aside. Mounted policemen, pistols in hand, galloped to the rescue, and clanging down the street in the best Keystone-cop tradition came a fleet of police autos filled to the brim with helmeted cops.

That Saturday similar dramas were being enacted across the city. A mob of several hundred men and boys attacked two Colerain Avenue streetcars. The trolleys that had just pulled out of the Brighton barn at 9:15 A.M. were waylaid on upper Central Avenue near the old Mohawk Bridge. In another incident, a sheepherder made his drove of sheep "mill" in front of another trolley on Baymiller Street. There were cases of small boys, by themselves, doing physical violence to passing trolleys. And a crew from a Madisonville streetcar was last seen being chased up Central Avenue at Main Street, pursued by a mob waving ice tongs.

But the major player in the finale was Elberon Trolley ⚡642, a cheerful summer car that loved everyone. As the open-air streetcar moved along Fourth Street Saturday morning, someone ran into the street and put a box on the track, obstructing its way. At the same moment, as if on cue, from almost every floor of the Union Central Building came a barrage of granite blocks, barrels of cement, and lead pipe—some from as high up as thirty floors. The streetcar's rear platform was crushed. The crew fled. The barrage continued. Barrels of plaster of paris came hurtling down, bursting at street level into huge clouds of white that covered spectators, police, and mob. By this time the police were firing up at the Union Central Building. Blazing torches were dropped down on them in return. From an upper floor, one witness said, a woman was shrieking at the trolley in hate. Meanwhile, throughout the action, workmen on the scaffolding outside the building stood as stiff as statues as bullets whizzed one way and concrete whizzed another. Because the street-level crowd was turning into a mob and could not be dispersed, one mounted policeman shouted to his cohorts: "Ride them down!" And in the midst of the screams, noise, shooting, and whizzing bullets, the little Elberon car stood, demolished. Its twin trolley poles pointed up and were crossed at crazy angles.

By Saturday noon, not a streetcar was on the streets in Cincinnati. The Mayor asked the Governor to send troops. The Governor refused. There was deadly quiet in the city on Sunday. On Monday came the headline:

No trolleys were running, but hope was in the air. The traction company had alerted its trackmen to be ready to oil the curves. On Tuesday, May 20, the headline said:

STREETCAR SERVICE IS FULLY RESUMED IN CINCINNATI

People, perhaps in a state of shock or perhaps troubled by the damage they had done, turned silly. As if to make up for the senseless bombing of that Elberon trolley from the Union Central Building, the first streetcar to pass that corner after the strike was settled was bombarded again—with flowers. Everywhere motormen and conductors were presented with bouquets. Traction cars that a few days before had been greeted with stones were welcomed with cheers. The strike was over. So much for serene Cincinnati.

The paper that announced the end of the strike offered two other headlines that indicated the temper of the times:

VOTED NOT TO INDICT GEO. COX
WATER IN CANAL IS WORST IN YEARS

1914 found Cincinnati at peace with its trolleys and thinking about being at war with Germany. The Gibson Hotel was built that year, where the Mecca Saloon had been, so Cox was without a mid-morning watering hole. The twelve-story Gwynne Building was built. So was the $1,000,000 Norwood High School. That July saw the first traction car move across the Ludlow Avenue viaduct. But traction cars, like elephants, never forget. The wounds they had received during the strike still rankled. Tossing roses had been no cure. The day before the viaduct was opened to streetcars, one trolley and one electric automobile mixed it up. A Winton Place man was tooling along with his electric runabout when, at the intersection of Mitchell and Sullivan Avenues, a streetcar in front of him stopped to board passengers. Unimpressed, the man swung left of the trolley and proceeded ahead—only to be nailed by a trolley coming the other way. Everyone walked away from the accident, but there was no doubt about it. The trolleys were seeking revenge.

The following year, 1915, Cox walked away from politics, but his machine was still perking along. North College Hill was annexed by Cincinnati, but the city had yet to catch up and pass Cleveland. The Cincinnati Women's Club was started.

In 1916, George B. Cox died.

The war occupied everyone's attention in 1917, but the winter of 1917–18 was a stem-winder that momentarily took their minds off the conflict. There was a blizzard on December 8, and in twenty-four hours the mercury plunged 50 degrees. The subzero temperatures lingered for several weeks, creating a gas shortage, which meant that ladies with gas stoves were hard-pressed to cook family dinners. On January 13 the trolley system was forced to shut down again, this time because of a coal shortage. Between 4 P.M. and midnight, only one trolley operated on each line.

But 1918 was also the year the war ended. Serenity was set aside and happiness reigned. Once again Fountain Square played host to a mob scene, but this one was happier. Automobiles tooted passageway through the pedestrian Emery Arcade, where an improvised orchestra proved an effective roadblock—and everyone danced. The city was at full cry. Businessmen traded their dignity for dime-store drums, marched around the Square, and added to the din made by sirens, whistles, and—heads up! Some nuts are shooting guns! In fact, a lot of nuts were. A bullet crashed through the third-floor window at the Princeton Hotel on Elm Street. Tied-down factory whistles shrieked the joy of the armistice. Church bells boomed and tolled and clanged. Got a tin pan? Beat it with a spoon! Add to the hubbub! Got a wash boiler? Make thunder! Scream, bellow, shout, wake the dead! Whoops, there goes a car towing a bathtub! Cheerio, my deario! Go kiss a bearded man! And you, sir, go kiss a pretty girl! Ladies! Tickle that man's beard with your feather duster! Celebrate! It's raining confetti, rice, ticker tape, and joy. The war is over! Burn the Kaiser! Put a coffin on Fountain Square, drench it with oil, then burn it, burn it, burn it! There's auctioneer Major J. B. Wallace auctioning the Imperial Palace of Potsdam! There's Judge William H. Leuders! The sign on his closed courtroom door says, "Closed! To hell with the Kaiser!" Drink up! Cheers! And so on, loudly and with great feeling, far into the happy night as skyrockets lit the sky.

But not everywhere. For some Cincinnati families the war had ended long before in places named Chateau-Thierry and the Marne.

Among the Johnnies who did come marching home were those forsaken men with far-fetched looks and funny stares who were reduced to peddling newspapers on a street corner until they died.

But soon another event was fighting for newspaper space, too; and it turned into an event that for a brief spell gobbled up every front page in town. The event was called prohibition. The headline in the *Commercial Tribune*, May 25, 1919, read:

QUEEN CITY BIDS GOOD-BY TO SALOONS
IN GREAT RUSH OF LIQUOR PURCHASING;
5,000 OHIO DRINKING PLACES CLOSE

Although they didn't have to close until Tuesday, May 28, most saloons shuttered over the weekend. It was either that or pay $305 for a license to operate the few remaining days. Only 163 of Ohio's 5000 saloons stayed open until the end. At that moment in history,

Ohio was the largest state to have prohibition. The state figured that Ohio residents poured 20,000 drinks down the hatch each day, enriching the state coffers $4,000,000 each year.

The last weekend in Cincinnati was one of Cincinnati's wettest. Said one newspaper, "the death watch was everywhere in the city." A few Cincinnatians, especially those who lived "Over the Rhine," didn't believe prohibition would last, so they didn't get too excited. Instead, they did as they had always done on weekends. They got sauced.

In the Mohawk section, every growler—can, bucket, jug, and pitcher —was in action. Breathing space was at a premium in Nick Frisch's Wine House on upper Vine Street, where everyone was foregoing wine to drink whiskey straight. The constant chant of the busy bartenders was:

"Buy your drinks now or go thirsty ever after."

Customers needed no urging.

Signs began to appear in windows. At Leo Morris's Liquor Store, 1229 Main Street, the store was no more than a shambles; empty whiskey cases, and the hastily scrawled sign in his window read:

SOLD OUT—OPEN MONDAY

At Joe's Place, on the southwest corner of Twelfth and Walnut Streets, two kegs of beer were placed on the bar and covered with black crepe paper. The laboring men, who frequented the place more than their homes, got sad and mellow, drinking until they dropped. Chester Park—advertising "the last cheer to the cup that cheers"—was the site of a funeral: a keg of beer was buried in a beery ceremony of goodby forever. Wieilert's Garden, where Cox used to spend his afternoons and evenings, started slow but picked up fast. By 9 P.M. the garden was reeling under the impact of merrymakers, and upstairs in a private banquet room August Herrmann was throwing one final blast. Wieilert's thereafter would sell only soft drinks and near beer.

Other entertainments—other than boozing, that is—were in the city, but that night few were attended. Claire Adams was featured in an aptly named movie at the Grand: *The End of the Road.* Mack Sennett's bathing beauties offered leggy visions onstage at the Lyric. At the Walnut, for $.15 or $.25, merrymakers could sober up watching Douglas Fairbanks in *The Knickerbocker Buckeroo,* a seven-reel extravaganza that took six months to make and cost $240,000 to produce.

Preparing for the dusty future, the Wheel Café advertised:

WILL REMAIN OPEN
AFTER MAY 27, 1919
Merchants' Dinner Lunch
Evening Table d'hôte Dinner
Non-alcoholic Drinks and Near Beer
Will Be Served . . .

84

And a brewery advertised:

There were altercations now and then among the merrymakers, but considering the whole city was on a binge, it is interesting to note that only forty were tucked away in the city's ten district jails. The rest of the brawls, said one newspaper account, were settled "by husky policemen."

And then, everything was over. An era had folded. And everyone went home to sober up and wish he were dead. There was no hair of the dog that bit them.

Also that year, 1919, the Cincinnati Reds won the pennant and the World Series, after which they, too, went into a twilight and didn't win another series for so long that Cincinnatians wondered at times if the city still had a major-league club. The new courthouse opened. East High School, now Withrow, was completed. P&G introduced Ivory Soap Flakes. And to answer the desperate needs of those who panicked at the sight of ice cream sodas, 3000 "blind pigs" were coming, where a man could wet his whistle on the sly. In a few years after 1919, it would be as if prohibition had never happened, but the lavish old saloons of old were gone forever. Most of the speak-easies were dreary little back rooms and dilapidated (and hard-to-reach) summer cottages. Where did the booze come from? Well, let's talk about George Remus.

Remus came to Cincinnati in 1919 after a stunning career as a criminal lawyer in Chicago, where in one year alone he defended eighteen people accused of murder. He started small here, but grew. His method was uncomplicated. He bought a distillery, got a permit to sell booze to wholesale drug houses, but his delivery system left much to be desired (if you were a drug house), because a lot of his whiskey was misdirected, ending up in a charming wooded hollow called "Death Valley" along Queen City Avenue. There the mis-directed whiskey was reshipped to—some say—as many as eight different states, to men who broke the law a little so they could buy it. Remus soon bought other distilleries. But don't frown. Look at it this way. On Cincinnati's wettest night, a street vendor cashed in by peddling black armbands for a dime. Remus, you see, wasn't the only opportunist. Also consider this. People didn't have to visit speakeasies. As they say, it takes two to tango.

In 1920 the canal followed the pattern of the nation, was drained, and went dry, too, ending another era. That same year, though, another era began when Mrs. Charles P. Taft, Mrs. Mary Emery, and Ralph Lyford formed the Summer Opera Association so that opera could be performed at the Cincinnati Zoo. Many world-renowned opera stars have begun their operatic careers there, singing duets with hungry lions. The opera company, now the nation's second oldest, heard Josephine Antoine sing Lucia for the very first time in 1939 in the same season Jan Peerce, then only a performer at Radio City Music Hall, came to try his hand at opera. Dorothy Kirsten debuted in opera here in 1941, singing a minor role in *Manon*. In 1938 James Melton had his first go at grand opera at the Zoo, singing the role of Pinkerton. Gladys Swarthout, to be honest, got started somewhere else, but at least, before her 1939 performance of *Carmen* here, she said, "It may not mean much to Cincinnati, but it's going to be one of the biggest thrills in my life." Rise Stevens, probably the greatest Carmen of all time, first sang that role here in 1943. Grace Moore first sang *Tosca* here in 1941. And when the Summer Opera stars are not using the Zoo stage, the *Post & Times-Star*'s Stan Dahlman, who can't sing a note, is up there running shows for the Zoo Food Show.

Price Hill was beginning to spread out in 1920. One of the most palatial digs ever built there belonged to, of course, the one man who could afford it: George Remus. You can't cast him in the role of the typical bootlegger. He didn't spit on carpets and he didn't talk out of the side of his mouth. He wasn't uncouth. If anything, he was about the couthest man on the scene. The *Cincinnati Guide* said he was "a plump little man who wore clothes fastidiously and had a taste for good food, exquisite art, and the joys of literature." His mansion at 825 Hermosa Avenue had a $100,000 Grecian swimming pool. The rooms were furnished in good taste, and there were rare books and inspired sculpture. Now, *presto!* all is history. A solid line of apartment houses has taken root where once at a lavish party Remus is supposed to have passed out $25,000 worth of jewelry as tokens to his guests. Perhaps when not counting his dollars or looking at his *objets d'art*, Remus tinkered with the cat whisker of a radio. He would have heard John Langdon Gates that August singing "On the 5:15." Radio, though not yet of age, was making itself heard with squeaks and howls.

The next year, 1921, wasn't a good year for George Remus. True, he banked $2,700,000 in just one of his many Cincinnati banking accounts—the money representing three months of foregoing that extra cup of coffee—but times were catching up with him. Federal agents raided his "Death Valley," seized every drop of joy tucked away, and charged him with conspiracy to violate the prohibition law. They arrested thirteen of his associates, too. A year later, 1922, he stood before Judge John Peck in the U. S. Circuit Court and heard himself fined $10,000, the cost of the trial, and sentenced to two years in the federal prison in Atlanta. You couldn't blame Remus if, at that point, he was feeling low. It had already been an expensive trial. He had raised a million-dollar defense fund, hired top New York lawyers to handle the chore, but there had not been a Perry Mason in the lot, and that was that. He fought the conviction straight to the Supreme Court—and lost every step of the way.

Even before the voters clobbered the Cox machine, the Supreme Court clobbered George Remus with word that his two-year prison sentence stood. On January 24—after passing out millions to his friends for safekeeping—jewels to his wife for stashing away, and a silk shirt to a porter for wearing—George Remus left Cincinnati in a special car to begin his two-year stint in the Georgia pokey. They say that as the car pulled away, Mr. Remus was preoccupied. He was reading Dante's *Inferno*. The next year, for good behavior, he was released and shipped straight to Dayton, Ohio, to serve another sentence. In the interim his wife sued him for divorce. The case, scheduled for trial in 1927, never got to court. Out of the Dayton, Ohio, lockup by that time, George Remus settled the case out of court hours before it was to begin. He settled it by shooting his wife in Eden Park. After doing that, he drove to a police station and gave himself up. His wife died, he was indicted for first-degree murder, and—acting as his own attorney—convinced the jury he was not guilty, because of insanity. He was hustled off to the Lima State Hospital, where three months later the Allen County Court of Appeals declared him sane, and again he was free as a bird. He flew to Florida.

Cincinnati wasn't *all* dirty politics and bootlegging in those days. In 1925, for example, Archbishop John T. McNicholas succeeded Archbishop Henry Moeller as head of the Roman Catholic Archdiocese of Cincinnati. An Irish Dominican, the new archbishop was a no-nonsense soul who promptly got involved in a campaign to get state aid for the privately operated Roman Catholic school system, which in his diocese was a whopper. Also, East High School in 1925 changed its name to Withrow. River Downs Race Track opened. The following year, 1926, the Burnet House closed its doors. And somewhere in the Congo, Susie—the trained gorilla that later won Cincinnati's heart at our zoo—first saw the light of day.

Having done wrong by our trolleys in the course of this chapter, we'd like to do right by them and end this section on a pleasant note that will make them feel better. Unfortunately, history will not permit this luxury. The trolleys didn't know it at the time, but in 1926 the streetcar company was considering the purchase of sixty-two gaseous and foul-smelling motor coaches. True, trolleys were still adored, but the adoration was waning. The 11-mile stretch of track that belonged to the dying Cincinnati, Milford, and Blanchester Traction Company —the track between Cincinnati and Milford via Terrace Park and

Mariemont, that is—was purchased by the Cincinnati trolley company so those (then) outlying communities wouldn't die on the vine. The company also bought the tracks, cars, and car barns of the Cincinnati & Hamilton Traction Company, thus extending city trolley service from the Zoo to Lockland, and from Hartwell Junction to Glendale. When 1926 ended, the company went on a buying spree, which showed that, as far as streetcars were concerned, the handwriting was on the wall. The company bought twenty-nine Mack motor coaches, seven Schacht motor coaches, eighteen Six-Wheel motor coaches, three Studebaker motor coaches, and three Biedermans motor coaches. As an afterthought, it bought five secondhand trolleys from upstate Ohio. By the end of 1927, the trolley line could boast of 278.61 miles of track, 400,000 passengers a year, 1500 employees, and the fact that the city-sponsored Rapid Transit—a subway where the canal used to be—was still little more than a hole in the ground. But honk! honk! the buses were taking over.

One final word about Cincinnati's now-you-see-it-now-you-don't subway. The Beelor Report in 1927, which represented a study of what to do with the hole in the ground, noted that the city of Cincinnati had already dumped $6,100,000 into the fiasco. To get it rolling would have required another $10,600,000. The Beelor Report said:

> . . . The new line will open up [new sections] and make it possible to reach an enlarged territory with a minimum cost . . .

It concluded that, if work were to begin at once (in 1927), the subway would be operating by 1930. City officials read the report with great interest, marked the report "file," went outside, climbed into their autos, and chugged home.

The subway? It never happened.

8

For a few years while Cincinnati enjoyed contentment, to live around here was the cat's pajamas. The city government, at last, was in good order; bootleg hooch dribbled down the gullets of the thirstier; Al Jolson sang about his mammy in the new talkies; and the stock market was everybody's darling. Now and then, home brew in the cellar would go boom, but such booms didn't bother neighbors, because at one time or other, their home brew went boom, too. 1927 was a good year, and so was 1928. Contentment and raw whiskey reigned.

B. H. Kroger, having journeyed from rags to riches in the best Horatio Alger manner, quit the grocery business in 1928 and sold his 6000-store chain. River Downs Race Track, which had opened in 1927, closed in 1928 for an uncomplicated reason: who wanted to bet on horses when betting on the stock market was easier—and on the cuff? Cincinnati neighborhoods grew fat, including Price Hill, which soon needed a public high school of its own; Western Hills High School opened in 1928 to answer that need. When the school opened, the trolley company extended tracks out to Ferguson Road, more families followed, and Price Hill grew fatter. Also, the trolley company opened its nearly five-acre streetcar repair shop on Mitchell Avenue and added nearly twenty-five miles of streetcar tracks to the city lines, but already in 1928, as we noted, the handwriting was on the wall. One symptom: the St. Christopher Shrine was dedicated at St. Vincent de Paul Church, River Road. Autos could pull by the shrine and be blessed, but the orange trolleys heading for the end of the line, in more ways than one, passed unnoticed, unloved, and unblessed.

Some inclines still operated. The Mount Adams incline hoisted streetcars up the slope to Eden Park, and the Eighth Street incline's self-contained little red cars hoisted passengers to Price Hill. The other inclines had died. These were the last of their tribe, and time was running out for them, too. As the Cincinnatians were lifted up the inclines and the city dropped away beneath them, the last sound they heard as the valley noises faded was the impatient honk of the auto demanding elbow room in the future. The Zoo-Eden trolley line was Cincinnati's last real link with history. After the trolley rolled on to the incline platform at the bottom, great gates would clang shut, and the streetcar full of people—some a little worried and others with faint hearts—would begin the adventure.

But, also, there was a line of autos following each trolley through the narrow Cincinnati streets. The congestion grew longer as the streetcars stopped at every corner, forcing the autos in their wake to stop, too. Nonetheless, in 1928, when new routes were considered, the trolley company still considered streetcars. "If traffic should give promise of becoming heavy, it might ultimately be carried more cheaply on streetcars," they said. "If it is likely to remain comparatively light, it might be handled more cheaply on motor coaches." Trolleys were a sound investment. They were less expensive to maintain than buses. Unless nailed by an irate motorist, a streetcar could pot around the city 20,000 miles before heading into a barn for a once-over.

But trolleys inspired no love in the breasts of motorists.

"Get rid of them!" they bellowed, furious because these great electric dreadnoughts could not be blasted out of the way with Klaxon horns. Anyway, in 1928, that beautiful boulevard called Central Parkway opened. It was the automobile driver's dream road: wide, devoid of trolleys, and luxurious. If trolleys must operate, said the motorists, experiencing new driving freedom, run them underground, out of sight, and out of our way. After all, wasn't Central Parkway the perfect answer for both: on the street level a stunning road, and underneath, subway tubes? In 1928 some Cincinnatians still felt that the subway would be completed. This area has always had dreamers on tap.

As 1929 rolled around, everything was coming up roses. Cincinnati was on the move. One had only to gape in wonder at the majestic building the Cincinnati Gas & Electric Company had built. And there was Holmes Hospital, brand new! The Eighth Street viaduct—a dignified concrete span that lifted street traffic above the tangle of the railroad tracks that plagued Mill Creek Valley—had been completed. The Cincinnati Clearing House reported new highs: banks were clearing nearly $4,000,000,000. True, now and then, there were less satisfying adventures. For instance, government agents around here had put the arm on 490 bootleggers, confiscated nearly 6000 gallons of liquor, closed down 31 stills, and seized 176 autos and trucks used by moonshiners. Chester Park, floundering, hopefully changed its name to Rainbow Park, but the pot of gold proved to be only a dream. Another name was changed in 1929: Bloody Run Boulevard (so named because of a long-ago Indian massacre there) was renamed Victory Parkway.

Also, in 1929, Cincinnatians were taking second looks at the Ohio River—and with good reason. President Hoover had visited here that year, dedicated that granite obelisk in Eden Park overlooking the river, and proclaimed that the stream was embarking on a new career. It had been completely canalized, as they say, and was ready for action.

Before the locks and dams had been built to make the Ohio River a year-round waterway, the stream at Cincinnati had flowed mostly by whim. It used to get so low in the fall that at times it was possible to "wade" from one shore to the other. To show its erratic range of yesteryear, on October 6, 1908, the river at Cincinnati was a little less than 3 feet deep; that April it had been more than 55 feet deep. It usually averaged lows of 3 to 4 feet deep, but the lowest it ever got was on September 17, 1881: less than 2 feet deep! After the stream was "canalized" and the dams were functioning, the new average low was 10 to 11 feet. Now, with even greater dams corseting the river, the normal pool stage for Cincinnati is 25.4 feet, which, of course, makes the river into a wide, wet highway that can handle deep-water traffic. The highest the river ever reached was in January 1937, but the official flood stage at Cincinnati has varied. Flood stage was 45 feet until 1898, was then changed to 50 feet, and in 1922 was changed to its present 52 feet. According to Weather Bureau records, the Ohio River used to flood nearly every year. More on that a few pages later.

Ice causes mischief on the river, too, though the dams have curbed this nettlesome problem a little. Between 1874 and 1964, ice has appeared on the Ohio River 62 of these 90 winters. The Weather Bureau says that, while "the formation of ice is directly related to the temperature of the water, which must be near freezing, the official minimum atmospheric temperatures at Cincinnati have averaged as follows: with the occurrence of light ice, 13°; heavy ice, 9°; and frozen, 1°." The Bureau adds:

> Light floating ice has usually been followed in about one day by heavy floating ice; and the river usually frozen over after three days of heavy ice. Actually, however, considerable quantities of light ice have appeared 66 times and heavy ice followed it only 49 times; while heavy ice appeared 15 times without light ice preceding it. The river has frozen over in only 13 winters on the 90-year record, always following heavy or gorged ice.

Since the Weather Bureau began keeping track of river ice in 1874, the Ohio River at Cincinnati has been gorged with ice 100 days in January, 58 days in December, 38 days in February, and only 1 day in March. Navigation on the river has been suspended because of ice 279 days in January, which is nearly 50 percent of all the days ice has made the river impassable. The longest period to date that navigation was suspended here was the 65 days between December 10, 1917, and February 12, 1918. During these 65 days, the river was gorged with ice 58 days. More recently, the river was frozen solid—but did not gorge—for 12 days in February 1948. The Bureau says that, "as the navigation dams increase in size, the deeper and larger pools retard somewhat the formation of ice in the river."

The gauge that measures how deep the river is at Cincinnati has moved around almost as much as the weather station has. From June 1, 1858, to October 7, 1908, the river depth was measured at the old waterworks. From October 8, 1908, to December 31, 1934, measurements were taken at the foot of Broadway Street at the Public Landing. From January 1, 1935, until December 31, 1946, the gauge was at the West End Power Plant. Since then it has been at the Suspension Bridge.

Back in 1929, though, the stock market proved even less predictable than the river. As *Variety*, the weekly newspaper of show business, put it:

WALL STREET LAYS AN EGG

The bubble had burst, merriment came to a screeching halt, and that was that. Cincinnati—and the nation—had been dealt a kick in the head called Depression.

Everyone—with work or without it—was touched by the Depression's gloom. Poverty became ordinary, but in this country ordinary poverty did not produce riots. No one threatened to overthrow the government. Not many, anyway. The Depression produced sorrow instead of anger. A feeling of helplessness filled every home.

"The lowest point in my father's life," one Cincinnatian recalled, "was the day we ran out of money and there was no food in the house. I was young then and didn't realize the enormity of the Depression, but I'll never forget the enormity of that one day. All I remember is that my sister and I had come home from grade school for lunch, and there was no lunch . . ."

Pawnshop windows were filled with mandolins and false teeth that told the story of each family's struggle to survive those first grim weeks. Wedding rings that had once pledged love found their way to stores that advertised WE BUY OLD GOLD. Soon the "Bean Wagon" visited the more severely stricken neighborhoods. It was a charity truck filled with boxes of food for those who had no food. The Depression years in Cincinnati were lean and forsaken years occupied by silent parents, silent factories, and children with no money to buy ice cream cones. The social worker was the only link some families had with hope. These bright young college girls traveled from flat to flat, inventorying despair, and signing little chits that said this boy could buy new shoes and that family could buy more coal.

Out Vine Street, where vaudeville was going into twilight, one man on the stage sang a timely tale of woe. Once he had built a railroad, then a skyscraper—his song went—had built this, that, and the other, but when these jobs were completed, there were no more. The song concluded:

"Brother, can you spare a dime?"

No one in the audience applauded, because they had entered the theater to forget and he had done an unforgivable thing: reminded them that there was no forgetting.

A thing called "public work projects" came along: a device of "make work" for men who had no jobs. Ultimately these diverse projects combined into one and became WPA projects that hacked paths through parks, erected stone walls, and constructed roads. Some of the citizens who still had jobs—not everyone was laid off in Cincinnati, of course—complained that men on such WPA projects spent their days leaning on shovels. It is not for this book to revive that old quarrel nor to decide it. Facts speak for themselves. Admittedly, some of the men were loafers. Not all were jewels. But on the other hand, wherever you go in the area today, you will find culverts, walls, and entire parks that bear the imprint:

WPA

Certainly not *all* the men leaned on their shovels. These things didn't spring into being by magic. At that point in our history, the world had run fresh out of magic.

To work on the WPA carried no stigma. With entire neighborhoods on relief, how could it? While those who quarreled with welfare could find legitimate items upon which to base their quarrels, there is one fact with which they could never quarrel: most of the WPA workers were not lazy creatures who didn't want to work; there was no other work to be had; and that is why they were there.

Life went on. Even though the Depression reduced many families to gloom, it took more than a mere depression to cancel the love stories each city must manufacture if it is to endure. Young couples full of hope and hopelessness met, talked, took long walks, and dreamed dreams that were sweet and impossible. As they courted along bankrupt lovers' lanes, they didn't plot revolutions; they plotted marriages and babies. There were instances in Cincinnati where the bride's family and the groom's family were both on relief, yet the marriage took place anyway. The hard-pressed case worker took such marriages in stride: established the honeymooners in a dinky flat, filled it with cheap furniture, and opened a new file on the new family. Some people who objected to that labeled it coddling, but coddling or not, it happened. Besides, in neighborhoods struck down by the Depression, it wasn't called coddling at all; it was called love.

The tide of the Depression ebbed and flowed. Sometimes there was work, sometimes not. And many people were not touched by the Depression's worst. They worked each day, fed their children, and wondered vaguely what was wrong with the rest of the world. Families either were bogged down by the times or moved ahead at the same pace. The same was true of the city itself. During the Depression years, many structures were added to Cincinnati. The Carew Tower, for example, was completed in 1930. Thus the Union Central Building, now the Central Trust Tower, was no longer the town's highest skyscraper and was relegated to second place. Four wings were added to the Art Museum in Eden Park. Depression or no, Procter & Gamble was on the move. In 1930, Richard Deupree was named P&G president; it was the same year P&G sales passed the $200,000,000 mark. The Ida Street bridge was built in 1931, so was Walnut Hills High School. But on the other hand, a landmark passed: Peeble's Grocery closed its doors for good. The store which had occupied the southeast corner of Peebles Corner since Hector was a pup had served customers as far as 500 miles away. Susie the gorilla had finally reached the Zoo, and William Dressman promptly began teaching her tricks that would win Cincinnati's heart. Eugene Goossens replaced Fritz Reiner as conductor of the Cincinnati Symphony. Chester Park, then Rainbow Park, changed its name back to Chester Park in 1932, but soon would close because of an unpaid water bill. The Stuart Walker Stock Company, after eleven years in Cincinnati, rang down the final curtain in 1932. Lane Seminary, once a Cincinnati fixture, in 1932 merged with the Presbyterian Theological Seminary in Chicago. Its building on Gilbert Avenue became an apartment house. The remodeled Taft Museum at 316 Pike Street opened to the public.

The next year, 1933, found Susie the gorilla happier than the zoo she was in. Running low on cash, the Zoo was teetering on the edge of troubled times. There were rumors that every animal would be sold, the park closed, and the land used to build houses on. Elsewhere that year, the double-decked Western Hills viaduct was opened, destined to become the only link during the 1937 flood between downtown and the western suburbs, but building the viaduct wasn't duck soup: foundations had to be sunk 200 feet to reach bedrock.

A year later, Cincinnati Zoo fans could breathe easier. The Depression was still around, but around also was the good word that the Zoo wouldn't close. On January 1, the Board of Park Commissioners took charge of running it.

Stories from Europe were making uneasy headlines as Greater Cincinnatians moved through 1935. Of local interest that year, the Cincinnati Reds played their first night game; Cincinnati's first hotel for Negroes—the Gordon, built in 1916 by Mr. Schmidlapp at Chapel and Ashland Streets—was remodeled into apartments; and the Spencer House at Front and Broadway Streets was torn down. A lot of Cincinnati history lingered in the dust of its rubble. Built in 1853, it had gradually dwindled from a posh river hotel whose guest register boasted President Johnson, Admiral Farragut, General Grant, General Custer, and Rousseau to a decayed and rundown rooming house filled with nameless wharfmen who lacked the price of better digs uptown.

In 1936, several things happened locally: River Downs Race Track opened again after having closed in 1925. In Norwood, John Uri Lloyd, who had lived in that most queer house on the southeast corner of Harris and Lloyd Avenues, passed away. The house at different times, depending upon the mood of the beholder, has been described variously as "interesting" or "that hilarious collection of roofs, turrets, and porches—each at a different height!" Mr. Lloyd wrote *Etidorpha*, a book about people who lived in subterranean villages. Norwood's John August Knapp—engraver and artist—illustrated the volume with moody and fetching drawings. And also that year, there was a flood. In fact, there were two floods. On March 8, 1936, the flooded Ohio River crested at 60.6 feet. A month later, it flooded again and crested at 54 feet.

When Greater Cincinnatians felt that the river would never get any nastier, they figured wrong.

Thunder in December is rare around here. And in December 1936, faint thunder was heard throughout the Ohio Valley. According to an old Indian sign, thunder in December means flood in January. Few bothered with the prophecy because, like old wives' tales, old Indian signs leave a lot to be desired. There's another old saying around here that floods come in pairs (look at 1936!), but statistically this premise is hard to nail down. As we noted, before the dams were built the floods didn't come in pairs; they came almost every year without fail. Even after President Hoover dedicated the Ohio River as an inland canal, floods still plagued the valley. Flood crests of 60 or more feet were considered major floods; anything less than that was shrugged off by Cincinnatians as penny-ante stuff. Most of the floods happen in January, February, and March.

That's why on January 14, 1937, when the Ohio River reached 44.8 feet at 4 P.M., no one in the city suspected anything. Families along the Little Miami River had been forced to vacate their homes and cabins, but that happened a lot in that valley. Anytime anyone spit in the river, up came the Little Miami, and families were forced to flee. The Ohio River had been higher than 44.8 feet every year since 1932. In fact, the Ohio River had failed to get that high only four years—1925, 1928, 1930, and 1931—since the turn of the century.

In the language of the Government, which watches over the Ohio River Valley the way a mother hen watches over her brood, floods happen here because ". . . the Ohio River Basin lies directly in the path usually followed by cyclonic disturbances as they move from west to east across the North American continent in the winter and early spring months. For this reason the watershed is frequently subjected to more than normal rainfall during the months of January to May . . . Other contributing factors to Ohio River floods are the precipitous slopes of the mountainous section bordering the basin to the east and southeast which occasion excessively high rates of run-off in those regions; and rain falling on melting snow which often covers the northern and eastern section of the basin in the winter and early spring seasons, resulting at times in rates of run-off in excess of the amount of rain . . ." Simply put, around January it rains, the rain melts the snow in the mountains to the east, this extra water comes sloshing down the Ohio River, and—taking a few hen houses with it—tries to reach the sea.

Even before this valley possessed hen houses, the valley had floods. Three brothers from Virginia—James, George, and John Medfee—visited here in 1773 and told of a flood stage of about 75 feet. Even before that, in 1763, the commandant of Fort Pitt, now Pittsburgh, said the river crested there at 41 feet. In 1884 the Ohio River crested here at 71.1 feet. In 1913 there was a flood here that broke the pattern and almost washed Dayton, Ohio, away in the process. Instead of coming west down the Ohio River from Pittsburgh, the flood came south down the Great Miami River and roared into the Ohio River below Cleves with such force that for a short distance the river ran east instead of west and flooded Cincinnati. The 1918 flood was a horse of a different color. Ice had formed on the river in December 1917, gorges had piled up in many sections, which backed up the river water until flood stage at Cincinnati was 61.2 feet. When the gorge at Sugar Creek, 53 miles downstream, broke, the river fell so fast that it either stranded beautiful riverboats on the shore or carried them downstream to their deaths in the ice floes.

Floods may come and floods may go, no question about that, but the flood in 1937 remains a grabber. Before it ended, 12 square miles of Cincinnati had been under water, damage was at least $65,000,000, eight people had been killed, and Cincinnati as a city had practically ceased to function: no water, no electricity, and the threat of typhoid was the day-in-day-out specter each family lived with. Happily, typhoid never happened, but who could tell that then? It was a river flood of the sort John James Audubon wrote about in 1820: ". . . The Ohio presents a splendid and at the same time appalling spectacle . . ."

When the people along the Little Miami River left their homes on January 14, the rest of Cincinnati was more concerned with the welfare of these evacuees than their own welfare. But then the rain began to come down in earnest. January in Cincinnati, unless the sun is dazzling and the air crisp, is a chilly and murky time of the year, making Cincinnati seem gray and gloomy. Rain only adds to the depression. But the most it usually rains in January is a few inches. That cheerless January the skies opened up and out poured 13 inches. By Sunday, January 17, the downpour had been so great the Ohio River had only one recourse: go higher. Wednesday, when the valley was drenched with rain, the river reached 59.9 feet by 5 P.M., and Cincinnatians began to get the feeling they were in for it. Anything, you recall, under 60 feet is a dinky flood, but the way the rain was coming down, the natives knew this one wasn't going to be dinky. By the next day, there was no question about it. The headline in the January 21 Cincinnati *Post* announced:

RIVER SOARS TO HIGHEST SINCE '13
NEAR 65 AND MAY REACH 68 FEET

The newspaper said that the river was rising two tenths of a foot an hour; Portsmouth, upstream, had reported 10,000 homeless; and that for thousands of miles the Ohio River was at flood stage. So fast had the river risen overnight that merchants along the waterfront had been caught by surprise. The first telling blow to the city was the levee giving way at Lunken Airport. That earthwork dike, built to keep flood waters out of the 1058-acre airfield, crumbled—and water gushed over it, flooding the field for the first time since 1913. The dike break caused damage everywhere. Telephone service via underground circuits to Mount Washington was drowned out. Telephone company crews, sloshing in hipboots through the swirling waters, attempted to establish communications again, but the task proved impossible. The best the harried linemen could do was set up emergency fire and police lines between Mount Washington and Cincinnati itself. Thus Mount Washington became the first of many Greater Cincinnati communities to be touched by this disaster that

97

was to reach ultimately into every home in the city, even those high on hills and safe from the actual flooding. As that Thursday dwindled into twilight, Mount Washington was as good as isolated.

Other reports came in. From New Richmond: 1700 wet and homeless.

Across the river our Kentucky neighbors were reeling, too. Water sloshed across the Newport industrial bottoms, gurgling first out of sewers and flooding streets, then, as the river got higher, merging with the main body of the stream itself—and no streetcars could reach Bellevue or Dayton, Kentucky. The telephone company estimated that it removed 1000 telephones that first day from Kentucky homes the river had made useless. Dayton, Kentucky, reported that thirty-five of its city blocks were inundated, with more blocks being added each hour. Making wakes as riverboats do, a dozen army trucks churned through streets, water up to their hubcaps, hauling furniture—and families—from the flooded bottom areas. One truck tooted along with a smoking stove as part of its load! The river had risen so fast the evacuees had no time to douse its fire.

From Carrollton, Kentucky, came word that State Route 42 into Louisville was impassable. Many of the Ludlow, Kentucky, streets were flooded. Five trucks rushed to Ludlow's next-door neighbor, Bromley, to rescue suddenly isolated families. Of the area's federal roads, only U.S. 25, the Dixie Highway, was free of detours by nightfall. Going north out of the city, U.S. 27 and 127 were blocked by water at Knowlton's Corner and, going south out of the city, by water at Eggleston Avenue. U.S. 52 was blocked at the western end of the Western Hills viaduct.

The rapid rise of the river had surprised Cincinnatians because they are used to more well-mannered floods. The nearly two inches of rain the night before, between 2 and 8 A.M., had made the river rise three feet. Generally Ohio River floods are not scary high walls of water that plunge like tidal waves through the valley—nor was the 1937 flood any such Hollywood production. The river rose gradually, and in 1937 it simply rose faster than anyone had anticipated. Thus, the surprise. As one man, after working all night rescuing stock from his Pearl Street warehouse, said: "Floods are floods, but this is ridiculous."

When darkness came, the two evening papers were hard-pressed to deliver to subscribers, but somehow they managed. In Cumminsville and Northside, where streets were already under water, the papers were delivered by men in johnboats to families who had stayed in their homes as the water inched higher. The country deliveries were the roughest. One circulation man said the only area where the papers couldn't be delivered was flooded Newtown. Elsewhere, after-dark deliveries to Lawrenceburg, Aurora, and New Rich-

mond, and other towns, were made by Rube Goldberg routes over
private roads, abandoned dirt roads, and sometimes straight across
muddy fields.

Once delivered, the papers made interesting reading. Other than
the flood news—soon the papers would contain nothing else—there
was a story about Major Bowes' Amateur Hour saluting Cincinnati
over WKRC that night. His All-Girl Review was on the stage at
the Shubert, where Olsen and Johnson were featured in the movie
Country Gentlemen. The *Post* also carried the item that WCPO
was preparing to broadcast *The Marriage of Figaro*, with Eugene
Goossens conducting, but the flood was to cancel that.

The first night found most Cincinnatians more dismayed than anything else. They weren't frightened. Supper was on the table. The
gas stove still worked. The tap water was safe to drink. And there
was electricity to operate the radio at 9 P.M. and hear the nice
things Major Bowes said about Cincinnati. If Cincinnatians worried,
they worried about getting to work the next day. With several major
intersections under water, traffic had become a crazy quilt of frustration and complicated detours. But, basically, except for those poor
souls huddled in temporary schoolhouse shelters, most Cincinnatians
felt safe. Even those who had remained in their homes while the
water seeped out of corner sewers and turned their streets into
canals weren't too excited. Their reasoning, at the time, was correct.
The river was high, but it had never got much higher, had it?
Thus, they chose to sit out the flood in their homes, watch moats
lock them in, enjoy the holiday, and wait the river out.

Friday, January 22, was the day that Cincinnatians began to worry
in earnest. The river, still rising two tenths of a foot an hour, had
begun to reach places never touched before. The evening papers, in
telling the story of the day, offered little assurance. Said the *Post*:

NEW CREST OF 73-FT. FORECAST
AFTER FLOOD BREAKS RECORD

Suddenly those who had stayed in their homes and watched their
front yards fill with water wished they hadn't. In Cumminsville,
nine gasoline storage tanks, loosened by the flood, floated off their
moorings and spread 135,000 gallons of gasoline on the surface of the
backwater that had accumulated around Beekman and Borden
Streets. The same thing happened at Spring Grove Avenue and
Arlington Street, filling that community with sour, thick, and deadly
fumes. These frightened Mill Creek neighborhoods were potential
infernos just waiting for one spark to set them off. People who had
stayed in their homes because they thought the river would not get that
high were warned with shouts from men in passing boats, shouts that

99

ordered them to keep their windows shut and under no circumstances to light a fire.

Robert L. Otto wrote in the *Post:*

> Night before last I was a passenger on a Spring Grove Avenue streetcar. The boulevard lights glowed dimly in the rain. Today I rode along the same section in a motorboat with two firemen. Only the tops of the lamp posts were visible above the muddy, swirling water . . .

To rescue all who had thought they could sit out the flood was a near-impossible task that somehow a thousand unrecorded dramas made come true. But there were so many to be rescued that at times it seemed not all would be saved. Meanwhile, floating swiftly down the swollen Ohio River came the bric-a-brac that a flood collects on its journey: telephone poles, boxcars, tangled trees, barns, and—now and then—a house itself. One family was rescued from such a house by a worker at Fernbank dam. How long had they been drifting? No one knew. The newspapers did not record their names. Even now, nearly twenty years later, all the stories of that flood have not been told. Back then, rescue stories were a dime a dozen because almost every neighborhood had its own, and there were simply too many to tabulate. Rescue was the important item. What did names matter?

On the high-and-dry hills Friday night, Cincinnati families faced problems of their own. The gas supply, barring a break in the mains, would hold. So far so good. Milk and food supplies were adequate. All right there, too. But travel had become impossible. Many still recall the king-size jam on the Western Hills viaduct. Traffic to the east side of town was a farce. Traffic to the western hills was the same. Mill Creek traffic? Where it existed, it was a nightmare, but mostly it didn't exist. But the thing that troubled the high-and-dry Cincinnatians far from the actual adventure of the flood was the electric service. Until the river reached 74 feet, the local utility could manufacture power, but a crest had been set for 73 feet, and the crest was being continuously revised. The electric company said that should the water reach 74 feet and stop its ability to make power, some power could be borrowed from nearby cities, but not enough for residential use. Only St. Bernard didn't have this worry; it had its own power plant.

Meanwhile, our over-the-river neighbors were being hit with everything but the kitchen sink. Suspension Bridge was still open, but the rest had been flooded out. The only link between Newport and Covington was the Eleventh-street Bridge. Those going to Newport from Cincinnati had first to cross the Suspension Bridge into Covington, then go into Newport via the Eleventh-street Bridge. How? Usually by walking. Most trolleys had stopped running in northern Kentucky.

A city of hills—dependent upon items it takes for granted: power, water, food—is like a high-rise apartment house filled with thousands of families. A disaster might cut the service to that structure and, *presto!* as a community it ceases to exist. Even those high in the sky and untouched by the violence of the disaster itself are also the victims. Elevator service goes out. There are no lights. Turn a faucet: no water. If there is a fire, there is no way to put it out. If there is food, there is no way to cook it. There is no way to shave, flush a toilet, or light a light to comfort a frightened child. There is nothing to do but wait. While waiting for the nightmare to end, the building's or the city's occupants can panic or stay calm. They have no other choice. Greater Cincinnati chose to remain calm. Corny or not, around here we are proud of the way the community reacted.

But this city was not without personal tragedy. The first drowning was that of Harry Vaske, forty-seven, an unemployed painter at 5173 Eastern Avenue. He had rowed to the second floor of his house to retrieve a small safe. When he climbed back out the window and stepped into the boat, the boat tipped and he fell into the water. Firemen with grappling hooks recovered his body.

There was greater danger out Spring Grove Avenue, where firemen battled a ten-alarm fire: a warehouse in the Baltimore & Ohio Railroad yards went up in smoke.

Help poured into Cincinnati from everywhere. From Toledo came thirty-three Coast Guardsmen and four boats big enough to battle the roughest Lake Erie ever dished out.

But the stricken city itself was slowing down. Ads in the newspaper announced that this and that railroad were suspending service. Candle supplies were diminishing. Afraid that any moment the electric power would sputter out, everyone was buying candles. One downtown restaurant bought 2500. No city is perfect.

But the absolute worst was the day Cincinnatians still call "Black Sunday." It was the day that Cincinnati as a city physically and emotionally hit rock-bottom.

The key to "Black Sunday" was fire, and in the worst of all possible locations. It began at 10:30 A.M. Sunday morning. Some say a power line dipped into the water and sparked it. No one can be certain. But in seconds an overturned gasoline storage tank near the Baltimore & Ohio roundhouse on Spring Grove Avenue was an angry orange smear in the sky. In less time than it takes you to read this sentence, flames galloped across oil-soaked waters—leaping in every direction. With lightning speed—and sometimes with terrible slowness—it consumed building after building and caused oil-storage tanks to writhe, rupture, and explode. The monstrous smoke cloud that turned Mill Creek Valley into night represented the worst fears realized. All Cincinnati radio stations crackled with cries for help to fight this monster blaze—and from everywhere, even as far as Columbus, came every kind of firefighter the area possessed: off-duty, retired, and volunteer. As thirty-five fire companies battled the inferno, Cincinnati was truly a crippled city. Crosley's warehouse had been gutted. Crosley's millwork shop had been gutted. "Flames shoot hundreds of feet into the misty rain-filled sky as tanks let go again and again," one reporter wrote. "Flames make the whole valley a yellow snarling lake—and the tops of more tanks keep blowing off . . ." One point of defense was a four-story brick warehouse and its frightening contents: tons of paraffin, industrial lubricants, and two 100,000-gallon tanks of oil. Prisoners from the city Work House casually risked their lives to drag heavy hoselines across still red-hot steel beams. Thirty-three different buildings burned to the water's edge. The flood itself handicapped exhausted firefighters, who couldn't use boats because "kickback" from the hose made boats useless. Hoselines were somewhere beneath the water. Firemen waded through these waters, at times five feet deep, to do battle with the blaze. Icy winter winds added torture to the nightmare. Dr. Fred C. Swing rescued one fireman whom the water had slowly frozen fast. Before the fire was put out, it had raged forty-six straight hours and had ravaged three and a half square miles of the Mill Creek area.

The fire itself did not, of course, threaten the entire city. In many neighborhoods—Westwood, Bond Hill, College Hill, etc.—people were only aware of its grim reality through a distant siren or a radio announcer's urgent plea.

Monday papers told the story of that sickening weekend and told, also, of terrible events to come, because no relief was in sight.

RIVER NEARING 80.5 PEAK;
WATER SITUATION IS ACUTE!

Streetcar service? None. Electric power? None. Stores? All but banks, restaurants, drug and food stores closed. Schools? Closed. Water supply? Unless drastically conserved in three days, there would be no water. The only time water was pumped through the city pipes was between 6 and 7 P.M. The city itself? Silent. Terribly, terribly silent. The headline said:

MONDAY IS JUST
A SECOND SUNDAY

Martial law had been declared in Dayton, Kentucky. The Cincinnati city manager had been given the powers of a dictator. He ordered Cincinnatians to burn one light only per home. Take a bath? Impossible. It was a high holiday for children.

Tuesday, January 26, found the city exhausted but calm. The

102

city, as a city, though, had practically ceased to function. All were concerned with the flood. The fire, which began Sunday, was officially out at 8 A.M., but there was no reason to cheer. The headlines that evening said:

RIVER STARTS RETREAT
FLOOD CRISIS LESSENING

Lessening? That meant little, really. The river was still higher than it had ever been. Ruptured gasoline-storage tanks still coated backwaters with that dangerous and heady slick. Except for taxicabs and private cars that flew Red Cross banners, downtown Cincinnati was a ghost town. At night there were no street lights on. Sightseers were steered away from the waterfront, which was Third Street. Schools were crammed with refugees, who slept in gyms and classrooms and wondered what they had to go back to. Twenty thousand barrels of water had been delivered to the city to bolster the dwindling supply. The Burger Brewing Company on Central Parkway opened its three wells (capacity 800 gallons of water per minute) to all comers. Shillito's opened its artesian well to the public. Hillside springs around the city, long since ignored, had been retapped, and neighbors lined up at these trickly pipes with buckets and pans, waiting their turn, and chatting.

"The thing that most impresses me about this flood," said Chicago *Daily News* writer Leroy Vernon, "is the calmness of Cincinnatians. Everyone seems to be . . . taking this in his stride."

Not quite everyone:

A lady called the police and asked for aid in removing her piano from a flooded apartment. The harried policeman told her, "Play 'Beautiful Ohio' just once and get out."

In another instance, the police had to call for assistance from the Coast Guard to rescue one lady from her home. She weighed 400 pounds and would have swamped the policeman's johnboat.

Not all citizens were behaving. Boats patrolled the Little Miami River area to prevent looting. In Cincinnati alone, police confiscated three-dozen "unauthorized" skiffs and canoes. And in Cumminsville, one reporter told of a man sitting on a roof and blasting away at looters with a shotgun. No, not all were good, but most were. Every crisis has exceptions.

By Wednesday the river had fallen, but not too far. By evening, it had dropped only nine inches. The city, though still its victim, had stopped reeling from the river's body blows. Electricity had been restored to two thirds of the homes, and that made everyone feel a little better—unless his home was one to which power had not been restored. But caution had been advised. Conserve, they said, or the supply of electricity will not last. Telephones once again could be used for regular calls. Thousands of Cincinnatians suddenly found voice, broke silence, called friends, and compared notes. But the fire tower was still averaging ten calls a minute, and the threat of fire was still around, especially in Cumminsville, Northside, and Riverside, where oil-storage tanks were still ripping loose and spilling. Already there was talk of "swishing parties"; that is, before the river leaves your home, you row inside, swish and stir the water with a tree branch, thus loosening the sediment. Then, when the river retreats, at least some of the mud will go with it.

With dictator's powers, the city manager ordered that no automobiles in Cincinnati exceed 20 miles an hour. This was to prevent accidents. His powers had teeth in them. Violate one of his decrees and a Cincinnatian found himself faced with a $500 fine or sixty days in jail.

Most sightseers stayed clear of downtown and went, instead, to the high ground to witness the havoc. They crowded places like Mount Echo, Mount Storm, Ault, Eden, and Alms Parks. Some went only because there was little else to do. Others went to see the flooded neighborhoods in which they lived. A reporter said that more than one person, looking down at the damage, saw his own home and wept.

Perhaps, as they looked, they could see that Campbell County lifeline: the Chesapeake & Ohio passenger train shuttling back and forth from 5 A.M. to 11 P.M. between Cincinnati and Dayton, Kentucky, fare $.10. It was that town's only link with Cincinnati. Unfortunately, many who rode were merely sightseers. They'd stay on at the southern end and come right back to Cincinnati again. But the train was needed. The railroad said that 102,688 people had used it during its operation. Oldtime railroad lanterns that smelled of kerosene had to be used to signal the shuttle train along; with no electricity, the modern signal was deader than a mackerel.

A *Post* photographer showed how some Cincinnatians solved the problem of no water: they erected old-fashioned outhouses. The *Post* picture showed several, side by side, on Michigan Avenue near Erie Avenue in Hyde Park. George Bentley, then of 36 Plum Street, was the official "de-louser" at the Red Cross shelter in the St. Peter Cathedral at Eighth and Plum Streets. With no water available for baths and much flood work to be done, men had need of his services. He did a land-office business, running through 250 gallons of disinfectant before the flood was over. In those tattletale-gray days when a bath was hard to come by, Norwood residents (with water supplied from Norwood's own well, and thus enjoying full service) were inundated with close friends and slight acquaintances from Cincinnati who popped up all hours at their doors, towel in hand and hope in their eyes.

But one thing *did* irritate Greater Cincinnatians, and that was the coast-to-coast radio broadcast Floyd Gibbons made over the Columbia Broadcasting System. Cincinnatians to this day insist Gibbons "over-dramatized the whole story." That Thursday, at 10 P.M., Cincinnatians listening to his broadcast over WKRC did a slow burn. Although Gibbons broadcast from the complete safety of WLW's Union Central Annex studios (WLW let WKRC use the studios when Gibbons complained that WKRC didn't have one big enough to hold his staff), to hear Gibbons tell it, the building was in danger of washing away and—not only that—as he broadcast, he was witnessing the collapse of another building. Just as the building "collapsed," he is supposed to have said, he saw a woman on its roof holding a baby in her arms and screaming. In fairness to Mr. Gibbons, a building *did* collapse on the street he said it did, but not at the time of his broadcast, and certainly with no woman on the roof yelling her head off. Although he told a good flood, the flood he told wasn't Cincinnati's, and that got everyone here angry. The Cincinnatians who objected had a good point: the flood was soul-wrenching enough, and it didn't —and still doesn't—need embellishing. Its facts are simple and compelling. Period.

Friday, other than talking about Gibbons and wanting to get their hands on him, Cincinnatians were talking about several things. Normal electric service had been promised for the first part of the next week. Food, as it had been throughout the flood, was still plentiful. Though the river was still high and, because of floating gasoline tanks, the danger of fire was ever present, Cincinnatians had learned to live with this problem and refused to get unduly upset. There were still problems. Water service, between 6 and 7 P.M., was available, and a few curious souls had found they could open the tap anytime and water would come out. The city manager said this wasn't playing the game, because there wasn't that much water available, and he threatened to withdraw water service from anyone who dared violate "the water hours."

By Saturday, the river was dropping at a good clip. Cincinnatians began to look around and pick up the pieces of their lives. Thus, for many that weekend, there was nothing available to them but heartbreak. The *Post*'s headline for Monday told the story best:

RIVER FALL BARES DESTRUCTION . . .

The Northside wreckage was typical of the rest. The water had been 15 feet deep at Knowlton's Corner. When it receded, it revealed a bedlam of buildings pitched at crazy angles and flopped-over garages, each festooned with mud and slime. As the water went down that scene repeated itself over and over again, in neighborhood after neighborhood.

Railroads were beginning to return to normal schedules. Five thousand had been inoculated for typhoid. Electricity was still in short supply. Weird travel routes still operated. The only way to reach Sedamsville by public transportation was by a roundabout taxi-and-bus combination. On Monday, seven streetcar lines resumed service. Two thousand WPA workers started to clean up the muddy city. The Missing Persons Bureau, which had averaged one call a minute during the disaster, had moments when the telephones were silent. On Wednesday, February 3, the ten-day "holiday" was officially over and it was (almost) business as usual. The ban on liquor was lifted, the C&O announced the shuttle train would make its last run, and newspaper ads warned people that if their refrigerators had been inundated, not to plug them in until they had been inspected. By Wednesday, also, 50 trolleys were operating. By Friday, 150 trolleys were making their rounds, and the following Sunday would find most of the city's 450 to 500 trolleys operating at regular schedules. That first Friday the movies opened. Although there were no lights permitted in department-store windows (power was still painfully short), the shopkeepers braced themselves for—and got—a most busy Friday. Those magnificent steam engines were once more chugging through the valley and headed to the Cincinnati Union Terminal. Mount Washington, heaving a tremendous sigh, had been reconnected with the city, and—well, the adventure, suddenly, was over. When the weathermen figured out that in twenty-five days more than 60,000,-000,000 tons of rain had fallen into the Ohio Valley, not a soul in the city disputed that estimate.

Exhausted, Cincinnati returned to the everyday. Now and then, amid flood reminiscences, there was talk of the rest of the world: Roosevelt was trying to "pack" the Supreme Court, and isn't that a terrible war in Spain?

William P. Devou died in 1937. Perhaps the sight of his flood-damaged property in the West End hastened his passing. He had made a mint as a slumlord, but Cincinnatians couldn't tell that by looking at him. He was a real character. He lived in squalor worse than any tenants in his tenements. His West End flat was practically devoid of furniture. He refused to buy an automobile and never rode a streetcar. He had ridden a dilapidated horse from building to building to collect his rents and, when not doing that, had pushed a rickety two-wheeled pushcart through the district to collect rags and old iron he could sell for scrap. When he died, he left his money to charity.

In 1938, private developers had begun to develop Roselawn, but federal housing was still the key word. Federal housing projects, begun earlier, were beginning to open. One was Laurel Homes, downtown, with low-rent apartments for 1303 families. Another was

Greenhills, the "model community" the WPA constructed on 5930 acres north of the city. It offered low rentals, too. And, after seven years, Columbia Parkway was finally opened. But 1938 was the year that saw the death of B. H. Kroger. The Price Hill House, that hefty structure with the hefty veranda at the top of the Eighth-street incline, went out of business.

The next year, 1939, saw more government projects completed. For instance, the Post Office Building on Government Square became a reality. On the nutty side, Susie the gorilla appeared in a movie that was shown around the world. And Cincinnati finally had cause to celebrate. The Cincinnati Reds won their first National League pennant since 1919! The next year, they did even better. In 1940 they not only won the pennant, they won the World Series. Also, in 1940, Garfield Park, that little patch of park downtown across from the library, was renamed Piatt Park to honor John and Benjamin Piatt, who had donated the land in the first place. The National Theater at Third and Sycamore Streets was torn down. Built in 1837, it had been the city's finest playhouse until the 1880s. Most everything had appeared at the National at one time or another: Shakespearean drama, burlesque, concerts, and even Lola Montez. But in the theater's dotage, it became a tobacco warehouse. In 1940, it was gone. 1940 found another WPA project started: English Woods, a 107-acre English Village of sorts, a poor man's Mariemont that would ultimately house 750 families. The community was named after David English, whose family had come to Cincinnati around 1800.

Rookwood Pottery atop Mount Adams was listed for sale in 1941, catching Cincinnatians by surprise. They had considered the pottery as solid as the hill it was on, but that world-famous organization had reached the end of its line. And so had Chester Park. Although its amusement devices had long since been dismantled, it had struggled through the summer as a swimming pool and a skating rink, but in 1941 gave up even those diversions, shut its gates, and that was that. No more fun and games.

But fun and games had become luxuries the world could scarcely afford. Because in December of that year on a bitter cold Sunday when it was spitting snow, Cincinnatians listened to their radios in disbelief. Next they asked one another where Pearl Harbor was.

9

Twenty-five years have passed since Pearl Harbor, but many of you can recall where you were and what you were doing when war came, and so Pearl Harbor seems like only yesterday. Perhaps to that slim and leggy typist you admired on Fountain Square last week, Pearl Harbor is as remote as World War I, and unless she is bright at history, she regards both happenings as "something Dark Age-ish." Indeed, she might have been only a nagging worry to two lovers who met months earlier over doughnuts at a USO. To write about this accumulation of "only yesterdays"—this quarter-century between 1941 and 1966—becomes difficult because the more recent the history, the more diverse the responses of the readers. What to one is a faint and childish memory is to another a grownup and frightening recollection.

We can only presume that, viewed by our great grandchildren when they are middle-aged, pot-bellied, and disenchanted, these last twenty-five years in Cincinnati's life will seem as sad, satisfying, silly, and wondrous as any quarter-century that preceded it.

In 1942, naturally, this community was concerned with war. If a recruiting office didn't get you, a draft board did. The Cincinnati Union Terminal concourse teemed with a thousand love stories and a lot of kissing. Our industrial complex made war machines. The cloth stars hanging in windows meant that someone from that three-room flat or that three-story home was somewhere else and lonely. Gradually, as the war progressed, many of these blue stars turned to gold to complete the loneliness for keeps. Other military men—strangers to our area—passed through, and Cincinnati opened its doors and its heart to such wanderers. Cincinnati acquired the happy reputation of a "good liberty town."

There was no shortage of shortages. Silk stockings? A luxury. Cigarettes? Hard to get. Frustrated advertisers with nothing to advertise ran ads that reminded defense workers not to sleep the hangover off at home. "Our boys over there have no day off," the ads said. Everyone collected tin foil and metal; Fountain Square at times had the appearance of a convention of secondhand-saucepan sales-men. Lucky Strike green had gone to war. Slogans, slogans, slogans. If slogans had been bullets, World War II wouldn't have lasted one weekend. Ernie Pyle wrote of enlisted men. Society balls were held for officers. Men in defense plants made passes at nubile riveters. We must be fair. Such incidents were exceptions. Riveters belted them, and that was that. Mostly the men and the women left at home worked long, hard hours and were lost and lonely, too. Moments of happiness were rare. They came in the form of V-Mail, a surprise furlough, or a long-overdue letter that said, "Mom, I'm okay. I got through that one all right." Lady bus drivers appeared; in July 1943, the Greene Line in Kentucky hired several; Mrs. Harriet Lalley was one of the first. In stores hard-pressed to keep inventories up, at times grumpiness replaced patriotism as frustrated clerks complained:

"Don't you know there's a war going on?"

Chances were, the customer would snap back:

"I wondered why my son was in Africa."

Without fanfare and unnoticed except for those who used it, on July 31, 1943, the Price Hill incline made its last run. The incline house was locked, no one mourned its passing, and that was that. There was simply too much to mourn.

Oh, there was merriment. When Mussolini quit, Cincinnati's 7500 Italians were beside themselves with joy. They had three good reasons: (1) their old country relatives would now, perhaps, fight on our side; (2) they personally hated his guts; and (3) they blamed him for the shortage of meatballs in their spaghetti.

Rationing was the key to civilian survival. Stamps were more precious than money. When anticipating a young warrior's leave, the family did without and saved stamps to offer him a feast and perhaps a cigar and a slug of good booze. Often such feasts featured the wrong items. For instance, because fruit cocktail was hard to buy, mothers assumed it was a luxury, so they served it proudly to their sons, who ate it and said nothing. How were mothers to know the military had more fruit cocktail than powdered eggs? But furloughs were always so brief. They were filled with ten thousand jokes about Spam, K rations, crowded trains, and everybody kept laughing. Why did they laugh? To keep from crying. Each goodby contained the unspoken thought it might be final.

Cincinnati had two celebrations: the first when Germany sur-rendered, and the second when Japan fell. Fountain Square was the focal point each time, joy rang, girls got kissed, everybody cheered, people shook hands with strangers, and it was a duplicate of the scene staged at the end of World War I.

The celebration of V-J Day on Fountain Square, some say, will be the last such celebration the fountain will witness. When the Korean War ended in stalemate, there was no celebration. There was nothing to celebrate. And, at this writing, there is Vietnam. The conclusions of such little wars are never conclusive. And should there be another big war, some say, it is certain to be a whopper that might destroy the Square in the whirlwind. That is why many today believe V-J Day on Fountain Square marked more than the end of a war. It marked the end of an era and was Cincinnati's goodby to an innocence that the fireball over Hiroshima destroyed.

After the war the men came marching home. They had been mustered out in about every state of the Union and, with ruptured ducks sewed on their uniforms to signify they had parted from the military, they came to Cincinnati by crowded day-coaches, chartered buses, and now and then by airplane. The Union Terminal was a mob scene. The reunion of lovers was a wild, sweet affair on the crowded concourse. Then, in taxicabs and buses and trolleys, everybody went home, and that huge station fell silent. Just as the V-J Day noise of Fountain Square was a collector's item, so was the noise the train station had made. The city's love affair with passenger trains was over. Passenger planes shoved antiquated day-coaches into history.

Today from downtown, in about the same time the transit company's noisy bus can deposit you at the train station, an equally noisy airport limousine can take you over the river to the Greater Cincinnati Airport. That's where the passenger action is now. What started as a 900-acre facility in 1947 has blossomed into one of the nation's twenty busiest airports. Our airport now handles 1,500,000 passengers each year and, to make the wait at the luggage counter more fun, another 1,000,000 passengers yearly are expected to use the airport by 1970. The airport has a two-mile jet runway which, the brochure says, is "completely free of fog and smog. Bad weather rarely causes interruption of service . . ." Also, if you care for that sort of thing, planes can land when the ceiling there is only 20 feet and visibility a half mile.

The last twenty-five years have brought many changes to the area, one of the biggest changes being the end of "old" Cincinnati and the start of the "new" city. Although the city has had a Master Plan for years, and has shown it to anyone who would look at it, it took the haphazard migration of its citizens to jar the city fathers into doing more than muttering how sweet the plan was. The "new" Cincinnati, really, is more the creation of its returned veterans, who said an abrupt "No, thanks" to the old city they had left. Once back from the wars, these returned warriors moved from the old neighborhoods, which seemed suddenly drab to them, and planted roots in distant subdivisions that had once been cow pastures. Easy credit, FHA, and the GI Bill accounted for the hundreds of tasteless homes built for home-hungry veterans. Both the veterans and the builders were products of postwar America, so don't blame the developer too much. He saw a need and answered it—at times, badly. The veteran couldn't be blamed. Houses for rent were nonexistent. Apartments were few and far between. While he was away, his wife had lived with his folks or hers. But now he was home. He had fought for the right to eat blueberry pie, boo the Dodgers, and do a couple of other things best done without the in-laws in the next room. Soon there was to be in Cincinnati a spate of those boxlike four-family apartment buildings. To build one after the war was to invest in a gold mine, but now these structures litter each neighborhood like intruders, and vacancies are a dime a dozen.

The developers built "far out," where the land was cheap and building restrictions were less complicated. Postwar families followed the pied-piping developer, and thus the older and closer-in neighborhoods of Cincinnati went down a few notches. One neighborhood after another was deserted after the war by all who could desert it. Sedamsville, for example, moved bag and baggage out Delhi Pike to Delhi Township and created a newer version of the old, a kind of community that proved about as satisfactory as the Edsel. Everywhere in the distant townships beyond the city's corporation line, new and undedicated streets were slapped down, soon to be ripped up again as city services caught up with the loping developers, repaved, widened, and potmarked—to become, as they say Wyatt Earp became, legendary in their own time. Or was that Bat Masterson?

A side benefit—or ill—of the rush to the suburbs is that now certain townships themselves may become extinct as dodos. During the twenty-five-year period, seven new communities have developed in Sycamore and Columbia townships (Amberley Village, Mariemont, Indian Hill, Golf Manor, Evendale, Fairfax, and Blue Ash), and thus, victims of incorporations or annexation, two townships may disappear from the face of the earth. They've already lost nearly 80 percent of their land area to the new incorporated communities. Sycamore Township dropped from 39.1 square miles in 1940 to 7.6 square miles in 1965. Colerain Township dropped from 19.3 square miles in 1940 to 4.7 square miles in 1965. Both Montgomery and Blue Ash would like to annex land north of their boundaries to the county line. Reading, Cincinnati, and Arlington Heights would like to annex neon-lit and bubbling Reading Road, where the Carrousel Motel complex is. Also, Reading, Blue Ash, Montgomery, and Madeira wouldn't mind grabbing off township slices of the Rossmoyne and Beechwood sections. Only Indian Hill is not interested in annexing anything. It doesn't want to bring more people in. It wants to keep them out. To each his own.

Shopping centers which were first only dinky afterthoughts followed the people out to the new developments. Gradually the shopping centers became grander. For example, Western Hills Plaza had a magic ring to it. It was vast, vital, antiseptic, and so modern that western Cincinnati flocked there to lock bumpers and shopping carts. Meanwhile, watching the customers go elsewhere, the business district of Cheviot gradually changed into one vast chili parlor. Now there are more shopping centers in the Greater Cincinnati area than any reasonable person would care to admit, while in the older neighborhoods musty little "mom and pop" stores are approaching the status of whooping cranes. Many of these new and sprawling shopping centers boast of a "downtown" department store. They *all* boast of a glittering supergrocery. These shopping centers have become the "new" villages and neighborhoods—a place where everyone mingles but no one meets. WCPO-TV's Uncle Al draws a crowd to this one. WKRC-TV's Skipper Ryle draws a crowd to that one. Each has a Santa Claus at Christmas time. Go downtown? No reason to. The shopping centers followed the customers—and on the heels of both came industry and offices. Everything headed for the suburbs. Well, not really everything. The Carew Tower was too hard to move. And there sat the city fathers, wondering what had happened. No one wanted to see the Master Plan anymore. Everyone was out at the shopping center, watching Uncle Al. Gradually, in the last twenty-five years, "downtown" Cincinnati began to cough like Camille. The downtown area our fathers and some of us knew as children was dying.

Can numbers tell what happened? Perhaps. In 1958, Cincinnati had 98 apparel stores "downtown" and 38 in the suburbs. Five years later, downtown had only 80 apparel stores and the suburbs had 51. Sales in the men's apparel stores downtown dropped from $12,500,000 in 1958 to $10,200,000 in 1963—a drop of $2,300,000! Sales in suburban stores of the same category increased from $2,600,000 in 1958 to $5,400,000 in 1963—an increase of $2,800,000! Add more numbers to the pot: in 1952 there were 345 doctors downtown; 140 have since moved to the suburbs. And during the 1950s, suburban banking got its biggest shot in the arm. In the ten years between 1950 and 1960, branch banks increased from 51 to 83. Now there are 97 branch banks in the Cincinnati area. The Fifth Third Union Trust Company has 31 branches. In 1950, it had only 20. The First National Bank increased its neighborhood banks from 2 in 1950 to 21 in 1965. The Central Trust Bank had 11 branches in 1950, and in 1965 had 21. The Provident Bank has added only 2 branches since 1950, but it had 18 branches to start with and now has 20. The Southern Ohio Bank, which had no branches in 1950, now has 4.

But let's add a dash of happier numbers to see if Cincinnati as a city will last. Well, by the year 2010—according to Arthur D. Little, Inc., a research company which studied the Ohio Valley Basin for the U. S. Army Corps of Engineers—Greater Cincinnati will have a population of 1,642,000. The fourteen-county area of which Cincinnati is the hub will have, by then, 2,052,400 fidgety people looking for a place to nest. Five out of every seven of those will be in the tri-county area of Cincinnati! Other predictions: employment in the fourteen-county area will nearly double. Manufacturing will double, and double again. Eight out of every ten persons will be city dwellers. The counties in the forecast are Hamilton, Clermont, Brown, and Adams in Ohio; Boone, Campbell, Bracken, Gallatin, Kenton, and Mason in Kentucky; and in Indiana: Dearborn, Ohio, Switzerland, and Wayne.

Cincinnati, happily, didn't sit around and let its downtown die. There was exciting chatter everywhere about a "new city." But the birth of the new city is no snap. With bulldozers for midwives, the dream is becoming a reality. Still, many Cincinnatians cross their fingers and hope that urban renewal here will not take on the slap-dash appearance that housing did after the war. In the early 1960s, Cincinnati voters approved the issuance of nearly $16,600,000 in bonds just to make our waterfront pretty and to build a fancy convention hall. Also, downtown Cincinnati was—on paper—chopped up into checkerboard-like sections, each section labeled Block This or Block That. The blocks in good repair would be allowed to remain. The rest, those filled with decaying buildings that were only eyesores and empty lofts, would be bulldozed into oblivion. In their place, the "newer" city would be built: a Buck Rogers kind of metropolis with gadgetry galore: traveling sidewalks, stunning high-rises, an actual Alpine cable car swaying high above the traffic to carry passengers by the score to Mount Adams—such beautiful dreams! The nice part is, Cincinnati has a way of making dreams come true. Don't underestimate this town. When it comes to dreams, this place swings.

Talk to a Cincinnatian before World War II about a "moving sidewalk" and he'd give you funny looks and edge away. But now, talk to him about anything—cable cars to Mount Adams, moving sidewalks, a whopping new stadium, a downtown so breathtaking it doesn't seem real—and he will look at you, shrug, and say:

"So what else is new?"

Consider the Mill Creek Expressway (some call it I-75, others call it Intrastate 75) and the double-decked Brent Spence Bridge that hurls the Expressway drivers into Kentucky. No need to stop in Cincinnati at all! Consider that spaghetti bowl called the Third Street Distributor. Before the war, these items were pipedreams that appeared only on the covers of science-fiction magazines. What else is new? Well, each week new patches of expressway come into being, and soon high-powered roads will crisscross the city. A lot of history has gone down the drain so cloverleaves could be erected, but common sense tells us this is a city and not a museum piece. Museums are silent and whispery places. Right now, Cincinnati is not. Right now, Cincinnati is where the action is. Look at the Kroger Building. Agree with it or not—and some Cincinnatians look upon it in horror—it is one of the first skyscrapers to be built here since the Depression days. If your tastes go for something a bit less dramatic and a lot quieter, consider the new Procter & Gamble Building. It doesn't shout at you the way the Kroger Building does. Add Midtown Tower, which the Galbreath-Hall-Stone entente is planting at Fifth and Walnut. Another flashy structure, it is thirty-three floors of offices for rent, garages, and retail stores. There's the Prudential Tower at Fourth and Vine. So what else is new? Just about everything.

But Cincinnati is still the grand old gal she used to be. What other city would pass an ordinance forbidding wreckers to touch Dayton Street between Linn Street and Freeman Avenue? That valentine of a street must remain, the city fathers said. Thus Dayton Street, with its trim little red-brick townhouses where Cincinnati's rich used to live, might just remain.

Nonetheless, prettying up downtown has made hash of neighborhoods, especially the drab and gray neighborhood that was removed to make room for the $10,000,000 Cincinnati Convention-Exhibition Hall. That center is bounded by Fifth, Sixth, Elm, and Plum Streets. At the end of World War II that neighborhood had little to brag about, but it did have a mood of its own. The Cincinnati *Post* in its grimy but solid two-story brick building helped set the mood, and so did the neighborhood flophouses. Also, around the corner on market day, what could compare with the Sixth Street Market—that noisy line of stalls filled with ten thousand sweet and sour scents! Gone, all is gone! Where such items were, the convention facility is now: 28 meeting rooms that can hold 8000; 20,000 square feet of storage space; a first-floor exposition area of 97,000 square feet; 13 loading docks; and parking galore, but not one wino.

Alfred Segal, writing as Cincinnatus in the *Post & Times-Star*, recalled one restaurant that urban renewel displaced:

> This departing café . . . Oh yes, Cincinnatus himself knew it so well when the *Post* stood on Elm Street . . . that happy place for lunch and sherry wine at 115 West Fifth Street. It was just around the corner, and was known as the Manhattan Bar.
>
> Cincinnatus was a friend of its gracious hosts, Messrs. George Stamos and Paul Dimitri. He used to speak with them

there, about life in the world and how to make it better maybe. They cared about much more than their own success at 115 West Fifth.

They have been there 20 years and on Saturday they are going out of business, because there's to be much renewal of the block in which they've been serving. So many of us of the neighborhood knew it as a happy spot to enjoy, away from our jobs.

Messrs. Stamos and Dimitri don't seem too sorry to be losing it all, even after 20 years. They are going on a visit to their native Greece to enjoy the time of their youth there for a while. Then they'll return to Cincinnati to start at business anew . . .

Si Cornell, in the same newspaper, wrote of another:

The New England Hat Manufacturing Company, a downtown fixture for 48 years, will close its doors and disappear by July 18. Downtown business reshuffling due to the urban renewal will put the Maisonette in the hat firm's address at 118 East Sixth.

New England Hat always has been a partnership between Conrad Focht, of Hungarian descent, and Miss Margie Crolley, of Irish ancestry. Conrad bossed the making of men's fine hats. Margie sold them.

Their hats weren't cheap (as a young reporter I bought my first snapbrim there), but their customers included most of the city's prominent names. For years, the shop also had an annual mystery—some unknown person dumped green sawdust in front of the place on St. Patrick's Day. Turned out the late Judge Joe Goodenough arose very early in the morning to play that prank.

Conrad, 72 next week, and Margie, nearly that age, have never had an argument in all the years. Says Margie: "That's because every time I fussed, he put on his hat and walked out."

Though subsidized momentum is underway, the Fourth Street Area Association prefers to tackle the redoing of its own posh shopping area. Gidding-Jenny, for example, earmarked $150,000 to make the front of its store look even nicer than before—a thought that struck most Cincinnatians as a hopeless task. Gidding-Jenny store windows have been soul-wrenching artistic coups even in the early days of this last quarter-century, when Gidding and Jenny were hating one another instead of hyphenated. The Fourth Street Area Association, incidentally, is something of a misnomer. It includes not only Fourth Street but both sides of Walnut and Vine Streets as well as the south side of Fifth from Walnut to Vine—encompassing the fashionable area where a husband can go broke window-shopping with his wife.

Cincinnati in the last twenty-five years has gone through a political upheaval that only Cincinnati could have survived. For years since the George B. Cox "machine" was sent to the boneyard, the Charter Committee—that curious blend of Republicans, Democrats, and Independents more interested in good local government than party labels—had maintained that the only way to elect city councilmen without the candidates resorting to political machinery was by a system of voting called "proportional representation." That is how our councilmen were elected. Proportional representation? Well, each voter lists his choices for council with a number instead of an X on the ballot, from one for his favorite choice, two for his second choice, to as far as he cares to number or until there are no candidates left on the ballot to vote for. No party labels are indicated on the ballots. Block voting—that is, voting an X under this party and that and electing its entire slate—is impossible. Each candidate is selected on the strength of his own merit and not his party affiliation.

Since the close of World War II the Republicans (those not members of the Charter Committee) tried to ditch the PR method of voting and go back to the straight X ballot. They were opposed by the Republicans (and Democrats and Independents) who were on the Charter Committee. Each time the Republicans tried for a referendum on the matter, the Charter Committee would scream bloody murder—and both groups would throw whatever mud was handy.

In 1957 the Republican party tried once more to get PR voted out. They got an okay for a special city election to be held prior to the general election for councilmen that November.

After the votes were counted, the headline in the *Post* said:

PR DEAD AFTER 33 YEARS

Our last twenty-five years brought many changes in the political structure, but no change made Cincinnati sadder than the 1952 Republican Convention in Chicago. It marked Senator Robert Taft's last try at the presidential candidacy—and history pulled a rug out from under him. Dwight D. Eisenhower was the name of the game, his name glittered with votes, and the Republicans needed all the votes they could muster. That hot July, Ike got the nomination over Senator Taft. If Cincinnati has a heart, and it has, its heart was breaking then.

Most Cincinnatians remember the late senator as "Mr. Republican"—local boy who made good—and not as the man he was. Senator Robert Taft's haughty front was really a shy man's veneer. But when the need came, he could out-heckle any heckler, could be as ruthless as the next, and he pounced on inaccuracies the way cats pounce on mice. Lyndon Johnson, surprisingly enough, was one of the few senators who dared heckle Taft back without being clobbered by

Taft's icy stare. Different as night and day, they each had a deep-rooted respect for the other's ability and beliefs. As a person, Taft was solid gold. Fuss and feathers left him cold. For a long time he drove to fancy Washington receptions in a timeworn Buick, instead of being chauffeured in a limousine. When the Buick went the way of all flesh, he bought a Plymouth and drove that for years, too. In 1951 he bought a robin's-egg-blue Oldsmobile and suffered immediate pangs of misgiving. He said:

"Do you think it's too flashy for me?"

Senator Robert Taft died on the morning of July 31, 1953. Herbert Hoover said: "He was more nearly the irreplaceable man in American public life than we have seen in three generations"; General Douglas MacArthur wrote, "He was the indestructible bulwark . . ."; and Lyndon Johnson said, "Bob Taft was one of the truly great men who have walked our way . . ." Although most members of the Taft family are buried in Spring Grove Cemetery, Senator Robert A. Taft was not. He sleeps forever in a little cemetery in Indian Hill.

But not all such political items in the last twenty-five years had such a solid base. Consider the "hearings."

Apparently impressed by the Kefauver crime hearings that made excellent television fare in the 1950s, Cincinnati ran a medicine show called "The Towing Racket Probe," complete with television cameras, wondrous innuendo, scary revelations, black headlines, and all that jazz. The premise: certain tow-truck operators, thanks to payoffs, were making a mint because cops favored them over other tow-truck operators when it came to calling one to accident scenes. Payoffs? Kickbacks? The Mafia? Tune in tomorrow. Same time, same station. The city watched the proceedings on television and heard names and trivia bandied about, but the local spectacular lacked the magnificence of the Kefauver hearings. The city hasn't televised many hearings since.

Another adolescent charade that occupied the city's attention for a while was the penny-whistle fury created by the question: Should Cincinnati's drinking water be fluoridated? WKRC news commentator Tom McCarthy was dead-set against fluoridation and made no bones about how he felt. The dentists, on the other hand, were in favor of fluoridating the water. The battle lines were drawn. McCarthy aired his quarrel over WKRC. The dentists answered over WCPO. Ollie James, writing of the impasse in the *Enquirer*, observed that fluoridating drinking water was dangerous. "Drink 50,000 gallons of fluoridated water a day," he pointed out, "and a person will have enough fluorides in his system to be poisoned to death." And Mr. James added that there was also the danger, drinking that much water, of drowning. Again the voters chugged to the polls. Who won? The McCarthy forces did. And there you are. Some things just don't change that easily.

But every time you turned around, you could sense the change in the air. Even once-delightful street names were reduced to dull and prosaic labels. In the eastern part of Hamilton County, for instance, Round Bottom Road was reduced simply to Round Road; and Twight-wee Road was changed to—of all things!—Kemper Road. But for years, ponder as they might, the men who painted street signs found no way to simplify Devil's Backbone Road, because no other name was so apt. Old sites were vanishing. Carthage Fair Grounds, where Hamilton County fairs used to whoop things up, exchanged grandeur for shabbiness; its stands became rickety, and finally ramshackle oblivion claimed the park. That Mabley & Carew clock at Fifth and Vine Streets is no longer the Mabley & Carew clock; Mabley's moved across the street to occupy the building where Rollman's used to be; and Pogue's, already in the Carew Tower, continued the game of musical chairs by occupying Mabley's former space. On Broadway Street, six floors up in the old *Times-Star* Building, the once crackling *Times-Star* city room stands stripped, silent, and forsaken. When the *Times-Star* merged with the *Post,* the *Post* occupied the building where the *Times-Star* used to be, but the *Post* established its city room on the fourth floor, nearer the composing room. Thus, the sixth floor was left with only ghost whispers of long-ago voices shouting for copy boys.

Floods still visit here, but the new dams have tended to gentle them. In one good-sized flood in 1948 the river reached 64 feet. Little Miami residents, of course, were routed; river waters played hob with the Cincinnati bottoms; but the flood worked its worst mischief in Newport, Kentucky. Soldiers from Fort Campbell were rushed to the city to build a sandbag dike to keep the rising waters out of the Newport lowlands. They filled $40,000 worth of sandbags! But on the Ohio side of the river, the Mill Creek Barrier Dam worked fine. It saved the industrial valley from an estimated $2,000,000 damage. Water seeped into only fifteen basements in the area of Knowlton's Corner.

But while the 1948 flood was grabbing headlines that April, few noticed that on April 15 the Mount Adams incline stopped running for good. It was Cincinnati's last incline. The three newspapers, filled with more urgent flood items, had little room to give that hillside structure a proper farewell. By the time the river returned to its banks, the incline story was old hat, and gaseous buses were grinding up and burping down the steep, twisty streets of Mount Adams—and that was that.

Anyway, any alert downtown newsboy could have told you that a lot of his customers didn't buy the newspapers to read. They bought the papers to hold over their heads so that, while they waited for buses and trolleys, the starlings didn't drop on them. Starlings were a problem here. Each building ledge was lined with the cheerful beasts, who killed time by muttering amiably among themselves while waiting for the five-o'clock rush, when their sport was best. Various devices had been tried to route the pests—spreading paste, firing shotguns, and shouting mean things—but no device proved more spectacular in conception and failure than Stanley Dahlman's Starling Safari.

Stanley Dahlman is better known to most Cincinnatians as that cheerful *Post & Times-Star* cherub in charge of the newspaper's public-service efforts. A veteran Scripps-Howard employee, he goes through life "not mad at anybody," the keystone of his philosophy being, "Personally, I like the guy, but . . . ," and he applied this attitude to the starlings. A master at staging, Mr. Dahlman reached a kind of zenith when presented with the starling chore by Bob Linn, then the *Post*'s managing editor. First, from somewhere, Dahlman secured the recording of a starling in distress, then hired a sound truck, rented a pith helmet, and his starling safari began. The idea: when starlings hear the cry of a fellow starling in distress, they fly away and don't come back. Well, Dahlman's picture, complete with sound truck and pith helmet, appeared in the *Post* (some readers looked upon Dahlman with sympathy because he looked terribly disenchanted), and that night the plan was put into action. The sound truck made its rounds, the distress call was broadcast, and the starlings took off. So far, so good. However, the sound truck disturbed other flocks, too. The recorded screechings, being interdenominational, also frightened a flock of worshipers in a downtown church, and the choir director came out to register protest. But, as you know, Cincinnati stories have happy endings. So does this one. The next day the flocks were back at the churches, the starlings were back at Fountain Square, Mr. Dahlman—pretending that all was well—went around muttering, "Personally, I like starlings, but . . . ," and street sales of newspapers continued to warm the cockles of each circulation manager's heart.

Other silliness has preoccupied Cincinnati since Pearl Harbor. Right after the war ended, everybody and his brother started radio stations. Before, Cincinnati had only five: WLW, WSAI, WKRC, WCKY, and WCPO. But the Federal Communications Commission opened up "daytime" stations—those that sign off at sunset so they won't interfere with distant stations that share the same dial position—and suddenly, in 1947, Cincinnati had two more stations: WZIP, which Arthur Eilerman put on the air, and WNOP, which James Lang put on the air. But the silliness was FM radio. Before anyone could reason with the investors, FM stations multiplied like rabbits, and each community had its own broadcasting station that no one listened to. For a brief spell Cheviot had an FM radio station upstairs over a movie house. Now both the station *and* the movie are gone.

Television was filling the neighborhood bars. Crosley opened its lavish Taj Mahal, called Mount Olympus, on April 17, 1948, up there on that hill: hippodromes for studios in which WLWT intended to create television programs, but Mount Olympus didn't last too long. Before cab drivers could learn shortcuts to the hilltop setting, WLWT moved its studios downtown, across the street from Jack Abrams' Bar. WCPO-TV came on the air, and so did WKRC-TV. Chapter 12 tells more of this weird art form.

The Cincinnati Public Library (properly: the Cincinnati and Hamilton County Public Library), which had originally occupied a building that was originally a theater, moved a block or so north on Vine Street to quarters more suited to storing books. Now the library resembles a hushed supermarket that features music at noon and Faith Baldwin. Another emporium of culture has changed its name. The burlesque house, next door to the library, used to be the Empress and is now the Gayety. Other diversions have folded. The Cat & the Fiddle Night Club, a watering hole for out-of-town salesmen and visitors to whatever conventions our city attracted, closed. Lately many little bars that have tried to emulate the racier or pseudosophisticated holes-in-the-wall that bigger cities possess have come and gone with such regularity that to catalog them is to catalog the misguided thinking of entrepreneurs who thought Cincinnatians were ripe for plucking. The more standard saloons remain—and that's Cincinnati for you. Leo Hirtl, who wrote the "Seven Hills" column in the *Post* for many years and is now the *Post & Times-Star*'s city editor, capsuled Cincinnati best. The key word, he said, is "unconcerned." He's right, too. That's why young men who flip-flop through the city in sandals and grow beards before they can are stared at only by other flip-flopping beard-producers.

How to bring Cincinnati up-to-date? Well, let's try it this way. On April 29, 1951, William H. Klappert, 936 Seton Avenue, was a motorman on streetcar number 129 that ran on the North Fairmount line. At exactly 5:55 A.M. that Sunday morning, he piloted the orange dreadnought from Fifth and Vine, his only passengers being some sleepy young men who had hitchhiked from Columbus, Ohio, for the occasion. Twenty-three minutes later, the trolley swung off the streets and into the gloom of the car barn. Mr. Klappert removed the paraphernalia of his trade (watch, change-maker, transfers, and lunch box), climbed from the trolley, and said to the men who waited:

"All right. You can have her now. I'm finished."

Thus the last trolley ran in Cincinnati. From then on, buses and, for a little while, trolley buses took over. The last lines to run streetcars were North Fairmount, Vine-Clifton, Westwood, Lockland, and

John Street. When they pulled into their respective barns that Sunday morning, that was it, the end of the line, there weren't any more . . .

The last green trolley in northern Kentucky—the one that potted through the hills to reach Fort Mitchell—was already a memory.

And there you are. We have journeyed a long way together since the dinosaur rooted through your flower garden, haven't we? And, in some fashion or another, here we are—at *right now*, the stopping point for this history. Histories have stopping points, cities never. As this is written, somewhere within a building downtown a bell is clanging, and soon the building will rumble because the running of presses makes buildings nervous. Thus, depending on the hour, another *Enquirer* or *Post & Times-Star* will hit the streets—and another day is history.

10

The second half of this book will be about Cincinnati today. As much as possible, the city's facts and moods have been updated. But to update our city *continuously* requires a fresh history be written each day. Happily, history *is* written each day. In fact, two histories are: the *Enquirer* and the *Post & Times-Star*. Not only do these two publications continuously update our city, but so do radio and television newscasters. In days of old, minstrels sang the news. We have Peter Grant, Al Schottelkotte, and the rest.

To picture present-day Cincinnati in words is like taking a snapshot at a family reunion. However good the intentions of the writer or photographer, if grandfather doesn't wiggle, a grandchild will. Families don't stand still, and neither do cities.

The best we can do is gaze at today's Cincinnati with affection, try to "fix" it in time, and know full well the moment this book says the city is one thing, it will have outgrown that and become another. This book may fit Cincinnati no better than last year's blue jeans fit a fidgety teenager who won't stop growing.

Also, it would require dozens of volumes printed in smaller type than you're reading right now to do an encyclopedic study of where today's Cincinnatians live, fathers work, mothers shop, and children play. Yet, these things *are* Cincinnati. When young couples go out to dine, where do they go? And in what atmosphere? Are there band concerts in the park? Where's the nearest nudist colony? Who owns the Ohio River? Which part of town is best to raise kids in? Who on earth are those local personalities on television? Will the Cincinnati Reds stay here forever? How much booze does Cincinnati pour down the hatch? Is Coney Island everything the ads say? Where's the best place to fish? Questions, questions, questions! Dozens of volumes would be needed—and a cast of thousands to write and edit them—if Cincinnati is to be completely explained. Only an idiot or a starry-eyed lover would attempt the task single-handed. So be gentle with your criticism, and let's get started.

At one point, it was the intention of this book to emulate that wonderful *Cincinnati Guide* published in 1942. Harry Graff, R. D. Sims, Myron Flechtner, R. C. Downes, and a host of others put together a whopper of a book about Cincinnati, taking us by the hand and guiding us along Fifth Street—for example—pointing out, as we walked, the history of the thoroughfare and every building we passed. These men offered "Basin Tours" that carried us from the riverfront to Central Parkway, west to the West End, and east to Pike Street; "Suburban Tours" that sent us through Walnut Hills, the East End, Pleasant Ridge, the upper Mill Creek Valley, the Mohawk, and west to Fernbank; and "Hamilton County Tours" that took us from Newtown to Elizabethtown—as far east and as far west as proper Cincinnatians would care to go. The *Cincinnati Guide* propelled us gently through Newport, Covington, Ludlow, and the other northern Kentucky communities. But this book you're holding can't do that. As soon as we started down Fifth Street, we'd meet an obstruction that said "Construction Ahead." Downtown Cincinnati, at this writing, is being torn down and rebuilt. Architect's sketches of the "new" Cincinnati only confuse things because some of the buildings are not turning out the way the dreamers planned. Example: the high-rise office building on the southeast corner of Fifth and Vine Streets was supposed to be much taller. So we hesitate to describe how the city will look by the time you read this book. Things are happening too fast to allow us to emulate the *Cincinnati Guide*. Where historic buildings used to be there are vacant lots—and see one vacant lot and you've seen them all.

Beyond the downtown area? Well, though they're not changing as fast as the core of the city, nonetheless entire neighborhoods are changing, too. But let's be brave and look at these neighborhoods anyway. First, you must recognize that Cincinnati is a clannish town. Families love their neighborhoods. Some would never think of moving to another. The same holds true for the side of town you're on. It's the best side of town Cincinnati has. For instance, people on the east side of Cincinnati—Hyde Park, Mount Washington, Milford, and the rest—consider themselves wiser than the people on the west side of town—Westwood, Price Hill, College Hill, and the rest. Why? Because when eastsiders drive to and from downtown each day, the sun doesn't shine in their eyes. In defense, the westsiders could point out that, statistically, the east side is dangerous. In 1964, four people were murdered on the east side; only two were murdered on the west side. Fourteen were raped on the east side; on the west side, only ten. The east side had 398 burglaries to the west side's 259. And on it goes. These statistics aren't forced. Police District Six, which *is* the east side, and Police District Three, which *is* the west side, both possess the same variety of neighborhoods: some ritzy, some sleazy, but most middle-class. District Six covers twenty-two square miles, one mile more than District Three, so area isn't the factor. But let's not get involved in that quarrel, which, at best, is a friendly one.

Rather, let's assume you're new to Cincinnati, know nothing about the community bickerings, and you're in need of a house for your family. To you, as a stranger, one neighborhood seems the same as any other. Even the odd names—Corryville, Covedale, and Finneytown—don't panic you or make you giggle. But they do worry you. Which is suburbia and which is a slum? Which has ticky-tacky housing, and which has palatial old homes for a song? Rest assured, there are many fine homes for sale each day in Cincinnati, and a few lemons, too. The happy part about Cincinnati is this: within reason you can buy exactly the house you want at exactly the price you want to pay in most any neighborhood in the area. But if you're a stranger here, that's no help, either, is it?

Let's go through the HOUSES FOR SALE columns in the classified advertising section of one of our two newspapers. This will give you an idea of the character of some of the neighborhoods. But fair warning: each Cincinnatian has his own strong opinions about this neighborhood and that. One man's meat is another man's poison. Some neighborhoods will appeal to you more than others. Some you wouldn't touch with a ten-foot pole. You might favor suburbia. Cincinnati is up to its ears in suburbia. You might hate suburbia. No strain. Cincinnati has many fine neighborhoods like mother used to make. Perhaps high-rise apartments appeal to your soul. Cincinnati has them, too. And, to be honest, Cincinnati has several neighborhoods that have deteriorated into slums. But each neighborhood creates a distinct and, at times, shattering reaction in the hearts of those who live in it. There are as many distinct reactions as there are Cincinnatians. All the reactions are personal, and this book's reaction must be personal if it is to have meaning. But bear this in mind, also. As suggested at the start of this book, if we seem to quarrel with this or that in Cincinnati, accept it for what it is: a lover's quarrel—and nothing more. Now, let's look at the classified ads, be as cheerful as we can, and find the character of Cincinnati's many neighborhoods. Then we can put all the neighborhoods together and have a reasonable idea of what Cincinnati is.

First, there's Addyston, the downriver municipality west of the Cincinnati corporation line. This neighborhood has seen better days, but unless you're an oldtimer, you'd be hard-pressed to recall when those days were. Addyston started out to be the "Pittsburgh of the West," acquired the drabness that Pittsburgh once possessed, but little else. Now it is a dinky community that is, for the most part, bypassed by the widened U.S. 50 that carries you west into Indiana. Paul Landfair, a professor of architecture at Miami University in Oxford, Ohio, and a traveler who has studied cities and housing in just about every country on the globe, said of Addyston:

> I would judge that it had once been a pleasant middle-class community, but it has since become a ghetto for a much lower income group. Addyston degrades gradually. There will be one house well maintained and right next to it a house that is falling apart, with fourteen junked cars parked out front.

Amberley Village is next in the classified columns. A sedate and well-maintained corporate entity, it is located north and a hair to the east of downtown Cincinnati. It is typical suburbia. As with most such communities, you must cultivate a taste for the music the power mowers make. If Forest Park is the place where the rising young executive lives, Amberley Village is where he relocates after he's risen a bit more.

Far to the east is Amelia, Ohio, but not so far that Cincinnati toilers in search of tranquility avoid the place; and when they drive back and forth into downtown Cincinnati, of course, the sun does not blind them. Naturally, being distant from the central city, housing in Amelia can cost less and you can get a bit more for your money.

Avondale, which is *in* Cincinnati, is the next neighborhood in the advertising columns for the newspaper that day. The prices and the kinds of houses offered tell the sad story of Avondale's twilight. Avondale streets are lined with stunning and massive homes that used to be single-family dwellings, but now that is generally not the case. When the West End was gutted to make way for civic improvement, the displaced Negroes were forced to move. Most of them came to Avondale, and through no fault of their own, the ghetto came along with them. In Avondale and adjoining Walnut Hills are about 1600 families who receive welfare assistance. In the same area, more than half a hundred homes are dilapidated. And in that same area, nearly 1500 families earn less than $2000 a year. If you hanker for such diversions, hang around Reading Road between Melish and Ridgeway Avenues, where, according to Police Captain Elmer Reis, "ladies stand on corners and flirt with passing motorists."

In the northeastern portion of Greater Cincinnati is Blue Ash, which got its name because blue ash trees once grew there. Now it is just another suburban area, and its one distinction is the Blue Ash Airport. At one time, before the Greater Cincinnati Airport was built in Boone County over the river, the Blue Ash Airport site was being considered as *the* site. There was a bond issue. And a radio commercial to the tune of "My Bonnie Lies Over the Ocean" ended, "Bring back our airport to us!" (Ohio vs. Kentucky, you see). But musical Cincinnatians voted the issue down, and that was that. Now homes ring most of the airport field, but the idea of converting the facility into a busy metropolitan jetport that would serve Dayton, Ohio, as well as Cincinnati still comes up now and then, causing young brides to look with quiet desperation at their new bone china. Some Cincinnatians assume that Blue Ash real estate prices fluctuate, depending on how hot or cold the airport "rumors" are, but this is not so. Blue Ash residents have lived under this threat too long and have grown most blasé about the entire shooting match.

Bond Hill, next in the classified ad columns, is, at this writing, a collection of middle-class families living in an assortment of middle-class housing. But slowly the main streets of this northern Cincinnati community are going commercial. This does not detract from the side streets and byways, of course, and fathers can still travel between Bond Hill and downtown on the Mill Creek Expressway in nothing flat, so one can't quarrel with the community too much. Just as in neighboring Roselawn, Bond Hill finds itself each year with additional motels and trailer courts. Basically, Bond Hill has individual homes and apartments, but a quick glance makes one feel the community has more apartment houses than you can shake a stick at. For the most part, Bond Hill is without color or personality, but many Cincinnatians would live nowhere else. Actually, to have color and personality can, at times, be a bad thing for a neighborhood to possess. Avondale is acquiring a personality it would like to get rid of.

Bridgetown is in the western part of the area, beyond the Cincinnati city limits. Once it, too, possessed personality: the rustic charm of the country. Them days are gone forever. Now subdivisions cover its hills and fill up its valleys. Old trees have been chopped down, and the new trees are still adolescent. Nevertheless, a few roads still maintain the "feeling" of the way things once were: ancient trees, sudden hills, and the whiff of a barnyard. But generally the hillsides are well manicured, and if your home doesn't have a REAL WOOD-BURNING FIRE-PLACE!!! the house next door will. Search long enough and you'll find the right house for you. Search too long and you'll get discouraged. They will all begin to look the same.

Camp Washington is within Cincinnati and "close in." A crowded little community whose center, if it had one, would be at the intersection of Hopple Street and Colerain Avenue, Camp Washington is a workingman's neighborhood. Most of the housing consists of flat buildings and a scattering of single-family dwellings—and both kinds look exhausted. Industry lines Colerain Avenue, and so do little groceries and all-night hamburger stands. The police are still trying to solve the murder of one Camp Washington couple, shot to death in their own garage. But the neighborhood is more musty than murderous. Camp

Washington is like many old Cincinnati neighborhoods: a raffish accumulation of buildings in varying degrees of disrepair; retired and bent old men sunning themselves on front porches; young men with funny haircuts tearing around in souped-up cars that aren't paid for; and teenage girls, overdressed, lonely, walking the evening streets in a ritual as old as time—waiting for the world to happen to them. It is a neighborhood of babies crying on sultry nights and the noise of ten thousand semitrucks gearing down. But it is one thing the newer communities aren't. It is a *neighborhood!* And there is in it, however old and noisy and musty the neighborhood, a feeling that people care.

Another community—and next on the list—is Cheviot, Ohio, on the western edge of Cincinnati. If Camp Washington is a community of workingmen, Cheviot is a community of better-paid workingmen. Apartment houses are springing up in Cheviot, but not too many. Mainly, Cheviot is an amiable corporate entity of pleasant middle-class homes, of which 99 percent are in excellent repair. Side streets are lined with low-slung brick and frame houses that are shaded by trees which have been there for ages. The lot sizes are not large, but now and then you'll find a whopper of a lawn and a whopper of a house. More than workingmen live in Cheviot, of course. If Cincinnati is serene, Cheviot is more so—though, at times, against its wishes. For instance, its business district, centered at Harrison and Glenmore Avenues, has lost much of its momentum. Now everyone shops at nearby Western Hills shopping centers. The family businesses in Cheviot are slowly fading away. Where they used to be, now there are chili parlors.

Some listings in the advertising columns are marked "CITY," which can mean most anything. Usually, it means a flat building in that teeming basic area that time and apathy are disfiguring: the Mohawk —and the creaking "Over the Rhine" section. If "City" could be pinpointed geographically, its northern boundary would be somewhere around Mulberry Street halfway up Vine Street hill, or perhaps along drab McMicken Avenue—but McMicken Avenue wiggles so. Simply put, the northern area is ringed by the hills and climbs a little up the hillsides on dangerous streets that would give San Francisco boosters a run for their money. The western boundary would be as far west as you could go before the Mill Creek Expressway stopped you. The eastern boundary would be as vague as the northern boundary. Perhaps Sycamore Street, perhaps halfway up the Sycamore Street hill— or Liberty Street hill? The housing there is just as gloomy. Maybe it's along Eggleston Avenue or in that degrading section around "old" Woodwood High School. South, of course, would be the river. In reality, the "City" is anywhere in the basin area you want it to be. "City" housing, nine times out of ten, is nothing more than a lonesome flat building filled with bedbugs.

Cleves is down the river, west of Cincinnati, and over the hill from Addyston. Widened U.S. 50 makes the drive between Cincinnati and Cleves a breeze. But a word of caution: don't breeze over 45 miles an hour. U.S. 50 becomes River Road when it reaches Cincinnati, is a dream road to drive, but Captain Tolbert Frances—the policeman in charge of District Three, where River Road is—says:

> The ten-mile stretch of road from the 3200 block of River Road to the corporation line is a real speedway. We can look for four or five automobile deaths on River Road every year.

Well, if you survive *that* problem and don't get nabbed by a Cincinnati policeman in a relatively unmarked but powerfully souped-up police car, you'll arrive safely in Cleves. Paul Landfair said:

> Coming into Cleves from the west, one sees a litter of degrading little service shops that look as if they had been thrown together. But as we approached the eastern section of Cleves there was that marvelous house high on the hill. It looked as if it were something Charles Addams might have designed. For some reason, there are four or five old and terribly huge homes in Cleves that don't belong there. They seem much too big and much too expensive for the president of a bank in such a small community to build. What sort of family would live in Cleves? Well, they probably don't, but working artists should. He could get into Cincinnati in thirty-five minutes, and along the river it's most interesting . . .

Next in the classified advertising columns is Clifton, a touch-and-go hilltop community that is a neighbor of the University of Cincinnati. On some of its streets are homes that leave you spellbound. Turn a corner, walk a few blocks, and you'll find the spell broken. The same kind of home has been whittled into a multifamily dwelling and is going downhill fast. Clifton is filled with surprises. Some are happy ones. Others can break your heart. A hilly community shaded by ancient trees, it is crisscrossed with streets and byways (some actually gaslit!) that take aimless turns and occasionally end up nowhere. It is a neighborhood of great homes that, now and then, have "modern" homes for next-door companions, but these modern homes are as out of place on some streets in Clifton as pop art at a Rembrandt festival. French doors, verandas, turrets, wrought-iron grills, porticos, fluted stone columns, floors of hammered-dress stone, carved marble fireplaces, and hand-carved mantels—these are the delicacies that Clifton mansions have feasted upon. Serenity is the password to many streets in Clifton. The password to others is despair.

The password to Colerain Township is growth. That's where Groesbeck is. Colerain Township is north and slightly west of the Cincinnati city limits. If Bond Hill has forgiven us for saying it lacks personality, perhaps Colerain Township will be equally forgiving. Builders are taking over this area, erecting attractive and comfortable homes: suburbia is rampant. There are few surprises in Colerain Township, but the same goes for Green and Delhi Townships, too. At least in Colerain Township you're out of the city in mushrooming suburbia, if that's your heart's desire. In Colerain Township you don't get the feeling of being in a crowded elevator.

Next in the listings is College Hill, northwestern Cincinnati beyond the Mount Airy Forest preserve. College Hill is a mixture. Like Cheviot, parts of College Hill have side streets lined with amiable one-family houses that were there before World War II. Other parts of College Hill present street after street of one-family units that represent the pride and joy of developers after World War II. Downtown Cincinnati is a short roller-coaster ride down Hamilton Avenue. The *Cincinnati Guide* said:

> [College Hill] is notable for its many beautiful homes and the light annual fall of soot . . .

The Ohio Military Institute on Belmont Avenue is a College Hill fixture, and so is the Methodist Home for the Aged at 5343 Hamilton Avenue.

Straight up Vine Street hill, a hair north of McMillan Avenue, is an older Cincinnati neighborhood called Corryville. It is a hilly community of red-brick multifamily dwellings, wrought-iron fences, sudden side streets, and second-floor flats. Downtown is close. The University of Cincinnati is close. And so are the mansions of Clifton and the band concerts in Burnet Woods. Corryville was never a grand neighborhood, never presumed much; it was always a workingman's kind of neighborhood, and time has done little damage to it.

Covedale means "outer" Price Hill, its main roads being Covedale Avenue, Cleves-Warsaw Pike, and Sidney Road. Actually, Covedale has no exact boundaries. Mostly it is filled with pre-World War II homes that are single-family dwellings and a middle-class homeowner's delight. If Price Hill becomes a slum, Covedale, being out so far, will be the last community to go under. Whether Price Hill becomes a slum—well, that's difficult to say. Price Hill is vast. In the Gay Nineties the brow of Price Hill, which one can now see from the Carew Tower, was *the* place for the middle class to live. As the city grew, Price Hill expanded westward, back from the brow of that hill, electric trolley cars aided the expansion, until finally, before World War II, Covedale—far west—was the nice end of Price Hill, and the brow of the hill—far east—was getting dowdy. For those who get fidgety in modern suburbia, Covedale is an excellent choice. It's certainly not suburbia. It's a neighborhood. The houses in Covedale are for the most part better built because, as oldtimers keep saying, they don't build houses the way they used to. Some of the homes are roomier, too. Covedale is the community that radio's Vic and Sade would have lived in.

Cumminsville is not. Lorenzo Jones would have lived there. Cumminsville has a last-century look about it. A workingman's neighborhood north of downtown Cincinnati along the Mill Creek Expressway, Cumminsville used to be where children gathered to see the circus trains unload. Before that, it used to be called Helltown, but times have changed. Cumminsville has settled down into a neighborly lower-middle-class section of red-brick houses and uncomplicated frames, most in good condition. The community has the appearance, because of its narrow streets lined with houses, of being tightly packed, but it's really not. Cumminsville goes on and on. Industry is there and the trains go through, but these items don't interfere too much with the neighborhood's complacency. Hamilton Avenue (U.S. 27) and Colerain Avenue (U.S. 127) cut through the heart of Cumminsville, but go a few blocks either way from these noisy things, and everything is peaceful again. Most of the bars are beery neighborhood establishments, uncomplicated, and without fuss or feathers. One of Cincinnati's earliest communities, Cumminsville has a lot of staying power. It has gone down a little, true, but not that much.

Deer Park follows Cumminsville in the classified column's alphabetical list of HOUSES FOR SALE. Deer Park, simply put, is a pleasant community of pleasant homes located in the northeast part of Greater Cincinnati. Deer Park has a variety of neighboring communities around it, nearly all just as middle-class. South of Deer Park is Silverton, north is Rossmoyne, west is Amberley Village, and to the far east is not-so-middle-class Indian Hill. Pretty soon—whenever that is—there will be an expressway to hurl you into downtown Cincinnati. At the moment, though, the expressway is little more than a dotted line on a map and a gleam in a road-builder's eye.

A gleam in the developer's eye, to be brutally frank, is Delhi Hills, a lofty name which means Delhi Township in western Greater Cincinnati, where years ago truck farms and greenhouses were the order of the day. Delhi Township, like Green Township, its neighbor to the north, was once rolling countryside, creeks, and cows grazing in vast and lonely fields. Only a few cows remain. Shopping centers have taken root in the pastures, the rolling hills are now covered with a vegetation called suburbia, and as for the creek—well, the old creaking mill is still, Maggie. Close-in along Delhi Pike, you can't tell where the city of Cincinnati stops and the "country" begins. Out farther—at the other end of Delhi—there are still some open tracts in the vicinity of Mount St. Joseph-on-the-Ohio, but don't count on them staying empty. Occasionally, you see an old farmhouse left over from Delhi's yesterday and looking like an old-maid aunt who never got the word. On certain roads in Delhi Township are some expensive houses, too. Mostly, present-day Delhi Township represents the handiwork of many different developers, which is a kind of blessing. If you don't like the way the houses on one street look, try the next street. Want something modern? Try this development. Want something rustic? Try that development. Whatever your heart's desire is in a home—be it bland, ornate, complicated, gingerbread, or dull—Delhi Township has it. Or if it hasn't, wait a week.

But it is better to live in Delhi Township than to live in some sections of the East End, particularly that dreary stretch of bad dreams they call houses on Eastern Avenue. East End is next in the listings, you see, but it is certainly not dear to Cincinnati's heart. But since communities are difficult to sweep under rugs and forget, let's look it over. Columbia Parkway is up there on the hillside, zooming traffic into town from the nicer sections of eastern Cincinnati. Paralleling Columbia Parkway is Eastern Avenue, which travels along the river. It is a poor neighborhood. Trucks grind along the narrow street; cars are parked to make it even narrower. Frame houses that haven't been painted since Hector was a pup stand guard—or they sleep at crazy angles. Sometimes the Ohio River floods the street, but as far as Eastern Avenue is concerned, the flood is simply another inconvenience. The neighborhood's real kick in the head has been time. Now and then you see traces of once-beautiful frame houses that have gone to seed. They bulge weirdly in the most unlikely places, as imperfectly corseted fat women do. But you can still see traces of another day's grandeur: fancy wood carvings and ornate scrollwork. No, the neighborhood's majesty has fled. The old frame houses look so dry, crackly, creaky, and frail that you're almost afraid to light a cigarette.

Farther out, in the East End, is Linwood, which struggles to maintain its dignity. Linwood is mostly an oasis of old-fashioned homes that sprouted long, long ago. Linwood, at times, has the appearance of a village plopped down—mistakenly—into the middle of a city. Expressways torment it. Trains make noises at it. But here and there, undisturbed, are little flower gardens tended by little ladies as old and charming as the neighborhood itself. True, Linwood does have charm, but it is also true that Linwood is pooped. One more expressway, one more cloverleaf, one more widened street, one more freight train's shriek and—well, there will be no little gardens or little old ladies to love them.

Evanston, now part of Cincinnati, was named after Evanston, Illinois, where Northwestern University and a lot of pretty girls are. Before that, Evanston was called Idlewild. Now it is a suburb of Cincinnati, has industry on tap, and, like most near-in suburbs, is feeling the aches and pains of age. Multifamily dwellings are taking over. Some of the homes were originally beautiful, old-fashioned, and huge. Now many of them are simply cheap.

Fairmount might be considered a typical Cincinnati neighborhood, vintage World War I. It's in the hills and hollows across Mill Creek, between Cumminsville and the Western Hills viaduct. Because it is situated along Mill Creek itself, the neighborhood looks about as disembodied as a neighborhood can get. On one hill the houses are bunched up, on another they are farther apart; and on the hillsides themselves, some houses hold on only by imagination. The streets of Fairmount go in different directions every chance they get, but the people are relatively stable. Fairmount is a blue-collar community that time and the railroad yards in the valley have turned to gray.

Finneytown lies north of Cincinnati between Hartwell on the east and North College Hill on the west. It is rolling-hill country in parts, a rural setting that is rapidly becoming a population center for the Greater Cincinnati area. Hence: developments by the score! Some of the roads are straightaways and some are sharp-cornered. The Finneytown area doesn't give you the jam-packed feeling some sections of Delhi and Green Townships do—or, at least at this writing it doesn't. The area is growing too fast to pin down.

Forest Park—far north but close enough to the Intrastate to make commuting to downtown Cincinnati or the Mill Creek Valley industry an interesting jaunt—is an antiseptic development of curved streets lined with antiseptic houses that developers get a kick out of building and young moderns, whatever their age, get a kick out of buying. Split-levels, dining L's, and trees struggling to take root abound in this stereotyped suburbia, where cooking steak on the backyard grill is a tribal rite. Most houses have three or four bedrooms—not all finished, of course—which means Forest Park is a community of mothers, fathers, teenagers, and smaller fry, plus dogs and cats and ten thousand bicycles. The neighbors are a friendly sort, cheerful, and it is one of the nicer suburbias, where everyone gets along because they have the vague feeling that somehow they are all in the same boat.

Glendale is still farther north, but the expressway is handy, the homes have a gentle beauty, and the town itself has a yesteryear gentility. There's no feeling of rat race or rush. Some of the homes are big, and most are old-fashioned. Glendale exudes a feeling of posh, which is no manufactured item, because Glendale in its quiet way *is* posh. Here and there, developers have tried to work their mass-produced magic, but Glendale makes stronger magic of its own. The magic lies in its sense of quiet, the tree-lined streets, and the timelessness of its lawns. Many rich people live in Glendale, but you don't have to be rolling in the stuff to enjoy its charms. You simply have to have a few spare bucks—and good taste.

Next, alphabetically, in the real estate listings is Golf Manor, another reasonably "near in" neighborhood off Reading Road past Bond Hill. Golf Manor is a coterie of dwellings as bland as those in Bond Hill. It is a dormitory community that has been there awhile; hence, the trees are shadier than those in Forest Park.

Greenhills, in the vicinity of Forest Park, is a gem of a community that the United States Farm Security Administration made come true on nearly 6000 acres in northern Greater Cincinnati. It was built between 1935 and 1938 to give work to the unemployed. It is one of the few "planned developments" that have created any sense of "community." Its trees and parks help. They're everywhere.

As you go out Vine Street beyond the archaic Carthage Fair Grounds and get involved in a mishmosh of used-car lots, you will be in Hartwell, which is not as bad as it seems. True, the main drag is something to make you think twice because it gets more commercial each year, but a community is more than its main street. Hartwell is proof of this. It is a community that was there before World War II—indeed, it was first settled in 1792—and its side streets wind in and out among trees that have witnessed more history than the residents. Hartwell has been part of Cincinnati since 1912, which means some of its homes are old. But it doesn't mean they're falling down. Hartwell, mostly, is a tidy community of both big and little homes that aren't pretentious.

After Hartwell in the listings comes Hyde Park, where all young P&G executives go when they first get hitched. (If they climb high up on the P&G ladder, they end up in Glendale, of course!) Hyde Park's main street is Erie Avenue from the Withrow High School Clock Tower to as far south as your imagination will permit you to travel. It used to be farmland, centuries ago. Then it became the setting for magnificent estates. Hyde Park is now the stomping grounds of the upper-middle-class, and Hyde Park Square, between Edwards Road and Michigan Avenue, is just that: a pleasant village square ringed with shops that are as well mannered as the neighborhood they serve. If you like big old homes, you'll like Hyde Park. Also, if you like big new homes, you'll like Hyde Park. But if you're suburbia-inclined, seek elsewhere. Hyde Park is a community no planner could blueprint. It is a neighborhood in the purest sense of the word. Apartments are there as well as single-family dwellings, but all are in good taste. In Hyde Park you'll find some dead-end streets so quiet the sound of a truck's backfire will send you into orbit. But after circling the globe, you'll always return to Hyde Park. That's the kind of neighborhood it is. It's close in, minutes from town if you drive that fast, and it's the kind of neighborhood they just don't make anymore.

Next we have Indian Hill. Now, there's a neighborhood for you! Said the *Cincinnati Guide:*

133

This hilltop community of great estates is called Indian Hill. While practically all Indian Hill residents are wealthy, some of the homes reveal the plebeian origin of the first families of the community. Many of the estates have extensive farms, and casual talk concerns the prospect of a tomato crop as well as the condition of the stock market . . .

Located in the eastern reaches of Greater Cincinnati and in the rumpled Little Miami River Valley, Indian Hill has for neighbors Madeira, Milford, and Terrace Park, but this doesn't mean that Indian Hill is neighborly. It also has its own police force, private cops who have been appointed deputy sheriffs, charged with the task of keeping Indian Hill the way its landowners like it: quiet. Although the roads are dark, narrow, and spooky, and would make delightful passion pits where young lovers could park, the cops frown upon that as gauche. There *are* some small homes in Indian Hill—by comparison with the others there, that is.

Kennedy Heights—bounded by Pleasant Ridge, Golf Manor, Silverton, and Madisonville in northeast Cincinnati—is out Montgomery Road and one of Cincinnati's older communities. A few years ago it nearly died. White families watched the arrival of Negroes; "For Sale" signs sprouted everywhere. But the panic which started was nipped in the bud fast by a hastily formed Kennedy Heights Community Council, originally a gathering of eight families at the Kennedy Heights Presbyterian Church. A nod here must be made in the direction of P&G, which encourages its people to become involved in community affairs. In Kennedy Heights, one of the P&G employees did. He is Stan Lambert, a P&G product researcher. Said Mr. Lambert of the Kennedy Heights Council:

> We started listing what we as individuals thought was important in a neighborhood. When we finished we found that the problem was not "Negro" or "white" but . . . that these were the ideas of people interested in the place where they lived. Then we decided to form an organization . . .

Emil Dansker reported in the *Enquirer*:

> Rumor-scotching has kept members active running down sources of errant information and ideas in order to prevent panic and alleviate problem situations . . .

Said Mrs. Robert M. Starr:

> Once a rumor starts, we think it's important to go to the source. I don't think there's one that has started that we haven't been able to run down and do something about. We participate effectively in problems between Negroes and whites, and we often solve them just by the third person being there.

Mr. Dansker wrote in the *Enquirer:*

> Rumors tracked down and proven false include one about an $18,000 home purchased with CORE and NAACP funds, and put on sale for $10,000.
>
> A tale that a child had been molested turned out to be two children who shoved each other.
>
> When word spread that the schools, now about one-third Negro, were deteriorating, an investigation was made, a principal invited to speak, and residents learned that the rate of college qualification was as high as ever . . .
>
> Much of the early emotional impact of the Negro migration has begun to wear off, spokesmen said.
>
> Some of the residents who were all set to move were prevailed upon to wait and see and decided later to stay; some who put their homes up for quick sale took them off the market.

P&G's Mr. Lambert summed up the situation in 1965 with this thought:

> We have had people move into the neighborhood onto streets on which Negroes have been living. We look upon this as a significant achievement in reaching stability . . .

Lest you think Cincinnati has all such problems behind it, the same day the *Enquirer* ran Mr. Dansker's story about Kennedy Heights (May 16, 1965), the *Enquirer* ran this story alongside it:

> The first Negro family to move into the Kenwood area just across from Rossmoyne on Pine Road Saturday found the initials of a terrorist group scrawled on their car and garage windows . . .

Kenwood, next alphabetically in the real estate listings and a neighbor of Kennedy Heights, is a refreshing community of reasonably well-heeled homeowners whose houses are big and little, and which sometimes, apparently, sport KKK signs soaped on the windows. But let's not belabor that. Loving thy neighbor takes a bit of doing, but happily, more and more Cincinnatians seem to be doing it.

Speaking of love brings us to the next community: Loveland. (How sneaky can a book get?) If ever a town seemed to be misnamed, it's Loveland. But then, when one thinks of Loveland—in his imagination —he pictures something corny as an old-fashioned valentine. Loveland, Ohio, is not an old-fashioned valentine, or any other kind, for that matter. In the far northeastern part of Greater Cincinnati and so far out it can hardly be called a suburb, Loveland just sits there, affable and rustic. It seems a farm village of another day. The Little Miami passes near. So do trains. Loveland has some industry, and—well, you can always go fishing. Or watch the trains go through.

Madeira, closer in, is a bit more current. Live in Madeira and go next door to Indian Hill, walk up to a mansion, and borrow a cup of sugar—or money. Madeira is a sociable middle-class gathering of sociable middle-class people who live in sociable middle-class houses and watch sociable middle-class color television.

Madisonville is a mixture. Some sections are attractive, but some are not. Some are one-family dwellings. Some are apartments. Some can be had for no money down. Some will cost you your eye teeth. Madisonville, at this writing, is difficult to define. Northeast of downtown Cincinnati, it is in a kind of industrial area (Oakley is next door with its industrial complex), and the result is, Madisonville is filled with toolmakers who have lived there for ages and with lower-income laborers. In Madisonville you can see potbellied, baggy-pantsed mill-workers who look as if they had just stepped out of the *Out Our Way* comic strip. There is a stability about Madisonville, because Cincinnati craftsmen are a stable lot. They pay their mortgages when due, carry tin lunchboxes to work, and on Saturday nights drink beer. They live in World War I houses tended by wives who get a kick out of potted plants. But is Madisonville changing? One ad said you can buy a house there for no money down. Is this the staid and unconcerned Madisonville of old? Time was in Madisonville—and most everywhere else in Cincinnati—when buying a home was a once-in-a-lifetime adventure. You sweated to pay the mortgage, raised your children in that house, retired, sat on the front porch in your undershirt, drank beer, and died—all in that house. But the mortgage would have been free and clear, paid up. To buy a house for no money down—whatever the financial hocus-pocus—is not to buy a house at all. It would be nothing more than a joke you played on the money-lenders—or one that they played on you. That doesn't seem like Madisonville, but there it was in the classifieds: NO MONEY DOWN. Was the stability we thought we saw in Madisonville just something we wanted to see? Drive through Madisonville and make up your own mind. Let's read down the list of HOUSES FOR SALE.

Mariemont! A happy hop, skip, and jump to the east of Cincinnati is what many have called the "perfect planned community," a point only developers who peddle ticky-tacky housing would dispute. Says the *Cincinnati Guide:*

> Mariemont was designed to create the atmosphere of an old English village. It has winding lanes, Georgian Colonial homes, and shops with mullioned windowpanes . . .

Mrs. Mary M. Emery donated the original 423 acres upon which Mariemont now rests. Started in 1922, people began moving in two years later. Said Paul Landfair:

A fine community! Although the Mohawk and Mount Adams are visually exciting, Mariemont is architecturally perfect. . . . I saw there what they call in New York a *cul de sac*, a little dead-end street. It went in a few hundred feet and ended. It had no more than seven houses, which were either reversed or identical. There were only four variations, but this captured, as some of Greenhills does, the essence of "community." Today's subdivision developer gives you only different fronts. The houses are all the same. In Mariemont on this dead-end street were similar houses *outside—only*. This dead-end street was an oasis carved out of all the dilemma Cincinnati faces. Mariemont has continuity, which most subdivisions lack . . .

Farther out is Milford, a pleasant community that has aged well. Milford itself used to be one-part metropolitan and one-part hayseed, but those days, along with the interurban, are gone forever.

Montford Heights in the northwest part of Greater Cincinnati is like Groesbeck, Bridgetown, and the rest: suburbia is taking over the woods and pastures. In a few years it will be impossible to tell one outlying community from another; they are losing identity that fast.

Montgomery, in the far northeast portion of Greater Cincinnati, got started in 1794, gained momentum when the old Cincinnati-Zanesville State Road went right along its main street, and lost momentum again when U.S. 22 was straightened out, bypassing the town. It is an assortment of old homes and suburbia, far enough "out" to be nice and close enough "in" to commute.

Mount Adams doesn't have many houses listed for sale; the classified column we checked, in fact, showed none. But apartments are available. The apartments are a mixed bag because, as suggested in Chapter 1, Mount Adams doesn't exactly know where it's going. Other neighborhoods are in a state of transition, too, but their individual directions are more predictable. Which way Mount Adams goes is anybody's guess, and a lot of investors are guessing with their shirts. The *Cincinnati Guide* described Mount Adams of the mid-1940s:

> Mount Adams is less affected by change than any other important eminence in the city . . . When seen in silhouette from Eden Park reservoir, Mount Adams looks like an Alpine village; and even upon closer inspection, its streets, residences, and shops retain something of an Old World appearance . . . The houses are small boxlike structures of brick and frame, securely attached to the hill . . . Sitting quietly alone, with traffic whizzing round its feet, Mount Adams has the ascetic majesty associated with spiritual things . . .

But that was twenty years ago. Now Mount Adams is a neighborhood that has suddenly been "discovered." Its latter-day discoverers have been young moderns emulating couples in Pepsi Cola commercials, and a few guys—some with the best of intentions—interested in peddling culture. In other words, Mount Adams is hip, gear, camp, in, or whatever term applies *this* week. Mount Adams, which once sported nothing more exciting than the jukebox din or a neighborhood brawl, now sports a bookstore that has not only books but a liquor license and a jazz combo. The neighborhood borrows whatever culture it can by its proximity to Eden Park (the Art Museum, Playhouse in the Park, a handful of lovers' lanes, summer band concerts, and the Cincinnati Historical Society), but to some Cincinnatians the sight of Mount Adams has become as delightfully unreal as a Steve Crane Kontiki Ports restaurant. Said Paul Landfair:

> It's a confusing place to drive around. I think other Cincinnati areas—say, the Mohawk—should have been developed more rapidly than Mount Adams. But Mount Adams at the moment is a "fashionable" thing. Although it is being developed by private developers, they haven't really developed it or solved its problems. You can't get down to the city easily from there. . . . Arty folk pay exorbitant rents for a house next door to one that a family has been living in for years and paying next to nothing.

Mount Airy is that hilly section of homes that for the most part borders Mount Airy Forest. The joker is, not *all* Mount Airy homes border the forest preserve. Some are little more than a hasty development, so Mount Airy as an address might sound posh, but it doesn't always end up that way. Still, some of Mount Airy's streets surprise you with excellence; others offer only monotony.

Mount Auburn is a different story. It is a changing neighborhood, and the direction of its change is as plain as the nose on your face. Perched atop one of Cincinnati's nearer hills that overlook downtown, Mount Auburn is a neighborhood of streets that can't decide which direction to go or whether to go at all. Some of its houses cling to the sides of the hill for dear life. Others are once-stately row houses upon which time has had a field day. Great single-family homes are mostly multifamily dwellings, and have gone to seed just as the ornate and sweet row houses have. Still, here and there, you'll find an old man or old woman, remnants of a family, living out their years in the only house they ever knew, but they are generally the last of their tribe. After they die, their houses will die, too. Some help has come in the form of commercial development. William Howard Taft Road, between Vine and Highland, used to be lined with fine homes. Slowly these fine homes are giving way to modern office buildings.

Next on the list is Mount Washington, which is as different from Mount Auburn as night and day. Mount Washington in eastern Cincinnati, beyond the oldtime neighborhoods, is an area of suburbia that's a shade better than most. At one time it had the appearance of a village, but the neon signs along the main drag have dispelled that notion fast. Beechmont Avenue each Saturday morning is a bumper-to-bumper adventure when husbands go shopping for power tools and wives go shopping for chow. But no town is its main street. On the byways are homes of every size and shape, lots of trees, and the feeling of "community."

Norwood, the city entirely surrounded by corporate Cincinnati, is a stable community that has the right blend of industry and residents. Most of the residents are middle- or laboring-class. Many have lived in Norwood all their lives. Some of the residential streets are quiet as a mouse, and a few are not. Cincinnati isn't perfect. We mustn't expect Norwood to be.

Between Madisonville and Hyde Park is Oakley in eastern Cincinnati. Oakley has nearly everything a homeowner might want: serene side streets with well-maintained houses shaded by ancient trees, a busy main drag lined with businesses, a gigantic industrial area, and a last-century village square that contains old trees and a flower garden. Some of the Oakley residents work at the Mill—which in Cincinnati means the Cincinnati Milling Machine Company. Others work downtown. Thus, Oakley is a mixture of professional people, office managers, time-study men, and skilled machinists. Oakley has a scattering of apartment houses and those little postwar one-family affairs on postage-stamp lots. Oakley is not suburbia; it is several old-fashioned neighborhoods rolled into one, each with its own income level.

A far piece from Cincinnati—thirty-five winding miles up a federal highway that shouldn't happen to a dog—is a Shangri-La of sorts called Oxford. Oxford is the site of great big Miami University and great little Western College for Women. Thus, its chief preoccupations are education and students' dirty laundry. There are medical doctors in Oxford, but most doctors are not. Some will not make house calls unless you have a sick Elizabethan. But nonacademic people live in Oxford, too, and for good reason. It's as near-perfect as a village can be. Chicago and New York developers would give their souls to manufacture a village business section that Oxford let happen naturally. Of course, there are tons of culture in Oxford. The university and the college are forever tossing that stuff around; name guests are the order of the day; and when both schools are going full-blast, the village has more beautiful young ladies than Hollywood could ever muster. Housing is reasonable, but commuting to Cincinnati takes an hour. The bars sell only beer, but most homeowners drink at home—theirs or someone else's. Hueston Woods is five minutes away. Oxford is an amiable and alert little community with restaurants that generally cater to the galvanized stomach linings of the young. But the Rainbow Restaurant in Millville is ten minutes' distant, the steaks melt in your mouth, and so do the martinis Mary Ruth Wooten sloshes together at the bar. This is where true Oxfordians gather. The Oxford *Press*—the only weekly newspaper published by a tap dancer who collects antiques—is head and shoulders above most dailies published in cities with much larger populations. By the way, the Oxford post office was cited by the President's wife—no less!—because the villagers got together and prettied it up.

Pleasant Ridge, northeast out Montgomery Road beyond Norwood, is exactly what the sign says: a pleasant ridge. While parts of the neighboring communities are beginning to feel the pinch of change, change has yet to pinch this friendly Cincinnati neighborhood. But it *is* difficult to tell where Pleasant Ridge and Kennedy Heights change from one to the other. Pleasant Ridge is primarily a community of one-family homes with beautiful lawns and fine shade trees. Cincinnati has many stable and well-kept communities like Pleasant Ridge.

Price Hill is not one of them. It is too diverse. It's the *big* neighborhood on the first hill to the west. But don't let the real estate ads lead you astray. Sometimes, in their enthusiasm, real estate men advertise homes in what they call "lower Price Hill." Lower Price Hill, simply put, used to be Storrs, that brawling and exhausted neighborhood which centers around Eighth and State. The *real* Price Hill is up there, on top of the hill, from the brow west until you run out of city. Eighth and State, unfortunately, has seen better days, but not much better. "Lower Price Hill," if it must be called that, is much like Camp Washington. Oyler Junior High School is there, surrounded by narrow little streets lined with tired little row houses, mostly red brick. It is a noisy community but not terribly naughty. Many fine old families live along its Neave, Staebler, and Hatmaker Streets. Many nice kids grow up in that section.

But back to the top of the hill! Well, the brow of the hill used to be elite. No more. Huge and ancient homes and townhouses, decorated with wooden scrollwork until some of the ornate front porches look like dusty wedding cakes, are there, but their original owners have long since departed. Decay has set in. Decay is slowly creeping west from the brow of Price Hill and giving some homeowners the willies. Far out on Price Hill in the community of Covedale there is little panic yet. Decay is too distant, something their children or grandchildren will have to worry about. That's how vast Price Hill is. In limbo, between the complacency of Covedale and the deterioration at the brow of the hill, are thousands and thousands of one- and two-family dwellings on the main and side streets, each house seeming as solid as the Rock of Gibraltar. Only a few of the homes have elegant touches, however. Price Hill does not have as beautiful or expensive homes as those in Hyde Park. If Hyde Park is upper-middle-class, Price Hill is so middle-

class that even its beatniks shave every day, take baths, and comb
their hair.

"In Covedale," Mr. Landfair said, "there are homes built just as
compactly and just as close together as the ones in Delhi Township.
But there is a difference. Each house has its *own* identity, and a
streetful of such homes creates the feeling of 'neighborhood.' The
area's homes are prewar, old, and still in a good state of repair. But as
you move east on Eighth Street to the brow of the hill that overlooks
the basin, the housing changes. They become more rundown. The big
homes, once beautiful, were hacked up into apartments. They weren't
maintained. But there, on the brow itself, stands that fantastic building
(the modern high-rise apartment building called the Incline House).
I'd just love to live there. There's the Ohio River, the valley of Cincinnati, and the rest—all at your feet. But around this building, the area
is too dilapidated . . ."

Reading—out Reading Road, of course—is a mixture of homes and
industry. Evendale with its industrial complex is close by. At one time
Reading, Ohio, was farther out than it is now. Expressways and high-
powered cars have brought it "closer in." The housing in Reading is as
mixed as the town itself. There's more to Reading than noisy Reading
Road. Don't let that road's traffic lead you to think the town is little
more than a valley truck stop. Many of its streets are as charming as
Mariemont's.

Riverside is that long and narrow stretch of Cincinnati west of Mill
Creek in the Ohio River Valley between Sedamsville and Anderson
Ferry. In most places Riverside is scarcely two streets wide. The valley
is narrow in spots. Riverside has only two main streets. One is rambling
and quiet Hillside Avenue; the other is River Road, which has a hotshot 45-miles-per-hour speed limit. Riverside is a community of old
homes that railroad families used to live in when the Riverside Roundhouse was in its heyday. Now the roundhouse is little more than a
memory, and the neighborhood is somewhat less. Trains parallel
River Road, thundering west through the tight valley to Indiana,
rattling windows as they go. Industrial sites are strung along the road,
too. Petroleum companies have huge river terminals there. Some
houses along Southside Avenue are available, some are condemned.
Floods have visited that street too often.

Roselawn is much better. Located north, it is another Cincinnati
neighborhood that is gradually changing. It used to be heavily residential. New motels, trailer courts, apartment buildings, and shopping
centers have been added. The Mill Creek Expressway is near. Roselawn, in reality, is a lot like Golf Manor: street after street of homes
without much distinction.

St. Bernard is a worker's paradise—of sorts. Procter & Gamble is
there, and many lower-echelon P&G employees live in St. Bernard

houses that their fathers lived in when they, too, worked at P&G. Its main street is busy, but its side streets are reasonably sedate affairs filled with a sense of yesterdays. St. Bernard could be the scene of a workingman's convention that would never get out of hand. Certainly not a suburb, it nonetheless is a fine place to raise a family. The children can always work at P&G and live at home.

Sayler Park (and with Sayler Park we lump Fernbank and Delhi) is incorporated Cincinnati's most western river community—and one of Cincinnati's nicest. Said Paul Landfair of that neighborhood:

> One of the first things that struck me were the little brick culverts and little brick drains—and the boulevards! The very fact that someone created boulevards with strips of old trees down the center adds charm. Here and there, of course, are little subdivisions, but in the old part, huge homes stand. . . . When River Road was young, Sayler Park had lavish homes lining it. But now the expressway is where the great backyards used to be, and some of the homes seem to be deteriorating. Sayler Park ten years from now? I don't know. It has pride now. In ten years, its pride might be gone completely . . .

Next is Sedamsville, a railroad community which never had much pride to begin with—and, anyway, Sedamsville is hardly there these days. The *Cincinnati Guide* described this "near in" western river neighborhood as a "grimy little community wedged between the bluffs of Mount Echo Park and the Ohio River . . . Its old brick houses string along River Road, Delhi Pike, and the . . . streets that clamber the slopes and continue as footpaths through the brush on the Mount Echo hillside." When River Road was widened, the bulldozers bulldozed most of Sedamsville into the backs of dump trucks and hauled it away. Now only its side streets exist. The rest is expressway. But the steam locomotive has bitten the dust, and Sedamsville, whatever remains of it, is cleaner now and quieter. Sedamsville looks like a postcard village of red-brick houses splattered on the Mount Echo hillside. Time hasn't improved Sedamsville much. And you know how unreal at times picture postcards can be.

Another railroad community still going strong is Sharonville up the Mill Creek Valley to the far north. Actually, Sharonville doesn't like to be called a "railroad community," and technically, it has more going for it than that. It has become another suburban dormitory community. It hasn't the sadness of Sedamsville nor the grime.

Silverton, to the north of Cincinnati, is surrounded by varying degrees of suburbia. In 1860 it was little more than (1) a tollgate, (2) an inn, and (3) a place to get your nag shod. Now it is a middle-class residential accumulation complete with shade trees, beautiful lawns, and a quiet sense of pride—on its side streets, that is. Its business section is a bustling affair. Silverton is where you can always play word games with one of its chief residents: Aron Mathieu, one of the guiding lights of *Writer's Digest*, who looks and acts like Cincinnati's answer to the *New Yorker's* Harold Ross.

Terrace Park, to the east, is another one of Cincinnati's more beautiful communities. It has managed to keep its "village" mood, though its residents are so metropolitan they could hardly be cast as hayseeds. Most are business executives who have climbed up a few rungs in the corporate world. Great trees, winding streets, and fascinating homes make Terrace Park a sanctuary of sorts. Although many of its homes are reasonably new, most don't look like it—which is a compliment when you consider the saw-and-hammer artisans at work on Cincinnati today.

Walnut Hills is a gargantuan neighborhood up there in the hills to the immediate northeast. Walnut Hills goes in every direction from its base, Peebles Corner. To the north, it is a musty neighborhood of Negroes forced to live in once-lavish homes that time has reduced to tenements and rooming houses. To the east and southeast toward Eden Park, Walnut Hills offers old and new homes, each in parklike settings of their own, and some expensive. To the southwest from Peebles Corner along Florence Avenue, Walnut Hills is another one of Cincinnati's many "little Italies": graying frame dwellings inhabited by workingmen whose wives brighten the window sills with potted plants. Walnut Hills is a complicated area. It is whatever neighborhood is next to it. Where you live in Walnut Hills depends on three things: the color of your money, the color of your face, and how you feel about spaghetti.

Westwood is another gigantic blend of just about everything—mostly middle- and upper-middle-class, though. Go a few minutes in any direction and Westwood changes personality, sometimes subtly, but sometimes abruptly. A western community whose main street is Harrison Avenue (U.S. 52), Westwood covers a lot of ground. Harrison Avenue, as you start up the hill, has ceased to be an elegant neighborhood. Apartments are there. Older homes—some of them mansions—are hidden, and the highway itself is a busy, noisy thing. But the nearer you get to Cheviot, the nicer Westwood becomes. As you reach Cheviot, though, Westwood starts coming unglued all over again. Very commercial. "Dead man's curve"—that interesting turn on Harrison Avenue just west of LaFeuille Avenue—is not half so deadly as the commercial establishments that take over at about Montana Avenue and gnaw away at the tranquility that street once possessed. Glenmore Avenue also has become a rat race, and so has Boudinot Avenue, which has been widened into a drag strip, much to the dismay of people who live in the great and beautiful homes that line it.

Where there used to be woods in Westwood, there are now apartment houses. Westwood is also dozens and dozens of hushed side streets and cheery homes, with not a split-level in the bunch. Some Westwood homes are expensive. Some are not. And beyond Westwood lies suburbia: Green Township and the rest. Westwood is Cincinnati's last neighborhood on the west side.

You might hear the Western Hills area mentioned, or see homes advertised in "Western Hills." Well, as any oldtimer will tell you, there is no such animal. There's Delhi Township, Green Township, Price Hill, Covedale (perhaps), Westwood, Bridgetown, and Cheviot. All —or any—of these could be considered "Western Hills." To define Western Hills geographically is as impossible as to define Walnut Hills. Neither has a geographic "fix." But Walnut Hills does something Western Hills doesn't. It exists.

But if anyone asks you where White Oak is, you can answer: White Oak is northwest beyond Mount Airy and Cheviot on the way to New Baltimore. It's a hilly place, suburbia is making its mark, but some homes have stunning settings as well as prices.

Winton Place, which is out Spring Grove Avenue and just this side of where Chester Park used to be, is a secluded neighborhood of both fine- and sad-looking homes. Much industry is nearby. But on some of the streets the quiet seems constant. Winton Place is another "old" neighborhood. Though some of its streets are shabby, its heart is not, and for the most part Winton Place seems to be holding its own.

Wyoming—straight north out Springfield Pike beyond Hartwell—is a well-heeled city that, at times, you must turn off Springfield Pike to enjoy. Well-tended homes and well-tended executives are everywhere, but now and then there is the tedium of an apartment house. Wyoming might be considered upper-middle-class in every sense of the word. Although many of the homes have charming personalities, there are a handful that look like someone's maiden aunt; happily, Wyoming has an abundance of shrubs, and shrubs can hide a multitude of sins.

Over in Kentucky, there's Newport and Covington: old cities for the most part, but on certain side streets (Garrad in Covington, for example) you'll see ponderous last-century housing so magnificent it will take your breath away. Unfortunately, most have become multi-family affairs these days, and pride has fled. Up on the hill, keeping watch on Cincinnati, is a happy community called Fort Thomas, an orderly collection of middle-class one-family homes and some apartment buildings. Most refreshing. Southgate is much the same, but Bellevue and Dayton—being river communities—lack such amenities. Park Hills is a roomy place with some posh homes in the Devou Park vicinity. Lookout Heights, farther out Dixie Highway, is northern Kentucky's version of suburbia but, in places, rather expensive. As you go out this stretch of Dixie Highway, you are in the tail end of the horse- country that is headquartered mostly in Louisville and Lexington. Ludlow and Bromley are pint-sized river communities to the west. They lead most quiet lives. Erlanger, Florence, and Elsmere have blossomed considerably since the end of the Second World War, but before that they mostly slumbered out beyond the reach of the trolley line which ended at Fort Mitchell, another Dixie Highway community that is much nicer now that Intrastate 75 has siphoned off much of the traffic.

Put these various and diverse communities together; mix thoroughly with traffic lights; season with the Cincinnati Reds, Procter & Gamble, opera at the Zoo, and Fountain Square; add a sinus condition or two; and what you have will be a city of homes—all kinds of homes for all kinds of people. But, up to now, we have neglected one kind. And we must be honest and mention this, too.

There is in Cincinnati, as in most metropolitan areas, that animal called "government housing." These trim and spartan high-rises were designed to replace rat-infested ghettos, and it must be said in their favor they look nice—from a distance! (Example: on Chicago's South Side they are lined up in an orderly line; at night they glitter a satisfying glitter; they are much better than the ramshackle tenements they replaced. The same is true in Manhattan: commuters riding the New York Central can glance up and become instant sociologists by comparing the many-windowed flat buildings with the many-windowed "government housing" structures that replaced them.) Each block of tenements and each new housing project is a city unto itself— by population count, that is. But these buildings replaced neighborhoods—and many neighborhoods have died. True, a mother can sleep easier at night knowing no rat will bite her baby, and this is important. But reduced to basics, these high-rises are little more than prisons that operate on the honor system. You can go out, no questions asked; but what do you come back to? Cincinnati's first such projects were Laurel Homes and Lincoln Court, bounded by John, Linn, and Liberty Streets and Lincoln Park Drive. Lincoln Court started eight months before Pearl Harbor, has 53 different buildings with 1015 apartments, and in this "city" live mostly Negroes. Laurel Homes, next door, has 29 buildings in its complex with 1303 apartments. Before Laurel Homes was built, 1600 families lived in the same area. But, as we suggest, from a distance these complexes look nice. It is only when you take a closer look that you want to cry. We have replaced old rabbit warrens with new, and in the process human dignity has somehow got lost.

Paul Landfair was asked:

If you could design a city and say, "This is really what Cincinnati is," what would your city look like? Mariemont? Or Republic Street? Mount Adams, Cheviot, or Delhi Hills? Which?

Mr. Landfair replied:

Architecturally, I would say that Cincinnati is a red-brick town. Chicago, on the other hand, was a timber city before the fire. Actually, Cincinnati is whatever the people want to make it. It can be a city of the arts or it can be a city of the burlesque. It can be anything—and everything—that the people desire. But the trouble is, Cincinnati is an indecisive city. It's not progressive. It simply can't make up its mind whether to be this or that . . .

At least we've got Greater Cincinnatians under roof. So far so good. But when they go out, where do they go and what do they do? In other words, as teenagers might put it: is there any action in this place?

11

Cincinnati is where the family action is, and a lot of it is either free or terribly inexpensive. As is the case with all modern American cities, Cincinnati is responding rapidly to the approaching twilight of that tranquil era when children were seen and not heard. In those long-ago years, family outings were major undertakings labeled the Fourth of July Picnic or the Family Reunion. The rest of the time, parents went one way and children another. The children fended for themselves in an utterly unorganized childhood uncomplicated by Blue Birds, Little League competitions, or organized playground activity. They caught lightning bugs. They swam in the canal. They swiped apples. They belted one another. They kicked tin cans, and those who did not die of diphtheria lived to kick a can the next summer or, if the corner saloon was going strong, shoot the can for their fathers. Those were the good old days.

Now *togetherness* is the magic word. Families *do* things together. Whether this is an improvement or whether it is not, each Cincinnati family decides for itself. Meanwhile, over the years, the Children's Hour here has evolved into a year-round activity. Togetherness is the cry—and to meet this cry Greater Cincinnati has built a lot of parks and filled them with things that families can do together. Now the poor father is bewildered by choices. If a Cincinnati family decided to cram everything offered here into one weekend, consider what they could do!

Saturday morning everybody in the family buggy! First stop, Winton Woods for horseback riding. Guides provided. Next stop, the Playhouse in the Park at Eden Park. Hustle! Must be there by 10:30. The Children's Theater is doing *Hansel and Gretel*. The play over —*zoom!* Destination: Ault Park. Must see the Municipal Rose Garden

147

there. Pause for lunch—*zoom!* To the Natural History Museum. Hurry, hurry. A simulated space trip to Mars aboard the Mariner. Splashdown! To the Art Museum in Eden Park, where the work of Art Academy students is on exhibit. *Zoom!* To the Zoo. Dinnertime. Gobble your hotdog, watch the monkeys, and away! Back to Eden Park. Outdoor folk singing. Hurry to Public Landing. Teenagers board the Johnson Party Boat: moonlight dancing. Go, go, go! Sunday morning. Church? No time, no time. *Zoom!* To the airport playfield. Rent bikes. Ride, ride, ride. Puff, puff, puff. Pitch horseshoes. Shoot arrows. Here we go again. Winton Woods. Picnic. Ride on paddle-wheel boat. Hurry to Burnet Woods. Paddle canoe full of family. *Zoom!* To Cincinnati Tennis Club. Tony Trabert in exhibition match. *Zoom!* Coney Island. Hotdogs for dinner. Merry-go-round, Lost River, Dodge'em—ride, ride, ride! *Zoom!* Eden Park. Curtain time. Playhouse in the Park: *She Stoops To Conquer. Zoom!* Winton Woods again: moonlight horseback ride. Anyone for family fun?

The point is, this is where the family action is, and the range of choice can stagger you. Consider the park system in this area. No matter where you live, it takes only a few minutes in the family buggy or a few minutes' walk to reach the quiet of a city park. Minneapolis considers itself a city of many parks, and we won't quarrel with that. Its parks are well kept and charming. But Cincinnati is a city of parks, too; our parks are every bit as well kept and charming; and in some of them, thanks to the hilly terrain, the views are sudden and spectacular. Cincinnati families like the parks and spend a lot of time in them.

But when it comes to choosing the park with the best view, it is wise to say nothing. Each Cincinnatian has his own favorite. He likes it for private reasons he might not put into words. Perhaps he played on the park's hillside as a child. Or, perhaps one summer night, with the city twinkling below him, he didn't see the city at all, because he had kissed his girl for the first time—and that made the moment magic enough. Or, perhaps it is where he went to say goodby to his city before going to war, silently promising his city he would return, telling it not to worry, and telling it to look out for his mother while he was gone. Or, perhaps he is a dried-up old man looking at the city and remembering how sweet things used to be when his step had spring in it and when spring was in his bones. No matter. Each has his park and each has his view. When he looks out over his city, it is as Antoine de Saint Exupéry said in *The Little Prince:* "It is only with the heart that one can see rightly; what is essential is invisible to the eye."

Perhaps it's the view from Alms Park on Tusculum Avenue. The park is big: 93 acres of woods, swings for the children, trails, trees, a shelter house, and a calm. Perhaps it's the giant-sized view from pint-sized Bellevue Hill Park, 15 acres at the end of Ohio Avenue south of Parker Street. Maybe it's the sight of Cincinnati from somewhat larger Fairview Park, 28 acres on McMillan Avenue near Ravine. Or 73-acre Mount Echo Park in Price Hill, off Elberon Avenue. Each view is different. Each is stunning. Each offers its own adjectives to help Cincinnatians describe their city.

Such views have captured the imaginations of Cincinnatians since Cincinnati began. Charles Cist, writing in 1841, reported:

> One of the views most worthy, perhaps, of attention may be had at an early hour on one of the foggy mornings of August, or September. A spectator . . . placed upon one of these hills will find himself elevated quite above the dense vapors of the river; he will behold the sun rising free from all obscurity, while the plain below him is lost in one unbroken sheet of fog, presenting the appearance of an unruffled lake. As soon, however, as the rays of the sun fall less obliquely, [the] vapor . . . dissipates, and assuming the appearance of fleecy clouds, passes away to rarer regions, gradually disclosing the city, the river, the villages, the numerous steamboats, and all the various objects of the valley.

—Cincinnati in 1841

Where most of the views are, Cincinnati planted parks. Right now, as you read this, someone—at least one person—is in one of these parks, gazing at the city, seeing something no one will see but him, and thus adding another dimension to this love story of ours.

But the parks offer more than views of Cincinnati. When music lovers wish to mix music with mosquitoes, they go to Burnet Woods on Clifton Avenue in July and August, sit on the grass, scratch chigger bites, and listen to free band concerts. Or, while the music is playing, couples can stroll hand in hand along the darkness of the lake and pretend to watch the ducks. Eden Park supplies free concerts, too. Love music is played by Wally Johnson's orchestra, Charlie Kohrer's orchestra, Herbert A. Tiemeyer's band, or George C. Smith's band (known with affection by Cincinnatians simply as Smitty's Band). Under a mall between two dormitories at the University of Cincinnati, there's more music filling the summer nights. Associate Professor of Music Robert L. Garretson directs the University's summer-school chorus and band in everything from Strauss to Hungarian folk singing. To dance under the stars the Cincinnati younger set can go, as their parents did before them, to Ault Park at Principio and Observatory Avenues. The Cincinnati Park Board and the Musicians Association started weekend dancing in Ault Park in 1965 after two years of sitting them out. The dances run from 9 P.M. to midnight. Admission is $1 a head because passing the hat didn't work out. Girls must wear dresses—no shorts or slacks allowed—but the lucky males need not wear coats and ties. Warning: keep your shirttail tucked in. Another warning: don't present your girl with roses; she might think you filched them from Ault Park's rose gardens. Or worse, the cops might think that.

Cincinnati families like to go boating. After all, the Ohio River is here. Since the building of Markland Dam, which began operating in 1963, the Ohio River is not only a highway for commerce but a big, fat lake, pool stage now being 25.4 feet as compared with half that before. There are more marinas along the Ohio River than you can shake a stick at: forty listed, and more under construction. A few Cincinnatians sail, but most use powerboats. Tacking around an oncoming string of barges can take the fun out of sailing. In addition to the commercial marinas, the city itself operates three facilities for launching boats. On the east side of town the facility is in the Walter S. Schmidt Playfield at the end of St. Peter Street; on the west side, in the Riverside Playfield on Southside Avenue; and downtown, at the Public Landing.

For those who prefer more tranquil settings and no towboats to dodge, canoes can be rented at Burnet Woods, Winton Woods, Sharon Woods, and Hueston Woods. At Winton and Sharon Woods, Cincinnatians who hate to paddle, sail, or tool around in a low-powered outboard can take a ride on miniature stern-wheel riverboats. At Hueston Woods, beyond Oxford, Ohio, thirty-five miles north of Cincinnati on U.S. 27, sailboats can also be rented. These are in the Sunfish class: nothing more than a single sail attached to a surfboard. Each costs about $10 a day to rent, but Cincinnatians have smartened up: they rent them from one to four hours for $3.50 because a full day of sailing can be exhausting. Boats can also be rented in the Campbell County Park six miles south of Alexandria, Kentucky, on the other end of U.S. 27. The park has a 217-acre lake for boating, fishing, and swimming.

How's fishing for Cincinnatians? Well, Chapter 15 gives the full story on where the big ones are, where Cincinnatians *think* the big ones are, and how to explain to your bride why you brought home a steak instead.

As for golfing, Greater Cincinnati has twenty-one public courses as well as five practice driving ranges. Add private clubs to this list and you will see why James Dean, of MacGregor Sports, estimates that Cincinnatians spend more than $700,000 each year on equipment for the game. Once again, the city itself operates several courses. The city courses are open to the public every day from March to November. From November 1 to March, they're open holidays and weekends. Clubs can be rented. The eighteen-hole courses the city runs are Avon Fields at Reading and Paddock Roads, the California Golf Course out by the waterworks, and the Neumann Golf Course on Bridgetown Road near Fiddlers Green Road, plus eighteen-hole courses at both Sharon and Winton Woods. Cincinnati operates a nine-hole course that's open every day of the year: the Reeves Golf Course on Beechmont Levee next to the Airport Playfield. Campbell County Park across the river has an eighteen-hole course open to the public. In fact, Park Manager Orville McAtee figures that 300 duffers show up there every weekend, thus paying with green fees for the park's other amenities. Although weekend golfing is crowded and some of the fairways have the appearance of Evendale at 5 P.M., the weekday golfer has better luck. McAtee says that seldom does a weekday golfer have to brood more than fifteen minutes before teeing off.

This area has parks for just about everything. Some parks are whoppers, and some are no more than play areas where tenement children gather to play games. Lytle Park is an acre and a quarter dot of memories set down in the middle of downtown, its claims to fame being George Barnard's 11-foot statue of Abraham Lincoln, the U. S. Marine Corps' 500-pound memorial, the Mullen Memorial Bandstand named after long-ago ward councilman Michael Mullen, and at Christmas time the Nativity scene with live animals that give this little metropolitan park a barnyard smell. Some of the children who played in this park once lived in the tenements along Third Street. Now, where their coldwater walkups used to be, is only the Third Street Distributor's steady hum of cars.

A park not for children—or anything else, for that matter—is Piatt Park, no more than a divider strip along Garfield Place between Vine and Elm Streets. Trees and benches are set in this long and narrow affair which was called Garfield Park until 1940. It is a lonely little place, and its benches are filled with old folks killing time. On summer afternoons it resembles—as someone once said of St. Petersburg, Florida—a great motionless streetcar.

Washington Park, which occupies one city block, used to be a Presbyterian cemetery before the city acquired it in 1855. A time-worn park bounded by West 12th, Race, and Elm Streets, it has horseshoe pits, swimming pools, benches, an unused bandstand, and trees. But there are better places young lovers might meet. The neighborhood has changed, a feeling of sadness and decay fills the park, and slowly the park is changing, too. Each twilight it is the depository of old people and, some say, young men who look like girls. Yes, Cincinnati has parks for every purpose, whether the purposes be approved or not. But no need to feel gloomy. Most Cincinnati parks are cheery affairs, just right for family fun. The Cincinnati cops, an efficient lot, make certain of that.

Parks, parks, parks! Cincinnatians have many from which to choose. There's 78-acre Stanberry Park at Corbly and Oxford Avenues, where fat men, if they desire, can play softball. There's tiny Salway Park, hardly bigger than a minute, on Spring Grove Avenue across from the cemetery; thus, it seems much bigger and touched, at times, with reflections of eternity. In Price Hill there's 50-acre Rapid Run Park, which on a map looks like a piece of spaghetti that went astray. It dips down from Glenway Avenue at Sunset Avenue into the winding valley that eventually leads motorists to Queen City Avenue and Little Italy. There's Mount Storm Park, 59 acres of calm, picnic tables, and trees at LaFayette and Ludlow Avenues. There's River Park smack beside the river. Cross the railroad tracks off River Road at Thorton Avenue, and there you are: 15 acres of park, a view of the river close-up, and the roar of freight trains heading west. Consider the Fleischmann Garden, another city park, but no picnicking, no ball playing, no horseshoe pitching, just *looking*. It's 3 acres of nothing but well-behaved flowers. Located at Forest and Washington Avenues, its feature attraction is tulips.

For a park where anything—within the framework of fun and good taste—goes, Cincinnatians have only to go to the Airport Playfield at Beechmont Levee, where the community of Columbia was founded long, long ago. Open from the first of April to the first of October and lighted every night to attract families and bugs, the Airport Playfield is a hodgepodge of archery, badminton, table tennis, shuffleboard, horseshoes, golf drives, and batting ranges. Bikes are for rent, too. For the younger set, the Playfield has Kiddieland, the Land of Make-Believe, and the problem of what to do with the lightning bugs they've collected.

When a Cincinnati family answers the call of the wild, it doesn't have to travel far. It heads to the western part of the city and to the 1476 acres of trails, hills, poison ivy, and lodges, an accumulation better known as Mt. Airy Forest, a city-owned and -operated preserve. What began in 1911 as 171 acres of timber has grown. More than a half-million trees have been planted in its silent gulleys and on its roller-coaster hillsides. The forest has eleven miles of horse trails, nags for hire, and, for those who would rather walk, ten miles of paths this way and that. Parks and forest preserves beyond the city limits are still close enough and civilized enough to interest Cincinnati families. On weekends these places at times get more action than Mt. Airy does. Butler County, north and west of Cincinnati's Hamilton County, is a mere hop, skip, and jump up the pike. Butler County has seven parks on tap, plus king-size Hueston Woods near Oxford. Indian Creek Park, north of Reily on Ohio 732, is the perfect year-round site. In summer, children can wade in its pint-sized stream without drowning; in winter they can ice skate there. The Miami-Erie Canal Park, on the other hand, has 16 acres of well-tended park and 28 acres of untended forest, but no canal. For a real canal-boat ride, Cincinnatians drive out near Metamora on the Ohio-Indiana line, where for a short stretch the old Whitewater Canal has been reactivated. A canal-boat trip on it costs a pittance, but the trip is short, and the canal boat itself is more Mickey Mouse than Disneyland. You don't get the feeling of antiquity. You get the feeling of having done something foolish.

Acton Lake at Hueston Woods, as noted, is for sailors—and swimmers and fishermen, too. Private sailboats are parked there each summer, and the weekend sailboat race is a must. Cottages can be rented as well as campsites and a spot to park your trailer. Swimming in the spring-fed lake is excellent, especially in the early fall and late spring when the man-made sand beach is dotted with those healthy young coeds from both Western College and Miami University. Then Cincinnati fathers don't swim much. They sit on the sand and gape slack-jawed at the scenery.

Butler County, someone said, has parks as some houses have mice; but while looking over the parks Cincinnatians attend, we'd be remiss unless Sharon and Winton Woods were included. Sharon Woods, on Highway 42 north of Sharonville, has 740 acres, a 40-acre lake with a paddle-wheel excursion boat, and enough picnic areas so that the place can be knee-deep in family reunions without having to merge strange families. Winton Woods is bigger. It has 2013 acres with a 183-acre lake with *two* paddle-wheel excursion boats. Winton Woods is next to Greenhills on Winton Road. The woods has a horseback riding center, plus ten miles of trails for the hay-burners to gallop. While relaxing at Winton Woods, Cincinnati children can be diverted by the ducks. Individual duck donors each year palm off at least a flock of ducks that have outgrown the magic of Easter. Children trot after these quackers, pick them up when they can, and dump them— *plop!*—back into the water. Great sport. On the other hand, according to Park Ranger Hillard Holbrook, the Canadian geese in Winton Woods will stand for no such nonsense, especially when they've just hatched their young. The geese bristle, glare stony-eyed at children, make angry hissing noises, and dare any urchin to pick them up. No urchin does.

But the younger Cincinnati set doesn't have to go to the woods to traffic with wildlife. Sometimes there's wildlife in their own front yard. Dale Balser, the game warden, said the community has its share of skunks, toads, raccoons, rabbits, lizards, and—in one heart-stopping incident—a black panther on the loose. No one has ever caught it. Actually, no one can say that it existed, or still exists. But every now and then the black panther story crops up in the western suburbs. County park naturalist Warren Wells offers advice on how to catch it: use catnip. Next question. The Cincinnati area has a lot of green turtles, some measuring 18 inches across. Basically from the western plains, they're brought here by returning vacationists, get loose, dig holes, and down they go. Horned toads are here. They sit around Cincinnati sidewalks and eat ant armies that conveniently march single file into their mouths. Some children keep these toads for pets, but Cincinnati mothers, unless squeamish, needn't worry. The toads are harmless. However, the area has chipmunks—and chipmunks, cute or not, will bite. Foxes? They usually hole up in Mt. Airy Forest between snacks. While no Cincinnatian has ever been bitten by a lion, several have been nipped by runaway monkeys, and one man was bitten by a pet honey bear. Around here the rabbits breed like rabbits, and raccoons are plentiful, too. Although baby raccoons are sweet, they lose their sweetness with age, and if not attended daily, can get waspish. Mostly for pets, children favor dogs, cats, parakeets, goldfish, and hamsters. George McDuffie, science teacher at Mt. Washington Junior High School, on the other hand, has for a pet a 75-pound snapping turtle.

A trip to the Cincinnati Zoo at Erkenbrecker and Vine Streets is the more practical answer when families wish to traffic with animals too cantankerous to housebreak. Everyone here is proud of our Zoo—and everyone has good reason to be. The Cincinnati Zoological Gardens had its beginnings in the spot where it is now back in 1868, when Andrew Erkenbrecker quit making starch to devote his time and dollars to creating an animal park. Opened in 1875, its first exhibits were not earthshaking: one circus elephant that had seen better days, a talking crow, some monkeys, birds, deer, and one terribly bored lion which didn't care about roaring, looking fierce, or anything else, for that matter. Twenty-three years later, with animals eating themselves out of house and animal park, the establishment went into receivership. The trolley company purchased controlling stock, the Zoo limped along through the years until 1917, when Mrs. Mary Emery and Mrs. Charles Taft started a fund-raising campaign, purchased the place from the trolley company, and the Cincinnati Zoological Park Association took over. Opera was established there in 1920. In 1932 there was disturbing talk of selling the animals and turning the park into a real estate development, but Cincinnati loved its Zoo too much, and it never happened.

The Zoo has improved with the times. Now it's as modern as a zoo can get: very few cages—and for children, a Children's Zoo where mother's little darling can stare dismally at pigs, and the pigs, if intrigued, can stare back. Farm animals are everywhere, children are allowed to pet them, and overhead—in the trees—monkeys chatter. For grownups—and children, too—there is the standard fare: elephants, giraffes, hippopotamuses, zebras, tigers, snakes, and a lot of other bad dreams, most in open cages, brooding in their natural habitat. Although the Zoo "season" opens in May, the Zoo itself is open every day of the year. Admission is low. More people visit in the summer. In 1964, between May 1 and September 30, more than 600,000 attended. From October 1 through April 25, 1965, only a handful more than 50,000 people showed up. Getting the animals cleaned up for the visitors is no easy task. Biff Hoff, executive director at the Zoo, says the elephants need three pedicures a year.

One of the places children aim for first is the Zoo nursery behind the Ape House. This is where the young animals deserted by their mothers or too young to fend for themselves are cared for. It's the same as a "people" nursery. It has several incubators, a custom-designed playpen, cabinets to store baby bottles, measuring spoons, food to make formulas with, and a ready supply of—of all things—diapers. Much to the chagrin of human mothers watching, baby gorillas sometimes sit at a table and eat with better manners than the mother's own children.

At this writing the Zoo has a lioness named Mary who, according to Zoo patrolman Stanley Reese, is in love with him. Either that, he feels, or she would love to have him as her dinner some night. Whenever he putt-putts his three-wheel motorcycle by her cage, the lioness watches him carefully the way a cat watches a mouse. She doesn't watch any others who pass by. Eerie. Si Cornell, writing of this in the *Post & Times-Star*, says that "Patrolman Stan has a theory about this. He thinks that Mary thinks the motorcycle is purring at her."

Some of the Cincinnati Zoo buffs aren't the stay-at-home type. Now and then the Zoo staff, along with other interested locals, take off on an African safari, traveling about the jungles in a Land-Rover through such places as the 1000-square-mile Tsavo Park, Kenya's largest game preserve. The souvenirs obtained are whoppers, inclined to be terrible tempered; thus, the Cincinnati safari recommends that children be left at home and that ladies not wear high heels. Most Cincinnatians feel it's better for their peace of mind—as well as their pocketbooks—to take the children to the Zoo instead of to Africa. At the Zoo the only wild beasts running loose are the swarms of bees in the picnic area, an occasional obnoxious child, or now and then a disenchanted tenor looking in wonder at the lions as he waits for his cue to sing in the Cincinnati Zoo Opera.

Opera at the Zoo? Odd but true. To us, it seems logical because, except for a few false starts elsewhere, the opera has *always* been at the Zoo. Where else? For children, there's the special Cincinnati Summer Zoo Opera, which features bits of this opera and pieces of that. In 1965 the children heard a digest version of Rossini's *Barber of Seville* sung in English. The program for children is usually sponsored by the Cincinnati Gas & Electric Company and the Women's Committee of the Opera, a hard-working bevy of ladies who knock themselves out each year trying to teach school children from the fourth through the eighth grades that there's more to the world than the music played on radio stations—those stations that play only the top forty glop, that is. A nod in the direction of these ladies is in order. For three straight years the children's program has played to full houses, something the regular opera playing to adults can't say.

For the Cincinnati daughter with stars in her eyes, music in her soul, and wings on her feet, there's always the chance she might get a role in the junior company of the Cincinnati Ballet Company as an understudy. Four girls were accepted in the audition in 1964.

While the daughter is doing that, the son may be answering an ad similar to this one:

WANTED
100 BRAVE YOUNG MEN

If you are accustomed to danger and have been employed in bridge building, sky diving, ex-policeman, race driving, fireman, etc., you must have plenty of guts, lots of nerve, and can stand the pressure of both mental and physical of CRASHING and WRECKING automobiles, then you must be the man we want . . . We now have 33 entrants with 67 openings left. You must be accustomed to risk life and limb as you will be part of the Second Annual
100-Car Destruction Derby

The ad went on to say, in grammar just as interesting, that $500 would be given to the winner. The affair was to be held in Union, Kentucky, on U.S. 42, and it was for Sunday night only. Family fun.

For young men who have brains as well as guts, consider the thirty-eight members of Boy Scout Explorer Post 303, whose interest is space-age scouting and who work under scientists at General Electric's Nuclear Material and Propulsion Division at Evendale. These young men can mix their own alloys from metal dust, heat and fuse the mixture, and test it with microscopic photography. Cincinnati youth, like Cincinnati fathers, have a Pandora's box of family fun just waiting to be opened.

If crashing cars together in Union, Kentucky, is not a native's speed, he can always join a walking club here. Cincinnati walkers organized themselves into the American Walkers Association fifty years ago. The club was organized in 1916 when five friends were walking from Westwood to Cheviot and, apparently to pass the time, elected officers. The five were an English doctor named Reeve; Sam Epstein, who was a clerk; Jacob Hoffman, who worked for a shoe company; a salesman named Charles Klusmeyer, and one other.

The club is still going strong. In its fifty years it has done more than walk; it has helped the community by planting trees, the last one an elm planted on Mt. Airy in 1965.

Not all activities are so amiable or worthwhile. Pick the right barn to visit and you'll find yourself as other Cincinnatians did: on the wrong side of the law, attending a cockfight. The police nabbed seventy during one raid in Warren County. They figure at least fifty others flew the coop. Thirty-nine birds were seized.

Then, too, some nature lovers around here go all out. Nudist colonies are illegal in Ohio, but there's talk that one such group has purchased a 65-acre tract down the river near Vevay, Indiana. They say three acres have been cleared and that the colony plans to put in a one-third-acre lake, sit around, sun a lot, swat mosquitoes, and get terribly healthy. The colony is said to have thirty to forty-five members. How Vevay, Indiana, a charming river town full of very nice people, feels about this is anyone's guess. Hence, if you head down that way to join up, keep your shirt on, because the colony just might not be there.

Most Cincinnati families, when they play together, don't mind if people see them. They indulge in more socially accepted sports. Consider Art Claxton, who lives in Summerville. He's a water-skiing buff, and so is every member of his family. They have become so good at it, in fact, they put on shows. They practice up and down the Great Miami River near Cleves, Ohio. While Mrs. Claxton drives their 100-horsepower motorboat, Mr. Claxton and the seven Claxton children travel along in the churning wake, performing a three-tiered pyramid and keeping a sharp lookout for low bridges. The youngest Claxton, now in her teens, learned to water ski when she was four. To make matters more interesting, none of them have seen a professional ski show.

This proves, at least, that Greater Cincinnatians love the water; but when it comes to swimming, few of them hang their clothes on a hickory limb and splash around in the murky Ohio River. For one thing, there are few hickory limbs. For another, this area has an abundance of pools—public and private. And the Ohio River is a fooler. It has treacherous drop-offs, queer currents, and an oozy bottom sometimes dotted with broken glass. Where do Cincinnati children learn to swim? Just about every public pool gives lessons. Princeton High School swimming coach William Renner, for example, actually gives swimming lessons to moppets as young as eighteen months. He calls it the Water Baby Program. Each summer the child, with its mother, shows up at Princeton High School and they take lessons together. The only reason the mother comes along, says Mr. Renner, is that she's the only instructor a young child will trust completely.

157

Some prefer flying to swimming. For a starling's-eye-view of the Queen City, families head out to Lunken Airport off Eastern Avenue, where, now and then, airplane rides are offered for a penny a pound. The family that's more earthbound heads for Dayton, Ohio—getting there is a breeze on the Intrastate—to the Air Force Museum at Wright-Patterson Air Force Base. Or they may head the other way, to the Public Landing, and, if the showboat *Rhododendron* is parked, see an old-fashioned everybody-hiss-the-villain melodrama performed by students from an assortment of West Virginia colleges. The boat makes a dozen stops during its summer season. Cincinnati is one of them, but oldtimers remember when the showboat was the towboat *Omar*—and used to visit more often, pushing tows.

For some families, St. John's Passion Play is a beautiful must, as is for other families the every-other-year May Festival. Those seeking the quiet life can find solace in the four—count 'em, four!—book- mobiles operated by the Cincinnati and Hamilton County Public Library. Each month these traveling parnassuses on wheels make 136 stops in areas from Loveland to Cleves. In the winter they make a few stops less because school stops are also included.

In this chapter about what Cincinnati families do in the pursuit of togetherness—and, as comfort for the father, where he can sneak out for a round of golf—some of the more commercial places have been omitted for obvious reasons. Every city has its movies: straight family houses, art movies, and those dismal little theaters where the sign says ADULTS ONLY.

Also, it has skating rinks, pizza parlors, pool halls, and shooting galleries. But this is not a commercial book, touting this place and that, nor can this book presume to be a complete amusement guide. However, in fairness, some commercial places have become as much a part of Cincinnati as Fountain Square, Ruth Lyons, and Izzy Kadetz. May we consider these in that light?

After all, in other days, when Cincinnati fathers were teething, children used to go to Chester Park on Spring Grove Avenue. But, as you may recall from our historical section, Chester Park fell into bad times. Prohibition came along; the last keg of beer was buried there in a noisy malty ceremony; its race track was weed-covered and its grandstand attended only by the wind; its name changed to Rainbow Park, then back again to Chester; and in 1932 it closed because of an unpaid water bill. John L. Sullivan fought there in 1885 and won, but that was the past. Chester Park has lost its magic, and now it isn't there anymore. In its stead, aided by the unpaid water bill of other years, stands a facility of the Cincinnati Water Works. Lagoon Park in Ludlow, Kentucky, with its five-acre lake, opened in 1894, when bicycles were the scourge of the streets; in 1915 a motorcycle got out of control, killed thirteen people there;

and shortly afterward a cyclone came along, clobbered the park, and that was the kiss of death. Tacoma Park in Dayton, Kentucky, was another remembered spot that time has bid goodby. But through the years of Chester, Lagoon, and Tacoma Parks, Coney Island remained strong, and it's still with Cincinnati today.

Not *quite* a park—rather, a facility that could as logically fit into the chapter about where Cincinnati eats—is the DX Ranch and Ghost Town east of Cincinnati on Route 25 between Amelia and Bethel. This is one place young children adore. Mothers and fathers like it, too, for several reasons. Family-style meals with hot biscuits are, of course, the place's reason for being, but fathers get as much kick as the children do, playing in the Ghost Town out in back of the restaurant. A perfect place for children to have a shoot-out while their parents relax over a second cup of coffee. No charge. For the Ghost Town, that is.

Fantasy Farm on Route 4 south of Middletown, open from Memorial Day to Labor Day, attracts Cincinnati families for several sound reasons. First, it's a first-class amusement park complete with the standard rides, all sorts of historical exhibits including a stage coach inn, farm animals the children can pet, a zoo filled with animals native to Ohio, and—as most commercial parks in this area do—occasional stage shows and special events. The second reason that Fantasy Farm pleases this area is that none of the rides cost money. Families pay as they drive in—and that's it. The children can ride until they're blue in the face. Cincinnati families bring picnic baskets and spend the day.

LeSourdsville Lake, the amusement park in Monroe, is nearly fifty years old, but it keeps up with the times. Like Fantasy Farm, it offers days when one admission at the gate covers all the rides; the difference is that this happens every day at Fantasy Farm and only on special days, usually Tuesdays and Thursdays, at LeSourdsville. But LeSourdsville has a lot going for it. Just as Coney Island has in Cincinnati, the Monroe park has a skyride (60 feet up) that goes out over the lake. The 1965 season at LeSourdsville featured a new attraction: a tombstone territory complete with Boot Hill for burying the dead. Cincinnati fathers like this: the saloon features 200 rare old liquor bottles. Cincinnati fathers don't like this: the bottles are empty. Bill Barr, one of the park's owners, looked all over the country for a buffalo herd, finally found one in nearby Camden, which shows you can find most anything in Ohio if you know where to look. The man in Camden raised buffaloes because he liked buffalo steaks, an item not often found at Kroger's. The LeSourdsville Park has attracted crowds through its forty-five years of operation, including 10,000 4-H members who descended on it *en masse* in 1965.

Finally, of course, there's Coney Island. Purists insist that the park lost some of its charm after the *Island Queen*—a gigantic five-decked sidewheeler that lugged Cincinnatians from the Public Landing upstream to the park—burned to the water's edge in Pittsburgh. Cincinnatians mourned its death. Yes, boats *can* die, especially if they are loved, and the *Island Queen* was loved. But today's pleasure-seeking children are not purists trafficking with history; they're trafficking with fun, and so are their parents. Hence, Coney Island's magic is as potent now for children as it was when their parents were children. The only item today's children miss is the ride back to town on the *Island Queen*'s last trip each night from the park. When the moon was right, the breeze was mellow, and the girl in your arms was primed with enough cotton candy, the top deck of the *Island Queen* was a floating passion pit. Also, if worst came to worst, you could always watch the lights of the city, as Cincinnati drifted upstream, twinkling at you out of the darkness. The top deck was called the Moon Deck, aptly enough. More Cincinnati marriages were made there, at least begun there, than were made in heaven. Homer Denny played love music on his steam piano—purists call it a calliope—girls got kissed, and all was right with the world. But we digress.

Now families travel to Coney Island several different ways: by bus, by outboard motorboat, by rowing, by family car, and now and then by a hydrofoil boat that skims the surface of the water between the Public Landing and the land in minutes. At Coney, families gape at the newest attraction: the Sky Ride, 90 feet up in the air! The rest is there, too. Lost River, the merry-go-round, the Dodge'em, the shooting galleries, the toy trains, and the scent of popcorn, cotton candy, beer, and peanuts. Some things never change.

The swimming pool at Coney is always a sight for sore eyes. It's a two-acre pool with one and a half acres of play and lounging space. It's the world's largest recirculating pool, but the real attraction, other than the water, is the collection of sleek and leggy young maidens sunning themselves, pretending not to notice that one muscular Adonis after another is on the horizontal bar, spinning himself silly.

No question about it. Cincinnati is where the family action is. Plenty to do. But then again, why go out? Sometimes Cincinnati families stay home and listen to the radio or watch television.

12

Cincinnati has a bunch of radio stations—and four television outlets. Most of the radio stations mimic the town's swinger: WSAI. Yet, once WSAI, along with WLW, was a staid "old-lady" kind of facility owned by the Crosley Broadcasting Corporation. When the National Broadcasting Company got rid of its Blue Network (thus the American Broadcasting Company was born), Crosley divested itself of WSAI. At this writing, WSAI occupies the site where the Price Hill House used to be, adjacent to where the top of the Eighth Street incline was —and WLW has long since moved from its Arlington Street studios to Ninth and Elm Streets, where it occupies a ponderous building that used to be a Masonic temple.

Our city also has the Taft Broadcasting Corporation, which operates WKRC-TV, WKRC-Radio, and WKRC-FM. Years ago, when WKRC-Radio had its studios in the Hotel Alms (its radio tower is still atop the building), a piano player one day found herself with a script to read, threw the script aside, ad libbed the program, and that was the start of Ruth Lyons. She's now at WLW-Radio, as well as on WLWT and those other stations: WLW-D in Dayton, WLW-C in Columbus, and WLW-I in Indianapolis. WLW used to operate WLW-A in Atlanta. More about that happy phenomenon called "Mother" elsewhere. When WKRC got its television grant, the Taft station originated its pictures from the *Times-Star* Building at Eighth and Broadway Streets. But when the *Post* took over the *Times-Star*, the WKRC stations moved bag and baggage to Highland Avenue, where WKRC-FM, before that, had been going it alone, broadcasting music and news to city bus riders. Now the city has fewer buses, and the ones that are left tool along the streets in, as far as radio goes, utter silence.

The Scripps-Howard station, WCPO-TV, will be touched upon later in this chapter. Don't think we could leave out Mort Watters.

WKRC-Radio—like the Taft family, which started it—treats Cincinnati listeners as an intelligent accumulation of reasonable grown-ups. The station does not hesitate to "talk" to its listeners. At this writing, the management gives its announcers a relatively free hand to broadcast whatever they please so long as what they broadcast is in good taste, doesn't insult the listener's credibility, and reaches a wider audience than teenagers with transistor radios tattooed to their ears. After all, teenagers might have "buying power" and be a good "market," but the adults in Cincinnati have greater "buying power" and are, when the figures are totaled, a much better market. One of WKRC-Radio's broadcasters is bespectacled Stanton Falls Matlock. He has been on the air nearly twenty years here. His air name has been reduced to Stan Matlock and, if ratings are to be believed, each morning 40 percent of Greater Cincinnati radios are tuned in to hear what Mr. Matlock will say next. He calls his morning stint the *Magazine of the Air,* and to fill it with facts of interest, Mr. Matlock spends seventy hours a week reading books, magazines, and news-papers for items that interest him—and, he hopes, will interest his listeners.

Another WKRC-Radio fixture is Bob Jones, who, with Jim Butler, operates in the afternoon and early evening on a program called *Kaleidoscope,* a smorgasbord of music, talk, features, and "conversations" with visiting firemen as well as locals, including Dr. Tucker of the Cincinnati Historical Society. Cincinnati native Bob Jones said that "brevity seems to be the *all* of modern radio, and that is not as bad as it sounds because of the choppy lives of our listeners. . . . Nothing we do on *Kaleidoscope* takes longer than two and a half or three minutes. In addition to being brief, it is also a . . . come-on, kindly compelling people to stay tuned. In that, of course, lie the advantage and disadvantage. Why does that idiot cut off this conversation with Mickey Rooney in order to play Tony Bennett, or hit me with a commercial? [But] the disadvantages can't be helped. Life is like that. It seems to me it is still possible to be sensible and still be commercial. It not only seems, it *is* . . ."

Bob Jones has conversations with just about everyone. He first chats with his guests ten minutes or so, records the conversation, then cuts the tape up into little bits and pieces and plays the chat throughout the entire five-hour program. The technique is most effective, but it requires a good announcer as well as a good guest to make a conversation worth listening to—and Bob Jones is that kind of broadcaster. A glance at his guest list shows the variety—and range—of the conversations. One day Mr. Jones will be talking with football player Johnny Unitas, and the next day with Dorothy Lamour, followed by—perhaps—Benny Goodman, Bob Hope, Jane Withers, or Countess Tolstoy. Also, judges, governors, and senators have been heard on *Kaleidoscope*. So have Rod Serling, Waite Hoyt, Dr. Albert Sabin, Sophie Tucker, Dorothy Kirsten, Glen Schnitker, Minnesota Fats, and Lawrence Welk.

Stan Matlock and Bob Jones are two of the most well-read men in radio.

WKRC-Radio also has Don Webb, the Woodward High School graduate who started his radio career as a WLW announcer when he was just sixteen years old. Mary Wood, *Post & Times-Star* radio and television editor, says that "when the fellows at WKRC want to dig up some obscure fact about oldtime radio, they call upon Don Webb. [He] seems to be a walking encyclopedia on the subject." And, as Ransom Sherman used to say, "Small wonder!" Mr. Webb has been in the broadcasting business nearly a quarter of a century, most of it at WKRC. Among his early chores was announcing the band "remotes" from Beverly Hills, Lookout House, and the Restaurant Continentale. He announced them at night—and during the day attended Woodward High School.

Webb is his real name, which is more than WKRC's Jack Remington can say. Remington's real name is Raab. When his first boss told Mr. Raab to pick another name for air use, he looked at the studio typewriter. It is fortunate it was a Remington; he might have gone through life as Elsie Smith.

Matlock, Jones, Webb, Remington, Butler, and the rest at WKRC-Radio are basically soft-spoken and mature—and a cut above the rest of Cincinnati stations, which sometimes change personalities as fast as it takes a wanderer to answer a HELP WANTED ad in *Broadcasting* magazine. At this writing, WKRC-Radio and WNOP seem to be the only two stations in town with personalities of their own. Most of the rest sound—in varying degrees—like jukeboxes or Musak. WCIN, of course, aims at the Cincinnati Negro "market," but it finds itself with non-Negro listeners, too—which shows how ethnic radio is in this city. At this writing, we do not have, as some areas do, stations that broadcast in Polish, Spanish, German, Italian, or French. On the other hand, some of the stations here don't broadcast in good English, either.

When L. B. Wilson was alive, WCKY went heavily into direct-mail advertising each night when the sun went down, beaming its 50,000 watts throughout the hillbilly hollows of the South, peddling in an excited voice such items as tombstones, secondhand work clothes, and—some say—Bibles that glowed in the dark. But during the daylight hours, WCKY would broadcast to Cincinnati in an ordinary manner. It was, back then, a Jekyll-and-Hyde kind of station. Mr. Wilson—a wonderful gentleman whose size was small but whose heart was bigger than human hearts should be allowed to get—died, and WCKY has since stopped peddling to the rustics. Now, its 50,000 watts are concentrated in this community day and night, haven't sold second-hand work clothes in years, and beam out the Cincinnati Reds baseball broadcasts as well as serve as originating station for the baseball network. At first, WCKY was in Covington, Kentucky; hence, its call letters. It occupied studios at Sixth and Madison Streets. WZIP, a daytime station Arthur Eilerman put on the air after World War II, later occupied the same studio space. Now both WCKY and WZIP are on the Cincinnati side of the river, but when you fly into the Greater Cincinnati Airport in Boone County, Kentucky, those towers on the adjacent hill are WCKY's; and as you swing down the Intrastate, that penny-whistle tower sitting in a vacant lot in Covington is WZIP's.

Powell Crosley, Jr., an auto-parts man, built 8CR, put it on the air in July 1921, but soon moved the station from his home to his factory, and in 1923 the Crosley Radio Corporation was formed. Then he began manufacturing radios. Then he began manufacturing refrigerators, washing machines, and—for a short time—an odd-looking little car called the Crosley, which was the forerunner of the Volkswagens and the Renaults, when, in this country, there was a market for none of them. Also, he tinkered with the idea of facsimile broadcasting: a morning paper printed by radio waves that came spewing out of your radio into your living room. At one time, under the call letters W8XEL, WLW operated with a whopping power of 500,000 watts. The station could be heard, literally, everywhere. Near its tower at Mason, Ohio, some said that it could even be heard without the aid of a radio receiver. They say that milking machines picked up the signal, and so did barbed-wire fences. When the Federal Communications Commission finished its experiment with such high-powered stations, WLW returned once more to 50,000 watts. No wonder, though, WLW is called the "Nation's Station."

Among the guiding lights at Crosley, one of the warmest and guiding*est* was James D. Shouse. He came to Crosley from St. Louis in 1937 to take over management of both WLW and WSAI. He introduced here the idea that radio stations should have a sense of civic responsibility. As a result, via Shouse, WLW supported the Cincinnati Symphony Orchestra and the opera at the Zoo. He beefed up the news department. And when television came along, he was as ready as Mort Watters was at WCPO-TV. Because of him, Cincinnati has that television institution called Ruth Lyons. Mary Wood of the *Post & Times-Star* described Mr. Shouse as a brilliant but shy fellow who possessed a fey sense of humor.

Well, he needed a sense of humor. When Carroll D. Alcott was a WLW "foreign affairs" commentator, Alcott introduced a rival "foreign affairs" commentator on the air:

"Next you will hear from Gregor Ziemer. Mr. Ziemer sees the world through a spyglass and the Encyclopedia Britannica."

That program, aired May 17, 1943, got terribly heated as it progressed, ending with Mr. Alcott belting Mr. Ziemer. Alcott was fired, but nearly 5000 listeners wrote and telegraphed him their sympathy. He worked at WCKY a little while after that, moved elsewhere, and returned to WLW for a short stay in 1947. From here he went to Hollywood and CBS in 1961. He died in 1965.

Mr. Shouse, of course, needed no sense of humor as far as Peter Grant was concerned. By the time Shouse got here in 1937, Peter Grant was already as much a part of the station as the call letters. He had started at WLW in 1932. Still at Crosley Square—and still very much unmarried—he is now known for his booming voice on newscasts and for his appearances on the Ruth Lyons Show. But he used to be better known for the poetry he read on "Moon River," the late-night radio program that parlayed many an errant lover headlong into matrimony. Also, Peter Grant used to confuse listeners in the 1930s. He sounded exactly like Franklin Delano Roosevelt. Some of his listeners had the uneasy feeling, when they heard Mr. Grant recite the news, that it wasn't Peter Grant at all, but the President moonlighting as a newscaster.

WLW, being something of an institution around here, has inspired a handful of trade jokes. During the early days of television, when the pay was poor at every television station, some wag said that WLW stood for "World's Lowest Wages." It is also said that one lad who quit to go to another station gave this explanation for leaving: "If I had known I was going to be at WLW this long, I would have brought more money."

There is one "air" personality at WLW who once didn't worry about how much talent is paid: retired Police Lieutenant Arthur Mehring. He rode over the city each morning and evening rush hour, reporting what he saw to WLW listeners, and the taxpayers underwrote him. Lieutenant Mehring got his "start" in broadcasting at WCPO-TV on a program that ran in 1952 and was called "Police Blotter," but now he seems as much a WLW staff member as Peter Grant. Still, he was a policeman first and a broadcaster second. In the summer of 1965 he had the shattering experience of looking down from his helicopter and actually seeing an accident *happen:* a little girl darted into the street, got hit by a car, and was thrown fifty feet. The officer immediately radioed for an ambulance, landed his flying machine in a schoolyard, and went to the girl's assistance himself. The WLW traffic broadcasts that evening had to wait. The Cincinnati police, you'll be happy to know, are a dedicated lot. Now retired from the force, Mehring still broadcasts traffic items—but as a WLW staff member.

Several educational radio stations are heard in the Greater Cincinnati area. One is an FM station operated by Miami University at Oxford, Ohio. The other educational FM station is operated by the University of Cincinnati. This is WGUC. Just how strongly Cincinnati feels about radio listening—and its own university station—is best illustrated in this *Enquirer* editorial (February 13, 1965):

> When radio station WSAI-FM announced a while back that it was abandoning—out of economic necessity—its classical offerings, the Queen City music lovers were understandably disturbed . . .
>
> The WSAI-FM fans had nowhere to turn, they felt, but to WGUC, the broadcasting arm of the University of Cincinnati. And their sentiments on the subject assumed the proportion of a flood of pleas for an expansion of WGUC's classical music broadcasts—especially during the morning hours.
>
> It must be a matter of satisfaction that WGUC has responded. It will now be on the air 85 hours a week . . . and three-fourths of its broadcast time will be devoted to classical music. There is additional satisfaction in the knowledge that WGUC's expanded schedule will cost the station a grand total of $75 a year—for electric power involved. And even this cost will be assumed by friends of good music in Cincinnati . . .
>
> Significantly enough, no tax funds are involved in WGUC's activities. Indeed, instead of draining the University's resources, we have a distinct impression that it enhances them.

Radio station WNOP will be treated in Chapter 19, the chapter dealing with unique Cincinnati institutions. The rest of Cincinnati radio—well, wherever you go, as broadcasters say, there's radio, which makes some Cincinnatians wish they hadn't gone. Cities will eventually all look alike. Radio has almost achieved that dubious distinction now.

This is also true of three out of the four television stations in Cincinnati; but in television, the fault for this does not rest with the stations themselves. Television *does* follow patterns. To be a nonconformist broadcaster means you'd run no situation comedies, no films whatsoever—and that would cost too much for any station to accomplish singlehanded. In radio, it can be done. In television, no. But Cincinnati television, more than any other metropolitan television, should get "A" for effort. The three VHF stations here love to telecast "live" stuff that's local. WLWT and its sister stations in Dayton, Columbus, and Indianapolis have a television network of their own! WKRC-TV, which is owned by the Taft group, on the other hand, has a sister station in Columbus, but no physical tie-in. WCPO-TV, the Scripps-Howard outlet, has no sister station near; hence, no private network. Then, there's WCET, UHF Channel 48. WCET is the community educational station operated by the Greater Cincinnati Television Educational Foundation, and guided by Uberto Neely, who put the station on the air by the sheer force of his beliefs and a handful of equipment borrowed from Crosley. As more and more sets come equipped with converters to receive UHF telecasts, more and more viewers will turn away from the colorful pap the VHFs offer. WMUB-TV is another educational television station, a UHF based in Oxford, Ohio, and operated by Miami University. Unlike WCET in Cincinnati, where those interested in working at professional stations can cut their teeth and learn something about television, WMUB-TV is used primarily to teach teachers how to use closed-circuit television in the field of education.

A closer look at one of the "professional" or "commercial" stations best tells the story of Cincinnati broadcasting. Cincinnati broadcasting is an Alice-in-Wonderland kind of world, complete with Mad Hatters, Tweedledees and Tweedledums, and an occasional tumble down a rabbit hole where people change size, sometimes against their better judgment.

Although it's in the act of moving from there to a downtown location next to the new convention hall, WCPO-TV is at this writing perched atop an ugly knoll halfway down Symmes Street from McMillan Avenue, kerplunk in the middle of one of Cincinnati's many Little Italies. WCPO-TV is a five-minute drive from the Vernon Manor, a two-minute drive from Spiders Cafe on Boone Street, and a stone's throw from the staff's home-away-from home, The Maisonette. Two men have made WCPO-TV what it is. One is John Fiorini, the burly "vice-president in charge of most everything": parking lot, brooms, mops, and the ids of the staff. Fiorini's voice is great, his anger greater, and his heart the greatest. The other man is Mort Watters. He is no longer general manager of the shooting match. Robert Gordon, who came from KTUL in Tulsa in 1960, has held that title since 1964. Watters himself is now executive vice-president of the Scripps-Howard Broadcasting Company, of which WCPO-TV is a part. Fiorini is in charge of most everything; Watters is in charge of most everything else.

The crew at WCPO-TV works hard, and they relax hard. They were not invented by Mort Watters. Rather, most are the same kind of people you'd meet at Cincinnati Milling Machine or at Shillito's. Some are Cincinnatians by birth, some by adoption. They are, it must be understood, normal people who pay mortgages, have headaches, and wonder what the younger generation is coming to. To most of them, broadcasting isn't an art; it's a business.

But WCPO-TV was not without its floor-stomping adolescence. It had—as WLWT and WKRC-TV had—its heydey. That was when the Paul Dixon Show was fed to the now defunct Dumont Network, Dave Stanley did a Katzenjammer-type cooking show, Walt Phillips wowed the town with one-liners, Glen Ryle did station breaks; and when that tall private detective came in looking for work, he had the unlikely name of Colin Male. Big Jim Stacey was doing the Cornhuskers Jamboree at noon, each Sunday Harris Rosedale's tap dancers practiced time steps in the lobby, and Waite Hoyt was simply himself. Al Lewis then—a nightclub song-and-dance man turned artist—had got down on his knees to talk to his first studio full of children. Wanda Lewis was there—shy and sweet—but capable of pantomiming a can-can that made Bill O'Bryan and George White, engineers, wonder about her Sunday-school upbringing. Len Goorian, a cigar stuffed in his face, was there. A New York City transplant, Goorian was a dance instructor-turned-producer; he reached a kind of zenith trying to teach Dixon to dance. Penny Pruden was there, doing a cooking show, and Dotty Mack (of all people!) ran camera and directed it! Abe Cowan also ran camera; Al Sternberg, now a television director in Florida, ran camera, too; Lee Hornback, now public service director at Crosley, directed WCPO-TV shows; and on the WCPO-Radio side (now WUBE), the staff announcers were Larry Brunner, Gil Sheppard, Cliff Baker, Bill Dawes, Walt Phillips, and Paul Dixon. Harry Hartman was a salesman. So were John Patrick Smith, Pat Crafton, Jack Kelly, Virgil Schmit, Vince Niemeier, Bob Cook, and Bob Reitman. That husky Canuck, Harry LeBrun, was Mort Watters' assistant; as program director, Ed Weston had begun his collection of feature films and things; Sid Barger was film editor; and working with Sid Barger was Tom Buskirk, who had gotten a Speed Graphic camera for his birthday.

On the engineering side, trying to keep the station glued together, was Paul Adams as chief engineer. He's still there. WCPO-TV had forty-two engineers in 1951 and 1952. Some have stayed. Some have moved on. There was Max Neal, Burnett C. Wayner, Roy Smith, Don Fry, and William Karches. John Hall was there then. Mike Bowden handled the "remotes." William Volkart worked the Dixon show, and so did Harold Briggs, Johnny Walcher, and Dick Cromer. Plus a cast of thousands.

And, as noted, Dotty Mack was there.

Dotty Mack is married now and has become more beautiful than ever, which seems an impossibility. She was with the Paul Dixon Show as Girl Friday, working with Wanda Lewis and Dixon in the pantomiming chores. Later she had a program of her own, Pantomime Hit Parade, with Bob Braun and Colin Male. She's a Price Hill girl and a charmer.

When the Paul Dixon Show first went on the network, in 1951, Watters hired, for the first and last time, a writer to feed Paul Dixon lines. The writer recalled:

I stood in the control room, watched Dixon "perform," turned to Mort, and said:

"Write what?"

Paul, ad libbing a commercial for Frito's, shocked my commercial nature by saying they tasted like dog food. Wanda Lewis was holding a cue card that Paul was ignoring, Dotty Mack was giggling about something, and the two floor men— one was Jack Tempfer, who before television had been a streetcar motorman—were playing cards, oblivious to the action. Only Cowan and Sternberg, the cameramen, paid any attention, but they had to. Well, the engineers in the control room were paying attention a little, but they seemed more concerned about something called "night maintenance" than the show.

"This isn't Chicago television," Watters told me. "This is Cincinnati television."

Mort Watters was wrong, of course. It wasn't Cincinnati television. It was Mort Watters television!

As executive vice-president of a corporation that grosses more than $17,000,000, Watters has come a long way since, one year after WLW's Mr. Shouse came to town, he arrived in 1938 to take over the wishy-washy radio station Scripps-Howard had purchased. In 1938, WCPO-Radio—formerly WFBE, and now WUBE—wasn't much. WLW had 50,000 watts of power, and the other stations on the air—WSAI, WCKY, and WKRC—all had more power than WCPO, which poked along on 250 watts and Bob Bentley reading the Sunday comics. Back then, WCPO was much more comic than anything Bentley found in the funnies, but to Mort Watters the radio station was no laughing matter. It marked his entry into metropolitan broadcasting. Before coming here, he had managed a Tinker-Toy three-station radio network in West Virginia. WCPO in 1938 was a dog, but Mort Watters proceeded to teach the dog a few tricks.

Soon his staff picked up his enthusiasm. Red Thornburg was broadcasting sports, and so was Harry Hartman. Paul Hodges, brought to Cincinnati to do the morning stint, later blossomed out into Train Time, a program in which he roamed the Cincinnati Union Terminal waiting room, buttonholed passengers, and demanded in his W. C. Fields' voice, "Arriving or leaving?" Along came Malcolm Richards, an announcer Mort Watters still considers among "the best 'morning men' ever to face a microphone." And if listeners couldn't hear the low-powered WCPO, Watters made certain they would at least *see* his radio station. He moved its news room to a storefront on Walnut Street between Fifth and Sixth Streets, and there it stayed until 1944, when WCPO had enough bucks to move to more lavish quarters in the Carew Tower. While on Walnut Street, the station attracted noontime crowds who wandered in off the street to hear a newscaster Watters had brought in from Washington, D.C.: Tom McCarthy. McCarthy later moved to WKRC-Radio, became a mainstay and power there, once waging and winning singlehanded a war against the city's fluoridating its drinking water. McCarthy has since retired and gone "down East."

Watters introduced in those early days the idea of around-the-clock newscasts. A studio was set up in a broom closet at the *Post*, five-minute newcasts originated from there every hour, news briefs originated every half hour, and—as they say—bulletins at once. Rather commonplace these days, this round-the-clock news coverage was a grabber then because radio news consisted of only an occasional newscast in the morning and afternoon—and Gabriel Heatter. With Watters' news pattern established, some say Watters forced the other Cincinnati stations to follow suit. The key news broadcasters were Tom McCarthy, Bob Otto, and Jack Fogarty. Mort brought in another from Chicago. "I was driving to a convention," Watters said, "and I heard this Chicago announcer doing a morning show. I thought his voice had the right quality for our newscasts, so I telephoned him, offered $50 a week, and he came to Cincinnati." His name? Paul Dixon.

Bill Gold wrote in the August 20, 1950, Washington *Post:*

> As news director of 250-watt WCPO, I often dreamed of the day we could compete with the Crosley station on equal footing. And [sob!] now that I don't work in Cincinnati anymore, that day has come. WLW still throws the best [radio] signal in town, but in the television field it's on equal footing with two competitors, WCPO-TV and WKRC-TV . . . When the *Post* at long last got a facility equal to WLW, things really began to happen . . .

Mort Watters said, "When we went on the air with WCPO-TV, July 1949, it seemed apparent that the income available from a few nighttime announcements . . . and network income would never get WCPO-TV out of the red, let alone provide profit."

Broadcasting magazine, December 1950, reported:

> So WCPO-TV from its inception started its telecasting day at noon and signed off at 11 P.M. seven days a week, although the other two television stations in Cincinnati operated only

from late afternoon to 9:30 or 10 P.M., and one was on only six days a week. When in October, 1949, WCPO-TV became connected with the network, it pushed its starting time back to 10:30 A.M., running continuous programming until 12:30 or 1 A.M. . . .

Bill Gold, in the Washington *Post*, looked with awe and misgiving at the idea of running a television station during the daytime. He wrote:

> The long-range effects of such programming are hard to guess. Mothers trying to get their kids ready for school while the small fry howl that they want to watch the Crunky Wunchy breakfast program may find themselves hoping that Mort Watters falls down a coal chute and breaks his leg. Husbands who expect their wives to sweep and dust and cook and mend socks may come home to find their women still glued to the television set—and it's entirely possible that a few irate husbands will eventually take direct action in the form of an ax applied vigorously and repeatedly to the receiver's working parts. On the other hand, of course, the long-range effects on cities which have been *Watterized* may be relatively mild. We humans have a way of adapting ourselves to periodic upheavals . . .

Cincinnati adapted—and adapted fast. Cincinnatians bought television receivers like crazy. They wanted to see the ball games. They wanted to see the wrestlers. And they wanted to see what Watters would pull next. With only a half-million people in Cincinnati—and perhaps twice that in the Greater Cincinnati area—by August 1950, a quarter of a million television receivers had been sold here!

Watters himself pointed out to the broadcasters at the 1950 broadcasters convention in New York that, "with the exception of one feature film WCPO-TV has at 8:15 A.M., *all* daytime programs are live and are run back-to-back in one studio. Our policy of news every hour comes in handy. We use these two minutes to move scenery, cameras, and lights for the next show." He didn't care much for television-station operators who were afraid to tinker with daytime television. He apparently didn't care too much for comptrollers, either, because he said:

> Every time we approached the break-even point in our operation, I added another hour to our broadcast day. That brought in more revenue to balance the additional expense and gave us a chance to expand again. Meantime, the additional programs sold thousands of additional receiving sets and built in Cincinnati a *mass* audience for television.

In 1950, Watters noted:

> Today, operating nineteen hours a day, five days a week, and twenty-four hours on the two other days, we are almost breaking even again, and should be earning a profit in a few weeks.

Bill Gold, in the Washington *Post*, sighed:

> . . . I can't argue with Watters, because that's like arguing with success. WLW's TV station has hopped on the bandwagon and is also in operation by breakfast time now, and even the Taft transmitter is trying to keep pace. The whole city is affected by the battle, of course, and is watching its progress with interest . . . But to all of us, it's going to mean a profound change in our living habits—and I'd kind of like to stick around for a few hundred years and see how it works itself out.

In December 1950, typical WCPO-TV schedule was:

6–7 A.M.	Morning Merry-Go-Round
7–7:30 A.M.	Kids Show (*not* Uncle Al)
7:30–8 A.M.	Santa Claus
8–8:10 A.M.	News
8:10–8:15 A.M.	Morning Exercises
8:15–9:30 A.M.	Morning Movie
9:30–10:30 A.M.	Coffee Club (audience participation)
10:30–11 A.M.	Bill Dawes Disc Jockey Show
11 A.M.–NOON	Al Lewis' Drug Store (adult variety)
NOON–12:15 P.M.	Man-on-the-Street interviews
12:15–1 P.M.	Midday Merry-Go-Round (hillbilly)
1–2 P.M.	Kitchen Show
2–3 P.M.	Meet the Ladies (audience participation)
3–5 P.M.	Paul Dixon's Music Shop
5–6 P.M.	Six Gun Playhouse (western movie)

And on and on and on . . .

If Mort Watters was setting the town on its ears, he was doing the same to his talent. Al Lewis recalls his first stint in Cincinnati television: Al Lewis' Drug Store. "It wasn't meant for children," he admitted. "It was just another variety show featuring whatever local talent we could beg, borrow, or steal. But one day some neighborhood children wandered into the studio, I talked with them on the air to kill time, drew pictures for them, and there we were!"

"That's how Al Lewis started the children's program," Mort Watters said. "A lucky accident. I was sitting in my office, watching the monitor, and I knew he had something there. As soon as the show was over, I told Al to find some more children to work with, and after that, things just grew."

Thus, Al Lewis—by sheer chance—became Cincinnati's babysitter. Meanwhile, Paul Dixon and Bill Dawes, both WCPO-Radio disc jockeys, were transferred by Watters bodily before the WCPO-TV cameras. Watters' only advice was:

"You'd better *do* something. You each have a lot of time to fill."

"Do *what?*" Dixon protested.

Mort Watters only shrugged. "It's your show. Run it yourself."

Later Dixon recalled:

"I was flabbergasted. I knew radio. But television? How do you spin records on television?"

But those were the anything-goes days of Mort Watters' plaything. In self-defense, prop men, wives with a little talent, engineers, and strangers off the street worked feverishly together. Lewis, who had just started working there ("Wanda and I were married on a Friday, and I started at WCPO-TV that Saturday!"), brought his wife to the station, suggested she draw pictures while records played, and that was her entry into show business. Dotty Mack—also by sheer chance, which seemed to be running WCPO-TV—was teamed up with Dixon.

"She was supposed to work with Bill Dawes," Watters said. "But one day, before the station went on the air, the engineers had cameras warmed up and asked if we wanted to do a dry run on a show to give them practice. Dixon was around. So was Dotty. They weren't supposed to be together, but they were—for that one dry run. One look at them and I knew they belonged together . . ."

Long-suffering Harry LeBrun, who once earned the admiration of the entire staff because he belted a minor executive and knocked him flat, is now with WESH in Orlando, Florida, but in those halcyon days of WCPO-TV he was right in the thick of things. He was Mort Watters' righthand man.

"It is true," said Watters, "that I dreamed up a lot of wacky ideas, but it was poor Harry's job to see that they were carried out in the most efficient way possible, with the knowledge that I would forbid him to tell me, 'It can't be done.'" LeBrun moved from WCPO-TV to a vice-presidency at Crosley, and then to Florida. He was—and is—one of broadcasting's most efficient and nicest guys.

Where Dotty Mack is concerned, some have labeled her story a "Cinderella story," but that's not correct. In those early days, WCPO-TV had more Cinderella stories than it could shake a transmitter at. Just as in the military draft, where any warm body was chosen, so it was with television then: if you could walk, talk, and were a pretty girl, chances were you'd end up as some announcer's "Girl Friday." Couch casting had nothing to do with it. No one had time for hanky-panky, and, besides, the couch was a prop on some show. A former announcer recalls, "Everyone and his brother had a chance there. Tell Watters you had a program idea, and the next day your program was on the air. You either lucked out or bombed. It depended on you."

Haphazard as it was, it wasn't quite *that* haphazard. Mort Watters said it another way:

> It was and is a matter of *talent*. In any other city, you can run a program or personality thirteen weeks and know whether or not the city approved. Cincinnati is different. Here you have to run a program or personality longer—at times, years. But once this city accepts a Dixon or a Lyons, the talent can do no wrong. Still, we can't put just *any* talent on the air. Cincinnati won't buy a face or a comic because we keep shoving him at the city. The people on camera must have *talent*. If they just have that, Cincinnati will make stars out of them.

But exactly what talent did Dotty Mack have? Or, for that matter, Dixon? Wanda Lewis? Or Colin Male? They only pantomimed. Bob Braun, who came that route, can at least sing.

A man who used to produce the Paul Dixon Show wrote:

> I've directed enough live amateur shows on television to know that pantomiming—*good* pantomiming—is in itself an art. Mack, Lewis, Dixon, Male, and Braun at WCPO-TV had it mastered; and over at WKRC-TV so did Dick Hageman, Shirley Jester, and some others. On the other hand, I have seen on these amateur shows too many mother's little darlings move their lips to records and think they're better than Dotty Mack. They were, in reality, light-years away from her ability. They weren't really pantomiming. Very seldom did any capture the *essence* of what they were supposed to be "singing." Rather, they were more concerned with admiring themselves on the monitors and hoping that when they got home their mothers wouldn't nail them to a cross because they didn't have it. So don't kid yourself. Pantomiming *is* an art.

The quarrel about pantomiming has diminished now because pantomime shows on local television have gone the way of shows where women roller-skated in anger. Those items are history. Now Paul Dixon is at WLWT doing what he does best: chatting with a studio filled with mothers. He's been there more than ten years now. And Dotty Mack is a mother herself. The others? Len Goorian is no longer active in television. He was at WKRC-TV for a while, and, thanks to him, Cincinnati has Skipper Ryle. Now Goorian is dabbling in real estate. Dick Hageman is dead. Bob Smith has gone to the networks. Colin Male is doing network commercials on the West

Coast. Shirley Jester, having married George Palmer, still noodles with the piano at the Vernon Manor, but her real love—and George's—is their little girl named Haven. Jana Demas is in Dayton, wowing them there. Bob Braun is at WLW and is most happy there, and Cincinnati is most happy that handsome Ludlow lad stayed in the area. He needn't have. With his talent, he could have made it in New York or Hollywood, but he's like a lot of Greater Cincinnatians: this area is home. Braun, if anything, proves the thesis of this book. Love anything hard enough and it will love you back. He loves Cincinnati. Only Wanda Lewis remains in front of the WCPO-TV camera, but as for pantomiming, she hasn't opened her mouth in silence for ages. Bud Chase is a top television producer in Chicago at this writing. And so it goes, and so they all have gone. But of the "good old days"—if they dare be labeled that—a writer for the Dixon show remembers some of the madness:

Though Dixon was an exuberant critter not given to reading scripts, still my job of "writing" the Dixon show was a snap. Paul's talent was and is ad libbing and letting the laughs, if any, fall where they may. But he needed a studio audience (I'm glad Crosley gave him one), and when I came to WCPO-TV he had no audience. I wasn't worried, though. The pay was good and, anyway, I needed a job at the time.

The Dumont Network had just signed the Dixon Show on the network opposite Arthur Godfrey and Ernie Kovacs, which meant only the master control room in New York was watching us. But Dixon wasn't worried about that. He worried about "getting rolling."

"Cincinnatians know the kind of show we do," he fretted. "But in other cities . . ."

I decided the best thing to write for him was to write absolutely nothing. Had I written anything he would have made hash of it, and besides, that wasn't his kind of show. So each Wednesday night before the program, Dixon and I would meet, and I'd give him three five-by-seven index cards, a one-line joke on each.

"Keep them handy," I said. "If you find yourself running out of steam, use one."

The plan worked like a charm. Each week Dixon and I met and I gave him three jokes. Since he hadn't used the jokes from the week before, I kept giving him the same three jokes I started out with. After all, so long as he had something to fall back on, he didn't worry, and he could relax and do the show as he'd always done.

After a year of writing the Dixon show that way, I quit and took the three jokes with me, my reputation as a comedy writer intact.

"Talented people," said Mort Watters, "are like children. They brood about unlikely things. Should they buy this house? or a car that color? They'll worry for months. I listen, and after they've fretted enough, I tell them to buy the house or the car that color—which they wanted to do anyway! But they don't worry about what to do with their programs. That's different. There, they're so sure of themselves, it is sometimes painful."

Being in front of the television cameras, as most Cincinnati talent was, five days a week and long hours each day, made their lives high-tension merry-go-rounds. The camera drains whatever talent a performer possesses, then demands more. Yet, Cincinnati managed to accumulate performers who actually became more human because of the camera. Ruth Lyons is an excellent example. So is Paul Dixon. Consider Glen Ryle (who is covered more thoroughly in Chapter 19), add Al and Wanda Lewis—and so many others. The camera didn't conquer these people. They conquered the camera, which was not an easy victory. Some others, strewn along the wayside, failed. These discards believed their press notices instead of their hearts, and so they were mere flashes on the local scene, coming and going, with Cincinnati not caring at all.

A classic example of real talent are Al and Wanda Lewis, who have not changed one iota in fifteen years. When Al gets off his knees and his children's program is over for the day, he becomes a grownup again: a thoughtful and mature artist who is not, as they say in the trade, "on." The greatest mistake anyone can make about Al Lewis is to consider him childlike, forever crawling around the studio floor among a pile of children. Yet, it's surprising the number of people who think just that—and some of them, being in broadcasting and advertising themselves, should know better. A man who manufactures widgets for children looks upon himself as a mature businessman, but looks upon Uncle Al as some kind of nut capable of trafficking only with smallfry. But don't they *both* traffic with smallfry? In reality, both are in the same business. There's more to Al Lewis than meets the eye and, being a good performer, he tries to keep it hidden. Wanda—now Captain Wendy on the Uncle Al Show—is Al's wife and the last of a long line of Cinderellas who worked with Uncle Al. Basically shy, she is surprised to be in "show business." She certainly didn't intend her life that way. Wanda met Al in a Cleveland art school, up came love, and there you are. She has a pixy sense of humor which, these days on television, has little chance of being seen. It is true that Al and Wanda Lewis make good money, but they earn every cent. If anything, chalk this up for the Lewises. They *are* themselves.

And Dotty Mack is herself, too. In the early 1950s, glamor was poured over her by the bucketful, press releases puffed her "image" beyond where images should be puffed, and wherever she went there were ohs and ahs, some with jealousy in them. Still, Dotty Mack remained the breezy kid from Price Hill. If she had not got involved with WCPO-TV, she would still have been beautiful. Price Hill is full of such charmers, and most of them—as Dotty did—chewed gum, respected their parents, went to church, went nuts over babies, and could—if pressed—be a tomboy as rowdy as the next. The difference was, Dotty Mack was lucky. She was at the right place at the right time. But she has never considered herself a glamor queen. That was press agentry. The surprising thing is this: she never considered herself beautiful at all. But, then, what truly beautiful girl does? In lonely moments of quiet—and these, too, existed in early television —Dotty used to sit off by herself and wonder, as a child wonders, when someone would come along and take the magic away. She had only one talent: pantomiming. She was its master. Have her pantomime a sultry tune, and her eyes would glitter with witchery. Have her pantomime a lonely tune, and somewhere inside and out of sight her heart would break. Have her pantomime a comedy number, and Dotty was every imp who ever was. She couldn't dance. She couldn't sing. She couldn't tell jokes. Happily, she didn't have to do these things. She did two things: pantomimed perfectly and made Dixon look good, as, in turn, he made her look good. Had either one an ounce of talent—dancing or singing—they would have laid an egg. Their real talent was being themselves, which, in front of a camera, is hard to do.

Just as Al and Wanda Lewis have not changed, neither have Dixon or Dotty Mack. Dotty, as noted, is married now. She lives in New York, her husband is repetitively named William B. Williams, she has a boy, and she is happy. But there were stormy moments at WCPO-TV and in her career. Talent can be fractious. But she was not the only performer in our city to get furious at the way things were. Dixon used to get furious. Lewis did, too. WCPO-TV back then was a high-powered world of high-powered emotions. Furies existed, but *this* is important: they were over as quickly as they appeared. Then the talent would brood, sulk awhile, and by and by, someone would smile at them again, they would smile back, and be themselves once more. There was always another show to do. The gang didn't have time to nurture hate.

Mort Watters brought Walt Phillips over to WCPO from another station, put him on radio—and for two hours each Saturday afternoon in front of the television cameras. Walt Phillips is presently the morning man at WGN-Radio in Chicago, where time and success have not tinkered with him one bit. Some performers—Milton Berle, Henny Youngman, *et al*—are perfectionists with Univac brains. Clickety-click! Out comes an instant one-liner that knocks them dead.

Walt Phillips has this same beautiful ability. It worked fine over WCPO-Radio. Converting it to television was something else again. He brought Jana Demas to help. Together one wintry Saturday afternoon minutes before air time, they sat around wondering how to fill the two hours. *That's* how planned television was back then. As air time approached, they hadn't come up with a single thing.

"I guess," said Walt without concern, "we'll have to use Plan X."

This bothered Jana Demas because, to be honest, there was no Plan X.

But Walt asked the prop boy to build a fire in a lard can and place it outside the studio in the snow. A hand mike was run out to this location, and a camera looked through the window, taking its picture. For two hours Walt and Jana huddled around the fire, the ice-cold sky their backdrop, and ad libbed. The idea: the station had locked them out, but they were going to do their program anyway! Well, Walt and Jana made that show into a gem, but now they're both gone: Walt to Chicago and Jana to Dayton. Cincinnatians, remembering, keep close watch on their picture tubes. In their hearts, loyal viewers know that someday, when it is snowing awfully hard, they will see two creatures huddled around a lard-can fire, talking happy nonsense, and when that moment comes, Cincinnati will be happy again, too. It will mean that Walt Phillips and Jana Demas have come back.

This was the caliber of talent Mort Watters assembled for his stations. Sometimes he picked wrong, but that was seldom. The ones he picked have gone on in the business. Glen Ryle, now Skipper Ryle, began his career at WCPO-TV. There was, of course, Dixon. Add Colin Male and add Bob Braun. Add Bud Chase, Walt Phillips, Jana Demas, Len Goorian, Art Garrett, and didn't Mort Watters put Al Schottelkotte on television—Schottelkotte! *Enquirer* writer, Western Hills graduate, and constant father, with a name only true Cincinnatians find logical—and thus update television news reporting so well that Al has traveled to other stations to show them how it's done in Cincinnati. Waite Hoyt is a WCPO alumnus, and so is Tom McCarthy. Add amiable and honest-as-the-day-is-long-in-summer-yet Jules Huffman, now with WSAZ-TV in Huntington. To be fair, it must be noted that Ruth Lyons was never at WCPO. And neither was Peter Grant. Leo Underhill has never set foot in the place—and some who did, wish they hadn't. At WCPO, via Mort Watters, people got exactly what was coming to them.

But not *all*. Watters missed the boat when it came to some talent. He wasn't perfect. There are many in Cincinnati who say he missed the boat where Bark Yeatts was concerned. Bark, like Dotty Mack, was a perfect foil for Paul Dixon. Then a prop man at the station, Yeatts had created from the prop room's assortment an outlandish costume. When he wore it and stood around, saying nothing, he had the impact of Jackie Gleason's Poor Soul. But Mort Watters was more interested in the stars. Bark Yeatts has long since deserted WCPO for the business world, where he has become a successful Cincinnati advertising man. But in his closet, gathering dust, still hangs the Poor Soul costume. Someday Cincinnati television will wise up and ask him to put it back on again.

Jack Fogarty, reporting on Watters' twentieth anniversary with the WCPO stations, told how one man looked with gloom at Watters and said:

"It never ceases to amaze me how a guy wrong so often . . . continues to breathe [and] confound the opposition with such regularity!"

It is true that Mort Watters is not perfect. At times his weaknesses stand out like a sore thumb. But his weaknesses are the weaknesses of broadcasting. Broadcasting is one part performing art and one part cash register. He is, as John Murphy at Crosley and Lawrence Rogers at WKRC-TV are, surrounded by high-keyed people who bombard their bosses with well-meaning ideas and directions. Watters, Murphy, and Rogers must sift through the debris the bombardment leaves to find if a new idea or new direction *does* exist. In sifting and sorting, each man must set his own standards—and all three do. Sometimes, in sifting and sorting, they make mistakes. But don't crucify them when this happens. Our mistakes we can hide. When Watters, Murphy, or Rogers make a mistake, all Cincinnati sees it. There's no way on earth to *un*televise a program. Good broadcasters—and these three *are*—should not be measured by their mistakes, but by their successes. After all, if we measure men and civilizations only by their failures, we might still be savages who sit under rocks and grumble—not because the sun has warmed us after a long winter—but because its glare momentarily bothers our eyes.

Television has, unfortunately for the viewers, settled down much since those early days, but not *too* much. Just the other morning, a child sat on Uncle Al's accordion and, unable to contain herself, got it wet. Can you imagine explaining *that* to an insurance company! And now, WCPO-TV has outgrown the ugly knoll upon which it fermented so many years. By the time you read this, perhaps WCPO-TV will have moved downtown. Well, WLWT left its Mount Olympus for Ninth and Elm Streets. WKRC-TV left 800 Broadway Street for Highland Avenue. Industries have moved. You have moved. Can't television stations move, too? Nothing—cities, television stations, or families—stands still. Each gets bigger and, perhaps, gets better. Time is the judge of that. And each, in getting bigger, loses the personal touch. You would have got more intimate service from the telephone company when it had only two hundred subscribers. When you bought candles from a P&G pushcart, the Procter pushing it probably knew you by name. But are these the important things?

The important thing is, Cincinnati isn't standing still. It doesn't shrink as some communities have. It keeps getting bigger. When we needed candles, Procter & Gamble answered that need. Now that same company answers greater needs—and for the nation. When we needed someone to make broadcasting mature, there was Mr. Shouse. When we needed someone to turn this town upside down via television, there was Mr. Watters. If P&G's growing bigger is wrong, Mr. Shouse and Mr. Watters are wrong, too. And Cincinnati should never have happened.

13

When Cincinnatians are not transfixed by television or by that stunning blonde down the street they read newspapers. They have a lot of newspapers to choose from. This area has more than fifty suburban weeklies and religious publications: the Milford *Advertiser*, *Northeast Suburban Life*, *Hilltop News*, *Catholic Telegraph*, *American Israelite*, Clermont *Courier*, *Western Hills Press*, Court *Index Press*, Price Hill *News*, *Valley Journal*, *News Enterprise*, and a bunch of others. Add the two dailies that serve all of Greater Cincinnati, the *Enquirer* and the *Post & Times-Star*, and there you are. The *Enquirer* is the seven-day-a-week morning paper, and the *Post & Times-Star* is the never-on-Sunday evening daily.

Some Cincinnatians might tell you that the *Post & Times-Star* owns the *Enquirer*, but purists will tell you this is an oversimplification that does not hold water. Let's untangle that situation right now. First, the *Post* was founded during a blizzard on January 15, 1881, by E. W. Scripps; the *Post* acquired its afternoon rival, the *Times-Star*, in 1958. Second, the *Enquirer* originally went to press as the *Enquirer* on April 10, 1841. It was an afternoon paper then, published by brothers John and Charles H. Brough. It became a morning paper two years later. It began its Sunday edition in 1848, and today is the oldest surviving Sunday newspaper in the United States. So much for the parentage of each. When the (then) *Times-Star*, in 1952, tried to buy the *Enquirer* for $7,500,000, the *Enquirer* employees and community supporters bought the paper instead. Now follow the bouncing ball carefully.

In April 1956, the E. W. Scripps Company (which owns Scripps-Howard newspapers, including, among others, the *Post & Times-Star*) bid $4,059,000 to acquire $1,500,000 in convertible debentures left over from the sale of the *Enquirer* by the McLean estate to the *Enquirer* employees and community shareholders. The E. W. Scripps Company next purchased additional *Enquirer* stock and became not the owner but rather the major shareholder of the morning paper. Although as major shareholder the E. W. Scripps Company could have a voice in the operation of the *Enquirer*, the E. W. Scripps Company prefers to keep hands off the entire shooting match. The *Enquirer* itself hires and fires whomever it pleases, and it sets its own editorial policy: local, state, and national. The *Post & Times-Star* follows the lead of the majority of the Scripps-Howard editors where national policy is concerned, but in matters concerning its circulation area (Ohio, Kentucky, and Indiana) the *Post & Times-Star* establishes whatever editorial policy it chooses—and the E. W. Scripps Company goes along. Thus, you might find a Scripps-Howard paper in Columbus at odds with the Scripps-Howard's *Post & Times-Star* over who should be governor of Ohio. The parent company, E. W. Scripps, actually has no more control of either the *Enquirer* or the *Post & Times-Star* locally than a father with two teenage sons has control over his two family cars. All fathers can do is insist that each son pay his own way. That's all the E. W. Scripps Company requires of its papers. How they do it is their business.

So independent are both papers that each possesses its own presses and advertising staff. In some communities where newspapers are linked, the only difference is editorial personnel. So you can't look upon our papers as blood brothers. Their attitude to one another is, Does Macy's tell Gimbels? At the *Post & Times-Star*, Dick Thornburg, the editor, is top dog. The publisher of the *Enquirer*, Francis L. Dale, sets that paper's editorial direction, and Brady Black, as editor, sees that it is carried out.

Which is the bigger paper? Actually, where these two brawling giants are concerned, size and numbers mean little. They're both whoppers. Both circulate in the three-state area. In fact, if you want a real bargain, buy their Kentucky editions. Each day, both put out a northern Kentucky edition that is bigger than most tank-town dailies. These editions are added to the regular metropolitan editions and sold for the same price as the Cincinnati edition—and the result is that some days these Kentucky editions are so big you can work up a sweat lugging one home. In addition to this special edition for Kentucky readers, both papers publish special pages each day for Ohio and Indiana communities. So don't ask which one is bigger. Neither is a lightweight.

Francis L. Dale, president and publisher of the *Enquirer*, said: "We ask not to be judged [by] our mechanical equipment, the size of our issues, the volume of our circulation, or the size of our profits. We ask instead to be judged by our devotion to truth, by our success in arriving at a position of leadership, and by our influence in making good things happen." Politics? Well, Mr. Dale said, "In local as in national matters, the *Enquirer* will be politically independent . . ."

The *Post & Times-Star*, too, is politically independent. When the paper was founded, E. W. Scripps wrote:

"We have no politics in the sense of the word as commonly used. We are not Republican, not Democrat, not Greenback, not Prohibitionist. We simply intend to support good men and condemn bad ones, support good measures and condemn bad ones, no matter what party they belong to. We shall tell no lies about persons or policies for love, malice, or money . . ."

Also, and this is important, the *Enquirer* and the *Post & Times-Star* keep their political beliefs out of the news columns. When they have axes to grind, the grinding is done on the editorial pages and, at times, by columnists who make no bones about how they feel about issues. But hard news is reported as hard news. It is not tinkered with. The men working the editorial desks bend so far backward to be objective, the force of gravity ought to send them toppling from their squeaky swivel chairs. Not all dailies in this area are that objective. One nearby has yet to recognize in its news columns that the United Nations exists. The emphasis in Cincinnati on good reporting has caused the two city rooms to hatch many good writers, not all of whom stayed in the business. For instance, one reporter on the defunct *Times-Star* is a Supreme Court justice: Potter Stewart.

But, in fairness, it must be noted that the *Enquirer* and the *Post & Times-Star* weren't always winning Bibles. Both dailies went through a hairy period of growing up.

In its youth the *Post & Times-Star* (then the *Post*) was that rowdy, two-fisted little operation that snarled a lot. This was in the days when snarling was more effective than smiling. Its snarling helped scuttle the Cox political machine. But along came Carl D. Groat, a finely textured gentleman who looked more like a university professor than the sharply honed reporter he really was. As editor of the *Post*, Groat introduced an aura of respect to the sheet. Its cops-'n-robbers heyday ended with a thud. Groat brought in newsmen like Robert Linn, who became one of the finest and (at times) fattest managing editors in the nation (see Chapter 19). Simply put, the *Post* became such a thoughtful newspaper that now, when *Post & Times-Star* reporters see the play or movie *The Front Page*, they gape in wonder and disbelief. When Carl Groat passed away, Dick Thornburg was appointed editor. Fortunately, he is as professional as Groat was. Editorial shabbiness has no place in his newspaper.

The *Enquirer*'s youth was equally colorful. You would hardly have recognized the "grand old lady of Vine Street." It was a Democratic newspaper then. It attracted such heady diatribes as: "The impudence and the low vulgar Billingsgate of the *Enquirer* clique . . . is only exceeded by their total disregard for the truth. The vilest epithets are heaped daily upon our oldest and best citizens to gratify . . . these unprincipled adventurers." What other newspaper could boast this endorsement: bumbling along in 1870, the *Enquirer* favored France in the Franco-Prussian War, and the Cincinnati Germans expressed their distaste by marching to the *Enquirer* building and groaning three mighty groans of protest! Alvin F. Harlow noted in *The Serene Cincinnatians* that "John R. McLean and his newspaper [were] a far cry from the *Enquirer* of today . . ." *That* is putting it mildly. But Vine Street—and Cincinnati—changed from rowdy to nice; and so did the *Enquirer.* Today the only place a reader can find muckraking here is in the dictionary under *m.*

Because "yellow journalism" went out in Cincinnati with button shoes doesn't mean that all became Alphonse and Gaston. When the *Times-Star* was still among us as an evening paper competing with the *Post,* the two evening papers engaged in all kinds of silly schemes to get new subscribers. Wonderful promotions were held: football lotteries and the rest. The prizes were usually substantial: a new car or new home. Of course, to participate, a reader had to read the newspaper the contest was in, and *presto!* up would go that newspaper's circulation. Trouble is, when the contest was over, *whoops!* the added circulation would fly out the window to the rival, which was then running an equally stunning contest. It was a weird tug-of-war. When the *Times-Star* ran a contest, it increased circulation; when the *Post* ran a contest it, too, increased circulation. Trouble was, both papers were trading the same handful of customers back and forth. Their regular subscribers couldn't be budged away from this paper or that. It finally dawned on the papers that they were spending more money than they were gaining in new customers—and circulation promotions went into a twilight. The newspaper finally realized what their readers had known all along: people bought papers because of the comics, columnists, and features. As for hard news, all three papers were at a standoff. Each of their city rooms trafficked only in excellence.

Now, with only one evening newspaper and one morning newspaper available, perhaps this is not so: the interest in features, we mean. Perhaps comics, columnists, and features are not as important as they once were. Some people by habit read evening newspapers, some read morning newspapers, and some read both. Whether this premise is correct will never be put to the test in Cincinnati because both newspapers not only keep their writing standards up but they keep raising them every time they turn around. And, happily for this area, Cincinnati does not have newspapers the way some other towns

have: newspapers filled with only wire news and the only local stuff
being the death notices. Both Cincinnati papers have more local
columnists and local feature writers than you can shake a stick at.

Since Art Buchwald is the same here as elsewhere, there is little
need to survey the papers' syndicated features. But a glance at the
local columnists and feature writers is in order. These natives (either
real or by adoption) are the most articulate of Cincinnatians. After all,
each day they struggle with words. Television performers can establish
rapport with a grunt or a grin, but our local writers must reach their
audience by using words artfully to say something that needs to be
said. Cincinnati readers who read only one of our two newspapers
miss half the daily sideshow of wit, wisdom, and whimsy because
they see only one side of the editorial midway. So let's assume we are
new to the city and take a fresh look at some of these writers who
give our city substance and meaning.

Had we looked only yesterday, we would have been reading Nixon
Denton, the *Times-Star* sports editor who strayed so often from the
subject of sports, one wondered if he cared for athletics at all. For a
long time, more amused then enraged, this writer was the amiable
cornerstone of the now defunct *Times-Star,* his column being a
pleasant thing that wasn't unhappy with anyone. We would have
read Joseph Garretson, who was a columnist first with the *Enquirer,*
then with the *Times-Star.* Garretson was a bulky reporter and
columnist of the old school who grumbled in type and rearranged
cities to suit his needs. A thorough newspaperman who had weathered
a lifetime of press handouts, Garretson ignored them all and wrote of
Cincinnati as *he* saw it, never hesitating to puncture a stuffed shirt in
the process. It is said he once went to the posh Gourmet Room and
floored the French chef by ordering a ham sandwich and a bottle of
beer. O. O. McIntyre, years before, had been a reporter for the *Post*
before going on to New York to become a syndicated columnist.
Irvin Cobb had been a *Post* staff member, and so had Roy W. Howard
himself. Add Lafcadio Hearn a century before, and you can see that
this city glittered with embryo literary lights. The *Times-Star* had
Clark P. Firestone, who wrote *Sycamore Shores* (1936), and Frank
Grayson whose *Pioneers of Night Life on Vine Street* (1924) is now a
collector's item. Leo Hirtl, now city editor of the *Post & Times-Star,*
wrote a column called "The Seven Hills" for so many years that,
since he no longer writes it, readers assume he is dead. Any cub
reporter on the *Post & Times-Star* can squash that rumor fast. William
H. Hessler of Connersville, Indiana, though, is no longer with us. An
Enquirer editorial writer, Hessler made his mark on the city as one of
the most thoughtful writers to come down the pike. He started at the
Enquirer under William F. Wiley, who paid Hessler the free-lance
rate of $5 an editorial, but Wiley soon found it was cheaper to hire

Hessler fulltime. Another *Enquirer* writer, Dave Roberts, left his mark as a travel editor, but few travel editors covered the beats he covered. He handled the story of Fidel Castro's takeover. After a quarter of a century on the *Enquirer,* Roberts retired. To what? To his three country weeklies in Batavia, Milford, and Loveland.

A writer you might have read only yesterday, but now retired, was Alfred Segal, who wrote the "Cincinnatus" column on the editorial page of the *Post & Times-Star.* Mr. Segal had been at the paper since Hector was a pup. Elsewhere in this book are one or two paragraphs extracted from his columns because, when it comes to describing "old" Cincinnati, no one can do it better than he. But his daily column was concerned with more than recollection. He was, in many ways, the conscience of Greater Cincinnati. He wrote of prisoners who needed jobs and babies who needed food. He wrote of how awful City Hall used to smell and gently reminded his readers that good government is no accident. He was not a crusty old prune but rather a pipe-smoking ancient who looked like a pixie. And he was not above sampling the sauce. For instance:

> ALL ABOUT DRINKING . . . Oh, Cincinnatus himself each morning takes a couple of glasses of sherry wine to stimulate his aging mind. Yes, just now as he writes this, he thanks sherry wine for alerting his mind to this column.
>
> Cincinnatus comes to this confession upon hearing in a letter from Marietta Camille of 808 Elberon Avenue, who is saying, "A little good wine in moderation . . . thank God for grapes . . . is good, but until alcohol is abolished entirely, our young and old will fast be destroying the prospect of keeping America the benevolent country for all mankind . . . God save America."
>
> Yes, dear lady, Cincinnatus long ago quit drinking whiskey. Whiskey? What for, except to direct the mind toward wrong ways . . .

On the other hand, sherry wine or no, Mr. Segal was not considered flaming youth zooming along the highway.

> THE WAY WE DRIVE . . . Cincinnatus hears about this from Mr. Joseph Heitzler of 1870 Hanfield Street. He is telling Cincinnatus in this letter of his ". . . there's one thing that disturbs me very much. It is this: you often mention that you drive 15–20 miles an hour. I agree with you that there is too much speed in the world today, but on the other hand, going too slow is dangerous. I am very much afraid that some morning you are going to get in front of the wrong guy, and bam! he will pile into you and knock you right off the road. And that may be the end of good old Cincinnatus."
>
> But, yes, Mr. Heitzler, so far the swifter drivers have re-

spected Cincinnatus enough just to try to blow him out of
their ways with their horns. And the other morning another
cautious driver stopped beside Cincinnatus and shouted:
"You're a good driver . . . going as slowly as you do. That's
me, too. Thanks."

Lest all of you think that Greater Cincinnati newsmen are sipping
sherry wine and racing slow-motion along expressways, think again.
Some of the reporters tinker with yesterdays, some tinker with todays,
and one even tinkers with ugliness. Not that anyone goes around
Cincinnati endorsing ugliness, but if there is ugliness, it will be
reported, and usually by a soft-spoken man named Arthur Darack, art
and book editor of the *Enquirer*. The ugliness mentioned here illus-
trates that although Mr. Darack can get as high-falutin' as any artist
(he writes book reviews for the *Saturday Review*), and does not
turn his back on the intellectual (he is an associate professor who
lectures on twentieth-century music as well as esthetics at the College-
Conservatory of Music), he is a working newsman when it comes to
art in Cincinnati. In 1965 he took one look at the American Ugly
Exhibition, a tongue-in-cheek display in Mount Adams, and, in part,
wrote:

> My favorite item in the show . . . is a wildly garish jukebox.
> It has a bright, squat, confident evil look about it . . . Perhaps
> it is a poor thing, but it is our own. Ugliness, as somebody
> said about sin, is very much a function of the eye of the be-
> holder.
>
> Most of the exhibit . . . is merely pathetic, like the wall
> hangings made out of flowered linoleum or the cheap paint-
> ings and the other attempts at decoration. Some [exhibits]
> seem merely innocuous or simply irrevelant. Irrevelance is
> not necessarily ugly. A child can answer irrevelantly and be
> altogether winning; so can a pretty girl . . .
>
> So long as Cincinnati tolerates the ugliness of its riverfront,
> its smugness and intolerance, its wrathful, strident insularity
> or, by contrast, its lethargy . . . we [will] have prize ugly
> exhibits.

As you can see, Mr. Darack is one of the people to read if you wish to
know which art gallery is exhibiting what—and whether or not the
exhibition is really worth the visit.

Musically in the *Enquirer*, Henry S. Humphreys is the man of the
hour. He learned his trade under his College of Music teacher, Dr.
Sidney C. Durst, who used to steal into Music Hall when no one
was about and play Bach on the 50-foot-wide and 30-foot-deep organ
whose pipes reached 60 feet straight up. Musically in the *Post &
Times-Star*, Mrs. Eleanor Bell, who is no bigger than a minute, is the

lady of the hour, and she suffers from unladylike but professional perfect pitch. Lady or not, she is not afraid to slug it out verbally with an audience, orchestra, or conductor. She floored the conductor of the May Festival one year when she reported dourly that "he failed to lead the chorus in a forceful manner." But she is forever the pint-size Pollyanna in pursuit of excellence. "All in all," she concluded, after shooting the Festival conductor down, "the concert last night was one of the weakest Festival openings I can recall, which"—her Pollyanna rising to the foreground—"may be taken as a hopeful sign for the rest of the program." Now and then, as Mr. Darack does, she looks over the galleries and attempts to make sense out of the occasionally senseless:

> Pat Kelly's welded art metal sculpture occupies Flair House's first-floor gallery, and the most eye-catching of the lot is the couple in the rusty iron bed. Most of Kelly's figures are female and high fashion, and the artist is adept at catching the 1965 postures and attitudes of expensively draped ladies. Most of them are burnished to a fine glow and on two of them Kelly has applied paint. This struck me as being less than successful.

E. B. Radcliffe, of the *Enquirer,* is a man of such well-defined tastes where the theater is concerned, and has been at it so long, that some national companies have the uneasy feeling that he personally invented the theater west of the Alleghenies. Readers aware of his distinct likes and dislikes have their own way of reacting to his opinions. If he proclaims one play good, some of his readers wouldn't go near it if you paid them, and other readers couldn't wait to get there. Thus, when you hear a Cincinnatian say, "Well, Radcliffe says . . . ," he will be saying it one way or the other: with a tone implying either that Mr. Radcliffe couldn't review his way out of a paper bag, or that God has spoken. There are no middle-of-the-road readers where Mr. Radcliffe is concerned. He calls the shots as he sees them, and will take sass from no theatrical advertising man.

Another such writer is book reviewer Edward Carberry of the *Post & Times-Star.* After years of reviewing movies as well as books—sitting through more reels of black-and-white, technicolor, narrow, wide, and *real* wide screen pap than a mortal should be forced to endure—Mr. Carberry now toils only with books, a toil which at times he finds as uninspiring as a grade-B movie. Each day publishers flood his desk with books, and each day, with quiet desperation, he palms the less fortunate books off on whoever will haul them out of his sight. Children's books—*Look at Jane! See Jane! Hello, Jane!*—do not warm the cockles of his heart, but mature books do. Thus, between Carberry and Darack, most of the better books get reviewed here, and as for the rest—well, movies aren't better than ever, either.

While sports writers are considered in more detail in Chapter 15, the one detail not covered there is that Pat Harmon, sports editor of the *Post & Times-Star*, doesn't have to fill up the athletic stadiums by writing prose that stimulates the fans. He could fill up stadiums with his own offspring.

The business pages of both newspapers here are equal to, and, at times, better than, the business pages you'll read in New York and Chicago. Business news can be drab if not well written. Ralph Weiskittel, the business writer for the *Enquirer*, and his counterpart on the *Post & Times-Star*, William Styles, are not drab writers. Stereotyped handouts find no home on their pages. Much to the despair of press agents, Weiskittel and Styles dig deeper, ask questions they shouldn't, and the result is a daily serving of hard business news.

Because Greater Cincinnatians are television-oriented (they can't name the Supreme Court justices, perhaps, but quiz them on Peyton Place and they can talk for hours!), television writers hold powerful sway over their readers. When the *Times-Star* was still going, its television writer was Charlton Wallace, a cheerful soul who loved children and dogs but hated bad television with a passion. Now that the *Times-Star* has expired, Mr. Wallace is back with his true love: writing a bridge column for the *Post & Times-Star*.

The conscience of radio in Cincinnati—if radio has a conscience—is Magee Adams, who has been writing a radio column for the *Enquirer* more years than even he cares to recall. There is little to review on radio these days because radio has turned itself into some kind of a jukebox, but Mr. Adams, undaunted, keeps trying, and praises where he can. When FM-radio was first introduced and considered a boon to broadcasting, Mr. Adams was one of the first in the country to recognize its possible worth. Afterwards, and with melancholy, he was one of the first also to recognize its gradual demise. Constant radio listening would have long since unhinged anyone less dedicated, but he keeps plugging away, writing a gentle radio column that is filled with one-part hope and one-part gloom.

James Devane used to be the television writer for the *Enquirer* for years; now Martin Hogan, Jr., handles the chore, which, he admits, bewilders him because he can't take the tube too seriously. He wrote:

> Have you ever been admonished to "get serious"? Like get serious about your studies, your job, your life? Well, I have, so I know the feeling. Some irritated fans are writing to admonish [me] that I am taking all that serious business of prime time just too lightly. Most of the communiqués just offer a difference of opinion. But some get downright nasty— like the love letter from the lady who reminded me that I'm

stupid. And who knows that better than I do? Meanwhile, I'd like to know what there is to get serious about?

Should we take seriously the horrible drivel of Peyton Place? All right, so it's clean. Big deal. But it's still lousy. It's like dirty jokes. Some are funny and some are just dirty. Should we get serious over Petticoat Junction, Moment of Truth, Beverly Hillbillies? Should we get serious about Gilligan's Island? Are we supposed to take seriously situation comedies that are funny only to the guys who are pouring the junk at you, telling you to buy their product, and then get nice and fat while the ratings go even higher?

I'll get serious over something that's well done—situation comedy, soap opera, musical show, drama. I'll get serious about Shindig and Hullabaloo. They're both well-constructed shows. I can get serious over The Man from U.N.C.L.E. and The Rogues.

I'll get deadly serious about anything that isn't an affront to the intelligence and taste of all of us. But I don't see why any of us should get serious about the type of non-entertainment that's a slap in the face to us midwestern nincompoops who aren't supposed to know any better.

And to prove that Mr. Hogan *can* get serious about television, the morning after a beauty pageant he glared at his typewriter and wrote:

This morning, students, we're going to raise our blood pressure over a hallowed, revered, and respected American institution—the beauty pageant.

Now, I like girls plenty. And I certainly enjoy the sight of a shapely lass who nicely fills out her bathing suit . . .

But do you know what? When you take 15 girls all under 24 years old and ask them to parade up and down a runway in a packed auditorium with millions more watching, it's like judging a cattle contest!

Pow! And on and on he went. Television may not be good, but, fortunately, the Cincinnati television writers are. Even if you don't have a television set, they make good reading.

Mary Wood, who writes the television column for the *Post & Times-Star*, has been in every facet of broadcasting and done everything but change tower lights. She is a usually cheerful lady with a Kentucky drawl, who is on a first-name basis even with those in broadcasting who are nameless. Like Mr. Hogan, she enjoys television, keeps looking for good programs, but the way television has been going, she has been looking more but enjoying it less. Now and then, utterly bored by the tube, she writes of other matters: like taking grandchildren to Coney Island, which was certainly more satisfying than listening to television's canned laughter. The laughter of grandchildren is real.

"No grandmother," she wrote, "should count herself a member of the club until she has visited the Zoo and Coney Island accompanied by at least two grandchildren. Any less and she's chickened out."

Her adventures at the amusement park made better reading than a rehash of a rerun would have made. "Since the Teddy Bear is the first roller coaster I've ever been really happy on," she wrote, "I was reluctant to leave it, particularly when Betsy, 3½, announced that the Wild Mouse was more her speed."

Taking her other grandchild, five-year-old Dougie, on Lost River—Coney's Tunnel of Love—raised knotty problems.

> Dougie and I embarked on the Lost River alone except for an amorous young couple in the seat ahead, locked in tender embrace.
>
> "Why is he kissing her?" asked Dougie at the top of his lungs.
>
> "Because they're friends," I explained frantically . . .

But Mary does not forsake her broadcasting chores too often, and readers don't blame her when she does. Most of them feel exactly the same. When Mary Wood attended the opera, everyone in Cincinnati knew what she had gone through. They had gone through it at one time or another themselves, and she was their spokesman.

> For some obscure reason—just lucky, I guess—each time my friend Bud Thomas and I seek to immerse ourselves in culture at the Zoo Opera, it turns out to be the hottest night of the summer. This probably accounts for the fact that I've seen the third acts of almost *no* operas . . .
>
> When we attended a beautiful performance of *The Tales of Hoffmann* the mercury, as usual, had reached an all-time summer high and the Opera Pavilion could be best described as a large Turkish bath with fully-dressed patrons.
>
> On stage, which had to be hotter than the pavilion, poet Hoffmann and friends were quaffing liberally in the neighborhood saloon as Hoffmann sang his heart out about his ill-fated amours.
>
> "What is this you've gotten me into?" I asked Bud. "Peyton Place set to music?"
>
> . . . We spent the third act at the Playboy Club, which is air-cooled, as are the Bunnies. If Hoffmann had his wits about him, he'd have been there, too!

When not attending opera at the Playboy Club or explaining smooching to a grandchild, Mary Wood minds the store: which is, of course, watching television until she's glassy-eyed with tedium. Watching a commercial one day aroused her dander. She stared glumly at the picture tube as Prince Charming appeared in the commercial to awaken Sleeping Beauty. In her column she asked: "But does he implant the traditional kiss on Sleeping Beauty? Indeed not. He hands her a can of hair spray."

Having written as much for broadcasting as anyone writing for local stations or the networks today, Mary Wood thought a minute and, with fiendish glee, wrote: "It boggles the imagination to think what artistic heights could be scaled by using the Very Grim Fairy Tales to hawk such mundane products as soap, detergent, shampoo, and so on!"

She proceeded to do just that. Her readers that afternoon were treated to her version of commercials: Goldilocks in a Lady Clairol pitch, the *Hansel and Gretel* witch touting Betty Crocker products, Cinderella peddling—of course!—corn plasters. And for a Planned Parenthood Association public-service announcement, the Old Lady Who Lived in a Shoe obliged.

"But," she wrote, warming to the task, "what I consider the absolute peak commercial of the entire lot, I saved for my final flight of fancy. Haven't you guessed? It's Old Mother Hubbard starring in a dog food commercial!"

Her final thought: "I don't know why I'm wasting my time writing a TV column when I could be making a fortune on Madison Avenue."

Two columnists who write about the city in general, or about whatever strikes their fancy that day, are Si Cornell of the *Post & Times-Star* and Frank Weikel of the *Enquirer*. Both are well-grounded, no-nonsense reporters who have labored long enough in the city rooms of their respective papers and thus do not pretend to be poets or to razzle-dazzle with high-flown phrases. They are reporters first and columnists second—and their assignment is the odds and ends of the city. Because both men know people in high and low places as well as every place in between, their columns paint a picture of the city that would otherwise never reach the canvas. Where else, for instance, could you learn that some of Cincinnati's cops are getting fed up and seeking police jobs elsewhere? And where else, for instance, could you learn that Judge C. Watson Hover has a perfect sense of direction? Plant him anywhere and he can instantly tell where north is. Between the two of them, Cornell and Weikel supply readers with so many conversation pieces that barbers have a hard time getting a word in edgewise.

At the moment the *Enquirer* is one up on the *Post & Times-Star*, but it's not the latter's fault; the fault is in the scarcity of talent. The *Post & Times-Star* has no column that traffics in local humor, whimsy, and occasional wildness. Such writers are rare and, anyway, humor is a chimerical gathering of words that not everyone can gather. Few papers have humorists these days, and sometimes when they do, the humorists are apt to bewilder the editors. The *Enquirer,* happily, has a working humorist on tap, a humorist who might even be considered the last of his tribe. And, as he would say, if you will all lie down in a neat circle (watch out for the wet spots), we will take a fond look at Ollie James.

He is a huge and highly organized man who works at a huge and highly disorganized desk, or at least it is said the desk exists. All one can see are mounds of paper: scraps of notes, memos, clips, and a bunch of other things that Mr. James says he will one day get around to reading. Mr. James writes the "Innocent Bystander" column that has appeared in the *Enquirer* for more than a quarter of a century. When not doing that, he writes editorials and helps out around the place. He is so well known as Ollie James the humorist that he lives a clean life, is kind to cats, and says that buttermilk is the only nectar. The price of fame is, at times, prohibitive. He is not an old man. He admits to being "twenty-nine and holding, as we space experts say."

His daily columns are labeled Monday Morning Mess, Tuesday Tripe, Wednesday Whoppers, Thursday Thurps, Friday Frivolities, Saturday Scrapple, and Sunday Scrunch. They are usually filled with jollies sent in by readers, editorial stands that teeter a little, and personal observations that search your soul or whatever else needs looking into. For instance, "People are forgetting the horrors of the last war. Somebody broke into a warehouse in Memphis and stole three cases of C rations."

Hiding behind the editorial "we," Mr. James has a fabulous sense of destiny ("We've just determined what keeps America going. Unplanned parenthood and planned obsolescence."), is terribly modest ("All we know about cooking is that water and flour make paste and you should never put sugar in cornbread."), is sober as a judge ("We never get crocked. The peril that we might start writing sensible things is just too dangerous to contemplate."), is an astute observer of the passing parade ("Maybe the government is going in for direct action . . . A sign in Washington said, 'Support Mental Health or I'll Kill You.'"), and when it comes to children, he is all heart ("School's on, so watch out for children. They may be driving the car behind you.").

Though he did stop girl-watching one year long enough to run for President, his interest in animal life—and the Ollie James Piece Corps—is enduring:

> We do not know whether to set aside a whale-watching division of our Girl Watchers, but it has been our observation that you can't watch two things very well at the same time. However, whales are easier to watch, and if some of our

members are experiencing failing eyesight we might transfer them to this new assignment.

So far we've done well because to our knowledge not a single whale has been killed in this vicinity for a number of years. If you see one, say, "Nice whaley, nice whaley," and feed it some plankton. If it is a friendly whale and wags its tail, stay out of its way—they wag pretty hard—and do not try to milk the whale. You could make a whale of a mistake.

Once, in a daring display of versatility, Mr. James drew a picture of a mouse and ran it in his column, but he was instantly filled with second thoughts:

This worried us a great deal because we had drawn a navel on the mouse and we couldn't remember whether a mouse was supposed to have a navel. Then we took a look at our *objet d'art* when it appeared in the *Enquirer* and saw we'd forgotten to put a curly tail on the mouse. We *always* put a curly tail on a mouse when we draw one. It gives it a nice touch of elegance . . .

Mr. James came to the *Enquirer* from Lexington and Louisville, and still lives across the river in a place he calls Bull Frog Hollow, which has become as famous as Stephen Leacock's Old Brewery Bay. Mr. James is a night owl, better known to the *Enquirer*'s night watchman than to many who work in the city room. He wanders in around two or three in the morning, takes one look at that pile of papers where his desk is supposed to be, and moves to another desk to write what needs to be written: a completely logical editorial or a completely illogical look at the world around him. Then, when the city is waking up, he takes one last look at his desk, wonders if it's really there at all, leaves the *Enquirer* building, goes home, and drinks buttermilk.

14

Greater Cincinnati restaurants offer everything from greasy hamburgers to snails. In earlier times, when this city was more German, German restaurants were everywhere. But of those early restaurants, only Grammer's and Mecklenburg's Gardens remain. Recently a new German restaurant has arrived on the scene: Old Vienna, at Ninth and Plum Streets. So Cincinnatians can still get their fill of sauerbraten, wiener schnitzel, beef roulade, Thüringer bratwurst, potato pancakes, and potato dumplings; and wash the offering down with steins of beer, light or dark. Nonetheless, it has been a long time since the Baker's Singing Society wet its whistle at Grammer's at Liberty and Walnut Streets. Grammer's is German, but the neighborhood now is not. Mecklenburg's Gardens, 302 East University Avenue, is in a neighborhood that is changing, too. Grammer's began in 1872 with Anton Grammer as its first *gasthaubesitzer*. Mecklenburg's Gardens began in 1865, with Louis Mecklenburg in charge there. Al Matthes' Old Vienna, downtown, though a johnny-come-lately at that location, has German fare equal to the other two German restaurants. Thus, all three seem to have lingered through the years like rare and mellow wine.

Of course, not *every* Greater Cincinnati restaurant can be listed here, for several good reasons: (1) there are too many, (2) many of them are too similar, (3) others serve terrible food, and (4) just as mom-and-pop groceries do, a few open and close so fast you hardly have time for dessert. It is not the purpose of this chapter to recommend this restaurant over that one. Each Cincinnatian has his own preference. We wish only to reflect the variety of these preferences by showing the variety of restaurants in the area. The writer of this book is not a gourmet.

In Cincinnati, the Italian influence has outlasted the German. Pizza parlors abound! Some are chains, some are not. Pasquale's is one of the chains. At last count, there were thirty-three Pasquale Pizza Carryouts. Their pizzas range from peewee to large, and can be covered with anything your heart desires: Italian sausage, anchovies, bacon, pepperoni, onions, or you name it. For more formal Italian cooking—spaghetti, ravioli, mostacciolo, manicotti, and even baked lasagna—Cincinnatians out in the valley go to the Wishing Well on Reading Road, where Reading, Ohio, and Cincinnati touch. Or, downtown, they go to Caproni's most elegant restaurant on Main Street, where, if they're not careful, they emerge smelling like a garlic factory. Or, their pasta headquarters might be Scotti's Italian Restaurant, 919 Vine Street. Scotti's used to be on Court Street, moved later to a Ninth Street basement, but now is in its own amiable building on Vine Street. But no one goes to Valerio's anymore, a thought that strikes melancholy in the true spaghetti-eater's heart. Valerio's used to be on the second floor at 114 East Sixth Street. Mary Valerio, daughter of founder Alfredo Valerio, said the restaurant was upstairs because "Daddy always thought a restaurant had to be on the second floor if it was to be traditionally Italian." Eugenie Cardinal Pacelli ate dinner at Valerio's and then went on to become Pope Pius XII. Mr. Valerio used to entertain his dinner guests with quotes from Dante's *Divine Comedy*.

Not *all* spaghetti in Greater Cincinnati is Italian. Si Cornell reported in the *Post & Times-Star*:

> "GREEK SPAGHETTI," said the sign in front of 104-year-old Arnold's Grill. What's that? "Bacon cooked in butter as the base for the sauce," said George Christos, co-owner, who is about as Greek as an American can get. "No Italian tomato sauce," added his brother, Jim. "Mother made it so well," said George. "We just tell our Irishmen how to cook it," said Jim . . .

There's the Balkan House, 8032 Blue Ash Avenue, for shishkebab. When Cincinnatians want to be posh, they try the Fox & Crow, 9769 Montgomery Road, where they can dine and dance, too. Zimmer's, in Oakley, has European fare. Lenhardt's, in Clifton, cooks Hungarian. For oriental food, to name only a few restaurants, there's the Formosa on West Court Street, Wong's on East Sixth Street, the Kon-Tiki in Pleasant Ridge, and the Mandarin where U.S. 25 and U.S. 42 intersect. Pick a month with an R in it, and the Central Oyster House on East Fourth Street is open. Cincinnati has more chili parlors than you have Tums for; some are good, some are greasy, but the Empress Chili Parlor at 234 East Fifth Street is the cleanest, healthiest, busiest, as well as one of Cincinnati's first. It used to be next door to the Gayety Burlesque Theater on Vine Street when the Gayety was called the Empress, hence the chili parlor's name. Ten thousand Greeks seem to work at the Empress, seem terribly angry about something, yell at one another a lot, but are nice to customers, fast and efficient, and serve the best Coney Island sandwiches in town. Actually, for *real* shouting among the hired hands, consider Izzy Kadetz's Kosher Restaurant, now on Elm Street. Compared to Izzy Kadetz's, the Empress Chili Parlor's rush hour is as hushed as the public library. Romantics who want to eat in a streetcar go to Al Lederle's Trolley Tavern on River Road. It's really a streetcar, but since Mr. Lederle added what he calls "The Flying Bridge," at times the beautiful streetcar is hard to see. Cincinnati's smallest restaurant at this writing is the Red Rooster at the corner of two downtown alleys: North and New Streets. They say "rush hour" there is anytime more than four people order lunch within five minutes of each other.

When gambling was in its heyday, the restaurants across the river in Kentucky boomed. But Kentucky has settled down, Beverly Hills went out of business, and many of the lesser eateries folded, too. Still, when Cincinnatians hanker for the "good old days," they go to the Lookout House on Dixie Highway. An ornate restaurant filled with more memories than a grand jury could ever find, the Lookout House seats more than 1200 in its eight separate dining rooms. A visit there transports Cincinnatians back to the shadowy days when the dice were as sizzling as the steaks and when the tables were covered with green fuzz. Half the time Cincinnatians feel they're in a tasteful speakeasy and keep looking over their shoulders for cops to raid the place. It never happens. Upstairs is the Little Club: capacity 145, postage-stamp tables, and a ceiling that rolls back to let the moon peep in. The real action is downstairs in a hippodrome called the Casino, which holds 550 people. The service is fast, and the roast prime ribs that go by are works of art. The Lookout House has something nice for everybody, but no one brings his dice. That craze has passed.

One over-the-river spot that hasn't a gambling pedigree is Carl Wooten's Town and Country, also on Dixie Highway. Olga Wooten, its housemother, possesses a grandmother's charm and decorating magic, both of which she lavishes by the bucketful on the restaurant. The sky could fall down and she would still go on, rearranging some of her dining rooms the way Mrs. Ralph Ross in Cheviot keeps rearranging her living room. Both women, being cheerfully preoccupied with interior decorating, are forever wondering if they've done the right thing. Over the years, Cincinnati's answer to Mrs. Wooten and to Mrs. Ross is that such ladies can do no wrong. For one thing, Mrs. Wooten has done almost as much for the apple business as Johnny Appleseed did. Children get a big kick out of seeing an apple tree growing smack dab in the middle of one of her dining rooms, filling the entire restaurant with sweet fragrance. The fragrance is real and so is the apple tree. But don't get the idea the Town and Country is a tearoom truck stop where you drown in chintz. It's one of Greater Cincinnati's better restaurants. Men like her combination plate: broiled lobster tail *and* a petit filet mignon!

The Dixie Highway, on which the Lookout House and the Town and Country are located, is a wide road that used to be much busier —and more scary—before Intrastate 75 lessened its traffic load. At one time, before the Intrastate was a reality, it was the main drag strip to Louisville and Lexington's horse country. True, the road contains some ticky-tacky houses and look-alike apartments, but it also contains a few horse farms. The *real* horse crowd has headquarters at the White Horse Tavern on the highway. On Derby Day the White Horse bar is as jammed as the Brown Hotel in Louisville. But there are no Damon Runyon characters. The menu at the White Horse has thirty-eight *different* entrees, everything from fried chicken to Maryland soft-shell crab. Outside one of its many dining rooms, huge rocks are poised inches from a diner's plate. The restaurant, it seems, has not only expanded west along Dixie Highway, but south as well, straight into the side of a hill. It's safe there, though. No landslides. Ben Castelman would permit nothing to upset his guests; thus, the White Horse Tavern, except on crowded Derby Days, is another place many Cincinnatians can take their mothers-in-law.

Cincinnati has several clubs like the Playboy Club—and it has a Playboy Club, too. Some of these clubs are private, some are not, but all the waitresses are leggy and bosomy creations. Also, some of the clubs last and some don't, which is why we'll not go into the subject. No need to describe the Playboy Club. See one and you've seen them all. There are some restaurants Cincinnatians will take their children to, but the Playboy Club isn't one of them. When Bob Graham is not around to make guests feel welcome—he's the den mother of the Bunnies—Jack Keating will be.

Although some Cincinnatians feel it is essential to go into Kentucky to find a good restaurant, or to stay on this side of the river to accomplish the same mission, it is possible by prowling the river bank itself for Cincinnatians to discover several interesting eateries. One is at 4609 Kellogg Avenue. It's the Four Seasons Marina, operated in the grand manner of the Vernon Manor's Forum Room. Another, if in the summer Cincinnatians can stand the whine of automobile tires on the steel-meshed floor of the Central Highway Bridge next door (the cars sound like swarms of disenchanted bees), is Captain Hook's Restaurant. It operates in an emasculated riverboat tied forever, Cincinnatians hope, at the foot of Ludlow Street. Chef Bob Christian operates in a galley the size of a broom closet from which come beautiful steaks and gallons of beautiful bean soup. Maître d' Wayne Weber will confide at the drop of a hat that the dining room is the former deck room. Should anyone get sauced at the bar, he's really where the steamboat's engines used to be. History along the Ohio River has been reduced to a gurgle, no keelboat men go around biting ears off strangers, but these riverside restaurants have a charm all their own: the charm of watching the river, a great wet mural that never stands still. And by night, the view from these restaurants is spectacular and glittery. Another remodeled steamboat restaurant is Sycamore Shores, which Pete and Alan Hahn operate at 7445 Forbes Street in Fernbank. It has two dining rooms because it also serves as headboat for a 75-boat yacht harbor. One dining room is for fresh-water sailors who aren't dressed to the teeth; the other is for landlubbers who are.

Another spectacular view of the city—and one that's scarcely two years old—is from the bar atop the Holiday Inn in the Queens Gate area just west of downtown. That's the Holiday Inn that keeps watch on the Intrastate 75 traffic that speeds out of the north and gets tangled up in the Third Street Distributor. The buffet up there in the sky is bountiful, and, as in the Playboy Club, the waitresses are bountiful, too. They are called Little Foxes. Cincinnati males can become instant authorities on such leggy wildlife because, whenever the guest sits down, along comes a Little Fox and pins a badge on him, making him a deputy game warden. Bunnies and Little Foxes, logically enough, are perpetually out of season.

If Cincinnati had a "jet set," it would use the Vernon Manor Hotel on Oak Street for headquarters. The Vernon Manor's 400 Room gets more ornate each time a stray wanders in to have a few. John Corcoran is the manager of the hotel, which houses—along with radio station WZIP, Uncle Al's Penthouse, and several old ladies left over from another era—one of the most elegant dining rooms in Greater Cincinnati: The Forum. When a guest gets a table by the window on a summer day, he can not only eat mock turtle soup laced with sherry but gaze out the window at the girls preening themselves at the Vernon Manor Swim Club. The Forum is neither stuffy nor highbrow, its staff doesn't sneer when someone orders beer instead of wine, and the waiters go out of their way to make sure children are served properly. The 400 Room across the lobby is a high-styled watering hole where each noon an assortment of executives wet their whistles. At times it has the sound of a rich man's discount house. Everyone is either going to Europe or working a deal. Should a local go in for a drink and not keep his head on his shoulders, someone will sell him a new car, a new suit, an apartment building, or a Chinese hand laundry. A good rule, they say, in the 400 Room is never to have that eighteenth martini.

While trafficking with the posh, there's always the Gourmet Room, that glass bubble atop the Terrace Hilton Hotel. But don't let its name frighten you. The sky may be the limit at the Gourmet Room, but Cincinnatians in the know can still get a fancy five-course French dinner for under eight bucks. And it will be cooked in the same grand manner used by Chef Vito Lecaputo to turn out the most expensive dish. Although it's not really the place the high school crowd gathers for Pepsi Colas and chili (Maître d' Henri Guglielmi might look pained if *that* happened), nonetheless the setting is stunning, the view of Cincinnati is stunning, and if you order à la carte the bill can stun you, too. But a philosophical Cincinnatian takes this viewpoint: "Where else these days can I suffer so elegantly? The Gourmet Room has a six-foot-high, six-foot-wide bronze chandelier that once hung in London's Army and Navy Club, a gift to the Club from Queen Victoria. Where else can I see Regency Period wall sconces from the Chateau Vistaero in France right next to an eighteenth-century terra cotta bust of Marie Antoinette?" Certainly the menu doesn't send Cincinnatians back to high school French. It's what is called Anglicized French. Anyway, if a Cincinnatian chooses not to dine at the Gourmet Room (let's be honest: his rich uncle left him out of the will), he can still enjoy its atmosphere. Many people don't go up to eat; they booze it up in the adjacent Panorama Room, which has chess sets and looks like a library but in reality is a high-class bar. Same stunning view. They can sit in comfortable easy chairs and watch the city's nightly twilight drama. Beautiful, beautiful. True, the sign atop the Kroger Building disturbs a few esthetic patrons, but when luck is with them, they can get lit up before the sign does.

Pigall's is another French restaurant. It's street-level at 127 West Fourth Street, and though it's prices are a shade lower, Cincinnatians hardly equate it with the B/G. Maurice Gorodesky's cooking has made Pigall's one of *the* places in the city—and indeed, in the nation—to eat. Every time this master chef turns around, he wins another award from *Holiday* magazine. Some of his specialties are *crevettes à la nage, beuree blanc, soufflé de capon,* and truffles. His menu is strictly in French. Before opening his own Pigall's, Mr. Gorodesky was the chef at the Maisonette and won the *Holiday* magazine award for that restaurant, too. The Pigall luncheon menu is a lot less expensive than the dinner menu (that's a hint), but there's no shading the quality. Simply put, whenever a Cincinnatian sits down to dine at Pigall's, he's in for a beautiful experience.

The Maisonette, of course, is *the* restaurant as far as many Cincinnatians are concerned. Its tagalong, La Normandie, is operated by the same outfit, the tab is less, and the food, though not offered in the same variety as the Maisonette, is still well worth the price of admission and usually head and shoulders above the tab. The Maisonette used to be downstairs on Walnut Street, La Normandie used to be in the same building but at street level; then, along came the wrecker's ball, and now both are on Sixth Street. No matter. Wherever the Maisonette operates, it operates with elegance. Lee Comisar and his brother Mike see to that; and so do the dozens of dark-suited gentlemen who are the Maisonette's floorwalkers. About the only way Cincinnatians can get a poor meal there is to bring it in a lunchbox. As at Pigall's, lunches cost less than dinners, but Pierre Adrian serves up both with the same subtle touches that make eating at the Maisonette an event. Some believe the *tournedos Wellington*—two charming petit filet mignons served with burgundy wine sauce and foie gras—are items of joy, but each Maisonette regular has his own item that brings gladness to his heart and turns him into a high-tipping Pollyanna. The menu is French with English subtitles. Because Mr. Gorodesky of Pigall's and Mr. Comisar of the Maisonette are both members of the Confrérie des Chevaliers du Tastevin, a sensitive sipper can order a bottle of bubbly from either and feel secure in its excellence. Simply put, the Maisonette is equal to or better than any restaurant in New York City.

Not every downtown restaurant is French, though. Some Cincinnatians wouldn't touch snails with a ten-foot pole, and menus in French bore them. No matter. No strain. There's always the Colony around the corner from Fountain Square. Where the Colony Restaurant is now, the Bismarck Restaurant used to be. (A grand place that! When the Bismarck opened its doors there was a lavish ceremony: the key was taken to the river and tossed in because the Bismarck was never to close!) The Colony Restaurant carries on the old traditions of the Bismarck—and has added a few traditions of its own. Cincinnatians find the food most satisfying. The fare is standard and the price is nice. Also, the bar is nice, too. The Colony martinis do not have olives in them. No lemon twist, either. They're served with a hazel nut swimming in the sauce. At noon, the Colony is practically a businessmen's hangout, but many attractive secretaries eat there, too, adding to the décor. The Colony, according to most Cincinnatians, is a good place to take the whole family because the waitresses are as helpful as they are beautiful, which means fathers like the place a lot. There's also a Colony Restaurant (same outfit) in the Swifton Shopping Center. Some say it's one of the area's most stunning restaurants.

Two of Cincinnati's "men-only" restaurants aren't with us anymore. One was the Palace Café on East Sixth Street, and the other was the Wheel Café on Walnut Street. Both were functional chrome affairs that were open around the clock. They had the appearance of a free-lunch counter. After forty years of operating twenty-four hours a day, the Palace Café finally reduced its hours from 5 A.M. to 9 P.M., and shortly after that, closed for good. Then came the wrecker's ball and, *whammo!* both restaurants bit the dust. An *Enquirer* reporter wrote in 1919, the morning after prohibition took over the nation:

> Midnight in front of the Wheel Café resembled the Klondike days . . . Two hundred men, each carrying a bottle, a jug, or a case of liquor, thronged through the ballroom.
> Fisher Bachrach, the manager, stood on the table. Coatless, and with sleeves rolled up, he waved his left hand filled with bills of all denominations.
> "The town is dry," he announced. "Outside everybody," he commanded.
> And so at 12:01 o'clock, Cincinnati . . . passed into the shadow of the valley of ice cream and ginger ale.

The old Wheel Café lingered, blossomed again, regained its old magic, but came Core Redevelopment. Bob Jones Restaurant, across from the *Enquirer* building on Vine Street, is about the last of the tribe. The old Wheel and the Palace Cafés are memories. No longer do white-shirted men hustle behind the bar and the steam table, drawing beer and making sandwiches, exchanging small talk with wanderers of the night. Jorges on Fifth Street south of Vine Street is open, but it casts a different kind of spell. A cheery place, it can't be considered a "men-only" affair. Remember when it used to be the Purple Cow? Anyway, downtown Cincinnati after dark—when the theaters have emptied and the bars have closed—is little more than a ghost town. The only people are old men selling *Enquirers*, charwomen waiting for owl buses, cab drivers in front of the Terrace Hilton, a police car cruising by, and maybe somewhere a burglar or two.

While on the subject of sandwich shops, back in the early days of television, when paychecks were anemic, one of the reasons most workers survived was the commercial that showed the announcer raving about a Frisch's Big Boy sandwich, the double-decker hamburger. For each "live" commercial aired, Frisch's would send a half-dozen sandwiches, only one would be needed on the air, and the other five would be eaten by the studio help. At times there would be terrible arguments, especially when six studio men went in pursuit of five sandwiches. To exist in those troubled times, it was essential to be prop boy on at least one cooking show, get to lick the pans, and to borrow as many Big Boy sandwiches as could be got away with. And so today broadcasters look fondly upon Dave Frisch and his wonderful sandwiches. Television has come a long way since then, and so has Mr. Frisch. He started out as a boy working in his father's restaurant at 711 Freeman Avenue. Some Cincinnatians might recall that his father, Samuel Frisch, once ran Frisch's Stag Lunch in Norwood at Montgomery and Smith roads. Dave Frisch himself opened his first Big Boy drive-in on Central Parkway opposite the testing land—and *zoom!* away he went! Now there are 150 restaurants in the drive-in chain, most of them franchised, but twenty-three are actually owned by Frisch Restaurants, Incorporated. When Cincinnatians with children think of dining out, their thoughts turn to such drive-ins as Frisch's. The menus don't change much, but then, neither do the eating habits of children. Give a local child a choice—the Maisonette or Frisch's—and he'll pick the drive-in every time. Dave Frisch says:

"If Junior knocks over a sugar bowl or Susie has an accident with her Coke, it's no calamity."

Of course, to be fair, it's no calamity at the Maisonette, either, but when given a choice of calamity sites, most mothers pick a drive-in. When the little monsters have learned table manners, mothers can celebrate—relaxed—at the Maisonette, because the Maisonette loves children, too.

Another Cincinnati hamburger heaven is the White Castle, a chain that began in 1921, the same year Procter & Gamble introduced Chipso, but there's no connection. Now 101 White Castles are operating in the system Edgar Waldo Ingram started. They're in New York, Minneapolis, Miami, Detroit, and many other places. There are eight in Cincinnati, three in Covington.

Shuller's Wigwam, at the intersection of Hamilton Avenue (U.S. 27) and North Bend Road, is not really an Indian hangout, and the prices are so reasonable no one has ever been scalped. The Wigwam is an attractive restaurant with dozens of turns and corners and private rooms, some so posh you're sorry your shoes weren't shined. Sol Shuller, one of the brothers operating the place his father started in 1922, says the restaurant can serve 1000 guests at a time, which gives you an idea of Cincinnati's "neighborhood" restaurants. The Indian motif is, of course, carried out in its menu. Cocktails are listed under "Fire Water." Sandwiches are listed under "Heap Good." But don't let this bother you. It doesn't bother Cincinnati. The parking lot, by the way, can hold 305 cars—or horses—or whatever your tribe rides up on.

Another example of a neighborhood restaurant is the Tiny Cove on Harrison Avenue in Cheviot. It should be called the Great Big Cove, because, like the Wigwam, it keeps growing, too. It has a pair of bars that satisfy the needs of the soul, and a kitchen that's carpeted—of all things!—which means the waitresses don't have aching feet and don't growl at the chef. The Tiny Cove began years ago as a dinky, nonessential little neighborhood bar with soft lighting where young lovers could stare soulfully at one another. But now the young lovers are

middle-aged, married, and terribly in debt, and the soulful stares
have turned to stony looks. The Tiny Cove has come of age, too. It
serves standard fare. Western Cincinnatians like the steaks, and the
hostess isn't a bad dish herself. The restaurant is operated by a friendly
gentleman who used to operate a gasoline station, but before anyone
panics, note that his grandfather ran one of the finest restaurants in
France.

Still other Cincinnatians head straight to the nearest David's Buffet
when an evening on the town is in order. Smorgasbord is the main
attraction; and as far as Cincinnati cares, need more be said?

Then, there's the Carrousel. It's just about everything: a smorgasbord of buildings. In 1965 two businessmen from Jenkintown, Pennsylvania, dropped in on this combination motel-restaurant-and-play-
ground via helicopter, but a car gets most Cincinnatians there just as
easily. The Carrousel is basically an inn, a Tony Elsaesser (he operates
the Cricket, Wiggins, and the Cincinnatian Hotel downtown) complex
of motel and convention facilities, restaurants, health clubs, swimming
pools, and other assorted mishmosh out Reading Road. A. J. Elsaesser,
called Allie, is its manager; retired merry-go-round horses are its
fetish; and Robert Harpenau is labeled "the driving force of its design." Harpenau, it must be noted, is the builder who mass-produced
acres of suburbia in the western reaches of Cincinnati which, thanks
to his architectural background, are a cut above those that most of
Cincinnati has acquired. He did right by the Carrousel, too. At the
moment, the Carrousel complex has more convention and meeting
space than any motel in Ohio. Also, it's recommended by the *Mobil
Travel Guide* as an "honor inn," one of the six best motels in the
nation. But do Cincinnatians go there to eat? Sure. It's a family place,
too. The La Ronde is the heart of the matter. The La Ronde main
dining room can match the décor of any other Greater Cincinnati
dining room—and when it comes to serving up a feast, the La Ronde
chef can match skillets with the best of them. Just as at the Vernon
Manor's Forum, fathers can sit in the summer at a window table, keep
the kids under control, and not miss the pool outside, where leggy
young things are on display. If there are no leggy attractions, he can
always excuse himself and go sulk in the La Ronde cocktail lounge.
Some Cincinnatians look at the Carrousel this way: it's equal to the
most lavish Florida watering hole and a lot closer.

A little farther north in that same general area is the Howard
Johnson Motor Inn, which, unlike most Howard Johnson units, breaks
away from sameness. It, too, is operated by the Elsaesser clan. It tries
to achieve the Hawaiian motif; the Mai-Tai bar serves drinks that
are almost Hawaiian, and on some nights the guests can sit around
the pool to see Hawaiian hula work. Children get a kick out of

watching, too, but after they age a bit, they enjoy the action a lot more.

Farther west—just about on the Indiana line—on U.S. 27 is the Rainbow Dinner House in Millville, Ohio. No hula dancers there. Mary Ruth Wooten runs the Millville restaurant, while her husband, Dick, runs its twin in Hamilton, Ohio. From the outside, the Rainbow Dinner House in Millville looks like something the cat dragged in, but that's the way with country restaurants. They can fool you. Inside is perfection—in the form of steaks that, some insist, melt in your mouth. Also, the Rainbow Dinner House in Millville is one of the few restaurants where now and then the house buys a drink. There are many fine restaurants out along the highways from Cincinnati, and there are some that shouldn't have happened. The Rainbow Dinner House is one of the finest.

The *pièce de résistance?* Izzy Kadetz's Kosher Restaurant, which we've mentioned before. Bear in mind that not *all* Cincinnatians drool when they think of Kadetz's, nor is it the only kosher restaurant the city has, but it's certainly a Cincinnati landmark. Just as some locals wouldn't go near snails, others won't go near Izzy's. But that's all right. So many Cincinnatians do, his place is always going full-blast. Kadetz's used to be on Central Avenue near Seventh Street, Core Redevelopment clobbered that location, and so he moved up to Elm Street near Ninth Street across from Jack Abrams' wonderful saloon, where radio announcers of yore used to get stoned. The move hasn't changed Kadetz's Kosher Restaurant one bit. He brought along not only the steam table and the pickle barrel, but all the shouts he hadn't shouted. No recorded music is needed to set the mood in his restaurant; Izzy sets the mood himself. He sets it with shouts. When he's not shouting at the help, he's shouting at the customers. The help and customers shout right back, all the shouts are friendly, and the din, at times, is beautiful.

More people eat lunch than dinner at Izzy's—if they can find room at a table, that is. The tables seat eight, the eight are usually strangers, but the atmosphere is friendly. Everyone talks to everyone else, commenting on the bowls of pickles, commenting on the shouts, or commenting on the size of the sandwiches. If Izzy has genius, and he has, his genius is demonstrated in each sandwich he serves. He has been described as the loud and angry master of the sandwich. This description is apt. He is heavy-handed with the roast beef, salami, corned beef, and pastrami. While waiting for your sandwich to be served, you can graze off cabbage and pickles, drink your fill of soup, eat potato pancakes, and listen to the noise. It has been said that at Izzy Kadetz's a sandwich is a full meal and a full meal is murder. Make up your own mind.

And so, you see, as stated at the start of this chapter, Cincinnati restaurants offer everything from hamburgers to snails—and in between. The choice is limitless!

But if you have doubts about which restaurants are which, do as many Cincinnatians do. Sit down and figure out what kind of food you'd like and how much you'd like to pay. Figure out how many will be in your group—two or two hundred. Toss in which side of town you prefer. And, for good measure, note the atmosphere you seek. Then, contact the Cincinnati Restaurant Association and dump the problem into their laps. That's the kind of problem they love to solve. But the Association will not suggest just one restaurant. Rather, it will suggest several that fit your needs, so you can make your own choice. The Association will no more tout you on this restaurant or steer you to that restaurant any more than this book will. But the Restaurant Association can open your eyes to possibilities you hadn't dreamed of.

After all, *this* is the beautiful secret about dining out in Cincinnati. Cincinnati is a family town, families eat out a lot, and they don't have to hock the family jewels to do it!

15

One thing that gets Cincinnati choked up is baseball. When in 1961, after a 21-year wait, the Cincinnati Reds—oldest club in baseball, first to have a farm system, and first to travel by air—won the National League pennant, Cincinnati went wild. Waite Hoyt, as much a baseball fixture as the club itself, said the crowd on Fountain Square that September night was bigger than on V-J Day. Jack McDonald wrote in the *Enquirer:*

> . . . Mr. Hoyt was right. It was something like V-J Day, and V-E Day, and all the other big days Cincinnati has known— all rolled into one. The raucous hilarity on the Square persisted until midnight [and was] reminiscent of an old-fashioned Halloween whoop-de-doo.

No book about this city would be complete without the story of its love affair with its baseball team. After all, weren't our Reds the first to have Ladies Day? And the first to play in a game that was televised? Ladies Day started here in 1876. The Reds were first televised in 1938. Also, the first time a wedding was held at home plate, it was held at ours. Before looking into the Cincinnati Reds though, consider the other sports that attract Cincinnatians.

Anyone for tennis? The Cincinnati Recreation Commission has fourteen divisions ranging from men's singles to junior boys. Championship playoffs are usually held at the Airport Playfield and at Withrow Courts. Don't forget that Cincinnati's most famous tennis player, Tony Trabert, now an executive with the Adler Company, still keeps his hand in. This Walnut Hills High School and University of Cincinnati athlete no longer plays competitive tennis, but now and then lucky

Cincinnatians can watch him in exhibition matches at the Cincinnati Tennis Club.

How about polo? Cincinnati has a polo club that plays about a dozen games a year in Blue Ash's Stark Field, Kenwood, and Cornell. The club plays teams from Louisville, Youngstown, Columbus, Dayton, Akron, Cleveland, and Beaver Valley; and at half-time, spectators can pet the horses.

There's archery, with its Ohio Valley Open. There's bridge, the indoor sport. The Cincinnati Bridge Association sponsors championships for men's and women's pairs, mixed pairs, open pairs, and open team. The association is connected with the American Contract Bridge League.

Cincinnatians can go to the dogs, and they do—5000 strong! That's how many attended the Cincinnati Kennel Club's forty-fourth annual dog show at the Cincinnati Gardens in 1965. How many dogs appeared? Nearly a thousand! The best in that show was a five-year-old terrier named Deko Druid, owned by Mr. and Mrs. T. H. Carruthers, famous for their wire-haired terriers. On the other hand, there's Grant McCauley. He raises Samoyeds—Siberian sled dogs that weigh seventy-five pounds each. He has a half dozen of them; and each week they eat five-dozen scrambled eggs, two whole beef livers, and fifty pounds of dry kennel food. He exercises his dogs by hitching them to a sled on wheels—and along Hamilton Avenue they go.

There's canoe racing here: 25 miles of it down the Little Miami River from Glen Island Recreation Park at Foster to the bridge in Milford, passing through Loveland, Branch Hill, and Miamiville en route. Divisions range from the six-man relay, Explorer Scouts, to men's, women's, and children's divisions. In 1965, nearly 400 entered the race.

Skin divers get their watery kicks at Sportsman Lake on Route 42 at Cedarville, Ohio. The 10-acre lake is 45 feet deep.

No matter where they live, Cincinnatians are close to a place to bowl. The National Bowling Association's 1965 Convention was held here, attracting 5000, the same number that went to the dog show. Perhaps the area's most unique bowlers are the members of the Cincinnati Blind Bowling League, which started in 1948. The League's ten teams consist of five bowlers each, one of whom is sighted to handle the scoring and tell his teammates which pins are still standing after the first ball has done its damage. How good are these blind bowlers? Bill Staehling averages 131 per game and has shot a 180 game and a 393 series.

There is plenty of drag racing in the area. At Columbus, the National Trail Raceway features Double-A Dragsters. Closer to home, the Greater Cincinnati Racebowl at Glen Este, Ohio, advertises stock-car racing as well as powder-puff derbies. The Lawrenceburg Speedway at Lawrenceburg, Indiana, just over the state line, claims to have the "world's fastest quarter-mile track." The Northern Kentucky Speedway on Route 42 off Intrastate 75 offers figure eights and late-model stock racing. Typical of the special events each track features was the event offered July 4, 1965, at Glen Este, Ohio. Cincinnatians could watch cars vroom off a ramp daredevil-style, the idea being that the driver whose car rolled over the most won something. On the other hand, some Cincinnatians get their kicks in unscheduled matches on Intrastate 75, and tooling along the Third Street Distributor can be eventful enough.

Horse players know River Downs, Cincinnati's mile-length track just east of Coney Island Amusement Park. The race track has stalls for 1039 horses and stands for 7000 losers. Also, there's beautiful Latonia track across the river. Add Churchill Downs in Louisville, where on Derby Day the prices are so outlandish few can afford a taxi—and that's horse racing in this area. If there are bookies about, no one has come right out and said so, and it's the sort of thing Cincinnatians shouldn't ask friendly policemen. However, the St. Patrick Church in Northside once had a drawing in which the winner got an expense-paid trip to Keeneland for himself and a friend, and $500 to bet; if he lost his roll, he would get it back when he returned.

Trots? There's Hamilton Raceway on Route 4 north of Hamilton— and county fairs galore.

For steamboat racing, the *Delta Queen* is pitted against the *Belle of Louisville* in a classic mismatch during the Derby events at Louisville. The *Belle of Louisville* has one third the power of Cincinnati's *Delta Queen*. When the two boats race one another from the Louisville waterfront to the Six-Mile Bridge and back again to the George Rogers Clark Memorial Bridge, the *Belle of Louisville* has as much chance of winning as a ten-speed bike at the Indianapolis 500. But the race, which began in 1963, was more of a sentimental gesture than anything else—unless you consider the civic prides of Louisville and Cincinnati. Martin Hogan, Jr., writing in the *Enquirer* captured the real essence of the affair:

> Speed records aren't set in steamboat races, but they are still as thrilling as your first kiss.
> And even if the great days of steamboats of the Ohio and Mississippi Rivers are now but a legend, [the] race between the *Belle of Louisville* and the *Delta Queen* stirred memories of an era no further back than the days when the happy summer sounds of the *Island Queen* calliope floated into a little boy's bedroom window . . .

Who says reporters in Cincinnati haven't the souls of poets?

Boxing is a spectator sport that has seen better days around here. The last heavyweight championship bout in Cincinnati was on December 6, 1950, when Ezzard Charles belted Nick Barone in the eleventh round at the Cincinnati Gardens to retain his title for the fifth time. Only 10,085 attended.

More tranquil sports are found on the Ohio River, a place where some Cincinnatians head every time they get an hour off. Boating and fishing are popular, but the river isn't what it used to be. This isn't a complaint; it's a compliment. The new dams have increased the depth of the river, turning it into a long, narrow lake, so that boaters don't have to "lock through" every time they turn around. One man says that the river tends to flood more often because of the new dams and wants to hire the meanest lawyer he can find to sue whoever is responsible. The U. S. Army Corps of Engineers, who baby-sit the river, say the new dams aren't at fault. There the matter rests.

Who *owns* the Ohio River? Ohio or Kentucky? Guess again, Cincinnatians. Kentucky has full jurisdiction. If a Cincinnatian fishes in the river—or even from a dock that juts out into it—he needs a Kentucky license. Bob Rankin wrote in the *Enquirer*:

> The problem goes further in hunting. When you kill a duck
> or goose on the Ohio [River] and it falls into the mouth of
> the Miami River, you must have both a Kentucky and Ohio
> permit.

This began in colonial times, when Kentucky was an extension of Virginia and everyone was quibbling over land and gravel rights. It was decided then that the Ohio River would be in Kentucky. But suppose, for the sake of argument, the Ohio River reverted to Ohio and, downstream, to Indiana. The Dade Race Park at Henderson, Kentucky, would shut down. People have to cross the Ohio River from Kentucky proper to reach Dade, Dade now in Kentucky would be in Indiana, and Indiana says no to parimutuel betting. Actually, unless you're suing someone or a game warden is giving you funny looks, it doesn't matter who owns the river. Both sides enjoy it.

Boats, of course, have to be registered. Well, not *all* of them. Kentucky waterways patrolman Elwood Faulkner was cruising along the river above Cincinnati when he came across a man in a 12-foot fishing boat powered by a 2½-horsepower motor. The boat had no registration number, the man thought he didn't need one on a boat that small; but when informed that because it had a motor it needed a number, he shut off the motor, unbolted it, lifted it into his boat, and rowed away.

When Greater Cincinnatians go out on the river, they go out in a variety of craft: some new, some old, some store-bought, some home-made, some sturdy enough to battle the sea, and some that would be unsafe in a backyard wading pool. But on a summer afternoon, the Ohio River is littered with this happy makeshift fleet. How many boats actually call Cincinnati home port? The Treasury Department's Custom Bureau has 1300 documented, which makes Cincinnati twelfth in "boat population." Which boats are documented? Only those 25 feet or more in length. And that leaves us with a riverful of shorter ones unaccounted for. Sometimes these weekend sailors can fill up the river completely. Captain Pat Monohan, of the Ohio Barge Lines' towboat *Lunga Point,* tied up one Sunday night rather than pass through. He was afraid, and rightly so, he'd run down a small boat in the dark. A few Cincinnati boat operators run their boats the way they drive their cars, believing that as long as the motor is perking they are blessed with the right-of-way. Kentucky waterways patrolman Lyman Wells one night said that off Coney Island Amusement Park at least 400 small boats were anchored midstream or were beached, while their occupants watched the Park's fireworks. Some anchored in midstream had no anchor lights showing. Small wonder Captain Monohan tied up and waited for the weekend to pass. Water skiers pose another problem. Bill Kinsler of the Columbia Marine Service said that one Saturday he counted more than a dozen people swimming off his harbor, having fallen from water skis—or from boats.

When it comes to swimming in the Ohio River, most Cincinnatians say, No, thanks. The same goes for the Little and Great Miami, Whitewater, and Licking Rivers. The currents are treacherous. The bottoms change from day to day. Cincinnatians would just as soon swim in Mill Creek as some sections of the Ohio River—and one look at Mill Creek tells the story best. Right now it's an open sewer. As some say about Pennsylvania's Schuylkill River, "You can't drink it, but you can always write with it." The same goes for Mill Creek. It's not healthy for people. It's not healthy for fish either—which brings us to that tricky subject: fishing.

Well, there *are* fish around here. Below Markland Dam, Wesley Haines and his wife, Bertha, have been catching trout, black bass, white bass, and that ugly-looking native we call the river cat. The trout, some say, come from pay lakes near the river. Rains cause these lakes to overflow their banks, out slither the fish, there sits Mr. Haines, and *strike!* Once he caught a brown trout that weighed almost three pounds. The last sturgeon, Bob Rankin of the *Enquirer* says, was caught more than twenty years ago below the Warsaw, Kentucky, dam by a retired Covington policeman named Jesse Craig. Muskies have been taken at Rocky Fork Lake. One was a whopping 18-pounder. Wally Forste of the *Post & Times-Star* wonders if Lake Grant is finally producing big crappies, because he says:

> Some anglers, knowing the secretiveness of their fellow fishermen, suspect as much. The reason? Several times in recent weeks outsize crappies have been reported "caught in the ponds."

When it comes to knowing where the fish are biting, when the hunting is best, and which camping site has more amenities, Greater Cincinnatians rely on Bob Rankin of the *Enquirer* and Wally Forste of the *Post & Times-Star*. Both are thoughtful and wise outdoorsmen with their own contacts and hunches—hunches that are invariably more knowledgeable than the hunches your neighbor, however good his intentions, might pass along. In fact, so many Cincinnatians have such faith in these two authorities that some anglers believe all they need for a successful fishing junket is a glance at what Rankin or Forste has written, a bent pin, and a pail of water. The two writers, of course, admit they are not infallible—but they're the only people in the area who believe it. If sportsmen wrote bibles, Forste and Rankin would have long since earned by-lines in each of the testaments.

Wally Forste, for example, found out from Stonelick State Park officials that one April the bass there were beginning to move into the shallows. Mr. Forste promptly concluded that "if Stonelick is O.K., so should be Cowan, Hueston, Grant, and Rocky Fork Lakes—other park lakes in southwest Ohio." If that kind of hunch doesn't start an angler thinking, nothing will. The same kind of advice comes from Bob Rankin, too. Both tell fishermen where the catfish are hungriest, when Acton Lake is warm enough for action, and where the smallmouth bass are snoozing. They point out the elbow room each park has, which parks charge admission, and the best place to pitch a tent. Because this information changes from season to season, and sometimes from day to day, it would not be logical to include any of it here. But it would be logical to suggest that new Cincinnatians do as old Cincinnatians have done: make the reading of Rankin and Forste a habit. Where else could an angler learn about fishing in the dead of winter? Early one spring from icy Lake Cumberland Rankin wrote:

> No matter how bad the weather or how muddy the water, if you use a jigging pole and work hard you can catch bass. But be forewarned: jigging isn't for the fireside fisherman. . . . I was dressed more like an Eskimo seal hunter than a fisherman, with the temperatures under the freezing mark . . .

Or, consider Forste's advice:

> If you venture a trip to Falmouth State Park and lakes from Cincinnati or northern Kentucky [don't] follow the park route signs on U.S. 27. They take you south into Falmouth and then back north to the park and 225-acre lake. The best way to get there . . . is via U.S. 27, turning left on State Road 609 direct to the park, saving many miles.

And, early one May, Bob Rankin wrote of Campbell County Park:

> The lake is still muddy and we found only small yellow-belly catfish, bluegills, and bass. But don't be fooled. There are bass up to four pounds and plenty of bluegills in the lake, plus channel catfish. All we need is for the water to clear.

Also, there are pay lakes stocked with fish and the comforts of home. It is to these that our fishermen—and their smallfry—head when the rivers are running out, the lakes are muddy, and the farm ponds are overflowing. Pay lakes around here are stocked with everything but the kitchen sink: yellow-belly catfish to rainbow trout. Some lakes let you keep all you catch, some don't. It's better to check first. Some of the lakes advertise this or that kind of fish, so study their ads in the newspapers and follow your heart. Now and then, for example, Springdale Lake at Springdale, Ohio, advertises Lake Erie channel catfish. Airy Hills Lakes Club on North Bend Road advertises channel cats, bass, and walleyes. Twin Lakes Club at Blue Ash advertises 20-pound catfish; the Starling Lake Club in Bethel, bullheads and bluegills; Lake Gloria on Pippin Road, crappies and walleyes; and Mueller's Lake Club in Loveland, channel catfish and sheepheads. Lakewood, north of Georgetown, not only has a fishing lake but an 18-hole public golf course. There are more than forty pay lakes in this area.

Cincinnatians are also hunters. The hunting seasons differ each year, depending on how many birds and animals got married and whether or not their marriages were blessed with issue. The 1965–66 hunting season set by the Wildlife Council tells much of the story.

The bobwhite quail may be hunted from November 12 to December 18 on private land. In public hunting areas the season runs from November 12 to January 29. The daily bag is six, and possession is not to exceed a dozen after the first day.

Cottontail rabbits can be hunted from November 12 through January 29, from 9 A.M. to 5 P.M., the bag limit being four, and possession eight.

Grouse are fair game from October 8 to February 26 any time from daylight to dark. The bag limit is three and possession is six. But don't try to nail a grouse in the southeastern Ohio deer-hunting zone on November 8, 9, 10, or 11. That's when the deer hunters are blasting away—and for those four days the grouse are taking a legal coffee break.

Deer hunting with a gun, as noted above, runs just those four short days in November, from 9 A.M. to 5 P.M.; and the bag limit is one male deer with antlers more than three inches long. If you try to luck out with a bow and arrow, you have a longer season: from October

15 to December 31, daylight to darkness, but the bag limit is the same as nailing one with a gun.

If you hate squirrels—or have cultivated a taste for squirrel stew—you can shoot them on private land from September 10 to November 11, from daylight to dark only. Bag limit is four, possession is eight. Squirrel hunting is permitted in the southeastern Ohio deer-hunting zone only from September 10 to November 8, then duck. Here come the deer hunters. *Pow!* On state hunting lands you can shoot squirrels from September 10 to Christmas Day, from daylight to dark, same bag and possession limits applying.

The girl-watching season varies with the temperature, the sun, and the strength of the wind gusts. In summer, try any public beach or pool. In the spring, try Fifth and Vine Streets on a gusty day. Other girl watchers concentrate on Fourth Street between Main and Race Streets, the Dixie Terminal Building, or the exits (at night) of the Procter & Gamble Building. There is no limit, and the season depends on your imagination, but bag one and she'll have the law on you.

Raccoons, opossums, mink, muskrat, and other Walt Kelly characters can be hunted from November 15 to February 15. Weasels, groundhogs, and skunks can be hunted any days but November 8, 9, and 10 in the southern deer-hunting zone and November 9, 10, and 11 in the northwestern deer-hunting zone. There is no closed season for trapping skunks. Common sense should prevail, though. On the other hand, beaver can be trapped only the first fifteen days in February, two per trapper per season, and only in Ashtabula, Columbiana, Trumbull, Mahoning, Carroll, Williams, Jackson, and Jefferson Counties.

Duck hunting? September 17 through September 25 was set in 1965 as a special season for the blue-winged, green-winged, and cinnamon teal. Bag limit for such brightly plumaged wild ducks is four; possession, eight.

Bear in mind that the hunting seasons vary from year to year. What has been listed here can give you only a general idea because these dates applied only to the 1965–66 season.

Golf was touched upon in Chapter 11, which deals with family recreation; but a few thoughts about the Cincinnati golfer as a sportsman are in order. Del Vaughn, owner of the Twin Oaks golf course in Covington, Kentucky, said that one morning he arrived at 4:45 A.M. to open shop and found—waiting for him—a pair of golfers itching to tee off. That's not all. By 6:15 A.M., eighteen groups had backed up on the tee, waiting *their* turn! Weekend golfers, regardless of the weather or how far away spring is, still go at it strong. A total of 1720 rounds of golf were recorded at the three city-owned courses at Avon Field, California, and Reeves Field one chilly April weekend. The *Post & Times-Star* together with the Cincinnati Recreation Commission each year sponsor a hole-in-one contest at the Airport Playfield, usually in July.

It makes sense that Cincinnati has the golf bug. After all, in 1875 in Covington, a company hung out a shingle that said:

P. GOLDSMITH—BASEBALLS

Baseball and golf? Well, there *is* a connection—at least around here. The Goldsmith company grew so fast, making and peddling baseballs, that several things happened. Twenty-two years later, it moved across the river to larger quarters in Cincinnati. In 1936 it bought the Crawford-MacGregor-Canby Company, the Dayton, Ohio, outfit that made golf equipment. Then, MacGregor Sports Products, Inc.—as it came to be known—was itself bought out by Brunswick, the bowling-ball people. Jack Nicklaus used MacGregor clubs and the MacGregor ball that advertising men call the DX Tourney to blast his way out of the amateur ranks to the top-money level of professional golf. MacGregor also makes gear for baseball, football, track, tennis, and basketball. Its football equipment is used by professional and collegiate teams from coast to coast, and so is its baseball and basketball stuff. As far as golf is concerned, it was MacGregor right here in Cincinnati that experimented and developed the golf glove and golf bag made of lightweight kangaroo leather. The company maintains an "advisory staff" of professional athletes, of which Jack Nicklaus is one. So you see, the jump from baseball to golf wasn't as farfetched as it first seemed—at least, as far as Cincinnati is concerned. And the look we take at Cincinnati basketball also fits right in here. MacGregor, as noted, makes basketballs, too.

Cincinnati basketball at the professional level means the Cincinnati Royals based at the Cincinnati Gardens.

Ambrose H. Lindhorst, chairman of the board for both the team and the arena, is an amiable lawyer with five-o'clock shadow. His fingers are, legally, in a variety of diverse pies. He's also a director of the Southern Ohio Bank, of the Buckeye Savings Association, and of the Victor Transit Corporation. He is also on the board of trustees at Good Samaritan Hospital and chairman of the Hamilton County Republican Executive Committee. A graduate of Xavier High School, he attended Xavier University and the University of Cincinnati, receiving his law degree in 1940 from the Chase College of Law, which has trained many of Cincinnati's better lawyers. The local basketball team could have no better—and no more local—board chairman. Face it. What other board chairman got his start as a milkman?

He tells the story of the Royals this way:

My association with [them] commenced in 1963, although the club was brought to Cincinnati about 1959. The Royals, prior to that date, were known as the Rochester Royals and

215

were owned by two brothers named Harrison. After the club was moved here by the Harrisons, it was sold to a group headed by Thomas E. Wood. Wood was a large shareholder at the time in the Cincinnati Gardens and . . . felt that the addition of a professional basketball team would produce a good tenant for the arena. A second major shareholder . . . was L. M. Jacobs of Buffalo, New York, who is widely known in the concession field. Wood had the original idea of making the ball club a . . . civic venture, and I do not believe that he intended originally to be the majority shareholder. However, when the civic-venture approach failed, he ended up with 56% of the stock in the Royals, and the remaining 44% of the stock was and is held by approximately 104 shareholders.

For the first two years of its operation after the sale to the group headed by Wood, it operated at a loss, but with the advent of Oscar Robertson and subsequently Jerry Lucas, the financial picture changed, and it has operated at a profit ever since.

Following the death of Thomas E. Wood in 1962, the executive leadership of the club was exercised by the three trustees of the Wood estate. Then, in April 1963, as counsel and attorney for L. M. Jacobs, I bought the controlling interest in the ball club for my client and also bought the interest of the Wood estate in the arena. That resulted in the Jacobs family owning over 80% of . . . the Cincinnati Gardens, and 56% of . . . the ball club.

The Cincinnati Gardens on Seymour Avenue started out to be *the* center of winter sports, exhibitions, and the spectacular type of show. The Beatles played there to a mob scene, dogs have won prizes there, and Judy Garland sang there in an ill-fated spectacular that found her sick at intermission time and unable to complete her show. The promoters of her show, when the curtain rang down, were a little sick, too. Charles Sawyer, before he resigned to become Harry Truman's Secretary of Commerce, was the first president of the Gardens. Others who followed him in that position—president of the Gardens, that is, *not* Secretary of Commerce—were Louis O. Richter, the late Thomas W. Wood, and at this writing, J. Thomas Grace.

The building is plunked down on a 30-acre site that was, in the beginning, 40-acres. The Gardens can seat 11,130 in permanent seats, up to 3000 more on temporary seats, and still have standing room for 1500 others. The main roof is 90 feet above the ice floor, or the basketball floor—it depends on which sport you came to see—which means the ceiling is high enough and the arena is big enough for a ten-story building to be tucked in there out of the rain.

The Royals, under Mr. Lindhorst, have been trying to move out of the National Basketball Association's eastern division and into the western one. Mr. Lindhorst says the team would like to move not because the Royals are tired of playing second fiddle to the Boston Celtics, but because the move would geographically correct the imbalance of the annual All-Star Game, which the East keeps winning. But when the matter of switching to the western division came to a vote in Boston in the summer of 1965, Boston and three other teams voted no. Boston, some Cincinnatians grumbled, wanted to keep its second fiddler fiddling second fiddle.

The Cincinnati sporting scene includes collegiate as well as professional basketball; add to these, college and high school football, baseball, track, and golf teams. Cincinnati is a city of highly defined neighborhoods (no one lives on this street or that; they live in this community or that), which tend to have their own athletic classics, like the Army-Navy game. Also, there is friendly rivalry between the Cincinnati-area public schools and the Roman Catholic schools. An example is the ancient feud in Price Hill between the football teams of Western Hills High School and its parochial counterpart, Elder High School. The conflict on Thanksgiving day attracts the attention that a prizefight would attract if Martin Luther were going fifteen rounds with the Pope. At the college level, the archenemy of the University of Cincinnati teams is Xavier University—or is it the other way around? It depends on which school the Cincinnatian attended, and even if he attended neither, how he feels about fish on Friday. Meanwhile, up in Oxford, Ohio, the Miami University Redskins can have the hottest basketball team in the conference, but no one outside of Oxford gets choked up about the matter. Most Cincinnatians—involved as they are with the UC-XU conflict—couldn't care less, an attitude that sometimes causes legitimate chagrin at the Purity, where Oxford students gather to brood, drink beer, and rave about their Redskins over the jukebox's din.

The one thing that makes these diverse rooters one is, of course, the Cincinnati Reds.

The Reds should not be accused of political taint, nor tied in with the Russians or the Chinese. When, in the summer of 1950, the newspaper in Beckley, West Virginia, suggested our Reds be called something else because those other reds were getting adverse notices, Cincinnatians shrugged and let the matter pass. To locals, the Communists and not the Cincinnati Reds are the upstarts. When Lenin was born, the baseball team had already been called the Reds for a year. And when Stalin was ten years old, the Cincinnati Reds were twenty! Thus ends that rhubarb.

But the Reds—our Reds—weren't always the Reds. Josiah L. Keck, first president of the team, nicknamed them the Porkopolitans. Sportswriters, struggling with that mouthful, in 1886 tried to nickname the team the Pioneers. They had no luck, either. The Reds were named the Reds because Harry Wright, British native and cricket expert, had come to Cincinnati in 1867 to teach cricket, took over the local base-ball team instead, and called the team the Red Stockings—because that is what the team wore. Lee Allen says that the lady who sewed the stockings for the team was named Margaret Truman and that she later married Asa Brainard, the Reds' first paid pitcher.

As the Red Stockings—with four paid players and with Manager Wright himself in the outfield—toured the country, they knocked off almost every team they played. In 1868 they played 66 games, won 65, and tied one with New York, 17–17. In fact, Wright's team didn't taste defeat until well into the second season, after they had 130 wins under their belt. The Altantics of Brooklyn beat them 8–7 in an eleventh-inning game on June 14, 1870.

The players didn't get rich in those days. Salaries ranged from $800 to $1400 a season.

Each Cincinnati generation has its favorites on the team—and also its favorite scapegoats. Consider Charlie Gould, who was player-man-ager in 1876, the year the Reds became charter members of the National League. Poor Charlie! When his team won 9 games and lost 56—and ended in last place, yet!—Charlie himself ended as a streetcar conductor on the ballpark line. The Reds were so terrible, after so stunning a beginning, that the team's first president, Josiah L. Keck, unloaded the team bag and baggage in 1877—and for three weeks Cincinnati had no ball team at all. But things brightened again when William and James White, called Will and the Deacon, captured the fancy of Cincinnati rooters in 1878. Will and Deacon were the first brother battery in professional baseball, and Will was the first player in the major league to wear glasses. Lee Allen reports that Will White had still another first to his credit. In 1879 the Reds played 81 games, and Will pitched in 76 of them. He started and completed 75 games, and appeared once as a relief pitcher. Allen says, "The record book shows 75 as Will's total, but the extra one was a six-inning tie against Syracuse that would count today."

Back in 1882, when the Reds temporarily "quit" the National League because, it was said, the League didn't want them to play ball on the Sabbath, the Reds won their first major-league pennant. The league was the hastily formed American Association, which not only permit-ted games to be played on the Sabbath but allowed the parks, in addition, to sell beer and whiskey. The stars of that first pennant-winning team were Bid McPhee at second and Rick Carpenter at third. Joe Sommer, one of the outfielders, died in Cincinnati in 1938. At the time of his death he was a retired apartment-house janitor—and we add a melancholy note to our Cincinnati love story: in none of Carpenter's obituaries was it ever mentioned that he had played for the Reds when they won their first pennant. Incidentally, second-base-man McPhee was noted for several things; one of them was that he refused to wear a baseball glove until 1896.

The first player ever to hit two home runs in a single inning was Charlie Jones, who joined the Reds in 1876. He hit eleven home runs for the Reds in 1883, his annual batting average nearly always topped .300, and he probably would have played for the Reds much longer, but his wife got angry at him one day and threw pepper in his face. With his eyesight failing, he quit as a player and became—of all things!—an umpire.

In 1892, Charlie Comiskey came to Cincinnati to manage the team for three years, but the doldrums were upon the team, and nothing much happened. In those three years the Reds finished fifth, sixth, and finally tenth. But one thing did happen during the Comiskey reign: in one game with Louisville, on Sunday, June 18, 1893, the Reds made fourteen runs in the first inning and won the game, 30–12. The easygoing Louisville pitcher was William Rhodes—nicknamed "Dusty," as is anyone named Rhodes; the pitcher went the distance, giving up thirty-two hits as well as hitting two batters and walking seven others.

William Ewing, nicknamed "Buck," took over where Comiskey left off, and in 1895 gave the Reds another first: a spring training junket to Mobile, Alabama.

In 1919 the Reds played in that murky World Series with the Chicago White Sox. After that series, eight Chicago players appeared before the grand jury, charged with throwing the series, but the jury acquitted them. Baseball's new commissioner, Judge Kenesaw M. Landis, on the other hand, was not so lenient. He blacklisted all eight players.

Ten years later, in 1929, Cincinnatian Sidney Weil bought the Reds, dumping many dollars into the team. He brought in shortstop Leo Durocher, who played here three years. He brought in Floyd (Babe) Herman as an outfielder. And he brought in that monument to Cincinnati baseball, catcher Ernie Lombardi, who stayed with the Reds ten years and became a Cincinnati institution. Ernie was not the handsomest devil to walk down Vine Street, but nonetheless that shy and massive catcher brought out the mother in most female hearts. The gals flocked to the field to cheer him. Anyway, there was little else during that period to cheer about. During those gloomy days of the Depression, the Reds suffered a depression of their own manufacture. They spent most of the time potting around in the cellar, wondering what the name of the game was. From 1931 on, the club ended in eighth place for four years straight. You couldn't blame the scattering of Cincinnatians who appeared at the ballpark because they went wild and shouted over Lombardi's big nose and interlocking grip. The only other item worth shouting for there was beer.

Happily, along came Paul Derringer. Even when the Reds were in second division, he was a twenty-game pitcher. But it took more than Derringer and Lombardi. In 1933, Sidney Weil gave up the team. It had become a luxury he could no longer afford. The Central Trust Company took over the franchise and hired Larry McPhail to get things moving again.

The first thing McPhail did was to sell Powell Crosley, Junior, on "temporarily" buying the team. Crosley bought it with the understanding that the ball club wouldn't lose too much money and that sooner or later someone else would come along and bail him out—or, that not happening, he would be free to peddle the franchise to another city and recoup his investment. The "temporary" purchase, however, lasted almost a quarter of a century. When Crosley died in 1961, he still owned the team. In 1962 William O. DeWitt, now the team's president and general manager, purchased the club from the Crosley Foundation, which Crosley himself had set up to control the team. And to the satisfaction of everyone, the Reds are still with us. DeWitt and Cincinnati's city manager worked out an agreement in July 1965: if the Reds would agree to stay here until at least after the 1971 season, the city would help with the Club's parking problem. When this agreement was announced, Cincinnati rooters sighed with relief. After all, baseball franchises travel more now than some players do.

It was during the McPhail-Crosley regime that night baseball came to the major leagues—right here in Cincinnati. In the first game under the lights, May 24, 1935, Paul Derringer defeated the Phillies, 2–1, with 20,422 fans witnessing the illuminated adventure.

After McPhail left, Warren Giles came from the Cardinal's International League farm in New York. In 1937, manager Chuck Dressen quit; the following year Giles appointed Bill McKecknie to fill Dressen's role. Derringer was around, of course, and a youngster named Johnny Vander Meer was brought up. The Reds paid $50,000 cash and traded catcher Virgil Davis and pitcher Al Hollingsworth to get another pitcher: William (Bucky) Walters.

Everyone remembers Johnny Vander Meer—and with good reason. On June 11, 1938 he pitched a no-hit game against Boston. Four days later, when next on the mound, he pitched another no-hitter, against the Dodgers in Ebbets Field. Incidentally, it was the first night game the Dodgers had ever played at home. That was the year Lombardi led the league, batting .342, and the Reds got a little hot: they ended in fourth place. The next year they got hotter and won the National League pennant but lost the series, four games straight. In 1940, the season after that, our Reds didn't fool around. They won the National League pennant, defeated the Detroit Tigers in the World Series, and for the first time since 1869 were the world champions.

War played hob with the team—and with everything else, for that matter. Ball players were hard to get and to hang on to. Warren Giles, faced with such shortages, used Joe Nuxhall as a pitcher in 1944 when Nuxhall was only fifteen years old. But fifteen-year-old pitchers, however good, can have problems. He got rid of the first two Cardinals at bat—and there stood Stan Musial. Before the inning was over, Nuxhall had allowed the St. Louis team to score five runs. Still, the Reds finished fourth in 1944. And at this writing, Joe Nuxhall is still pitching for the team.

What kind of park do the Reds have? They've been right where they are, at Findlay and Western Avenues, since 1884. The present grandstand was built in 1912, but the park has endured a flood or so and several face-liftings since. When the place was first opened, home plate was where the present right-field foul line joins the corner of the bleachers, but it was moved to its present location ten years after the park opened. The first player to hit a home run out of the park hit it thirty-seven years after the field was dedicated. He was outfielder Pat Duncan, who sent one winging over the left field fence in 1921. The record crowd for a single home game at Crosley Field was on April 15, 1925, when 35,747 paid to see the Reds play the Phillies. And here's something to win a bar bet with: the Reds have not always played their opening games at home. In 1887, because of heavy rain, the "home" game opener was played in Louisville. Add this: no matter how the team does during the year, the opening day of the next season is always an *advance* sellout. The Reds have an efficient farm system: five minor-league teams owned outright, and working agreements with a fistful of penny-whistle leagues.

If the lady fans were permitted their turn at bat, most of the gals would already be baseball habituées, thanks to the Rosie Reds. The Rosie Reds, now the Rosie Reds, Inc., was organized in 1964 by Mrs. Jeanette Heinze. It has a membership that now should be in the thousands. It is a club of ladies who get choked up about baseball and who won't take a back seat to any man when it comes to cheering the Reds on. As you can see, baseball in Cincinnati isn't limited to the boys at the corner saloon. Here it's not a sport. It's an institution.

This chapter began with Waite Hoyt's description of the frantic day the Reds won the National League pennant in 1961. It was, indeed, a momentous day. Fred Hutchinson—that big and silent bear of a manager—had led the Reds well. But time does not wait. Fred Hutchinson is dead. He guided the club five years and pieced together a winner. But cancer got him. He came to Cincinnati in 1959 to replace Mayo Smith. And it was here, Cincinnatians like to believe, that he had his finest hour.

The giants of Cincinnati baseball come and go—and their memories linger.

Another giant has passed. His name: Waite Hoyt. Happily, he only retired. But to Cincinnatians, Waite Hoyt, who never played for the Reds, was as much a part of Cincinnati baseball as the team itself. He was, until he retired in 1965, the radio voice of the Reds, broadcasting on several Cincinnati stations, and always for Burger Beer. When television came along, he stayed with radio. Only for a short time did he do the play-by-play for both radio and television. Most of the time, he and his familiar "Burger Beer Baseball Network" caused advertising men to become manic-depressives. Cincinnatians would watch the games on television, turn the sound off, and listen to Waite's description over the radio. Commercials were a hodgepodge. Waite would be selling Burger Beer while the announcer on television was showing another brand. But try as the stations might, none could find an announcer like Waite. They brought in good ones, but no. To Cincinnati, Waite Hoyt *was* the Reds.

In broadcasting, the Reds still maintained its collection of "firsts." WLWT, Channel Five in Cincinnati, was the first television station in the country to telecast major-league baseball in color on a strictly local basis. That was back in 1959.

As for Waite Hoyt, it is hard to say whether he felt that fifty years in baseball was enough or whether the economics of broadcasting caught up with him at last. It was as Magee Adams, veteran radio columnist for the *Enquirer*, pointed out on July 25, 1965: "The cost of sports broadcasting may seem of no concern to listeners so long as the games get on the air. But it does concern them in a way that makes a difference. For instance, three sponsors now share the cost of airing the Red's games on WCKY because the bill has grown too big for one . . ." That was the forerunner of events to come. A few days later, when August rolled around, the newspaper headlines said:

HOYT RETIRING AS REDS' "VOICE"

WAITE HOYT STEPPING DOWN . . .

WAITE HOYT TO QUIT BROADCASTING REDS

Magee Adams on August 9, 1965, picked up the loose ends with his uncomplicated summation:

> Waite Hoyt announced last Wednesday night that he is to retire as the radio voice of the Cincinnati Reds at the end of this season. It would be pointless to argue with the personal reasons for his decision. But I speak for thousands of his fans when I regret the prospect of baseball without him.
>
> In an extraordinarily real sense, Waite Hoyt has come to stand for baseball here in Cincinnati. It is not simply his knowledge of the game or his skill as a sportscaster, but the man himself who has won this singular distinction . . .

Waite Hoyt, the boy wonder of the New York Yankees when Babe Ruth was king, had come west, got behind a microphone, and for twenty-four years added to the broadcasting of the Reds that part of himself that was and always will be: pure gentleman. Around 9:45 P.M. on August 4, 1965, Cincinnatians were listening to Waite Hoyt and his partner, Claude Sullivan, broadcast the Cincinnati-San Francisco game. At the end of the fifth inning the score was tied, 3–3. Instead of the commercial, Waite Hoyt said:

> The big adventure is over.
> Late this afternoon after a conference with John F. Koons, Junior, president of the Burger Brewing Company, I decided to surrender my position as baseball broadcaster for the Cincinnati Reds following the final game of the 1965 season October 3, in San Francisco; and thus my career as your broadcaster will be brought to a close.
> Also my fifty years of association with the game of baseball will end . . .
> My association with Burger has been too delightful and my allegiance too strong to consider any other course after twenty-four years.
> To say I will not regret my departure from the game of baseball would be telling an untruth, for baseball has been my life, and my devotion to it will always remain a living thing . . .

One thing, as suggested at the start of this chapter, that gets Cincinnati choked up is baseball. Another thing, that night in August, was Waite Hoyt telling baseball goodby.

16

Does the world of industry—that is, people in offices and factories, smoke, cash register noises, the stock market's fluctuation, the acid stench of cauldrons, and the newsboy's garbled cry—have a place in this book which purports to be a city's love story?

Of course!

Without the clangings, shouts, and smells there would be no love story to write.

Each city has its own commercial and industrial fingerprint. Its characteristics lure fathers, who establish homes, which add meaning to a city. Thus the love story emerges, shaped by still another dimension.

But a city's commercial and industrial fingerprint can't possibly be simplified, and this book—unless it seeks only the blessing of the chamber of commerce's industrial committee—*must* simplify here and there. What follows in this chapter is not a clinical study of Greater Cincinnati's industrial muscle. Rather, it is one man's once-over of a commercial complex that grows more complex and gratifying each day. To some fathers, Cincinnati is a railroad center; to others, a place to make soap; to others, a place to make machine tools; and to Izzy Kadetz, a universe that eats him out of kosher corned beef every time he turns around. Yet, these items could be true of *any* major city. You can buy kosher corned beef in Chicago. Topeka, no doubt, makes machine tools. And what railroad center can compare with Chicago on a wintry night when the prairie winds howl through the vast Proviso yards? No, Cincinnati's industrial muscle is a dab of this, a smattering of that, and a particle of the other. Yet, these things make us—and have made us—the city we are. To find *that* out, all you have to do is read the civic section of the telephone book:

In the production of machine tools, playing cards, and soap, Cincinnati leads the world. Also a leader in the production of building materials, cans, chemicals, clothing, coffins and burial cases, conveyors, cosmetics, electric motors and machinery, electronic equipment, food products, foundry and machine shop products, jet engines, malt and distilled liquors, mattresses, meat packing, motor vehicles and parts, paper and paper products, pianos and organs, plastics and plastic products, printing inks, printing and publishing, sheet metal products, shoes, sporting goods, steel mill products and valves . . .

The Cincinnati and Suburban Bell Telephone Company and its good neighbor across the river, the Citizens Telephone Company, are as much in love with this area as any individual citizen can ever claim to be. They've sized up the Greater Cincinnati community, too, noting that we are smack in the middle of the bituminous coal-sales action— more than 600,000 coal cars each year carrying 32,000,000 tons, and on river barges an additional 3,000,000 tons of coal hauled. Cincinnati, they say, is the nation's largest inland coal port! Between 1955 and 1964, 132 new manufacturing plants came into the Greater Cincinnati area, 600 existing plants expanded their facilities, and, combined, these items produced 22,737 more jobs paying $101,273,100 per year. So, you see, there's more to Cincinnati than meets the eye, and there's more to the telephone book than telephone listings.

The telephone company itself will be bragged about in Chapter 19, but this thought in passing: the national average is 45.9 telephones for every 100 people; Greater Cincinnati has 55.8 telephones for every 100 people. A gabby town!

No strain. Cincinnati has as much need for the telephone company as it has for Izzy Kadetz, and both the telephone company and Mr. Kadetz, being thoughtful citizens, admit this. With *that* in mind, let's look at one or two businesses here because these will give us an idea of the rest. After all, there are just so many factory tours any civic booster can stand. Beyond a certain point, everything dwindles into the meaningless.

Elsewhere in this book, scattered about, are stories of most of Cincinnati's industry. For more information on any of them, consult the chamber of commerce or your next-door neighbor. Both are amiable authorities on Cincinnati commerce, big and little.

No question about it, though. Industry here *is* both big and little. On the whopper side, we invite your attention to the center ring and the Mill's nearly 10,000 employees. The Mill, of course, is the Cincinnati Milling Machine Company, with its home base in Oakley and branches in so many places the Mill's mailing room is a stamp collector's heaven. You'll find the Mill in Worcester, Massachusetts; Reading, Ohio; New Brunswick, New Jersey; Birmingham, England;

Biggleswade, England; Vlaardingen, the Netherlands; and Lyon, France. Then, too, consider its many-named subsidiaries: the Heald Machine Company; Carlisle Chemical Works, Inc.; Cincinnati Lathe and Tool Company; Hordern, Mason, & Edwards, Ltd.; Cincinnati-Nederland N.V.; and Cincinnati-Chemienne.

Romantic? You bet. Ever watch a big carbide cutter bite into a rough forging? They say the most hardened machinist passing by stops to stare at that! He might have witnessed the operation a thousand times, but no matter; each time it's new, compelling, and exciting. This makes sense, doesn't it? If there is passion involved in the shaping of a statue, there is passion involved in the shaping of a forging. Thus, Cincinnati has many love affairs.

In 1884 in a Cincinnati loft, a handful of men built a small milling machine for their own use in making screws and taps, and the Cincinnati Milling Machine Company was born. Sixteen years later the Mill was peddling to customers in this country—and in Europe! That first machine proved to be the grandmother and grandfather of the sixty-five different standard machine tools that the Mill hatches today. The offspring are all shapes and sizes. Some have definite weight problems: 65 tons. Some have even more definite weight problems: 100 tons! Some are 200 feet long. Some are so small they come 100 to a handful. Wander down the aisles of the Mill's Special Machine Division and you'll seldom see two identical machines side by side. One machine might make the teeth for mechanical cotton pickers. Another might mill aircraft wing skins from aluminum slabs. Another might machine the contour airfoil sections of 50-inch blades for a power-house turbine. Not everything at the Mill is custom-made, though. The Mill turns out standards from a 145-pound bench drill to a 175,-000-pound metal-forming machine.

Elsewhere in the Mill, the Meta-Dynamics Division is exploring new worlds of metalworking, using controlled heat via the acetylene's hot blue flame, manufactured gas, and now and then, *whammo!* a 50,000-watt jolt of electricity oscillating a million cycles a minute. They're playing with "chipless" machining, too. No more flying scrap. Great hydroform machines—using tons and tons of pressure—silently and systematically *squeeze* the reluctant metal into the desired shape. Such a machine can, with its bear hugs, turn out 600 silver coffeepots an hour, or, if tinkered with, produce metal punches with equal ease.

Look into another section of the sprawling Mill and you'll see men creating a wet, ladylike, dribbly, and pink substance called Cimcool, a cutting compound developed by the Cincinnati Milling Machine Company to save the wear and tear of the cutting equipment it sells. In Reading, Ohio, the Mill's Carlisle Chemical Company is producing chemicals used in the manufacture of oil, soap, textiles, wax, and inks. The Mill's Heald Machine Company in Massachusetts has developed an automatic machine so precise it can drill holes to a tolerance of .00015 inch into the inner race of a ball bearing no bigger than a house fly. The hole itself is no bigger than the period at the end of this sentence. The canny machine can drill one such hole with precision accuracy every fifteen seconds! Or, how about this: the Mill has developed a wheelhead that runs 100,000 revolutions per minute!

Add grinding wheels. Add the good food in the Mill's company cafeteria. And add the touch of Frederick A. Geier, who built the Mill's plant in Oakley. If Schlitz is the beer that made Milwaukee famous, the Mill is one of the names that did the same for Greater Cincinnati. But there's more to the Mill than that sprawling facility, its crowded parking lots, and the streetloads of traffic it unleashes when shifts change. For thousands of Greater Cincinnatians—husbands, fathers, uncles, sons—the Mill *is* Cincinnati.

Lest you think the Mill is the only facility like that on tap, may we suggest that there are many others that are not as big but just as effective. For instance, if you have a fondness for trolley cars (if not, *pretend* you have and humor us), there's the Tool Steel Gear & Pinion Company with 600 employees. Though the last trolley went to that Great Carbarn in the Sky, Tool Steel (the company's abbreviated name) is still the leading producer of carburized industrial parts: gears, pinions, and track wheels. These unpoetic items are used in steel mills from Pittsburgh to Tokyo, and in cement and mining operations from West Virginia to South Africa. Not bad for a company that started a little more than fifty years ago as a two-man bicycle shop, eh? Like the Mill, Tool Steel has subsidiaries, too: one near Chicago, the other in Toronto. Charles E. Sawtelle helped start the company when his son-in-law, Russell C. Bloomfield, invented a way to harden steel ball bearings for bicycle wheels. The company began in a North Bend, Ohio, blacksmith shop. Nearby U. S. Pipe and Foundry Company in Addyston suggested that the same hardening method be applied to gears and pinions. These pinions were used in the streetcar drive mechanism on the Cincinnati Traction Company's wonderful trolleys. By 1911, products bearing the company's TSP trademark were driving streetcars in New York, New Orleans, San Francisco, Chicago, and Philadelphia, as well as in Montreal, Paris, Berlin, and Rotterdam. When the trolley business petered out, Tool Steel didn't. It kept growing. Every other year, and sometimes sooner, Tool Steel expands. It outgrew its Sharonville plant in 1955, three years after the plant was built. Enlarged, it outgrew the addition in 1956. It expanded again in 1957, 1959, 1962, and 1964.

For a pint-size industry, take a trip up Ten Mile Road near Milford, Ohio, and visit Cread Calaway's sawmill. Lots of people do, and they take their children with them. Mr. Calaway rough-cuts lumber for barns, fences, and silos. The trees themselves come from the customer's own stand. They're dragged by tractor to the mill: a yesteryear building of logs, beams, and rusted tin siding, the likes of which haven't been seen since *The Perils of Pauline*. Ralph Gullet is Mr. Calaway's assistant. They manhandle the timber onto the graduated carriage and, *whrrrrrr-screeeeeech-whine!* there you are! An air full of sawdust, a truckful of lumber, and a vague feeling you're not in the atomic age. Mr. Calaway's mill is one of the last in southern Ohio.

How *is* business in Cincinnati? Well, the Cincinnati Stock Exchange in the Dixie Terminal Building at Fourth and Walnut Streets is doing very nicely, thank you, but there *is* a reason. Only the Cincinnati exchange and the one in Detroit at this writing allow brokers to split commissions 60/40 with brokers who are not actual members of the exchange. The result is that four out-of-state members have been added to the Cincinnati exchange, doubling the May 1965 volume over May 1964. In the first five months of 1965, 563,351 shares were traded. In the same period in 1964, only 382,792 shares were traded: a gain of almost 200,000 shares!

How *is* business in Cincinnati? According to one report, Cincinnati has kept pace with the rest of the nation—on paper, at least. Productivity gains show we haven't fallen behind. In other words, we're still producing a lot. But on the other hand, we have manufactured these things *with fewer workers*. Compared with Cleveland, Akron, Dayton, and Toledo, you'll find Cincinnati has actually reduced manufacturing employment. Still, the manufacturing businesses themselves are strong and healthy. It's just that they haven't added many new workers. New plants open. Old plants shut down. A balance is maintained. In 1958, in the Cincinnati Standard Statistical Area of Hamilton, Kenton, and Campbell Counties, there were 763 manufacturing firms that employed more than twenty workers. Five years later, in 1963—and adding Dearborn, Boone, Clermont, and Warren Counties to the original three—there were still only 766 such firms. In other words, some came, some went, and the final increase boiled down to three *new* major firms. While certain types of business have disappeared, others have strengthened themselves. Two of the more invigorating are electrical machinery and fabricated metal products industries. Declining are transportation equipment, nonelectrical machinery, and—surprisingly enough—food products.

Take a look at the changing labor pool. Add to the college graduates pounding the pavement here each June, 13,000 high school graduates. This makes for crowded chili parlors downtown on a summer afternoon. At least two thirds of the high school graduates will be seeking work. The other one third will be loafing. Half of those graduates seeking work head straight to the city's Youth Opportunity Center, which one sweltering June week was inundated with 690 applicants. Will they find work? Perhaps. Ohio employers have offered 2500 summer jobs to these kids. The joker is, not all the jobs are in the Greater Cincinnati area. Also, pounding the pavement is a new experience to many high school graduates. In Hamilton County alone, 42,000 never walk to school at all; they ride school buses. Thus, in June a lot of kids suddenly find that their feet as well as their souls are beginning to ache.

Even with aching feet, though, some find jobs. Let's add a few more numbers to the scene and then stop before we all get terribly confused. Hamilton County employs 11 percent of the state's 1,182,206 manufacturing employees. Cleveland hires 21.3 percent. Dayton—which includes Miami, Montgomery, and Green Counties—hires only 8.6 percent. Statistically, if it is a factory job an Ohioan seeks, he tries Cleveland first, Cincinnati second, Dayton third, and Columbus fourth. Columbus uses a scant 6.1 percent. Men have better luck finding factory jobs than do women, who fill only 18.6 percent of them.

Southern Ohio's industrial pulse is healthy. Consider Middletown. The Armco Steel Company's $300,000,000 expansion program creates 1000 new jobs. The town itself has only 50,000 people. Add to the mixture the 5000 new college students who will attend the Miami University branch being built there, and you can easily see why Middletown is suffering from what it calls "staggering growing pains."

The action is less exciting in Hamilton, Ohio, but don't let that fool you. There's action. Hamilton's population is 77,500, compared with 72,354 in 1960. The development of Hamilton's Southwestern Ohio Industrial District (288 acres) has been labeled "Hamilton's greatest single industrial development in history." Ryan B. Hall, executive director of the Hamilton Association of Trade and Industry, said that industrial employment in his city rose to the highest peak in nearly four years during May 1965. Hamilton has 14,113 employed in its industry. Each year for three consecutive years, $11,000,000 has been added to the city's industrial payroll.

In Cincinnati the employment in manufacturing industries for May 1965 was 426,900, up 1.5 percent over the same period in 1964. The average worker in Cincinnati earns $120.75 a week, compared with $113.90 a week in 1964. But he works harder to get it. In 1965 he worked 42.8 hours a week. In 1964 he worked only 41.7 hours a week.

He spends what he earns. In 1964, $1,698,083,000 was rung up on cash registers in Hamilton, Clermont, and Warren Counties. Most of the money went for food. In that year, area housewives gave the girl at the checkout counter $421,618,000. Think of that in terms of trading stamps, and it makes your head swim. In 1964 this area spent $150,000,000 in restaurants and bars, and $124,000,000 in drugstores. But not all the people were on a spending spree in 1964. Nearly one third of the families earned less than $4000 a year. Only 22 out of every 100 families earned more than $10,000.

As many as 44,000 people in the Greater Cincinnati area own stock. According to William Styles, *Post & Times-Star* business writer, the Cincinnati area is twenty-first among the nation's metropolitan areas in stock ownership. He breaks the figures down even more:

> The ratio of one stockholder for every nine citizens is well ahead of the Ohio average of one for twelve, and only second to Cleveland's one for seven. Shareholders in the nearby Hamilton-Middletown area are also on the rise . . . One out of every ten citizens there is a shareholder.

Women slightly outnumber men as shareholders, 51 to 49. Children represent 6.5 percent of shareholders.

Has automation hacked away at the labor force? Not in every case. Consider Aggie's Egg Farm in Milford, Ohio: 5400 laying hens clucking nervously in a single henhouse that's completely automated. The operator also has 7500 birds at another farm in St. Martins, Ohio. Each day from the Milford henhouse come 4000 eggs. Thanks to automation, the hens are fed automatically, and the operator doesn't have to do a thing except candle and pack the results. In this fashion eggs reach customers in forty-eight hours or less. In less automated times, farmers sometimes saved their eggs for a week or so before lugging them gingerly off to market. Without automation, the egg farm called Aggie's would be only a dream. As it is, it's practically an industry unto itself which requires a lot of people who can't be automated.

Thomas N. Stainback, executive vice-president of the Cincinnati Chamber of Commerce, is trying to build the Cincinnati chamber into an area chamber by following the example of Aggie's Egg Farm: put all its eggs into one basket. The chamber's "one basket" is the Greater Cincinnati area, and the "eggs" are the various individual chambers and communities that comprise it. Numbers bother Mr. Stainback as they bother the rest of us, especially numbers that indicate we're manufacturing more but employing less. He feels it's high time Cincinnati did a little more than break out in a cold sweat about the way some things are. He maintains, also, that the city has a tough row to hoe because of the increasing competition from other, more distant, areas.

"It is not sufficient to say that Cincinnati is a beautiful city and wants industry," he said. "In this day and age you have to show what you can do for industry and demonstrate the advantages of coming here and staying."

He added:

"There's no sense advertising if you don't know what you have to sell. We have to have an inventory of what is available here and then go out and merchandise it. We haven't done very well at this in the past. Too few people in the East know about Cincinnati. I'm not being critical of the past . . . but we are in a tough business, a very tough business, selling industry on sites. We have the goods here, but they just haven't been promoted to the fullest."

He stakes some of his hopes on urban renewal. "The good industrial land and parks available around here are no longer within the confines of the city. They're in the Greater Cincinnati area. As a consequence, what happens in those outlying spots is going to have an impact on the city and area as a whole. Therefore, it should be coordinated. As for Cincinnati itself, hemmed in by the suburbs and most of its industrial land in use, one of the few things left is urban renewal."

Mr. Stainback, a practical man who has no desire to become a "take-over" artist, says he seeks a cooperative program for the tri-state area of Hamilton, Warren, Clermont, Boone, Campbell, Kenton, and Dearborn Counties.

Will he succeed? Will Cincinnati survive? Don't be discouraged. If this Cincinnati story sometimes sounds like a soap opera, do as the soap-opera announcers do and look at the brighter side. Cincinnati, after all, has more bright sides than gloomy ones. For instance, Cincinnati is growing. For every 1000 who die each year in Hamilton County, 2000 are born. The exact figures: in 1962, 969 died and 2163 were born; in 1963, 956 died and 2118 were born; and in 1964, 948 died and 2012 were born. But even these figures do not completely cheer us. Each year in Hamilton County fewer people are born. But there are other ways to increase the population. In June 1965, a special trainload of 300 representatives of business and industry took a railroad tour from Cincinnati to Hamilton, looking at the many available industrial sites. The tour was sponsored by the Railroad Community Service Committee in cooperation with the Chamber of Commerce and the Cincinnati Gas & Electric Company. Did they find new sites that appealed to them? Were they excited about the prospect of moving their industry into our area? Time will tell.

Let's look at a few more businesses to establish that this area has just about every kind on tap.

There is the Stearns & Foster Company, which began in 1846. George Stearns came here from Bedford, Massachusetts; Seth Foster came only from his father's Woolper Creek Farm in Boone County, Kentucky. Together they trafficked in better cotton batting, which they created by spreading flour paste on a marble slab, rolling a sheet of cotton batting on it, peeling it off, and hanging it out to dry. The result was a cotton batting that wouldn't tear or stretch.

Each man put up $1500 and their first mill was opened at Clay and Liberty Streets. Thus, the cotton-batting and -wadding world had a brace of new kings. Now the plant is in Lockland, where just before the turn of the century the company began making mattresses, too. During World War II most of Stearns & Foster's output was absorbent cotton and mattresses for the armed services. Their cotton wadding now is everywhere—and in the unlikeliest places. Automobile makers use it for upholstery and trim. Milady wears quilted robes made from it. Everyone sits on it when he sits on an overstuffed chair. Did your wife powder her nose this morning? Stearns & Foster's cotton wadding helped take the shine away.

Now think about fatty acids. One Cincinnati company does, to the tune of more than $45,000,000 a year. It's Emery Industries Incorporated, which peddles fatty acids and fatty-acid derivatives to the nation. Emery is about one fortieth the size of Union Carbide and one thirtieth the size of Monsanto, but still it sells one fourth of all the fatty acids sold. What are fatty acids? You're not the first to ask that question. Fatty acids are used in just about every manufacturing process you can think of, the way wives use salt for seasoning. The end result is many things: urethane foams, textiles, agricultural sprays, and jet lubricants. Cincinnatian Thomas Emery started the business when the Queen City was up to its ears in slaughterhouses. He converted animal fats into tallow candles. His competitor: William Procter. When the Emery family began to dabble in real estate (they built the Carew Tower, and if you live in Mariemont, they built that, too!), the fatty-acid business and the real estate business got so tangled up, it took the founder's grandson, John Emery, Jr., to sort out the two. The company didn't really go in to the chemical business on a grand scale until right before World War II. Now it's growing every which way. In two years it has gone from 600 stockholders to 1300. Long-range hopes: $100,000,000 worth of fatty acids sold each year.

Add Formica to the list of home-grown Cincinnati industries, but don't forget to write it with a capital F or everyone at Formica will give you angry looks. It's not that Formica hires only angry men, it's simply that the Formica Corporation, now a division of Cyanamid, keeps trying to protect its registered trade mark. And well it should. If you've ever spilled beer on a new bar table, chances are the waitress didn't cry over it. Chances are the table wasn't wood at all but a Formica laminated surface that looked like wood. The company officially began in 1913 when Herbert A. Faber and D. J. O'Connor, both on the engineering staff at Westinghouse Electric & Manufacturing Company's plant in Pittsburgh, quit to go into business for themselves. Now, with its two major plants in Evendale and Winton Place and another abuilding in California, the company seems on firm footing. It is. But it wasn't in the beginning. Things were touch-and-go. In 1913 the company began with crossed fingers, high hopes, factory space at Second and Main Streets that rented for $30 a month, a half-hearted 35-horsepower boiler, and a gas stove. The first order was from Chalmers Motor Company for commutator rings. To fill it, Faber and O'Connor borrowed tools, donned overalls, and worked practically around the clock. It wasn't until 1918 that they could uncross their fingers and breathe a little easier. That year sales had reached $145,000. In 1919, Formica moved out to Spring Grove Avenue near the (then) Chester Park. By 1923 the company was on a firm footing financially and expanded some more. It went into the timing-gear business, turning out 6000 such items a day for cars with such heart-stopping names as Maxwell, Haynes, Graham-Paige, McFarlane, Auburn, and Willys-Overland. Next, Formica made parts for washing machines, vacuum cleaners, and refrigerators. Then came the frabjous day the company chemist found a way to use a printed sheet as the surface of a phonelic laminate and, *presto!* the granddaddy of decorative Formica on countertops from coast to coast. At the time, though, it was turned out mostly in walnut or mahogany grained sheets and used as the front panels of radio sets with wooden cabinets. Now, with gravure presses, sheets can be produced imprinted with almost any design. The first cigarette-proof laminate (foil is one of its layers) was sold in 1931. After that, color was added, and Formica was off and running. The 1937 flood slowed the company a little—water reached the second floor of its Spring Grove Avenue plant—but Formica by then was creating high-water marks of its own in sales and research.

Cincinnati's "Madison Avenue," the advertising row where men in Ivy League suits run things up flagpoles, is scattered all over the city. Although on a par with the more glamorous New York and Chicago agencies when it comes to ability, Cincinnati agencies are considered dinky, homespun affairs of little consequence. Are Cincinnati ad agencies perhaps too "small town" to handle national business with big budgets? Not at all. The Ralph H. Jones Company in the Carew Tower is a no-nonsense sharp shop that handles big spenders like Ashland Oil & Refining Company and Numaid Margarine. Stockton, West, Burkhart, Inc., another old-line Cincinnati agency (actually an outgrowth of the Jones Company years and years ago) has one of the nation's best copywriters on tap: Ran West. Leonard Sive & Associates is another mature, thoughtful agency that can roll up its sleeves and get out good advertising—advertising that equals anything Madison Avenue has produced. Jack Nolan, who heads up Nolan, Keelor & Stites (which used to be just Keelor & Stites), has accumulated a handful of advertising's best professional talent in John Healy and Art Radke. Ann Smith, one of the city's best "media buyers," could teach her counterparts in New York and Chicago tricks they never heard of. And Sam Levy has been in the advertising business here so long, some newcomers think he personally *invented* advertising. John Healy, one of the city's truly great advertising writers, once looked at the chimerical way accounts change hands overnight and agencies blossom and die, and remarked: "In three months any advertising agency can be an office full of secondhand furniture that nobody wants to buy."

Having said that, he gave up writing ads for a spell to write a book, *With Sunshiny Faces,* a charming recollection of Price Hill in the long-ago days when both boys and girls attended the (then) Seton Academy, streetcar rides were a nickel, and advertising men were treated with a modicum of respect.

Will Cincinnati survive? Of course! You can bet your boots on it. One Cincinnatian looked at the competition and said: "This is good for us. It means we must be alert and alive. It demands the very best in us and necessitates the strengthening of the organization to hold and improve our position."

The fact that his name was Richard Deupree and he said the above about Procter & Gamble and not Cincinnati is not the point. The point is that, to many, Cincinnati is the stuff Procter & Gamble, the Mill, and all the other industries are made of. To many who love Cincinnati, in fact, Procter & Gamble and Cincinnati are synonymous. Thanks to each, the other has grown. And just as there's more to Cincinnati than meets the eye, there's more to P&G than meets the eye.

P&G is more than that brunette on television peddling the merits of Ivory, Camay, Zest, Duz, Tide, Cheer, Salvo, Oxydol, Dreft, Dash, Joy, Thrill, Mr. Clean, Spic and Span, Cascade, Comet, or *premium* Duz. P&G is more than that other brunette hawking the benefits of Crisco shortening, Crisco salad oil, Fluffo, Big Top peanut butter, Jif peanut butter, and Duncan Hines prepared mixes. But you must admit, she's an eager-beaver gal like Mother used to make. No hussies on the P&G tubes, thank you. When she sells you Charmain paper products, White Cloud bathroom tissue, and Puffs facial tissue, she puts her heart and commercial soul into the pitch. And there she is again, touting a household bleach called Clorox. As a good neighbor she's always on hand to recommend either Crest or Gleam toothpaste; a trio of shampoos: Drene, Prell, and Head-&-Shoulders; a home permanent called Lilt; and to keep your secret a secret, Secret—the deodorant. This done, she slumps gracefully at the kitchen table, has a cup of coffee with you, and if the coffee isn't Folger's Instant or Folger's Vacuum-Packed, you can bet your boots that somewhere in the advertising world that night there's an advertising copywriter enlisting in the Foreign Legion. The P&G commercials on television are always well-mannered offerings. They will never shock you or be in poor taste, but now and then one will come along that will bore you to death. But P&G is more than something on your grocer's shelf or a bland invitation that interrupts bland television offerings. P&G, simply put, is a whopper of a company.

It all started because William Procter and James Gamble, as brothers-in-law, set up a partnership in 1837 to make and sell soap and candles to Cincinnati, hawking each day's output from a wheelbarrow pushed door-to-door. But Avon wasn't calling; destiny was. Today 85,000 people are shareholders in P&G, its net sales for 1963–64 were close to two billion dollars, and each year P&G gives more than a million dollars away to aid education. A half-million dollars of this gift is in unrestricted grants to universities, graduate schools of education, and graduate schools of medicine. P&G's common stock has paid dividends every year without fail since the company was incorporated in 1890. Fifty-million shares of common stock are authorized; as of June, 1964, 43,629,404 shares are outstanding. If P&G can be considered a soap opera, it's certainly the biggest soap opera this city—or this nation—has ever seen.

Rod Serling, before going on to grander horizons and adding *Twilight Zone* to the nation's vernacular, used to write here in Cincinnati, first at WLW, then at WKRC. It was his play, *Patterns*— a tale of corporate in-fighting—that sprung him free and sent him on to well-deserved fame and fortune. There are some Cincinnatians who maintain that Serling based that play on the life-and-death struggles of the local corporate world. Then, with a murmur, they would look in the direction of P&G's Ivorydale as if to say, "Well, there you are!" Erase such thoughts from your mind. If you talk like that, wash your mouth out with Ivory soap. P&G is big, and will probably get a lot bigger, but it will never get *that* big. The day it does, P&G will cease to exist. In fact, bring the subject up and P&G bristles with old-fashioned irritation.

". . . Let's face this fact squarely," P&G President Howard Morgens told the graduates of St. Louis's Washington University in 1958.

Some people are viewing the growth of large corporations with alarm. Books and magazine articles are appearing which talk dolefully about the "organization man." We read about the "corporate wife" who must follow some sort of rigid protocol. We hear about "robot executives" and "faceless men in a chain of command." These writers seem to imply that large organizations stifle individuality and individual expression and creativity. These are serious questions . . . raised by critics who are quite earnest in their views, even if they are short of facts to support them. However, I am not one who shares these views. I think most of them are nonsense. I can't speak with any authority about other fields, but I think perhaps I can speak with some authority about the field of business. Very possibly the conditions seen by these critics exist somewhere in some organizations, both large *and* small. But they do *not* exist in good organizations. It is the very essence of good management and good organization to see that they do not exist. In the main, organizations become large because they are good organizations and well-managed ones. They grow large because they steadily succeed in bringing new and better services and products to the public. And what are the basic elements behind new and better services and products? They are ideas, imagination, innovation, initiative, and a healthy dissatisfaction with things as they are. These are not the qualities you will find in a climate of conformity, or rigid protocol, or stifled expression. Ideas, imagination, and initiative can only come from men who are free to express themselves. And they can be put into effect to serve people only by organizations which encourage that freedom.

Starting in 1837, with two brothers-in-law making and peddling tallow candles, lard oil, and German soap, the company grew fast. In ten years they had earned $20,000. In 1859, P&G employed eighty men in its Central Avenue plant. After the Civil War, P&G helped reconstruction by extending liberal credit to its shattered southern customers. How the first "floating soap" came to be is mentioned in Chapter 6, as well as how it acquired the name Ivory, but it all happened forty-one years after the two men began the business. By 1879 the Central Avenue plant had grown to sixteen old-fashioned buildings that produced 200,000 cakes of soap each day. Five years after that, the whole shooting match caught fire, burned down, and P&G moved to Ivorydale. Three years later, P&G hired its first chemist to tinker in the corner of the Ivorydale machine shop.

Even in those early days P&G was working out the kinks in its employee-employer tangle. In 1886, P&G shook up industry by giving its workers a half day off on Saturday. The next year P&G further rocked industry by starting a profit-sharing plan for its workers. Five years after that, the company began its stock-purchase plan. And two years after that, in 1894, the company instigated its pension plan.

Even after the turn of the century P&G still manufactured candles, but not many households were buying them. P&G candles were used mostly in railroad and stage coaches. By 1910, P&G research was paying off: from the tinkerings had evolved a method for partial hydrogenation of cottonseed oil. This put P&G into the food business a year later, when Crisco—the first all-vegetable shortening—was introduced. In 1923, network radio began and Crisco was there. The year Wall Street collapsed, 1929, was the year P&G organized its first market-research department to find out what products housewives wanted and how they felt about the products they were getting. Now that department each year hires hosts of attractive college girls —another way P&G helps to make our city more charming.

Meanwhile the company's program for its workers was growing. In 1915 the employees' disability and death-benefit plan was set up. By 1923, P&G could guarantee its hourly employees forty-eight weeks of work every year. And while the stock market laid an egg, P&G laid a golden one. In 1930, its sales passed the $200,000,000 mark. During World War II, the Wolf Creek Ordnance Plant in Milan, Tennessee, operated by P&G's Defense Corporation, which the Government had asked P&G to set up, loaded shells—usually three months ahead of schedule, thanks to P&G production know-how. P&G also ran the Gulf Ordnance Plant at Aberdeen, Mississippi. After the war, the action was faster: new plants, new products, new people, and foreign expansion.

Now P&G has thirteen operating divisions, soaps and detergents are manufactured in eleven different locations from New York to California, food products are manufactured in nine, toilet goods in two, and paper products in three. Add the Clorox Company, which manufactures in thirteen different locations; the Buckeye Cellulose Corporation's crushing mills in five southern states; and the Buckeye Cellulose Corporation's pulp-producing plants in Foley, Florida, where wood pulp is produced, and in Memphis, Tennessee, where cotton linter is produced. Also, don't forget P&G's Folger Coffee Company in Houston, Kansas City, New Orleans, and San Francisco. Besides these, P&G has manufacturing operations in thirteen foreign countries (its first opened in 1915 in Hamilton, Ontario), and its products are also manufactured in partially owned P&G plants or under license in sixteen additional countries. P&G products are sold in more than 140 different countries!

We could go on forever telling about this industry and that. But let's end the matter here. There's more to Cincinnati than the salt mines each father seeks each morning. There are, in addition, salt mines for children. These items are called school. Let's brush up on new math and attend.

17

When Greater Cincinnati fathers hurry each morning to the salt mines, their children hurry to school, but the little red schoolhouse is only a memory in the minds of those tinkering with middle age. In the metropolitan area many of the schools are now sleek one-story structures that cover acres of ground and are as antiseptic as a hospital drinking glass. However, here and there stand fat, gothic brick piles of the past, three and four stories high. Even the schools built in the 1920s and 1930s look like one-owner secondhand Buicks; but built well, they have endured, so why sic the bulldozer on them? In townships beyond the corporation line, where the one-room schools made their last stand, the magic word was consolidation. Mushrooming suburbia has left these one-room relics to linger forgotten at country intersections where wind, rain, and time are doing the rest. Yellow school buses pass these antique structures, but the children-commuters never wave. Inside the city itself and sometimes lost among weeds and rubble are the remains of school buildings that have died. For instance, Riverside School is now a vacant lot on a steep hillside. *Old* Riverside School, that is. *New* Riverside School is a brick building on River Road. When it appeared, both *old* Riverside School and *old* Harrison School breathed their last. Children dusted erasers for the last time, emptied their desks, and left the ancient buildings for the wreckers to play with. Well, *old* Riverside is gone, but *old* Harrison had better luck. It was refurbished, turned into a flat building, and once again children run and play in its yard.

On the other hand, Woodward High School, which is nearly 200 years old, has roamed the city like a lost child, following the population. Now it's at 7001 Reading Road. More than 18,000 have been graduated from Woodward High School, either the Woodward on Reading Road or one of the three other Woodwards. Founded in 1831—somewhere else in the city—most recently Woodward used to hang around the intersection of Thirteenth and Broadway. Actually, Woodward High School didn't join the Cincinnati public school system until 1851. Before that, it was Woodward College, a combination high school *and* college.

Alfred Segal of the *Post & Times-Star,* recalled *old* Hughes High School at Fifth and Mound Streets as opposed to *new* Hughes, which has been across the street from the University of Cincinnati since 1910. When a shoemaker named Hughes died in 1824, he requested his estate sit dormant a few years, then some of its money be used to start a school. Mr. Segal, who had been graduated from *old* Hughes in 1902, recalled how Mr. Coy, the principal at that time, once spanked Mr. Segal's hand with a rattan, "by way of making me go straight," Mr. Segal added. The reporter also recalled Clara C. Jordan, who taught Life as well as Latin. She used to instruct her class with extracurricular thoughts like: "Care about people. That's the main purpose of your living in the world. It's more important even than these Latin lessons." Mr. Segal, a beautiful dreamer and a beautiful rememberer, wrote this melancholy recollection in the *Post & Times-Star:*

> Oh yes, Cincinnatus himself remembers when he as a kid resided among the many German neighbors "Over the Rhine." The two-story house which was his home stood at Elm and Central Parkway, but in Cincinnatus' time the Miami and Erie Canal was trickling by.
>
> The little brick house in which young Cincinnatus resided stood where the YMCA building now rises so magnificently. And across the street stood the 10th District School, now known as the Raschig School.
>
> And Cincinnatus also remembers his German teacher there, Miss Meinhardt. German was the language of many in the city then and German was spoken all "Over the Rhine." The German language was taught in all the public schools, together with English . . .
>
> Miss Meinhardt used to speak up, saying, "This is a German city and I hope you'll all learn the German language . . ."
>
> There was German singing in the classes. "Ich weiss nicht was soll es bedeuten das ich so traurig bin" was a popular school song which asked why should I feel so sad.
>
> And there was Fräulein Meinhardt, who used to tell us, "Smile and keep smiling always! What beauty is there in sadness on your face. Now, all of you, together: smile!"
>
> But the German language has gone from the city, together with the German lessons. German went out of our schools on the first day of World War One . . .

And before that, John B. Peaslee was superintendent of the Cincinnati public schools those dozen years between 1874 and 1886. A New Hampshire native who had been graduated from Dartmouth College, he took over the Cincinnati job when he was thirty-two years old. He introduced "lined" paper into grade schools to combat the students because, whenever they wrote, they wrote every which way. He ordered that slateboards be ruled, too. This was in the days when paper was a luxury; most children carried slateboards. Mr. Peaslee's insistence on precise and beautiful writing paid off. Samples of slateboard work by Cincinnati schoolchildren were the talk of the 1878 Paris Exhibition. Now Peaslee School, at 216 Woodward Street, is named in his honor, and slateboards, if they exist at all, are in some catch-all corner of a museum.

So much for recollections. The pretzel man no longer hovers near the schoolyard peddling doughy pretzels for a penny. Now schoolyards are not calculated by the square foot but by the acre. Let's put *old* Woodward, *old* Hughes, and all the rest back into the closet and look at the area school systems today: a whopping complex. Example: in the Cincinnati school system alone, 9000 school windows need new glass each year. This figures. The Cincinnati public school system in 1965 included seventy-one elementary schools, sixteen junior high schools, seven senior high schools, one senior-high college-preparatory school, one senior-high vocational school, and nine special schools.

To relieve overcrowding in fourteen elementary schools, the Cincinnati Board of Education rents sixty-nine neighborhood churches and community centers, and in addition, carts students by the busload from crowded neighborhood schools to others with more room. When school started in September 1965, Superintendent Wendell H. Pierce said:

"We'll be overcrowded as usual, but Cincinnati public schools are prepared to take care of . . . about 88,000 pupils."

The peak enrollment for 1964 was 88,440, a high caused by the arrival of 3000 first-grade pupils from the Roman Catholic schools in the Cincinnati archdiocese, which that year was forced to eliminate from its private system all its first grades. The Cincinnati archdiocese operates a privately supported school system almost as complex as the public school system—and almost as costly, too. Without the tax support the public schools have, these private parochial schools are hard-pressed to keep up with the population explosion. Parents whose children attend Roman Catholic schools pay both tuition for the private facility and taxes to support a public school system they don't use. Both school systems are bursting at the seams but have managed with luck, imagination, and crossed fingers to keep a little ahead of babies that seem to turn overnight into children of school age.

The *quality* of education has not suffered in this area. But to keep up with the rising school population, the Cincinnati public schools as an example hired 384 new teachers in 1965. In fact, if all the teachers employed by the Cincinnati public schools for the 1965–66 school year were crowded into one auditorium, you'd need an auditorium seating 3543. Some of these teachers are dolls, some are ancient, a few resemble Mr. Novak, a few others think they do, many are like Mr. Peepers, but they are all qualified—and isn't *that* the important thing?

Meanwhile out in Hamilton County beyond the Cincinnati city limits, if you put the teachers and administrators of just seven school districts—Finneytown, Forest Hills, Lincoln Heights, Northwest, Oak Hills, Southwest, and Three Rivers—into one auditorium, you'd need a hall seating 1265. Nearly 32,000 children from kindergarten through grade twelve attend school in these districts. Northwest School District has the heaviest load: it's slugged with a turnout of 10,000!

Two other school districts, Indian Hill and Madeira, have joined these seven so they can go shopping together and save a bundle when buying school supplies. Hanford Combs, assistant superintendent of the Oak Hills School District and chairman of the combined seven districts' purchasing committee, says that this committee awarded $50,000 in contracts for the purchase of a dozen penny-ante items alone, like pencils, crayons, and carbon paper. How does this save the taxpayers? Well, finger paints which used to cost $1.10 a quart now cost only $.596. Tempera paints, formerly purchased by the separate districts for $.93 a pint, are now purchased by the combined district in larger quantities for $.49. Combs said: "When you consider we buy 7200 pints of tempera paints and 900 quarts of finger paints, it is easy to see the savings grow."

A glance at several of the area schools gives you an idea of the others. The Bond Hill Elementary School at California and Matlock Avenues is a red-brick Georgian affair that has been called "one of Cincinnati's most beautiful buildings for lower-grade pupils." Another handsome structure is the Brown County Academy of the Ursulines, actually Ursuline Academy, at Reading Road and Oak Street; it's a semiprivate school filled with giggly but well-mannered girls taught by the Ursuline nuns. The majestic Clifton Public School, built in 1905 at McAlpin and Clifton Avenues, boasts a wet touch of history in its frontyard: a ten-foot-high fountain whose inscription says it's from Henry Probasco to the people of Clifton because "Thirsty and ye gave me drink." If you like schools with cupolas, there's the Hartwell Public School on Vine Street between Ferndale Drive and Hartwell Avenue; it has an imposing portico, too. Should the girls wish to know where the boys are—or the other way around—it depends which part of town you're in. Boys can be found at Purcell High School, a Roman Catholic school for boys only. Girls can be found at Regina High School in Norwood, a Roman Catholic school for girls only. In Price Hill, the girls are at Seton High School and the boys are at Elder High School, both Roman Catholic institutions.

Most names for Cincinnati's public high schools, by chance, begin with a W. There's Walnut Hills High School located on a fetching campus along fetching Victory Parkway. When it was built during the Depression years, according to the *Cincinnati Guide,* taxpayers grumbled at the extravagance of "erecting palaces with swimming pools" in the name of education. There's Western Hills High School on the western edge of Price Hill. It has a swimming pool, too; but it was constructed in 1928 when Wall Street was feeling fat and sassy, and not a soul murmured a protest. Since then it has acquired brick additions and has erected temporary classrooms where the front lawn used to be. Withrow High School on Madison Road is a beauty! What other high school has an impressive 114-foot clock tower? The school was called East High School until 1925, when it acquired a fancier name. And to complete the W's, there are all four Woodward High Schools.

Most students try to go on to college after high school, but even those who don't have a variety of "commercial" schools that can train them—and older people as well—for just about any occupation.

Want to learn advertising art and be an agency vice-president before you're twenty-five? Students can enroll in the Advertising Art School on Hackberry Street, one of many available. Want to work in a beauty shop and know if she does or doesn't? The Moler System is but one of several here that will teach you the tricks. Want to succeed in insurance, door-to-door selling, or as a bread-truck driver? Well, to be popular, glad, cheerful, overjoyed, enraptured, transported, and terribly successful, visit Dale Carnegie first. Cincinnati offers that, too! Want to master the slide rule? Welding? Blueprint reading? Consider, for one, the Ohio Mechanics Institute Evening College on Central Parkway. Is Hollywood calling? Look in first on any of the drama schools in the area. Is real estate your meat? Try classes in Dayton, Ohio, and prepare for your state exam. Perhaps you'd rather be a photographer? Among others, there's the Pazovski School in Mount Adams. Sculpturing? Landscape painting? The Art Academy in Eden Park is for you. Want to be a soprano, a tap dancer, or play the Hawaiian guitar? Cincinnati has schools galore. Want to be a secretary and marry the boss? We've tons of commercial schools. The Campbell Commercial School, for instance, will teach you to run the comptometer, too. And the Cincinnati Barber College can teach you everything about barbering except how to memorize batting averages. Want a college degree but have to work? No strain. Try our night colleges.

Streetcars may be only a memory, but the University of Cincinnati is still considered by Greater Cincinnatians as that "streetcar college." But when they say it, they say it with affection. More students lived at home—and used to ride streetcars back and forth—than lived on campus. Such was and is the way of a municipal university. Actually, since the University of Akron and the University of Toledo gave up trying and became part of the state system, the University of Cincinnati is the last city-owned university in Ohio. And as the last of its tribe, it has a couple of nasty problems, but even so, it's no dinky place. When it comes to educational excellence, U.C. takes a back seat to no one.

It's old (established in 1819). It's big (14 different colleges on 148.5 acres). It's crowded (22,580 full- and part-time students). It's growing (in 1961 it opened an additional two-year University College, and nearly 1500 attended). It has parking problems (three campus garages hold 886 cars). And it simply doesn't have room for everybody (each year nearly 4000 applicants go elsewhere—or nowhere).

To be honest, U.C. is a "municipal-supported university" in name only these days. And being labeled "municipal" has proved a handicap. Many private-foundation dollars go elsewhere because the foundations have the idea that Cincinnati taxpayers are picking up the University's tab. The truth is, the University gets more money from federal grants and contracts than from the $6.70 each Cincinnati taxpayer pays each year. Golf Manor pays, too, though it is a corporate entity; but by supporting U.C. this way, Golf Manor parents can send their young people to U.C. at the same low rate Cincinnatians pay. U.C. officials don't scorn the tax money that comes to them. The federal money and contract money look good, but so does every dollar that comes along. After all, the University of Cincinnati is "big business." The place costs nearly $28,000,000 a year to operate. Its physical plant is worth more than $100,000,000. It's light bill alone must be a whopper—thanks to its Evening College.

As many students attend the University of Cincinnati's Evening College as attend Miami University in Oxford, Ohio. U.C.'s night enrollment is 10,000 strong. During daylight hours, when these night students are working in local offices and factories, the U.C. campus with its 12,000 day students looks much like a regular campus filled with gangling boys and leggy girls. But after dark, the campus has the appearance of a defense plant going full-blast. To many Greater Cincinnatians, U.C. *is* its Evening College. But to call it an evening "college" is a misnomer: the courses offered are almost as varied as the curriculum served to the day students. The difference between the night students and the day students is—forgive us!—the difference between night and day. The day students are young, charming, and full of vinegar. The night students are every bit as charming and just as full of vinegar, but for many of them, youth went thataway. Look at the 1965 graduating class and see what we mean. Degrees were awarded to 144 Evening College seniors. There were only 11 women in the group. The youngest in the graduating class was 22, the oldest was 59, and the average was 31. Nearly all of the graduates were married—and the combined offspring totaled 273. Many attended the Evening College with no thought of acquiring a degree but to brush up on this or to learn that. But something happened. The atmosphere caught up with them, they plugged on, and eventually graduated. It takes longer to earn a degree at night than during the day because night students can't carry as heavy work loads as full-time day students. Miss Alberta E. Weisgerber, a Procter & Gamble librarian, attended U.C.'s Evening College for nineteen years before she earned her Bachelor of Science Degree. Xavier University, operated by the Jesuits, has evening college, too, and, you'll see ladies in the night classes as well as men. U.C.'s night program, by the way, is the third largest in the nation.

U.C. has more professors than Western College in Oxford, Ohio, has students. U.C. has 1063 full-time and nearly 800 part-time professors. If you combined the libraries of Miami University and Ohio University, you still wouldn't have a library the size of U.C.'s. It has 844,692 books.

But the real worth of a university is measured by its people, and in this category, too, the University of Cincinnati comes on strong. U.C. is the only university ever to supply three vice-presidents to the General Motors Corporation *at the same time*. The Golden Gate Bridge in San Francisco and the Pam Am Building in New York were designed by U.C. graduates. Two of the seven Ohio members of the National Academy of Sciences are U.C. professors: Dr. Albert Sabin, who developed oral polio vaccine, and Dr. Paul Hergert, who organized the Vanguard Computer Center. U.C. graduates cover the map. Ralph Seedorf stayed home and became a vice-president of Carthage Mills, Inc. R. W. Hutzelman went to Luxembourg to become a manager for Dupont. Eugene Agger is chief adviser in the New Brunswick, New Jersey, Urban Renewal Program. William Hesse is in advertising as chief executive officer of Benton & Bowles, Inc. Robert L. Rice is president of Graflex, Inc., in Pound Ridge, New York. Robert Moore is principal of Madeira Beach, Florida, Elementary School. Morey Gibbs is assistant head of the Control Systems Department in the Electronics Division of Aerospace Corporation in El Segundo, California. And Mrs. Letha Greene runs that oldtime river packet on the Ohio River. You can find her anywhere between Pittsburgh and New Orleans.

The University department that is creating national attention is in a building marked "Basic Medical Research." Inside is Dr. Herman C. Lichstein, formerly a professor of bacteriology at the University of Minnesota. He is the magnet that attracts top-caliber students to U.C. from everywhere in the nation to do research in microbiology: bacteria, viruses, yeasts, and molds. But Dr. Lichstein doesn't believe that professors should be heard from and not seen. He believes firmly in classroom teaching.

"You'll find some instructors whose most important thing is the paper they're working on," he said. "But *our* people are not that way. I don't want to be by myself in my laboratory, with teaching left alone. Our most important product is the student and our staff people are teachers."

Exploring the tiniest forms of life has brought both fame and dollars to the University. The National Institutes of Health have come through with a five-year grant of $250,000—which is not bad for a "streetcar college."

Meanwhile, the Cincinnati Bearcats are doing what they can to attract attention to the city and the campus. In case you've ever wondered how the athletic teams at U.C. got the nickname of Bearcats, the *Cincinnatus Alumnus*, the U.C. alumni publication, offers this answer:

"He's a bear! Who's a bear? Teddy Baehr!"
Fullback Leonard K. Baehr, Jr., class of '16, was in the thick of the U.C. varsity tangle with the Wildcats of the University of Kentucky in 1915 when that cry was first heard from the massed throats of the U.C. supporters who had traveled to Lexington for the game.
In the early moments of the contest the U.C. rooters weren't so exuberant. Their team had been struggling against heavy odds and had dropped behind long before the half. It seemed "one of those days."
All during the game U.C. cheerleader Norman M. "Pat" Lyon, class of '15, tried to infuse spirit into that disappointed crowd. As he watched the driving but futile efforts of Team Captain Baehr, he was suddenly inspired and turned to the crowd and shouted, "They may be Wildcats, but we have a Baehr-cat on our side."
The crowd took up the chant, "Come on Baehr-cat!"
The name inevitably became changed to Bearcats and became the standard appellation for all U.C. athletic groups. Incidentally, on that day in 1915, whether the new nickname was responsible, no one knows today, but it is in the record books that the new "Bearcats" went on to win that day by two points. Final score: Wildcats 11—Bearcats 13.

Each September, 800 Cincinnati students travel thirty-five miles northwest to Oxford, Ohio, and Miami University, which only the natives know is not in Florida. This sprawling land-grant institution is supposed to admit any Ohio resident who waves an accredited high school diploma in its face, but the truth is, the University doesn't have enough beds to tuck everyone in at night. Oxford is too distant for all but a few students to commute to. Thus, some applicants take one last look at the beautiful campus and go away, grumbling. The applicants' reasons for wanting to be a part of Miami University are reasonable: the University is academically sound, and the setting—trees, winding paths, cheery village, and stately buildings—is exactly the setting pictured by Hollywood and dreamers. Milton Caniff's cartoon strip *Steve Canyon* uses Miami's campus as a background prop when "Maumee University" appears in his strip. A look around shows you that not *all* the students get excited about their Redskins, be the Redskins dribbling a basketball or wondering why a football rolls so silly. There *is* excitement at game time, but win or lose, there is generally more excitement—and noise—at the Purity, an Oxford beer hall once an ice cream parlor, hence its name. By nightfall the athletic confrontations are forgotten. Then, under a full moon, the football stadium has other kinds of action as, in pairs, resembling walk-ons for the Ark, students enter the stadium's gloomy confines, where darkness swallows them up.

None of this tells how good the University is academically—and simply put, it *is*. University officials figure that by 1980 there will be 15,000 students at the University in Oxford itself, not counting those enrolled in the branches it has now and will have then. September 1965 found about 10,000 students in Oxford attending Miami University—and already elbow room was getting scarce. When the future rolls around, the University people hope to have another matter ironed out. Now basically an undergraduate school, Miami would like to climb higher on the academic ladder. Some want the burden of undergraduate work handled completely by neighborhood junior colleges that are closer to the homes of the students, and when that happens, goodby *rah rah* college! They feel the Miami facility would be better if it trafficked only in those seeking masters and doctors degrees. But this hope is still just that, a hope.

While the Miami Redskins may not get the volume of national publicity that other—and sometimes less deserving—teams are collecting in scrapbooks, the Oxford university has one distinction. If Ohio is the mother of Presidents, Miami University is the mother of football coaches. At this writing, Miami University men are coaching teams at Indiana University, Notre Dame, University of Virginia, Xavier, and Yale. Add to this list the Miami University men coaching professional football teams in New York and San Diego, and it becomes apparent that if all the football coaches who came from Miami University and are now coaching collegiate and professional teams should quit and open candy stores—football would be declared a disaster area.

On the academic side—the *true* university—there are many professors who have been stamped with all kinds of national and international approval. Dr. Reo Christenson and Dr. Daniel Jacobs in the field of government are two. Two others, but in the history field, are Dr. Harris Warren and Dr. Dwight Smith. From the Fine Arts College comes a pair of artists who have exhibited nationally and won applause: Professor Edwin Fulwider and Professor Philip Morsberger. Theatrically, Dr. Ronald C. Kern is rapidly making the theater in Oxford an item to be reckoned with. And in the literary world, both in Butler County *and* the world, Dr. Walter Havighurst has quietly carved for himself several niches as (1) a novelist, (2) a historian, and (3) a rare and sensitive teacher of creative writing who brings out the best in his students and fires them with enthusiasm.

The campus itself is filled with students mostly from Ohio (and most of these from the Cleveland area), but by no means is it a corny midwestern place of small intellect. There are foreign students, mostly from Asia and Africa. And the rest of the students seem to be from Illinois. In case you're interested in such matters, the girls generally outnumber the boys, especially in the education college, where there are about four girls for every male. In Arts and Sciences, however, the trend is reversed: for every twelve guys there are only seven girls. Thus, a student who goes to Miami University for both higher education and occasional hanky-panky should pick his—or her—college with care.

To sweeten the setting for the boys, however, Oxford possesses not only Miami University but Western College for Women right next door. Legally, the College is outside the village limits, but across the street is still across the street. At first glance—especially to men in the Miami University dorms—Western College for Women seems more like a delightful slogan than a college, but a second glance introduces everyone to a most interesting school in a most beautiful setting. Hidden by ancient trees, with a duck pond for a moat, Western College for Women is a genteel gathering of beautiful girls from about every nation on earth. These young ladies fill their days by studying hard, dating or not dating boys from Miami University, and by wandering down the paths to the duck pond, where in spring they can watch nature and in winter they can ice skate. Not a large college—and one that intends to remain tiny, top enrollment never to exceed 750—Western College for Women is better known to the East Coast than to Cincinnatians. To be honest, Western

College attracts more students from New York, New Jersey, and Connecticut (133) than from Ohio, Indiana, and Kentucky (101). For every two students from Ohio, there's a student from a foreign country.

The girls' college is vaguely associated with the eastern colleges of Wellesley, Vassar, Bryn Mawr, Smith, Mount Holyoke, Goucher, Barnard, and Sarah Lawrence. One Western girl, in a moment of desperate soul-searching or sheer frustration, announced that "when you can't make it at one of the other 'sisters,' you come to Western." But this, of course, is an oversimplification. Western College for Women is by no means a weak sister; rather, a few years back it was a Cinderella sitting around waiting for something to happen. Something *did* happen. The fairy's magic wand said "interculture"— advertising slang for a bunch of kids from a bunch of foreign countries learning things together, making do, and in making do, making a better tomorrow for everybody. What other college with an enrollment (1964–65) of a little over 500 girls had 37 students from 28 countries? Can you imagine that group meeting back at Western College after summer vacation and some wiseacre asking, "What's new?"

Academically, Western College for Women is an ideal facility that definitely is *not* a diploma mill concerned with piped-in lecturers, massive classes, and other frightening mass-production techniques that bigger places are forced to employ. Its upper classes are so tiny they are hardly more than bull sessions. Once the Western College girl sloshes through the tedium of subjects required for all freshmen and sophomores (but in classes that are never larger than thirty), she dives headlong into her major, where most classes contain scarcely a dozen. The College has only fifty-five full-time and a dozen part-time professors; like universities and colleges everywhere, when the school season opened in September 1965, even three of these were away on leave. The College also has only ten maintenance men, who, of course, are not on leave. And neither are the young stallions from Miami University. They're *always* underfoot, disproving the theory that Western College girls are dumpy grinds. But don't kid yourself. The girls *do* study hard. And when they let off steam, some of them do it dramatically—in the college theater, that is, which is managed by lean and handsome, sad-looking and perpetually exhausted Alfred Sugg, a professor whose father was a medical doctor in Ada, Oklahoma.

Another school for girls, as elegant as Western College and where drama is as well tended, is that superb combination of old and new structures called the College of Mount St. Joseph-on-the-Ohio. Located in the less populated western hills of Greater Cincinnati on the brow of an impressive hill that looks straight down into the Ohio

248

River Valley, this college is run by the Sisters of Charity. It first opened in 1869. But the way Cincinnati is growing, the campus will eventually be surrounded by the outcroppings of suburbia. Still, should ticky-tacky housing appear, the ticky-tackiness will stop with a thud at the college entrance—and from there on in, serenity will prevail. The College accommodates day students as well as residents, all being thoughtful girls who are as knowledgeable as they are refined because, frankly, the nuns run a tight ship. This doesn't mean the school is gloomy and lacks cheer. After all, no one can curb the exuberance of youth, but it does mean that Mount St. Joseph-on-the-Ohio turns out splendid young charmers by the busload, exasperatingly beautiful young ladies, some of whom know judo. The theater there, with Cecil Hale adding his two cents, has rapidly become one of *the* culture centers of the entire city, not just the western suburbs. Its artists series is a heady one. And because the nuns favor the history of the quiet hills that now surround the College, now and then Cecil Hale writes a play based on the western Cincinnati setting, a play which the students put on. The theater itself is no makeshift item. Nuns might look antique as they move about the campus, but there is nothing antique about the way they do things. They have created at their college a theater facility that makes professional theater owners and managers drool with envy. And in Cecil Hale they have the right man when it comes to theater. He's the one who, years ago, ran a radio program for Pogue's called "To Cincinnati at Six," a nightly hour of good taste, the likes of which present-day radio has forgotten how to do. Now he reads poems over WLW-Radio's "Moon River" in a beautiful voice that makes the rest of the broadcasters in this area sound like train callers. Mount St. Joseph-on-the-Ohio is but one of several colleges operated by the Roman Catholics in the Greater Cincinnati area. To list them all—and do justice to them— would make this book a bit too heavy to hold in your hand.

But we must look in on Xavier University, at least! It's on Victory Parkway behind the trees. Founded in 1831 as the Athenaeum, Xavier University is operated effectively under the watchful eyes of the Jesuits. Most of the students are male, but as suggested earlier in this chapter, Xavier Night College has women in attendance, too. The Xavier faculty isn't large, but being Jesuit-trained, it's about as good as any faculty can be. Many in Cincinnati—and not all of them Roman Catholics—agree on one thing: a school operated by Jesuits just naturally gravitates toward excellence because the Jesuit Order itself is an order of carefully selected and finely honed teachers, the cream of the crop. Incidentally, the faculty at Xavier University also serves as faculty for the University's school for Jesuit novices in Milford.

Naturally, Xavier University has a football team, and, naturally, its archenemy is the football team the University of Cincinnati puts together. Xavier teams are called Musketeers. Happily or unhappily (it depends for whom you're rooting), the stone lions in front of U.C.'s McMicken Hall can't be stolen when the rivalry gets to bubbling, but Xavier University has a symbol that can be. It's a statue only 27 inches high, depicting D'Artagnan in bronze-coated terra cotta. D'Artagnan was the musketeer of old upon whose diary Alexander Dumas based his novel *The Three Musketeers*. The statue, a gift to Xavier University by the 16,000 citizens of Auch, France, where the musketeer was born, now occupies a special place in the French Room of the University's new Center. Soft lights light it, but every time U.C. plays X.U. the Xavier students worry a little and watch it a bit more closely. President Father Paul O'Connor said the statue is "a symbol of honor and courage second to none." Being a true Jesuit scholar as well as interested in the outcome of the next Musketeer-Bearcat conflict, he added, "It is an inspiration to *all* our young students in *all* they do, on and off the athletic fields."

X.U. is another one of Cincinnati's no-nonsense schools of higher learning. You can find Xavier undergraduates at the University of Lyon in France as Fredin Scholars studying the French language. But the Jesuits back home have a way of keeping tabs on how these distant scholars of theirs are doing. An Xavier student may study overseas as a Fredin Scholar, but he takes his final examination back here in Cincinnati from the Jesuits. That's the sort of stuff that keeps him out of the sidewalk cafés.

Among the local colleges is, of course, the Hebrew Union College. More than 1100 Reformed rabbis have been graduated from its Hebrew Union College-Jewish Institute of Religion, the rabbinical seminary of American Reform Judaism. Both Jews and non-Jews attend the College itself because H.U.C. turns out some of the best Bible scholars in the world. Teaching of the Bible has been one of the important study areas at the College, and digging has been another. The Hebrew Union College is famed for its Biblical archaeology.

But whether the Cincinnati-area students go to college here in town, go to Oxford, Columbus, or across the river into Kentucky, there's one thing parents can look upon with a sigh of relief. Few of the students from this area look like Beatniks. Even when they live on campus where their parents can't see them, students from here for the most part are well-dressed and well-behaved. Fads don't get as *faddish* here. Actually, high school students are more extreme in their clothing than college students. But even in high school, students take a dim view of grotesque style exaggerations that more distant scholars go ape over. Now and then a weird creature will make the scene, but he's the exception.

Perhaps the most practical way to conclude this chapter on the area's educational plants is to look at Villa Madonna College in Covington, because somehow it has captured the mood of U.C., X.U., M.U., and all the rest. An editorial in 1965 in the *Enquirer* said it best:

> Just over a year ago, Covington's Villa Madonna College took a long, hard look at itself and the community it served. It looked at its past and at its probable future. And the result of that survey was the conclusion that Villa Madonna meets a need in Greater Cincinnati unmet by any other institution. Accordingly, there was a decision to build a new college on a 113.6-acre tract on Turkeyfoot Road, some six miles from the college's present home in downtown Covington—a home that embraces a former furniture store, a lodge hall, an abandoned firehouse, and a dozen other makeshift structures . . .
>
> The enterprises that make up this community are approached many times in the course of a year by similar appeals [for funds]. But few of them, we think, can present a more compelling case than Villa Madonna.
>
> For one thing, 90% of Villa Madonna's 800 day students [another 800 attend evening classes] come from the Greater Cincinnati area. The vast majority of them will remain in the area because this is their home. Some 80% of them are working their way through college—living at home and taking advantage of the college's relatively low tuition. If Villa Madonna did not exist, it seems safe to assert, a majority of its students would be denied the benefits of college training . . .
>
> As the Rt. Rev. Msgr. John F. Murphy, Villa Madonna's president, puts it, "There can be no real competition among colleges. All are needed. All of us together will not be able to provide what will be needed for higher education in the years of soaring enrollments which are already upon us."

That last paragraph tells the story of education in Greater Cincinnati—and everywhere else for that matter. But happily for this area, Greater Cincinnatians aren't simply sitting around and wringing their hands. They're *doing* something about it.

18

The children are at school, the fathers are at work, and what of
the ladies around here? After all, housewifery in Greater Cincinnati
has changed dramatically since the Treaty of Greenville. Shooting
Indians is considered poor taste. No one makes soap at home these
days. And when mother bakes bread, her neighbors cluck with
wonder at her ingenuity. We are hip-deep in the age of gadgetry.
Gadgetry, however, has turned milady into a master mechanic instead of a free spirit, and to run a home is no bed of roses. Anyway,
some of the ladies don't stay home. They work in offices, stores, factories, hospitals, saloons, restaurants, or wherever the buck is. Let's
look at the women's side of Cincinnati: where they shop, how they
get there, why the meter reader loves them, and how beautiful
they are.

Some of them have weird occupations. For instance, down in Cleves
husbands can't get jealous when the mailman visits because one of
the mailmen is Mrs. Dorothy Ritchie. She's the first lady mail carrier
in Greater Cincinnati and one of the few in the country. She took her
exam for clerk-carrier in 1961, thought it would be part-time, and
discovered, to her dismay, it wasn't. Although she wears regulation
mail-carrier's garb, she has insisted on one concession: specially made
slacks. Then, there's Mrs. Jane Miller, who is the lady barber of New
Baltimore and who also drives the ambulance for the New Baltimore
Fire Department's volunteer life squad. Trouble with getting a haircut
in her shop is, saving lives rates ahead of a neck trim, and when an
alarm comes in, she goes out. No one complains, though. She's one of
the better barbers around. And don't use her as an argument against
women drivers. She can drive that life-squad ambulance with no strain.
In fact, she can run rings around the best hotrodder on the pike.

Another one of Greater Cincinnati's more adventurous ladies is Mrs. Letha Greene, the "reluctant heiress" of the Greene Line, which is a one-steamboat steamboat line. The boat is the *Delta Queen*, last of the passenger-carrying river packets. The Greene family itself has been in these parts since Daniel Greene sailed here in 1796 on the schooner *Isabelle*. Later he took command of that schooner and sailed her down the Mississippi, into the Gulf of Mexico, and across the Atlantic Ocean, which was not bad for a boat built in Marietta, Ohio. The Greene family has actually owned riverboats since Dan's grandson Gordon bought the *Bedford* in Nashville. Said the grandson, "I dream about steamboats . . . Sometimes they are in trouble and sometimes it's just a nice moonlight night . . . but it's always steamboats." His wife Mary shared his dream and lived on the steamboats with him. But she did more than watch the trees go by or make lace curtains. She learned to pilot the boats. She had her master's license before her first son was born in 1898. The Greene family, with the women in there pitching, ultimately operated twenty-eight steamboats, but time and modern transportation have reduced their fleet to its present one. Of all the boats they operated, the only side-wheeler was the *Greenland;* the rest were stern-wheelers. Purists suggest that the present *Delta Queen* is not a true riverboat because it was built in Scotland, pieced together on the West Coast, and then operated as a ferry there. Besides, it has only one stack, they point out, and riverboats should have two. They forget that other Greene boat, the *Greendale,* also had only one stack, which accounted for its nickname, "One-Arm John." Anyway, these are idle quarrels. The important thing is that Mrs. Letha Greene, widow of the great-great-grandson who arrived here in 1796, still carries on the Greene family tradition.

Thus, each year the *Delta Queen* serenely chugs up and down the inland waterways, going as far south as New Orleans, lugging tourists on cruises that range from three-day respites to twenty-day journeys into the past. Derby Day finds the *Delta Queen* parked at Louisville (river people call it Lo'ville). When the Mardi Gras turns New Orleans into a playpen, that steamboat whistling 'round the bend is the *Delta Queen*, coming to play, too. Other times the *Delta Queen* slips through the quiet waters of the Tennessee River to whistle a throaty hello to Chattanooga. Then it huffs and puffs upstream to say hello to Pittsburgh. Now and then it sighs an enormous sigh and off it goes in search of St. Paul. Each cruise is a sentimental throwback to the gentler days of Mark Twain. People come from all over the world to Cincinnati, to board the majestic boat, and be thrown back into history with her. Everything aboard is as it was years and years ago—almost. They didn't have air-conditioning then. They do now. But there's even a calliope you can play; only don't be a rube. Aboard the *Delta Queen* they call the steamy pennywhistle a "steam-*pie*-anner." Now let's go ashore and look around at the rest of the Greater Cincinnati ladies.

Such ladies come in all shapes and sizes. Some wear well and some don't. Some are fat, dumpy grandmothers who speak broken English. Some are fat, dumpy teenagers who come from broken homes and quit school to get married. Some are sleek and sassy—grandmothers and granddaughters, both—who can cause truck drivers to look twice. On the other hand, there are some here to whom truck drivers would not give the time of day. Some of the ladies are high-spirited young animals, some are perpetually pooped, some are pregnant every time they turn around, and some drift lonesomely into middle age without ever having known the pain of childbirth. Some are white, some are Negro, and some—a few—are Oriental. They live in cramped flats, dull suburbia, littered furnished rooms, stuffy apartments, and (a few) in the Work House.

Greater Cincinnati ladies look their prettiest on Sundays as they go to and from church. On a crisp and sunny Autumn morning—or a mellow and sweet spring day—these charmers are a sight for sore eyes. Sunday and church represent the one occasion they can really put on the dogs *en masse*. Sunday in this area tells you more about the quality of these gals than any other day of the week. So check their beauty with care: tasteful, so fashionable you'd think the street was a Paris boulevard, and all teetering on high heels. Now and then one entry might jar your soul by making the scene with a dress suitable for vaudeville, but mostly, good taste is the rule rather than the exception. Even the lady you saw that day at the shopping center—hair in curling machinery, no makeup, dirty tennis sneakers, slacks, remote, stony-eyed, and fidgety—could give the fine ladies of San Francisco lessons in fashion when Sunday rolls around. Indeed, Sundays here are beautiful events. It's the rest of the week that sometimes hurts.

Religion seems to be the handiwork of these ladies each Sunday morning. While some Greater Cincinnati ladies may haggle about Zen till they're blue in the face all week long, Sundays find them polishing the family to a gloss and shoveling the children into Sunday schools by the thousands. These ladies are busy, busy, busy. They organize a thousand social events, hold rummage sales, slosh together church suppers, dust the pews, hold millions of meetings, consume oceans of coffee, and when the cops aren't looking, play bingo. But more power to them. Without their efforts, our churches would be turned into lecture halls.

Greater Cincinnati women who look beautiful every Sunday morning outdo themselves on Easter Sunday. Other than a few outlandish hats, these gals brighten the city with color and gladden the hearts of bus drivers. But Easter around here finds many worshipers not at church. They worship instead at sunrise in the woods, where God's handiwork is more apparent. Greater Cincinnati churches, you must understand, are not restricted to the ceremonial buildings that house them. Wherever God is, a worshiper is—and the other way around, too. This fact is crystallized on Easter Sunday morning. For example, in 1965, an interdenominational sunrise service was held in the outdoor band shell in Eden Park. The East End Protestant churches sponsored a community sunrise service in Alms Park. The churches of Greenhills, Forest Park, and Springdale selected an awesome setting for their sunrise worship: where the sun peeps over the lake in Winton Woods. The Community Church of Cincinnati offered sunrise services in Mount Storm Park; the Mount Healthy and North College Hill Methodist churches held theirs in the Mount Healthy and Arlington Memorial Gardens on Compton Road; the Kenwood Baptist Church held its services on the church grounds in the garden; the Pilgrim Holiness churches of Greater Cincinnati offered sunrise services in Devou Park across the river. The daffodils, blooming their heads off in parks that Easter, ran a poor second to the Greater Cincinnati ladies, who were gardens unto themselves.

Naturally, our ladies shop a lot. How are the stores in Greater Cincinnati? Well, whatever your taste—high, fair-to-middlin', low, or missing—Greater Cincinnati has places where you can shop and feel at ease. We have food stores that cater to every taste, even if they run to the extreme, exotic, or weird. If a major department store's gourmet department doesn't have your favorite on its shelves, chances are a neighborhood mom-and-pop grocery might. And don't write off supermarkets when it comes to fancy shopping. Actually, most food shopping is done at supermarkets anyway. Wherever a person lives here, there's a shopping center within whistling distance. Shopping centers boast of at least one supermarket, and the larger ones have several. According to one survey, Greater Cincinnati housewives choose one supermarket over others for these reasons: (1) the quality and freshness of the meat, (2) how easy the store is to reach, and (3) how high—or low—the prices are. Though most people here buy their meat in supermarkets, they don't hold much to meat that's precut or prepackaged; they'd rather trust a butcher they can see. The major food chains here are A&P, 16 stores; Albers (Colonial Stores), 31; Dot Food Stores, 10; IGA stores, 29; Kroger stores, 55; Liberal Markets, 6; Parkview Markets, 67; Thriftway Super Markets, 11; and White Villa food stores, 24. And there are hundreds of independent grocers who are not affiliated with any chain or cooperative. Some of these independent stores are huge, too, and have butchers who may occasionally remember your pooch with a soup bone. Independent butcher shops are beautiful places to shop. Some Greater Cincinnati housewives would shop nowhere else, but this depends on the neighborhood. Each neighborhood here is a separate and distinct world of sorts, so the best advice is to go exploring and find a butcher who loves you.

For a classic shopping adventure there's Findlay Market, the old-world last-of-the-tribe in Cincinnati. The market itself is located in the dilapidated Mohawk district on an Elder Street esplanade between Elm and Race. But the esplanade can't contain it. The market is so gregarious it spills out of the market place itself, and vendors line both sides of Elder Street between Elm and Vine, both sides of Race Street from Green to Elder, and the east side of Race Street from Elder to Findlay. Stalls, vendors, and seeming disorder are everywhere in this huge and unique open-air supermarket of yesteryear. On market days the din, confusion, and scents are beautiful. What can be bought there? Meats, poultry, fish, dairy products, fruits, vegetables, flowers, and special delicacies.

The Cincinnati area has well over 100 department stores, but don't be impressed by numbers. Not all the stores are big. Some are nothing more than dusty corners of antiquity that sell notions and thread. Some are sleazy discount houses with such murky reputations that more ethical discount houses—we have them, too—hate their guts. But consider our better stores. Mabley & Carew, downtown where Roll-man's used to be, is not only there but in four shopping centers as well. Jack Nolan is quick to point out that the five McAlpin stores—Cincinnati fixtures of good taste—are rapidly approaching the volume of Shillito's. Pogue's is downtown as well as in several shopping plazas; wherever you find it, you find elegance. Shillito's is downtown, and at several shopping centers, too. More about them later. Montgomery Ward has stores at Brentwood Plaza, Glenway and Werk Road, as well as in Covington across the river. Sears Roebuck & Company, everywhere these days, has its biggest store on Reading Road; others are in Covington, Oakley, Price Hill, as well as outlying places like Hamilton, Ohio, and Richmond, Indiana. The major department stores are really two stores: upstairs and basement. The basement stores aren't as costly as the upstairs stores, but the upstairs stores aren't staffed with bandits; you won't be robbed. The department-store suburban locations are more than mere make-do afterthoughts. For example, consider Pogue's in the Kenwood Shopping Plaza: two full floors of action plus a covered garage that can hold 300 cars, and escalators to hoist you up and down.

It seems Cincinnati has traveled a long way since Madame Trollope tried to foist her bazaar off onto us. Our better stores are as modern and competitive as stores anywhere, but one thing they possess that stores elsewhere lack is a certain Cincinnati "mood." A closer look at Shillito's might suggest that store and the others. Shillito's has more than a million square feet of sales area. Shillito's, like Pogue's and Mabley's and the rest, wasn't always the hotshot department store it is today. In fact, Shillito's was once such a sleepy little store in the 1920s that it almost went to sleep for good.

The store began in 1830 when John Shillito, twenty-two years old, started out with a couple of bolts of gingham and calico, a plain wooden counter, and heartful of hope. Two years later his store began to move: from one end of Main Street, between Columbia and Pearl, to the other, between Fourth and Fifth. Five years later, in 1837, it moved to the north side of Fourth Street between Main and Sycamore into what was considered at that time the most up-to-date and spacious emporium west of the Alleghenies. John Shillito stayed there twenty years, moving in 1857 west along Fourth Street between Vine and Race, but that also proved only temporary. He needed still more elbow room. But when he opened his next store in Shillito's present location in 1877, other businessmen gave him funny looks because the neighborhood then was strictly residential and so far from the commercial action they predicted he would lose his shirt. However, when Shillito's "Mammoth Dry Goods House" opened, customers came, and he ended up not only with his shirt but a beautiful building. Its main attraction was the open "well," which was 60 feet in diameter and extended from the first floor 120 feet straight up. From the first floor, customers could gape up the "well" six floors to the great glass dome that was the roof. And they could see, ringing the well, other floors filled with merchandise. To get upstairs was a breeze. Five steam elevators lifted the shoppers. Shillito was a showman as well as businessman. His delivery wagons were pulled by huge Palomino horses that all looked alike. Nonetheless, in the 1920s his store lost momentum. While the rest of the world was rushing ahead, Shillito's dreamily operated in the "old tradition." Store hours were from 10 A.M. to 4 P.M. because someone had once decided that was when most of the shopping was done. Palace or not, Shillito's fell into fourth position as a department store. Then the Lazarus crowd came along.

In 1928 the "Lazari"—that's what the family is called—moved in Fred Lazarus, Jr., as Shillito's new president. Fred's grandfather, Simon Lazarus, Sr., had come from Germany in 1848 to open a men's clothing store in Columbus. When the grandfather died in 1877, Fred Lazarus, Sr., took over the Columbus operation. During the panic of 1907, the father was persuaded by his two sons to expand instead of retrench, and he did. So when Fred Lazarus, Jr., arrived in Cincinnati to tinker with ailing Shillito's, he knew his way around department stores. The first thing he did was change the store hours—and in flocked the customers. Fred, Jr., also became the prime mover behind the plan that joined several of the nation's bigger department stores into the Federated Department Stores. Though Columbus was the starting point for the Lazari, most of them live here because Cincinnati is headquarters for Federated Department Stores.

Do the ladies still go downtown? A lot do. The Ohio-Kentucky-Indiana Regional Transportation and Development Study Agency says that each day more than a quarter-million people pour into downtown Cincinnati. True, not all of them are clutching credit cards, but enough are to keep the downtown-area stores going full-blast. Three out of four come downtown by private car. Most of the rest come by buses. Each bus averages twenty-one passengers. The buses are more crowded during rush hour, naturally—and empty as tombs sometimes in between. The buses are huge monsters called Dreamliners, cost about $32,000 each, are air-conditioned, and not half so much fun as streetcars. The bus company is privately owned. Not being subsidized, it has its problems. The fewer the riders, the higher the fare; the higher the fare, the fewer the riders; the fewer the riders, the higher the fare—and so on until service is cut back, resulting in fewer customers and higher fares and, *presto!* another cutback in service. Martin Hogan, Jr., summed it up in the *Enquirer:* "Someday you'll be waiting for a bus that will never come." But the president of the transit company, John Paul Jones, maintains that no one will be left out in the cold, waiting for a bus. "If the public wants to ride the bus and the patronage picks up," he said, "we'll add more buses. But since the period immediately following World War II, the transit business has slumped . . . We operate some lines where we don't collect enough fares to pay the driver his day's wages. There'll always be some bus service, even if it's limited to rush-hour traffic." The future of bus transportation, the company suggests, depends on the revitalizing of downtown Cincinnati.

Another utility—and one that seems to have more staying power than the bus company because of the nature of the beast—is the Cincinnati Gas & Electric Company and its Kentucky counterpart, Union Light, Heat and Power Company. Like the telephone company, the Cincinnati Gas & Electric Company—or CG&E to us homefolk—is a big company, but both exude such old-fashioned warmth, courtesy, and efficiency that people sometimes don't think them big at all. There are spoilsports who complain about any business or utility, but compared to some other cities, the phone company and CG&E have given Cincinnatians less reason to fuss. The telephone company will be rung up in the next chapter. Let's look at CG&E here.

The average Greater Cincinnati housewife has little association with the company. To her it's a light switch, a gas stove, and a man coming around to read the meters. Housewives here have so much faith in meter readers that 30,000 of them give these men keys to their homes and let them enter at will. Elmer John Heupel, who recently retired as head meter reader, maintains that the 150 CG&E meter readers are a special breed who would rather be bitten by a dog than kick

258

it and upset the pet's owner. *That* is true company devotion! He said that these meter readers can say "Good morning" and mean it. He added, "They like dogs and children. They are the kind of men who make good lion tamers." Besides not kicking dogs, they go about their business and don't "curb," either. "Curbing" means to sit outside on the curb and guess what the meter reads. In twenty-five years, only three men ever tried that—and were fired fast.

CG&E has been interconnected with other power companies since 1915, which means when one company runs out of electricity it can instantly borrow a cupful of kilowatts from another company. When Greater Cincinnatians light a porch light, they can never be sure where the power is from: nearby, or hurled across high-tension lines from who knows where. Doesn't matter really. The important thing to milady is, when she turns on the television to watch Ruth Lyons, there's electricity on tap. The electricity she doesn't use, the Federal Atomic Energy Center at Portsmouth, Ohio, uses. CG&E, you see, has all kinds of customers and tries to be nice to each of them.

It has all kinds of employees, too. Some are meter readers. Some run riverboats. Some put on cooking demonstrations. Some climb those high poles and hang on for dear life. Altogether, CG&E has about 4600 workers. Nearly a thousand have been with the company for twenty-five years. Nearly 1700 own stock in CG&E. Nearly 3600 belong to the CG&E employees credit union. CG&E has one of the largest telephone installations in Ohio, and certainly needs it: each year the company receives 1,500,000 calls. CG&E workers, other than meter readers on their appointed rounds, make nearly 500,000 service visits to home and schools each year. CG&E has nearly 800 passenger cars and trucks. More than a dozen crews trained in tree surgery trim more than 100,000 trees each year. CG&E's Home Service Department is filled with college-trained charmers who can teach anything: how to put light into your home, take lumps out of your gravy, and insert the pesky fuse into the pesky fuse box. In fact, CG&E seems to do everything but send out Valentines to its customers. Who knows? Next year they might.

19

This last chapter will be a grand finale—of sorts—in which we attempt the impossible task of completing the picture of Cincinnati this book has tried to paint. If a child can paint pictures by numbers, so can we. Grownups do it all the time. Ask a Westwood man to describe his house, he tells how much it cost. Ask a Mount Washington bride to describe her apartment, she tells how many rooms it has. Ask a businessman how business is, and he will shovel so many numbers at you that your head will swim. Only children and lovers are free from the spell numbers cast. Ask a child to describe his house, he tells of the tree that's aching to be climbed. A lover has no interest in numbers at all. To him, Cincinnati means only one thing: where *she* is. The only number that concerns him is *two*, because it takes two to tango. So let children dream and lovers sigh. And while they're doing that, we'll take one final look around at this city of dreamers and sighers.

First, let's wander one last time through the campus and smile at the pretty girls. There are so many students around here. In 1965, 2325 were graduated from the University of Cincinnati. Impressive? Only 167 were graduated from Villa Madonna College across the river. Not so impressive? Try to convince a Villa Madonna graduate of that! Or tell the 783 who were graduated from Xavier University that U.C. graduated almost three times as many as X.U. did. All you'll get is a look. Accept the look and say nothing. Had you got them terribly angry, they might have excommunicated you. And certainly the 1206 who were graduated in 1965 from Miami University in Oxford, Ohio, didn't fret because U.C. graduated nearly twice as many; the M.U. graduates watched the storm gather over the stadium and wondered if they were going to get drenched (they didn't; the storm passed). Greater Cincinnati has graduation classes of every size and description. Forty practical nurses completed courses at either Central High School or St. Francis School and got their licenses. Lawyers? The Salmon P. Chase College of Law awarded 35 law degrees. The Ohio College of Applied Sciences, the day division of the venerable Ohio Mechanics Institute, issued 155 associate degrees and certificates. Actually, the size of a graduating class means little, because each graduate is an individual. And whether the individual says goodby to the McMicken lions at U.C., that musketeer statue at X.U., the nuns at St. Francis, or the passion pits of Oxford, all the goodbys are touching, tremulous, and final.

After the goodbys are said, most graduates pound the pavements in search of work—or, having latched on to a live one as well as a degree, pound the pavements in search of a trousseau. Let's follow the horde of altar-bound graduates to the Hamilton County Courthouse and see the action there.

A lot of love affairs are authorized each year at the courthouse. And each year the number increases. In 1962, 5308 licenses were issued. Two years later, 5682 were issued. Ohio is not what you'd call a marriage mill, though. There's a five-day cooling-off period after the starry-eyed couples apply for a license. Deputy Clerk Louise Bosse says she has no way of knowing how many of the licenses issued are actually used, but she does say that about three out of every hundred couples are turned down for one reason or another. The reasons vary. The bride might not have been a resident of the county in which she applied. Maybe her blood test was made in another state; the girl's blood test must be made in Ohio; the lad can be tested anywhere. Maybe she was under twenty-one and didn't have the consent of *both* parents—one won't do—or her legal guardian. Or maybe she and the man she wanted to marry were closer than second cousins.

Let's look in on the Hamilton County Courthouse in June. Well, in June 1965, 612 licenses were issued. A closer look shows that 86 of the licenses were issued to those who listed their occupation as schoolteacher. But schoolteachers account for only 1 percent of the county population. How is it that 16 percent of the licenses were issued to them? Pursue the matter statistically, allow some of these June marriages to end in divorce and others to be blessed with issue, and only one conclusion can be reached: the Parent-Teachers Association is going to get a lot bigger. In Cincinnati right now it already has 20,000 members. What of the marriages that end in divorce? Divorce is costly. In three months, via the Domestic Relations Court, area husbands paid over $1,000,000 for support of ex-wives and offspring.

Cincinnatians love to keep records. For instance, in June 1965, in a photo finish, the Cheviot Branch of the Public Library of Cincinnati and Hamilton County won the monthly "book lending" championship from the Groesbeck Branch by a scant three books. Cheviot residents borrowed 21,747 books; Groesbeck residents borrowed 21,744. On the other hand, the Groesbeck Branch, which opened in 1963, loaned more books in 1964 than any other branch. The Madeira Branch was a fooler. In May 1965, it loaned out 4771 books; the very next month, 15,286! How come? Its new building, six times the size of the former one, had opened in June.

Altogether, the public library loaned 5,598,630 books in 1964. All but 3394 of the books were returned. In 1964, the library raked in 13,500,000 pennies in fines. Also, about $10,000 comes in each year from honest Greater Cincinnatians who are paying for books they've lost. Here's a happy thought if you're a slow reader: the library won't keep fining you $.05 a day, indefinitely. When the amount of the fine reaches the price of the book—plus a buck for handling, mailing, and worrying—no more is charged. But this doesn't work to the library's benefit. How does anyone determine the real value of a 1915 book that cost $2, for instance, when it would cost many times that to replace it? But the library still charges only what it paid for the book. Fair warning, though: when a book becomes *extremely* overdue, that man knocking at your door isn't the Fuller Brush Man. He's a collector from the library and he means business. Don't sic your dog on him.

President of the library trustees, John T. Nolan, Jr., also lends out books from his own private library, but he plans to halt that practice. Whenever he lends a book to strangers in Oxford, Ohio, the book never comes back.

According to our paint-by-number picture of this area, Greater Cincinnati is gabby. The Cincinnati Bell Telephone Company services a 55-mile radius with about 676,000 telephones. Although the community has a dial system, 207 telephone operators are still needed, and a few of these are 17-year-old charmers who work part-time while attending high school. The company says these young ladies are invariably the better students in school. Not only that, but they ached to become telephone operators. But don't think all the operators are schoolgirls. The average age of the operators is twenty-five to twenty-six years old. After working the long-distance board for a while, they move on to other chores: mobile, supervisory, clerical, customer service, marriage, and motherhood. During the small hours of the morning only five operators are on duty. During the busiest times—8:30 A.M. to noon; and 1 P.M. to 5 P.M.—at least thirty long-distance operators are working. The busiest days are Christmas and Mother's Day. On Christmas Day, 1964, 38,000 direct-distance-dial calls were placed. On Mother's Day, 1965, the calls totaled 36,219. Each day Greater Cincinnatians place approximately 3,397,000 calls. Overseas calls are serviced by operators in New York and San Francisco. Each month in Cincinnati, 11,000 overseas calls are placed. Each year the telephone company distributes 600,000 telephone books but retrieves only 400,000. The company likes to get the old books back for a very good reason: old telephone numbers are thus removed from the customer's clutches.

One last look at the telephone is in order. You must admit that the yellow pages aren't dull; they contain a multitude of accidental contradictions and trivia. For instance, the yellow pages list eight gymnasiums. They also list eight places that sell abdominal supports. Wild coincidence? Before you let your imagination do the walking, read on. Barber shops occupy only one page; beauty salons occupy seven. Now, that's the way things should be. But is there any significance in the fact the yellow pages offer two pages of delicatessens *and* two pages of dentists. Is Izzy Kadetz *really* painless? No, Izzy is fine and so are the yellow pages. These isolated items are plucked out of the mass. Each item is a dot. Put all the dots together and a picture of Cincinnati might also emerge. The yellow pages show us the variety of Cincinnati. There are nine chimney cleaners, four bridge builders, one drag strip, and one store that sells Hawaiian items. For the sportsman, the yellow pages offer forty-two places that rent boats and forty-three fishing lakes. Three companies make buttonholes, one makes bungs, one removes dead animals, and one restores antique cars. So complete is Greater Cincinnati that the yellow pages list fifteen different places that will groom your pooch. Should he die, three pet cemeteries are listed. Should your car die, five auto graveyards are listed. And if you'd like to build a greenhouse, look in the yellow pages. Two companies will build it for you. Want a private eye? The book lists twenty-nine. Let's drink a toast to them.

While toasting them—and the auto graveyards—why not take a final swing through the city and see how much toasting actually goes on. This will be a cheerful exercise. Why? Because Cincinnatians drink a lot. For every family in Hamilton County, $85 a year is spent on booze. The average for Ohio is only $79 per family per year. More than half around here buy bourbon. Eight out of ten buy straight bourbon instead of bonded. Only one man in ten buys scotch. Two in ten buy gin. Vodka is coming along. For every twenty gin drinkers, there are seven vodka drinkers. Most of the liquor is purchased in—of course!—December. In February, Ohioans buy the least. Does this loose statistic have any bearing on the report that February is also the slowest month for marriage licenses? Draw your own conclusion.

When it comes to fancy drinking, northeastern Ohio, where Cleveland is, outdrinks southwestern Ohio, where Cincinnati is, two to one in Galliano and Strega. They also drink twice as much Kahlua as we do. But when it's Kümmel, that's a different matter. We drink four jugs for every three they drink. We also drink twice as much peppermint schnapps. As for flavored vodka, both areas drink about the

263

same amount. But we're Cointreau country and they're Triple Sec. So much for the headier stuff. Back to straight drinking.

Hamilton County each year spends at least $24,000,000 on liquor. The state-operated retail package stores account for $17,000,000; bars, restaurants, and hotels account for the rest. About 1500 people—as many as used to run the trolley system back in 1927—are on the payroll of the state's Department of Liquor Control. This department operates the stores and, when not doing that, catches moonshiners.

Not too many moonshiners work the Greater Cincinnati territory; or if they do, they haven't been caught. About 5000 gallons of moonshine are destroyed each year by agents. In 1964 the ax wielders set some kind of record by seizing eighty-six stills, which, the department notes with mixed pride, was a 16.2 percent increase over 1963. 1964 was also the year the agents captured nearly 13,000 gallons of mash. The Cleveland area might outdrink us with legal liquor, but they also have the shaky honor of having more moonshiners. Nineteen were seized in Cuyahoga County in 1964 to only five seized in Hamilton County. Sadly enough for the image, Ohio has few hillbilly moonshiners. Six out of ten stills confiscated were in urban areas—which shoots another myth, doesn't it?

Each year the Ohio Department of Liquor Control returns permit-fee dollars to the taxing district from which they came. These figures give us a good idea which communities are more bubbly than others. For instance, terribly dry Oxford, Ohio, where only 3.2 percent beer is sold, got back only $900 in fees one year. Terribly wet Hamilton, Ohio, got back nearly $92,000. Batavia got back $7400; Loveland, nearly $6000; Milford, nearly $7000; Greenhills, $2000; Norwood, $43,000; and—hold on to the bar stool!—Cincinnati, $616,900! In Hamilton County, where Cincinnati is the wettest, Amberley Village is the driest. It got back $600. Reading and St. Bernard put away a lot. Reading got back more than $15,000, and St. Bernard $12,000. Lockland is in there pitching. It got back $7000. Green Township, in western Greater Cincinnati, outdrinks Delhi Township next door more than two to one. Colerain Township is a merry place. It got back $32,000 from the state. Miami Township received only $1700. If it's any kind of a race, Terrace Park outdrinks Wyoming, but call it a photo finish. Terrace Park, $705; Wyoming, $650. Neither should feel depressed, nor should Oxford, Ohio. Oberlin in Lorain County got back only $155.

If you want to look at it another way, Cheviot spends $780,000 each year on the stuff; North College Hill, $900,000; Loveland, $133,-000; and Cleves, $159,000. Greenville, Ohio, where Wayne made peace with the Indians, still spends about $250,000 a year celebrating the treaty. Norwood spends $280,000.

Where is the most hard liquor sold in the city? Well, in 1964 the store at 16 East Fifth Street downtown peddled $1,500,000 worth of joy. A close second, with $1,300,000 in sales, was the state-operated store at 3512 Reading Road. The only other store that year with more than a million-dollar volume was at 3862 Paxton Road, with sales totaling $1,100,000. Cincinnati, itself, has twenty-one state-operated stores.

Want a number that makes you sad? In one month alone in 1965, 925 dogs and 710 cats were left at the animal shelter on Colerain Avenue. Want to feel a little better? Forty percent of these dogs and cats found love again. They were adopted.

Some numbers, obviously, are numbers of the heart, and some are not. But our paint-by-number kit includes them all. And even numbers of the heart are not always items of beauty. The only thing some numbers can do to the heart is strike terror into it. Si Cornell in the Cincinnati *Post & Times-Star* wrote:

> Fifty years ago [a] great tornado hit Cincinnati, killing 36 people and injuring another 100. Mose Rosenbaum, 84, boss of Burton Furniture, had 11 relatives killed in that big blow.
> "I was only a block away from the worst of where it hit and I still do not like storms," said Mose.

Neither do other Cincinnatians, but on the other hand, the area is not overburdened with tornadoes. Cincinnati has fifteen to twenty tornado warnings each year, but how many have actually materialized? The Weather Bureau says the average is seven—in the past hundred years. Hail has proved no problem. The Bureau has no official record of the size of hailstones, but it admits that the public has reported some the size of golf balls. Smog? The Bureau begs off. "Smog, as such," it says, "is not reported."

When should you wear a raincoat around here? The Weather Bureau suggests June. Rainfall averages over four inches then—*maximum* rainfall, that is. But keep your raincoat handy the other months, too. Rain averages between three and four inches a month from January straight through August. Bear in mind, these are maximums, that is, the most it has rained. For real bad weather, consider August 7, 1920, when it rained nearly an inch in five minutes! The longest periods without rain usually come in the fall. In 1924 it didn't rain a drop those twenty-six days between October 5 and October 30. One of the wettest months recently was May 1964, when it rained nearly a foot! The wettest month on record was January 1937, when 13.5 inches of rain were added to the existing flood conditions. July, 1926, was a soggy month for picnicking. It rained ten inches.

Then, there's snow. While there have been traces of it in May, there's usually no snow in the Greater Cincinnati area between May and October. In October 1925, it snowed four inches, but the average for October is less than a tenth of an inch. Snow usually clobbers us in

January in time for the children to break their legs on the skis they got for Christmas. The average for January is a little over 5 inches, although in 1918, 20 inches fell, paralyzing the city. The most it has ever snowed in a 24-hour period was in December 1917, when it snowed nearly a foot, paralyzing the city again. The coldest day ever recorded was in January 1936, when the mercury dropped to 17 below zero. The hottest day was in July 1934, when the thermometer registered 109 degrees. January is the coldest month. Average temperatures range from 41 to 26 degrees. July is the hottest month. Average temperatures range from 87.5 to 63 degrees. These, of course, are the official figures. The Weather Bureau says:

"These temperatures were recorded at the Abbe Observatory . . . No doubt higher temperatures in summer and colder temperatures in winter have been noted at various other locations throughout the area."

The Weather Bureau itself has wandered around the city a lot. It used to be on the roof of Pike's Opera House at Fourth and Vine Streets. In 1885 it moved its gadgetry to the U. S. Customs House on Fifth Street east of Walnut Street, where it stayed until 1936. Then it moved a few blocks away to the Fuller Building at Eighth and Walnut Streets. It lingered there a little more than two years. At this writing it is in two locations: the Federal Building downtown and the Abbe Observatory, 206 LaFayette Circle.

Before leaving the whimsies of nature, here's a thought that will warm the cockles of Smoky the Bear's heart. The Weather Bureau has appointed a forest-fire expert to its Cincinnati staff. The warning system keeps an eye on Ohio, Indiana, and Kentucky. It comes as a surprise to natives to learn that we are in timber country, but we are. One out of every five acres in Ohio is filled with nothing but ants, poison ivy, and trees. Manufacture from this wood provides one out of every twenty jobs in Ohio, Kentucky, western Pennsylvania, and West Virginia. But these workers aren't the woodchoppers of yore. They work in factories that manufacture paper, furniture, and other wood products.

One last stroll by the river? All right, but she sure has changed. Consider the *Steel Ranger*. She's the 4320-horsepower towboat the Ohio Barge Line acquired. She operates between Pittsburgh and the Gulf, and she's a whopper: 168 feet long and 40 feet wide. That is as wide as an average residential lot in Cincinnati and deeper than most. An editorial in the Cincinnati *Post & Times-Star* summed up the river best:

The "work horses" of the Ohio River, the diesel tows and the sturdy barges they push up and downstream are busier than ever.

This year [1965] may be the first 100-million-ton year,

according to Brig. Gen. Walter E. Leber of the Army Engineers. His forecast is based on the just-completed cargo reports for 1964, which show 96.3 million tons.

The canalization of the river was completed in 1929 and the following year the tonnage was 22 millions. The dams of 1929 allowed year-round navigation; the high dams now under construction [5 of 19 finished] save time and thereby reduce transport costs.

The cargoes are typical of the basic industries of the expanding economy of the Ohio Valley—coal, coke, gasoline, steel, chemicals, building stone and gravel, and miscellaneous items. Not much glamor, no romance of the packet days, just heavy hauling on the valley "freeway."

Not *all* adventure, however, has departed from the river. In March 1965, a barge with a 136-foot crane broke loose from its moorings at upstream Foster, Kentucky. Drifting free, it threatened to rip down a half-dozen powerlines that crossed the river. The Cincinnati Gas & Electric Company's harbor boat, aptly named *Ready Kilowatt*, intercepted the runaway and beached it five miles away from the lines.

While on the river, let's go upstream for more numbers to paint. Up there is Coney Island. John W. Miles, with a Ph.D. in physical education and principal of Erlanger (Kentucky) Elementary School, is official "ticket burner" at the happy park. Each night he picks up the tickets after the park closes and, after counting from 200,000 to 300,000 ride and concession tickets to make sure the concessionaires get what's due them, he burns them all. How can he count that many? He weighs them on a sensitive scale that's accurate to one tenth of 1 percent. The biggest day he's had? The day he counted 850,000 tickets!

Practically everything in Greater Cincinnati, it seems, has been weighed, measured, counted, tasted, or tested by someone. For instance, as you cross the Brent Spence Bridge, the double-decker that carries Intrastate 75, you can't help but see that giant Tresler Comet gasoline sign. Well, the sign weighs exactly 2 tons, sticks 90 feet straight up in the air, and is supported by a pipe that's 5 feet in diameter. More numbers: the Cincinnati City Council law committee voted that the University of Cincinnati fraternity houses could allow only 25 square feet of bunk space per brother instead of the 50 square feet the building code requires. Cincinnati residents each pay $102 a year to keep their schools open. In a recent *Post & Times-Star* spelling-bee final, girls outnumbered boys 19 to 6. There are 433 certified life underwriters in Greater Cincinnati, and in 1965, 39 of these qualified for the Million Dollar Roundtable. Hamilton County every three months buys 7½ tons of coffee for Drake and Durham Hospitals, the county jail atop the courthouse, the juvenile detention home, Mount

Airy shelter, and the Glenview and Hillcrest Homes. In one five-week period, the Anti-Tuberculosis League X-rayed 6534 Greater Cincinnati chests and found 230 with symptoms of tuberculosis.

Cincinnatians put about $80,000 each month into parking meters—which figures, because when it comes to owning cars, Hamilton County keeps up with the Joneses. In the first six months of 1965, Hamilton County Clerk Robert Jennings said that 136,868 new- and used-car titles were handled by his office. In the first six months of 1964, his offices handled 6800 less than that figure. Adjacent Butler County, bracing itself for the 1965 July Fourth traffic, looked upon its registration figures: 81,000 cars. Then Ray M. Tayler, secretary manager of the Butler County Automobile Club, added these 81,000 to the 20,000 cars from other counties that would travel through Butler County, and said of the Fourth of July:

"If the holiday traffic expected through here was placed bumper to bumper, it would form a double line from Hamilton to Columbus."

The "killer" street in Cincinnati, statistically, is Eastern Avenue between Pearl Street and Columbia Parkway: sixteen deaths in five years, and it's only a six-mile stretch! Another killer street is the Mill Creek Expressway—or, if you like, call it Intrastate 75. A dozen have been killed on it in five years. River Road, though, ties the Expressway: a dozen deaths there in five years, too. Other dangerous roads: Columbia Parkway, with eleven deaths in five years; Reading Road, ten; Central Parkway, nine; Vine Street, eight; and Harrison Road, Madison Road, Gilbert Avenue, and the Westwood-Northern Boulevard, seven each.

Meanwhile, *under* the streets is more action. For instance, underneath the intersection of Fourth and Vine Streets are a Western Union electrical duct; a six-inch water main; an abandoned 6-inch gas main that now holds an electric cable that has the voltage of an electric chair; the Cincinnati Gas & Electric Company's electric circuits for traffic lights, fire, and burglar alarms; telephone lines; a 10-inch gas main; a Postal Telegraph line; and underneath this hodge-podge: a great big sewer!

Let's flesh out the picture with people. We'll add William L. Dressell, who, although blind, operates the concession stand at the Hamilton County Courthouse. The blind operate such stands in City Hall and the Post Office Building, too. There are 110 blind-operated stands throughout the state. Each year they take in more than $3,000,-000. Let's add some girls to the picture. We'll add those charmers who hang out at the Catholic Bible Reading Center near Eighth and State Streets, not the best of all possible neighborhoods. When the Glenmary nuns, who run the place, asked the girls what recreation facilities they wanted, the young ladies voted unanimously for—of all things!—a pool table.

268

We'll add a touch of Scotch to the picture. Cincinnati has the oldest Scottish group west of the Alleghenies. The Caledonian Society was organized here in 1833 and, according to City Health Commissioner Dr. Kenneth MacLoed, the group is still going strong. It does have a wee problem, though. Originally organized to assist destitute Scotsmen, the group is hard-pressed these days to find one. Add Emily Kimbrough to the Cincinnati scene. It was in a hotel here that she tried to open a bottle of ginger ale on the wall-opener in the bathroom, and the wall-opener came loose, the bottle split, and—they say—the wash basin broke, too. Remember O. O. McIntyre? Add his widow to the Cincinnati story. Once each year Mrs. Oscar Odd McIntyre revisits Cincinnati, where her husband used to work for the Cincinnati *Post* before he moved on to fame and fortune as a New York columnist. Add the Westwood dentist who belted a fidgety kid; the unlucky check passer who got arrested three hours after he tried to pass his first check here; and Mrs. Ruth Braun of Mount Airy, who found five double-yolked eggs out of the dozen she bought at the supermarket.

Cincinnati has a little of just about everything, including a big heart.

In 1964 the city coughed up $13,000,000 for its various charities. On the other hand, the Community Chest has needy groups coming and going. Withdrawing from the combined appeal for funds are Christ Hospital and the Fresh Air Farm and Convalescent Society. Both decided to go it alone and raise money on their own. Eighteen other groups had applied to join the combined drive. Since the fund-raising drive started, ninety-one groups have joined, only to resign.

Some organizations wish they had stood in bed. At the Ku Klux Klan rally in Warren County in 1965, the newsmen almost outnumbered the members. The *Post & Times-Star* said it best:

> The invisible Empire drew a crowd to match.
> It once had called for 25,000. It had whittled that to a hope for 5000.
> It got 200.
> That was last night's Ku Klux Klan rally in Warren County.
> One out of every four who showed up was a reporter or cameraman.

So add a dash of bigotry to this picture of Cincinnati. But add *only* a dash. That's all there is.

And add both sides of the Cold War. One former Cincinnatian has pleaded guilty in Richmond, Virginia, to the charge of selling missile data to the Russians. On the positive side, at Nike missile bases near Dillsboro, Felicity, Oxford, and Wilmington, nearly 150 soldiers are keeping the faith. It takes all shades to paint this picture, doesn't it?

For Keystone comedy relief—though it wasn't terribly funny to him—add the 20-year-old man who, clad only in a sheet, stole a taxicab. He had been taken to General Hospital by the police to be patched up after a brawl. Attendants took his clothes, he took a sheet, and took off. Said the cab driver when the sheet-clad customer got in: "I suspected he was a runaway."

The driver drove the 20-year-old back to General Hospital, and while he went inside to report his suspicion, his passenger zoomed off in the stolen cab.

Comedy? Perhaps. But sad, too.

All these items form the mosaic that is Cincinnati.

Cincinnati is Dr. Victor Greenebaum, who suggested "mass immunization" of children against diphtheria thirty-five years ago. He was told that if anything went wrong he would have to stand alone and that no one would defend him. He went ahead and vaccinated anyway—and diphtheria was wiped out in the city.

Cincinnati, also, is Miss Ethel Price, who heads the service here that mails out "talking books" to the blind. In March 1965, for example, she and her staff mailed out more than 21,000 such books. The most-wanted book? The King James version of the Bible.

Cincinnati is a bunch of badly dressed and big-bucketed women. *Enquirer* Fashion Editor Janelle protested:

> There ought to be a law—against some of the garb worn by women walking around on city streets!
> . . . While the sights are deplorable in wintertime, they're even worse in the summer . . . Shorts appear and legs are bared . . . Shorts and slacks, even when the wearer is well built, are not meant for the downtown area. Neither are the ugly hair rollers, pin curls, and the like . . . It's a shame such people can't be included in our next campaign to "clean up, paint up, and beautify."

Is the picture of Cincinnati emerging? Did you, somewhere between the Ice Age and Janelle's legitimate protest, find what Cincinnati and Greater Cincinnati are? Or are you like me: bewildered by numbers, faces, and things? An adding machine can be used to explain any city. Except for the variety of totals, the answers are all the same: nothing but numbers. A quick glance at the people of this city (the man in the sheet stealing a cab or the man in the sheet attending a rally) tells us nothing. At times we are as disinterested as we would be if forced to examine a high school annual published by a school we did not attend. I don't know *how* to explain Cincinnati to you. Everything here has a private and personal meaning. As individuals we even have our own institutions: places, things, and people that for us give Cincinnati a richer meaning.

To some, Robert A. Linn was a Cincinnati institution. As managing editor of the *Post & Times-Star*, he was at times as James Thurber was: a logical man at grips with an illogical world. He demanded simplicity from the city room—and the city. Those who figured him shallow, figured wrong. "Kid," he would say, "your trouble is, the world isn't complicated enough for you." Ovid wrote *Ars est celare artem* (art lies in concealing art), which fitted Linn to a T. But Linn wouldn't have approved of Ovid. "Kid," he would have said, "cut out that Latin jazz and just write what you know." Linn went through life editing out jazz wherever he found it—and he found it everywhere.

He cast such a long, fat shadow over his city room, it is difficult to believe he is dead. But he is. God finally caught his eye. He died in March 1963, at the age of 58, to end a 38-year newspaper career that never took him far from this valley. He started in Wheeling, West Virginia, as a reporter on the Wheeling *News*, was city editor there by 1926, went to the Akron *Times-Press*, and in 1938 came to the *Post* to work at the copy desk.

"Hell," one reporter said, "he climbed into the driver's seat the first day he sat down at that desk, and he never got out."

Physically, he was short and dumpy. Sometimes he was terribly fat. Sometimes he wasn't so fat. He had more chins than necessary, pudgy fingers, a pencil-thin mustache, a nose for talking through, a cigarette always within reach, and had it not been for bursts of boyish glee, he might have been mistaken for the vice-president in a tank-town bank. The important thing was, he was one of the best newspapermen Cincinnati has ever seen.

He rarely got involved in silliness. One time he did, though. He was named Indian Chief (BIC-Ta-Huh-Ka) by a movie press agent touting a film. He received this dubious title from Chief Fire Thunder assisted by Dan Dull Knife and a disenchanted Indian princess named Run-of-the-Arrow which, by coincidence, happened to be the name of the movie. When Linn got the title, he smiled a bewildered smile and flashbulbs popped: one of the rare times the *Post*'s readers met Bob Linn. Anyway, publicity nonsense was not his cup of tea. He was never off the telephone long enough to make a good Indian chief.

When he was city editor, Bob Linn was fastened to the city by eleven telephone trunk lines. Even at home he was never far from a telephone. He called everybody, and everybody called him. Had the telephone not been invented, he would have been serviced by exhausted platoons of exhausted runners. Linn didn't stay city editor for long. In 1945 he was appointed managing editor. From then on, *gangbusters!*

Whenever news was breaking, Linn fidgeted too much to watch the city room's action from his office. He hustled to a desk in the middle of the city room, hitched up his sleeves, and played, too. He actually maintained a second desk in the city room. When editions were closing, that's where he could be found: grubbing among the typewritten oddments and the wet galleys, nervous as a cat, but having himself a ball. He was a "first hunch" newspaperman who never waited for the second hunch. While others were troubling over one decision, he had made decisions by the tubful with no trouble at all and was drumming his fat fingers, waiting for the rest of the world to catch up. The world couldn't catch up, of course. By the time it did, he wasn't there. He was somewhere else.

Linn was a high-pressure cooker that once in a while exploded. Because he acted fast—with an idea, an angle, or a lead—he expected those who worked under him to move fast, too. He spoke shorthand. Giving an assignment, he would rattle off this angle or that lead, and then lapse into gibberish which reporters were unable to sort out. He scribbled notes the same way: the frantic scrawls and hieroglyphics of a man who has much to write and a train to catch. When queried, he couldn't decipher his own notes. Why? By then he had scribbled thousands more.

If Linn had an archenemy, it was not a person. It was the *Times-Star* until the *Times-Star*, as such, ceased. After that his archenemy became the *Enquirer*. It wasn't that he hated the *Enquirer*. It was simply that competition fed his soul.

Bob Linn made enemies all the time, but no one stayed his enemy long. Walk through the city room any day and you would have found at least one enemy scowling in the direction of the managing editor's office. On a good day you would have found a city room filled with scowlers. Bob Linn was that way. But he was also this way: the next day any one of those scowlers would have died for him. Simple as that. It was impossible to find anyone who hated him more than a week. On the other hand, those who considered him a friend are so numerous that to list them is to list every other name in the telephone book. His grin could charm the pants off anyone who came along. Also, he was the All-American softie. He was, like Diogenes, a sucker for an honest man. But cross him with a con job, and his office had the chill of a deep-freeze.

He was forever going on diets and forever getting fatter. Once, though, he did lose 100 pounds, which he went right out and got back. Anyway, he liked to cook outdoors too much. He grilled every chance he got. He would lug his grilling paraphernalia to a city park, invite a clutch of staff members, and grill there. When he wasn't on the telephone at home, he was out in the backyard, grilling. With no shirt on and sweating, he looked like a big-bellied Buddha horsing with temple fire.

In some ways, Bob Linn never got around to growing up. He was ruled by a boy's enthusiasm. The world fascinated him. The city fascinated him. People fascinated him. Things fascinated him. Each day was an exciting adventure to him. He would be up at 5 A.M.—if not at 4 A.M.—padding around his home, his mind an early-morning litter of leads and vague stories. He said he got his best ideas while shaving, but that is wrong. He got ideas everywhere. By 8:30 A.M.— never later—he would be at the newspaper, scribbling incoherent notes and taking shorthand, passing along the "half" stories to luckless reporters and wire men who had to make sense out of them. He was the Rudolf Bing of trivia: sidebar stories tacked onto the main story. If they were good stories, they tickled him pink, and he would be pleased for days.

He was not above breaking rules. When word came over the wires that President Roosevelt had died, Bob Linn and only a handful of people were in the *Post* building, because the day was over. He personally handled the story from wire to composing room. Some say he even touched untouchable type and set the headlines for the extra himself. If he did, no one will confirm. Noah Castle, the compositor, was asked about it, and he made no comment. You know how sticky union things can be. But to Linn that day the newspaper was the important thing. If he did set those heads, he probably muttered:

"What a hell of a way to run a railroad."

He was always muttering that or its equivalent. He ran a good railroad and expected others to do the same. When a story came in that two police cars chasing a bad guy had smashed into each other instead, he had no sympathy. He shook his head and said:

"What can you expect from Keystone Cops?"

Filled to the brim with corny and old-fashioned Right and Wrong, he chugged through life in a constant state of excitement. "Kid," he would say, "if you lose enthusiasm, get out of the business." He was a do-er you could depend on. "Once he handled a chore," *Post* editor Dick Thornburg said, "it was a finished product."

We will not suggest that he was happy or sad. Even now, such suggestions seem private and too personal. Rather, we will suggest he favored the underdog so much he could easily lose all sense of proportion. When an underdog appeared, Bob Linn was as sentimental as an old woman weeping at a wedding. The underdog didn't even have to be a person. In Akron it was a spider spinning a web on the hands of a clock. Each time a strand was completed, the clock hands would move and the strand would break. But the spider refused to give up. It began over and over again. This was the way Bob Linn's life was. Each day he created a newspaper, each day time pulled the plug, and he had to start from scratch. In some ways—

though Bob Linn himself would never have admitted it—he was a kind of poet. He was like Don Marquis, when that long-ago columnist wrote:

> My heart has followed all my days
> Something I cannot name . . .

Bob Linn had many fine hours, but *this* was his finest. When Carl Groat died and Linn was acting editor of the *Post*, people crossed their fingers and hoped that Linn would be appointed editor for real. As the days dwindled into weeks and still no word came from the newspaper owners, the *Post* continued to function as a well-oiled piece of machinery because everyone wanted to make Linn look good. What Bob Linn was thinking, no one knew. He didn't say. But you could sense the tension in the staff. What was management waiting for? Didn't they know Linn was the greatest? But the bottom fell out when word came that Dick Thornburg, not Bob Linn, had been chosen. One word then from Linn, and the precise machine called a newspaper would have ceased to function. It didn't matter that Dick Thornburg was qualified. What mattered was, Bob Linn had not been named. Everyone looked to him for a clue and waited to follow his lead.

"As I was flying to Cincinnati for the first time," Dick Thornburg said, "I wondered, too. I had met Bob before, but only casually. I had some doubts about coming in as editor. Without his cooperation, I was in for a rough time."

When Dick Thornburg's plane landed, Bob Linn broke away from the others who had also come to the airport to meet their new editor. Linn moved straight to Thornburg, stuck out his hand, and—in his finest hour—said to a man he hardly knew:

"Welcome home."

Can you see why Bob Linn is considered a Cincinnati institution? We've all kinds here.

Ruth Lyons is an institution that's practically an industry. Simply put, she's the lady who has been talking a blue streak, first on radio and then on television, since Hector was a pup. Her "Fifty-Fifty Club" over Crosley's four television stations (Cincinnati, Dayton, Columbus, and Indianapolis) and over WLW-Radio is a midday fixture like the noon factory whistle. It doesn't concern her that most people swear by her and a few others swear at her. She keeps right on, alternating between corny and complicated, and has mastered on television that ability few performers have acquired: the ability to be *herself*.

It would be easy to attach meaning to her in numbers: the number of dollars advertisers have spent on her program, the number of women who have been in her studio audience, the number of times she's bawled out the Government, the number of children she has made happy with her Christmas Fund, the number of celebrities she has put down, the number of hours she has appeared before television cameras, or the number of hankies she has used watching tear-jerker movies. But numbers are dull, and she is not. Anyway, numbers would rob her of meaning. No set of numbers can capture the essence of her any more than a motor number describes the color car you drive.

Part of her charm is that she is, at times, the twin of every woman in her audience. Another part of her charm is that now and then she is not. Most television performers exude so much phony happiness that your living room is hip-deep in affected Pollyanna glee, but Ruth Lyons never pretends to be anything she isn't. When she's happy about something, you know her happiness is genuine. When she's not happy about something, you know that fast. She can be sweet. She can be exasperating. But aren't all women that way?

Men watch her program and grumble at her gabbiness, but so what? Men have no more reason to watch than they have to read *Good Housekeeping* or *McCall's* from cover to cover. Her program is directed at women, who accept her gabbiness as natural. In reality, her program is a woman's magazine that is broadcast instead of printed. Her program and those magazines have identical ingredients.

To compare the Ruth Lyons program with a woman's magazine is not far-fetched. Her program runs ninety minutes a day, five days a week, a total of seven and a half hours, which certainly requires more substance and variety than a single half-hour or hour program once a week. The contents must be varied. The contents of her program, we suggest, are as varied as the contents of *Good Housekeeping* and *McCall's*. She is to the program what an editor is to a magazine. A magazine selects its audience, and so does Ruth Lyons: housewives. And, as a magazine does, she sometimes shakes her audience with opinions they don't want to hear and leads them along avenues they don't wish to travel. Don't magazines carry articles about subjects you disagree with? A good editor invariably gives an audience a little more than it can digest. A good editor is not afraid to make an audience think.

A magazine has two basic ingredients: editorial and advertising. The Ruth Lyons program has the same. Both the magazines and Ruth Lyons would fall on their faces without advertising—and not just because advertising dollars pay the freight. Women like to read advertising that informs them about new products, a new way to cook this, or a new method of cleaning that. Good advertising in magazines has as much readership as good editorial content. And consider this: *Good Housekeeping* and *McCall's* do not endorse products that they themselves don't believe in. Neither will Ruth Lyons. Just as advertisers line up for the *Good Housekeeping* Seal of Approval, they line up for Ruth Lyons' endorsement. If you doubt this, check any advertiser or advertising agency.

Does this comparison, though, hold up beyond advertising? You bet. A magazine has its editorial content, and so does the program Ruth Lyons operates. A magazine might have a good article about how the President's wife hates billboards. You should hear some of the things Ruth Lyons hates. A magazine traffics in recollection when life was sweeter. You should hear Ruth Lyons talk about how things used to be. A magazine has articles by or about famous celebrities. The same celebrities appear on the Ruth Lyons show. A magazine offers fiction. Well, fiction is entertainment. On the Ruth Lyons program, they sing. No question about it: the comparison is valid.

In fact, you could do this: make a list of the household hints, recollection, humor, entertainment, and commentary that appear in any issue of either *Good Housekeeping* or *McCall's*. Check the service information offered by the advertising. Then compare that issue with a month of Ruth Lyons programs. You'd be in for a surprise. While the magazines put out one issue, the Ruth Lyons program actually puts out two. Her monthly output in such items as recollection, hints, celebrity time, *et al,* is twice that of a national magazine. Other ladies try to do what she does on television, but they can't hold a candle to her because they neglect to edit. She's one of the best "editors" that television has ever seen. This is her real secret. This is why Ruth Lyons is an industry and an institution around here.

For instance, consider one of her programs picked at random. It will contain advertising, of course. But look at some of the *other* things it offers: a quarrel with the national anthem.

> The whole thing as far as I'm concerned is wrong. I can't stand that song. It may be our national anthem but I don't like it. I can't sing it. Who can? Only people like Marian Spelman. I can't even sing alto on it half the time. Don't you think we should have a song we can *all* sing? Why not "God Bless America" or "America, the Beautiful"? I just love "America, the Beautiful." Beautiful words and melody, too. Not an old tavern song. Why does it have be a military anthem anyway?

She considered the Canadian anthem beautiful and she loved the "Marseillaise." "God Save the Queen" tore her apart. "When they play it," she told her audience, "I just go right through the ceiling." The subject of anthems—and her quarrel with some—could easily have been an article in *McCall's,* because when Ruth Lyons is reduced to a printed page, you discover another surprising thing. She doesn't ramble, as most television talkers do. She speaks precise and coherent paragraphs.

Next on her program was an advertisement for Creamettes, but it was no ordinary pitch. Ruth Lyons told of a recipe called Halloween Hash that she had personally concocted. A stock film commercial could never have been as effective. Then Ruth Lyons touched on a variety of subjects we can only suggest here: how doctors and salesmen listen to her on car radios, how she finds it impossible to marry off her announcer Peter Grant, how her daughter Candy likes to make pie crust with Crisco (log a commercial fast!), how Crisco was her first sponsor nearly twenty years ago, and how she felt about children: "I love *all* children! I love boys. I love girls. All of them. Period!" Somehow or other, she wended her way back to Crisco:

> I haven't had a homemade biscuit for I don't know how long. Candy used to make them for shortcake. But Candy hasn't made any for a long time. They're all on diets at my house. They're all trying to lose weight. So I have to starve to death. But there's nothing as good as a homemade biscuit. If you make them with Crisco, they're light and fluffy and delicate . . .

Out of a clear blue sky came a paragraph of recollection that could be inserted verbatim into any magazine:

> Did your grandmother have a jelly cellar or a fruit cellar? I can remember my grandmother's. I can still see those jars of cherries. She used to make pies from them at Christmas time.
>
> Oh, there was everything in that cellar! Pickles, peaches, peach juice, and all kinds of jellies and jams.
>
> Women used to work harder in those days than they do now. They even used to can vegetable soup. String beans and lima beans, too, and loads of tomatoes.
>
> I can still see that bag of grape jelly hanging there with the drippings in it. My grandmother never made apple butter outside in a big crock, but that is so wonderful, too . . .

Magazines have humor. So does the Ruth Lyons program. That day she got involved in an Emily Kimbrough-type tale of sailing:

> Don't mention catamarans! I almost fell off one—right into the ocean. No, not too much poi. Too much *boy.* There was a boy, and he had his girl there. He was showing off. We were sailing around Diamond Head, where the big waves are. I held on to an old man and saved his life. Herman [her husband] wasn't afraid and neither was Candy, but I

was frightened to death. I kept sliding off and that old man kept sliding off. So I grabbed him and hung on to him for the entire trip . . .

A feature about marriage? Well, when asked if she had to do it over again would she still choose Herman, she didn't hesitate. "Of course I would choose Herman," she said. "But it's not a question of getting used to husbands. You can never get used to them. You never know what they're going to do next."

A feature about shopping or dieting?

When Candy and her father go to Kroger's, it's pitiful. I think all she buys the food for is the Top Value stamps. We never eat the food. We eat the stamps. We lick them and get our energy that way.

Of her television cameramen, she said, "We have balding ones who can't stand us more than ten minutes at a time. I think they go out for oxygen. But we kind of like these old engineers." Of yesteryear styles, she said, "Do you remember when we used to roll our hose around our legs below our knees? You had to hold them in the back and twist them around. Remember how they'd leave a lump in the back? Then you wore a real short skirt and your bare knees showed. Those were the wild Twenties. Remember the galoshes flopping open? Remember the yellow raincoats?" About gabbiness, she said, "I don't talk constantly, just mostly." She also said her husband loves banana nut bread, that you can tell how cold winter will be by the thickness of a cat's fur, and that she must have commented on how pretty 100,000 dresses were.

Maybe you can explain Ruth Lyons better. She's difficult to pin down to this or that. But in explaining her, be careful and do not oversimplify the lady—or don't look smug and write her off as wrong. If she is wrong, so are busloads of white-gloved ladies who show up every day at Crosley Square to see her. True, Ruth Lyons has been around a long time, but she wears so well, so gracefully, and so gabbily, that to many in Greater Cincinnati her first visit into their homes seems like only yesterday. They don't make many institutions like that anymore.

Another Cincinnati institution is not a person. It's a radio station: WNOP.

Whether WNOP still operates with the halcyon format it used in 1964 and 1965 is not terribly important. The surprising thing is that it ever operated that way at all. What happened was that it stopped trying to sound like the other radio stations. No swinging disc jockeys. No rock-'n-roll. Not even classical music. And certainly no hillbilly tunes, which purists call "country and western." WNOP began to play nothing but blue-ribbon jazz to an audience of Wayne King rejects, Lawrence Welk dropouts, and bewildered teenagers who had tuned in by mistake to discover WNOP had betrayed them.

The station assembled the most unlikely assortment of announcers a radio station could accumulate. At one time it had (1) a hillbilly guitar player from the Kentucky hills, (2) a solemn jazz musician who knew so much about jazz he was lost discussing anything else, (3) an ex-actor and ex-newscaster turned ex-politician, and (4) a radio announcer whose grandfather once owned a mountain in West Virginia. These men were Ray Scott, Ty Williams, George Palmer, and Leo Underhill. Right after World War II, WNOP was put on the air by James Lang, a onetime Kentucky sheriff whose wife ran— and still runs—the shooting match.

Most broadcasting stations are triumphant and posh affairs, with lavish studios and monumental conference rooms to impress clients, plus a manager's office fit for a sultan, mikado, nawab, or negus. This is known in broadcasting as "putting on the dog." Well, WNOP studios in Newport, across the river, look like something the cat dragged in. If a client wants to sit, he'd better bring his own chair. When the office telephone rings, the ringing is broadcast, because no one ever shuts the studio door. The studio itself is a depressed area filled with war-surplus radio gear that now and then functions in Rube Goldberg fashion, aided by a swift kick. The station manages to stay on the air by a combination of luck, spit, and wild surmise.

But a radio station's physical plant means as little to its listeners as a disheveled kitchen means to a diner in a restaurant which has five Cuban busboys for each table. The customer is interested in the excellence of the feast, not the disorder in which the feast is prepared. Lest you think the feast that WNOP offers is bland and ramshackle fare, be advised that its announcers are no-nonsense professionals who traffic daily in jazz records and grownup nonsense like radio used to make. For instance, Leo Underhill sounds evil in an innocent way—or should that be reversed? One listener suggested that he sounds evil even when he's saying nothing. "He grunts dirty," the listener said. But who but Leo Underhill would have thought of calling WNOP "Skid Row Radio," "Radio Free Newport," or "Make-Believe Radio"? In a ticky-tacky world where radio stations can be labeled "stylized" and "meticulous," WNOP can be labeled "casual" and "random."

Ray Scott, the impeachable hillbilly guitar player, turned into an unimpeachable jazz authority on that station. He would be considered the cool cat at WNOP if it were not for Ty Williams, who when there was so astonishingly cool that anything not connected with jazz left him perplexed. For the record, Ray Scott is listed as program director of a station that has no program. Each of the four announcers works a shift and plays what pleases him. The station manager's office has become an announcer's lounge filled with paper cups of cold coffee.

Who listens to WNOP? Other station managers are quick to trot out surveys to show that no one at all listens to WNOP. Jazz, they will suggest, is not exactly what Cincinnati wants, and WNOP is not really a nice station to have around. Some station managers, between martinis, will murmur: "They *drink* over there."

Even Hal Hall, the WNOP commercial manager, suffered misgivings and wanted to turn WNOP into a station that plays nothing but hillbilly music. Who really *does* listen? Well, simply put, WNOP might be called "sneak radio," because more people listen to it than the other station managers would care to admit. WNOP is truly a free spirit. The staffs of other stations listen because, as one confided, "WNOP is the way radio should be. You can be yourself on the air and act grownup." People in advertising agencies listen because many of them are prisoners of conformity and, as such, recognize real broadcasting when it comes along. It comes along so seldom. To the chagrin of stations that blare rock-'n-roll, college and high school students listen to WNOP, too. In fact, at Miami University the station was so far "in" it was considered "out." WNOP quietly sneaks into Greater Cincinnati homes of young moderns—and into homes of ancient moderns. It sneaks out of car radios. Who listens? Lots of people. That's who.

True, it is sometimes called the "beatnik" station, where unwashed announcers wear sandals, grow beards, and play jazz. But this is as ridiculous as saying all who like jazz must stop bathing, grow beards, and sit in coffeehouses that smell of disinfectant. Jazz—like popular and classical music—is appreciated by people in every walk of life and is no more restricted to beatniks than rock-'n-roll is restricted to teenagers. Jazz belongs, so WNOP threw away its pop records and went all out for jazz. That's why we suggest that WNOP is an institution. It dared to be different and, in doing so, proved that Greater Cincinnati has many facets. Radiomen, in fact, come from all over the United States to sit in at WNOP, listen in wonder, and wish they could go back home and broadcast the same way. But they can't. To do that, they would have to take Leo Underhill with them. Radio professionals do not grow on trees.

Getting away from broadcasting, there is another Cincinnati institution around here. This one is called Aron Mathieu. Like WNOP, he is a free spirit, too.

The New York publishing world may have had Harold Ross, but Cincinnati has Aron Mathieu, who looks and acts in the grand manner of that *New Yorker* editor. Big-boned and owlish, he even looks like Harold Ross. Aron Mathieu has been an editorial fixture at

Rosenthal & Company, printers and publishers on East 12th Street, for years. His fingers have been in just about everything the Rosenthal clan has published: *Farm Quarterly*, *Writer's Digest*, and a bunch of other magazines that have come and gone through the years. *Automotive Digest* is one. *Minicam* is another. As "business manager" of *Writer's Digest*, Aron Mathieu has seen a lot of writers come and go, and knows firsthand more famous writers than a writer's agent does. Sometimes he overwhelms writers and other times he bewilders them, which is par for the course. He bewilders and overwhelms whoever crosses his path.

Technically, he has never been an editor at Rosenthal's. *Writer's Digest* once listed an editor on its masthead when Aron Mathieu was operative, but no real-life editor existed; Mathieu had made up a name for an editor who existed only in Mathieu's imagination. The photograph of this "editor" was really the photograph of a press-man who worked on another floor in the building. "But he *was* distinguished-looking," Aron Mathieu said. This Alice-in-Wonderland state of affairs existed until someone came in, magazine in hand, to quarrel with the editor. The pressman hastily scrubbed and climbed into a suit. He was presented and, happily, the shaky affair ended fast. After that, an announcement appeared that the editor had retired. There was even a touching farewell column he was supposed to have written. "Gone fishing," was the heart of it.

In 1946, Aron Mathieu conceived the idea of a farm magazine more elegant than the earthier journals then being published. He dreamed of a slick magazine as posh and informative as *Fortune*. He dreamed of editorial text so thorough and imaginative that a reader could chug out and grow tobacco, corn, or what have you and need no help other than the magazine. Aron Mathieu had never been on a farm in his life. Thus the *Farm Quarterly* was born, making his dream come true.

"His hiring methods were strange," one *Farm Quarterly* writer said. "I had just gotten out of the military, had planned to collect 52-20"—returned warriors after World War II could collect $20 a week for 52 weeks while trying to readjust or find jobs; many took the 20 bucks each week and loafed—"and write a book. But the United States Employment Office suggested I ought to at least try to find a job first. Well, I agreed to go through the motions. I went over to Rosenthal's because they were listed in the telephone book as publishers. I didn't know what they published. I didn't care. I told the elevator operator I was a novelist, figuring that would queer the deal fast, but he said, 'Come on. You want to see Aron.' He rode me up to the fifth floor, left the elevator to itself, and guided me through a loft filled with typists to the far corner where

Aron's glass-enclosed office was. When the elevator man told Aron, 'Here's a writer looking for work,' Aron brightened. I told him I wanted to write only novels, but Aron's enthusiasm didn't dim. He didn't ask if I could spell. He hired me. The only instruction he ever gave me was a whispered, 'Don't sleep with any girls in the office.'"

In two weeks the would-be novelist was in Tipton, Indiana, doing a definitive story on—of all things—hybrid corn.

They say Aron Mathieu no longer runs the *Farm Quarterly*. And they say he no longer has a hand in the *Writer's Digest*. In fact, they will tell you he has retired, but he's still in the building and still going strong, only on the sixth floor instead of the fifth. He is involved, apparently, in the publishing of school textbooks. His methods in that field are as unorthodox as his methods were in farming. Now and then, manuscript under arm, he will lumber out of the office, head for the nearest playground, and round up whatever small fry are on the loose. He'll read the manuscript to them. If it appeals and makes them happy, he is happy, too; if it doesn't satisfy them, he is disenchanted—not with the children, but with the writer of the manuscript. Of course, standard tests and procedures are used to measure the academic worth of the textbooks, but as far as Aron Mathieu is concerned, the real test is a crowd of kids. He got involved with school books because he discovered retirement wasn't at all simple. In fact, when he was considering retirement he had got too involved in a book that said what retirement was. "People should retire *to* something," he would say, "and not *from* something." So he didn't retire at all. He kept right on going.

To say that he never was an editor is wrong. Years ago, when a student at Ohio State University in Columbus, he was assistant news editor of the *Lantern*. As such, he got himself involved in a quarrel with the U. S. Marines, who were in Nicaragua at the time. He wrote a story based on a Nicaraguan student's letter about "gunboat diplomacy," and before he knew what was happening, the Hearst syndicate had picked it up and run it under the headline, O.S.U. STUDENT SEES RED. Aron Mathieu says that at the time he wasn't exactly sure what a "Red" was. But the Ohio Legislature got furious with the University's president, and Aron Mathieu was booted out of journalism school.

He came from Columbus to Cincinnati, saw a "Boy Wanted" sign in the Rosenthal window, took the sign upstairs, and announced: "I'm your boy." When Joseph Rosenthal said the job helping put out their magazines paid $25 a week, Aron Mathieu was so pleased to be back in the publishing world he blurted out, "I'll work for $20!" He has been with Rosenthal's ever since. He began *Writer's Digest* in 1928, the *Writer's Yearbook* two years later, and he was off and running.

Another writer recalled:

> Because of Aron I met my wife. But it wasn't an ordinary meeting. At times Aron is so innocent, he gets complicated. I had left a manuscript with him, he was supposed to look it over and call me in a week or so, but the next day I began to get outlandish telephone calls from girls who said they were artists and that they wanted to illustrate the book they heard I was writing. They also said I shouldn't drink so much. Fortunately, one let slip that she had heard about me through Aron. I called him up and asked him what the big idea was. He sounded hurt. "I thought you'd like to meet beautiful girls," he said. "They're very nice. All I did was tell them you were a great writer and if you didn't drink so much you could finish a great book which needed illustrating. Somehow that brought out the mother in them and . . ." Well, one of the girls *did* turn out to be my wife, but only after a long courtship. I had to convince her I didn't stagger around in a stupor.

An editorial meeting back then, with Aron Mathieu in attendance, was never formal. It included everyone within shouting distance. His office door was always open. People walked in and out as if his office was Grand Central Station. Old men working for Western Union would peer over his shoulder and make comments about the magazine layouts. Secretaries—some from other floors and some from other buildings—would stop in, read proofs, pass judgment, and wander away. The elevator operator was as much a part of management as Mathieu or any of the Rosenthal boys—and the Rosenthal boys numbered in the thousands. Aron Mathieu welcomed the intrusions. In fact, he would have been lost without them.

"Suppose I shut the door and kept people out," he said once. "What good would that do? Who says the elevator operator doesn't know what he's talking about? He's made some darned good suggestions." He looked around his office thoughtfully because he was in a moment of rare quiet. "If everybody helps me put out these magazines," he went on, "no telling how big we can get. Maybe as big as the whole world. But if they bear my imprint and only mine, they can only get as big as I am. Magazines deserve better than that, don't they?"

And that's how Aron Mathieu chose to operate. Perhaps he had once read of Harold Ross and had tried to emulate that *New Yorker* cornerstone. But things didn't work out that way. Mathieu turned out far better than a carbon copy of someone else; he turned out to be himself. He is perpetually wide-eyed and young—and his wife

Rosella possesses this charm, too. Once on a train trip upstate, Aron Mathieu, Rosella, and their two children turned the ride into a *Life with Father* outing. They boarded the train at the station, they carried an enormous wicker hamper filled with fried chicken, and they immediately took over the empty smoker section at the end of the day coach. The feast was spread, everyone grabbed drumsticks, and they waited for the train to start. It is true that the children waited with the impatience of the very young, but when the train —with a lurch—began to move, it wasn't one of the children who got excited and shouted:

"Here we go."

It was Aron Mathieu.

And if that isn't the stuff a city can make institutions out of, this city has no institutions at all.

Let's look at another. We'll make this one for the children of the area.

There are two ways to "do" a children's show on television. You can return to childhood yourself, wobble around on your hands and knees, look pop-eyed, and let the children look upon you as one of themselves: another child. This is Uncle Al's technique on WCPO-TV. Or, you can stand up on your hind legs and treat the children as the grownups they must someday become. This is Skipper Ryle's technique on WKRC-TV, and it has made him one of Cincinnati's more acceptable institutions.

As the operator of a television show for children, Skipper Ryle is a Johnny-Come-Lately, whereas Uncle Al has been around since women roller-skated themselves silly on television. Both got involved in their children's shows by accident, though. Al Lewis had gone to WCPO-TV as a combination off-the-air artist and on-the-air song-and-dance man. Glen Ryle had gone to WKRC-TV as a staff announcer. But that's Cincinnati television for you. Now we have Uncle Al *and* Skipper Ryle. Martin Hogan, Jr., in the *Enquirer*, tells best why Skipper Ryle has become an institution here. He wrote:

Dear Skipper Ryle:

You're not as sexy as Sophia Loren. You probably can't sing as well as Goulet. And, as an actor, Gielgud, maybe you're not.

You're probably not as smart as William Buckley and Norman Mailer, either. I say "probably" because, having heard both of them, you couldn't prove it by me.

But I'll tell you what you are, Skipper. You're the best host of a kiddie show that I've seen.

And I'll tell you why I think you're the best, Skip. You don't talk down to the children. And, as you probably know, the little ones can spot a phony faster than us big, smart grownups.

You know something else, Skipper? That Saturday morning show of yours moves along faster than the kids do. The kids don't have a chance to get restless.

The show is balanced, too, Skipper. It's not ALL games and dancing. I've seen you read to the children. And I've seen you do a bit of an educational job, too. Like bringing in the actors from community theaters to talk to the children.

The kids go for "Connie Kangaroo," too, Skipper. And "Fritz-Fritz" usually manages a boffo line or two for Mom and Dad if they happen to be around.

How do I know how well the children like you, Skipper?

It's my two-year-old son, a great little guy who is fascinated by three things at this stage of his life—food, sneaking into the street, and Skipper Ryle.

Although Glen Ryle's on-the-air mustache is as phony as Groucho's, now and then a child will ask if it is real. Ryle's stock answer is: "It's as real as you want it to be."

The same can be said for Glen Ryle, too. He's really a bunch of people. To neighbors in Cheviot, he's simply another father. The mothers nearby are more concerned with his wife Jackie's bowling score than Glen's ratings. To ex-Marine buddies, he's that gung-ho Marine raider who fought in World War II and in Korea. When ex-warriors pass through town and hear that this tawny bruiser is now doing a kid's show on television, they are inclined to belt the person who tells them, because that's not the Glen Ryle they knew. To river buffs, Ryle is a guy studying for a license to pilot riverboats. To airplane enthusiasts, he's the fellow shooting landings at Lunken Airport. He has done a lot of things and wants to do a lot more. He wants to operate a fishing boat in the Mexican Gulf. He wants to run a real ranch—no dude stuff—in Colorado. He wants to do this and that—and chances are, sooner or later, he will. Right now he's learning to play the guitar. When he's mastered that, he might start collecting guns, or books, or bugs, or bottle caps. Or keep on with his judo until he gets a Black Belt. He's really a bunch of people. Pick the one that appeals.

But he's one other thing, too. He's typical Cincinnati Dutch. The "Cincinnati Dutch" are not necessarily German or Dutch, of course, never wear wooden shoes, and don't speak with a corny guttural. It's more a state of mind than anything else. Such people generally avoid the flash and glitter of young moderns, support churches and building-and-loan associations by the score, save so much for rainy days they could buy a fleet of Arks for cash, favor a simple neighborhood tavern to an erotic cocktail lounge where the waitresses get

285

chapped knees; and should one of their kind find himself in any form of show business—beyond the high school operetta, that is—he looks upon that occupation questioningly. Show business is foreign and embarrassing and illogical. Cincinnati Dutch of every persuasion are honest-as-the-day-is-long, uncomplicated, and usually outspoken people. When they get married, it is for keeps. They become such old-fashioned parents you would swear they were aping Clarence Day. To most of them, credit cards are the work of the devil, and the thought of being out of a job gives them goose pimples. The only time you read about them in the newspaper is when they celebrate golden wedding anniversaries or when they die.

This makes Glen Ryle and the rest of us sound drab, but don't think that. It simply means that deep down inside, the real Cincinnatian has never been much of a swinger. Perhaps this is why Cincinnati parents feel a kinship with Skipper Ryle. He refuses to giggle or act the country idiot. He refuses to traffic in nonsense when children are present. And when worst comes to worst—as it will now and then on a television show for children—Skipper Ryle is the typical Cincinnati father. He does not hesitate to step out of character and read the riot act to children who have got out of hand. Uncle Al glosses over the mischief his audience creates; Skipper Ryle does not. This figures. Uncle Al is not Cincinnati Dutch. That's all Skipper Ryle ever was.

Credit must go to Len Goorian (Leonard P. Goorian, if you wish to put his name on a Pullman car) for creating the television character called "Skipper Ryle." Goorian is that cheerful New York transplant who has adopted Cincinnati so completely you'd think he'd been born in Cumminsville. Goorian worked a while at WCPO-TV, where the Uncle Al program originates. When Goorian found himself at WKRC-TV as executive producer, it was logical to apply some of the knowledge he had acquired at WCPO-TV, and that was the beginning of Skipper Ryle. Whether Goorian ever wanted to turn Ryle into a Lewis is not the question. The task would have been impossible. Lewis could never do Ryle's program. Ryle could never do Lewis's.

Point is, Skipper Ryle has been on Cincinnati television a long time now, since the mid 1950s, and unless Cincinnati runs out of children, he is likely to stay around for a long time to come. There are so few sensible programs on the tube that Ryle comes on smelling like roses. Whether his program would work well in another city is hard to judge. Cincinnati is Cincinnati, and Glen Ryle is a Cincinnati product. Anyway, where else but Greater Cincinnati (because Cheviot is a city unto itself) could you find living on the same street a man who runs a children's television show and a Playboy Bunny? But this is Cincinnati. Chances are, when they met for the first time, they didn't discuss show business or the weather. Being true Greater Cincinnatians, they probably asked the question all Greater Cincinnatians ask one another: "What high school did you go to?"

There are thousands of institutions here. Some have been included in this book. Some have not. Here we are at Page 287, we've only scratched the surface, and suddenly the task seems hopeless. We didn't write of Carolyn Williams, we hardly touched upon the May Festival, we've glossed over the Fire Department . . . There is no one way to put this city between the covers of a book, tell its *full* story, touch all its facets, and do a thorough job. This city has done right by me. I'm afraid, though, that this book hasn't done too well by it. Forgive me my errors and omissions. They were not intentional. Forgive me my quarrels with the city. They are as I have said: no more than lover's quarrels. To those who say I goofed this chore, I have only one answer:

"You may well be right. But this is the best that I could do."

I am a man in love with a city. I am not a surgeon who explores, dispassionately, its innards, so let us conclude this love letter in this fashion:

A long time ago there was a little boy who lived on that stretch of McMicken Avenue where the crosstown streetcars ran. Actually he was middle-aged, but that is not important; his mind had simply never left childhood. Whenever people passed, he would announce, "I am going to the end of the rainbow." One day I asked him where that was. Without hesitation he pointed downtown.

Corny little story? Perhaps. But never to him and not to me. Children see things grownups can't. They see the magic in things. He saw the magic of Cincinnati. So let's stop kidding ourselves. Let's put aside statistics, dates, historical markers, and the comings and goings we have accumulated here and take a real look at Cincinnati. Let's see it as a child does—and see the magic of it.

Without the magic that comes from the heart, Cincinnati has no meaning. Take away the magic, and the city's thousands of love stories will come to a screeching halt.

INDEX

Trollope, Mrs. Thomas Anthony, 26–27
Tucker, Dr. Louis Leonard, 47, 49–52, 70, 162

UHF television, 166–67
Uncle Al. *See* Lewis, Al
Underground Railroad, 44–45
Underhill, Leo, 30, 279
Union Central Life Insurance Company, 56, 80–82, 94
Union Terminal, 9
U.S. 50, highway, 128
University of Cincinnati, 48, 128–29, 149, 166, 217, 243–45, 260
Urban renewal, 7, 112–15
Ursuline Academy, 7, 241

Valerio's, restaurant, 156
Vernon Manor, 198–99
Villa Madonna College, 251, 260
Vine Street Hill, 6

Walking club, 156–57
Wallace, General Lew, 50–51
Walnut Hills, 6, 125, 143
Walnut Hills High School, 242
Washington, Fort, 17–18
Washington Park, 151
Water sports, 157
Watters, Mort, 167–80
Wayne, General Anthony, 19
WCET, 167
WCIN, 163
WCKY, 163–64
WCPO-Radio, 169–70
WCPO-TV, 167–80, 284, 286
Weather, 265–66
Webb, Don, 163
Weikel, 192
Wells, Warren, 153
West End, the, 7, 68
Western College for Women, 139, 247–48
Western Hills, 144
Western Hills High School, 242
Western Museum, 27–28
Western Spy & Hamilton Gazette, 21

West side, 123–24
Westwood, 55, 143–44
WGUC, 166
Whiskey industry, 75
White Castles, 203
White Horse Tavern, 198
White Oak, 144
Whitewater Canal, 153
Wildlife, 153–54
William Tell Tavern, 25
Wilson, Charles R., 47
Wilson, L. B., 163–64
Wine, 35, 55, 60, 67
Winton Place, 76, 144
Winton Woods, 150, 153
Wise, Dr. Isaac Mayer, 59
Wishing Well, restaurant, 196
Withrow High School, 242
WKRC, 161–63
WKRC-TV, 166, 284, 286
WLW, 29, 161, 164–65, 170, 172, 274
WLWT, 166
WMUB-TV, 167
WNOP, 30, 163, 278–80
Wong's, restaurant, 196
Wood, Mary, 163–64, 190–92
Woodburn, 55
Woodward High School, 238–39
Wooten, Olga, 197
World War I, 82–83
World War II, 108–10
WPA, 93, 107
Writer's Digest, 281–82
WSAI, 161, 166
WUBE, 169
Wyoming, 144
WZIP, 164

Xavier University, 217, 249–50, 260

Yeatts, Bark, 178–79
Yononte Inn, 77

Zimmer's, restaurant, 196
Zoo, Cincinnati, 59, 86–87, 94–95, 154–55